John William Colenso

Lectures on the Pentateuch and the Moabite Stone

John William Colenso

Lectures on the Pentateuch and the Moabite Stone

ISBN/EAN: 9783741171536

Manufactured in Europe, USA, Canada, Australia, Japa

Cover: Foto ©Lupo / pixelio.de

Manufactured and distributed by brebook publishing software (www.brebook.com)

John William Colenso

Lectures on the Pentateuch and the Moabite Stone

LECTURES
ON THE
PENTATEUCH
AND
THE MOABITE STONE.

WITH APPENDICES CONTAINING

I. THE ELOHISTIC NARRATIVE.
II. THE ORIGINAL STORY OF THE EXODUS.
III. THE PRE-CHRISTIAN CROSS, ITS UNIVERSALITY AND MEANING.

BY THE RIGHT REV.

JOHN WILLIAM COLENSO, D.D.
BISHOP OF NATAL.

'Every one truth is connected with every other truth in this great Universe of God. Therefore, to accept as a truth that which is not a truth is an evil having consequences which are indeed incalculable. There are subjects on which one mistake of this kind will poison all the wells of Truth, and affect with fatal error the whole circle of our thoughts.'

DUKE of ARGYLL, *Reign of Law*, p. 34–5.

SECOND EDITION.

LONDON:
LONGMANS, GREEN, AND CO.
1873.

The right of translation is reserved.

PREFACE.

THESE LECTURES have been suggested by the New Lectionary of the Church of England, which in various places, and especially in the First Lesson for the morning of Septuagesima Sunday,¹ directs the attention of all thoughtful members of that Church to some, at least, of the important results of Modern Biblical Criticism. Henceforth, therefore, so far from its being forbidden within the Church of England to pursue such enquiries, the law itself, by commanding and enforcing the use of this Lectionary, prompts or, rather, requires us to enter upon them. It will surely now be necessary that, from the Pulpit and in the Sunday-School, more full and sound information should be imparted on these points from time to time than has hitherto been commonly supplied in English schools and churches.

Moreover, the New Bible Commentary, 'by Bishops and other Clergy of the Anglican Church,' admits that we have no correct copy of the Ten Commandments as really uttered by

See p. 1

the Divine Voice on Sinai, and that 'the two distinct statements' of them in Exodus and Deuteronomy, though 'differing from each other in several weighty particulars,' are 'apparently of equal authority,' and 'each is said, with reiterated emphasis, to contain the words that were actually spoken by the Lord, and written by Him upon the stones.'[3] Further, it instructs its readers that, generally, wherever they read in the Pentateuch, 'And JEHOVAH spake unto Moses, saying,' they are to conclude—not that there was any audible utterance, but only—that Moses felt himself moved by an inward Divine impulse to enact certain laws, which, however, he not unfrequently copied from heathen institutions, 'adopting existing and ancient customs, with significant additions, as helps in the education of his people.'[2] And it informs them also that '*it is by no means unlikely that there are insertions of a later date*, which were written, or sanctioned, by the Prophets and holy men, who *after the Captivity* arranged and edited the Scriptures of the Old Testament.'[4]

Under the above circumstances, the time seems to have arrived for preparing a work 'in which the latest information may be made accessible to men of ordinary culture,'[5] by one who has studied the question from a different point of view from that of these commentators, and has arrived at very different conclusions.

I have attempted to prepare such a work in these Lectures, which are intended to lay before English readers, who cannot devote the time and thought needed for the study of larger and more technical works, the most important results

---

[1] *B.C.*, I. p. 335.
[2] *B.C.*, I. p. 494.
[3] *B.C.*, I. p. 717.
[4] *B.C.*, I. p. iii.

of the criticism of the Pentateuch, and incidentally of other portions of the Hebrew Scriptures. The labour bestowed by me during the last ten years upon the Pentateuch and Book of Joshua, the results of which are given in Parts I-VI of my work already published, and in Part VII now in the press, has enabled me to produce here, in a compact and readable form, the main facts elicited by that Criticism, unencumbered with Hebrew quotations and the mass of minute investigation which that work of necessity contained. And I venture to hope that these Lectures may be found useful especially to Teachers in Day-Schools and Sunday-Schools, as well as to Parents among the more educated laity, who desire to impart to their children an intelligent knowledge of the real nature of these ancient books, which have filled all along, and still fill, so prominent a part in the religious education of the race.

I have here, of course, adhered to the views set forth in my published volumes, which I have seen as yet no reason to abandon, though in some respects more, in others less, conservative than those of some eminent continental writers. But such differences of opinion exist only on questions of secondary importance. These three facts may now be regarded as established by a very general consent of Modern Scholars not pledged to the support of traditionary views—(i) that no part of the original story of the Exodus can have been composed *before* the time of SAMUEL, (ii) that Deuteronomy was written not long before the Babylonish Captivity, (iii) that the Levitical Legislation originated during the Captivity—by which the notion of the Mosaic authorship and infallible Divine authority of the whole, or indeed of any portion, of the

Pentateuch is shown to be untenable. At all events the reader will here have afforded him, as it were, a bird's-eye view of the field of controversy, and will thus be able to enter with more lively interest into any discussions which may yet arise with reference to some of the details.

In App. I I have given at full length the Elohistic Narrative as extracted from Genesis and Exodus, and in App. II the Original Story of the Exodus, as it appears in the Books of Exodus, Numbers, and Deuteronomy, when stripped of all later additions; and the reader will be able to judge for himself how far, as thus exhibited, these two sets of passages have the appearance of being continuous wholes.

In App. III I have added some information about the Pre-Christian Cross, derived from the *Edinburgh Review* for January 1870, to which, or to my Part VI, App. 122, the reader is referred for further information.

J. W. NATAL.

BISHOPSTOWE, NATAL: *January* 8, 1873.

NOTE.—The readers of Part VI are requested to take notice that on further consideration I have seen reason to assign E.x. 28,29, to the O.S., (see *New Bible Commentary, critically examined,* Exodus 42,43, where, however, the last four lines in the Ans. to 43 have been inserted by a printer's mistake,) and the lists of Canaanite nations in E. iii. 8, 17, xxiii. 2, J. ix. 1, 2, xi. 3, to D., in addition to those already assigned to D. in PartVI (E. xiii. 5, xxiii. 23, 28, xxxiv. 11, D. vii. 1, xx. 17, J. iii. 10, xxiv. 11).

PART VII, which will be found to be occasionally referred to, is *in the press.*

CONTENTS.

LECTURE		PAGE
	Preface	v
I.	The Elohist and Jehovist in Genesis	3
II.	The Age of the Elohist in Genesis	15
III.	The Jehovistic Passages in Genesis	29
IV.	The Age of the Jehovist in Genesis	41
V.	The Age of the Jehovist in Genesis further considered	57
VI.	The Origin of the Name Jehovah	71
VII.	The Age of the Jehovist in Numbers	85
VIII.	The Ten Commandments	101
IX.	Human Sacrifices in Israel	115
X.	The Laws on the Stone-Tables	129
XI.	The Book found in the Temple	143
XII.	Jeremiah the Deuteronomist	157
XIII.	The Contents of Deuteronomy	171
XIV.	The Later or Levitical Legislation	185
XV.	The Later Legislation compared with the Original Story	199
XVI.	The Late Date of the Levitical Legislation	215
XVII.	The Ark and the Priesthood in the Original Story	231
XVIII.	The Priests and the Levites	245
XIX.	The Origin of the Pesach or Passover	261
XX.	The Real History of the Exodus	275
XXI.	The Worship of the Baal in Israel	291
XXII.	The Historical Books from Genesis to 2 Kings	305
XXIII.	The Books of Ezra and Nehemiah	319
XXIV.	The Fictions of the Chronicler	333
XXV.	The Moabite Stone	349
XXVI.	Concluding Remarks	367

APPENDIX.

I.	The Elohistic Narrative	381
II.	The Original Story of the Exodus	397
III.	The Pre-Christian Cross, its Universality and Meaning	435

'For its essentially valid belief Religion has constantly done battle. Gross as were the disguises under which it first espoused this belief, and cherishing this belief, though it still is, under disfiguring vestments, it has never ceased to maintain and defend it. It has everywhere established and propagated one or other modification of the doctrine that all things are manifestations of a Power that transcends our knowledge... No exposure of the logical inconsistency of its conclusions—no proof that each of its particular dogmas was absurd—has been able to weaken its allegiance to that ultimate verity for which it stands. After criticism has abolished all its arguments and reduced it to silence, there has still remained with it the indestructible consciousness of a truth which, however faulty the mode in which it has been expressed, was yet a truth beyond cavil. To this conviction its adherence has been substantially sincere. And for the guardianship and diffusion of it, Humanity has ever been, must ever be, its debtor.

'But... while in great part sincere in its fealty to the great truth it has had to uphold, it has often been insincere, and consequently irreligious, in maintaining the untenable doctrines by which it has obscured this great truth. Each of them has been age after age insisted on, in spite of a secret consciousness that it would not bear examination. Just as though unaware that its central position was impregnable, Religion has obstinately held every outpost long after it was obviously indefensible... How truly its central position is impregnable, Religion has never adequately realised. In the devoutest faith, as we habitually see it, there lies hidden an innermost core of scepticism; and it is this scepticism which causes that dread of inquiry displayed by Religion when face to face with Science...

'Of Religion, then, we must always remember, that amidst its many errors and corruptions it has asserted and diffused a supreme verity. From the first, the recognition of this supreme verity, in however imperfect a manner, has been its vital element... The truly religious element of Religion has always been good: that which has proved untenable in doctrine and vicious in practice, has been its irreligious element; and from this it has been ever undergoing purification.

'And now observe that, all along, the agent which has effected this purification has been Science. We habitually overlook the fact that this has been one of its functions. Religion ignores its immense debt to Science; and Science is scarcely conscious how much Religion owes it. Yet is it demonstrable that every step by which Religion has progressed from its very low conception to the comparatively high one it has now reached, Science has helped it, or rather forced it, to take, and that even now Science is urging further steps in the same direction.'—HERBERT SPENCER, *First Principles*, 3rd ed., p. 101.

LECTURE I.

SUMMARY.

THE new Lesson for Septuagesima Sunday; the New Lectionary, the New Commentary, and the New Translation; two important admissions in the New Commentary; the Elohistic and Jehovistic accounts of the Creation in Genesis; the characteristic differences between them; the Elohistic narrative almost continuous throughout, composing the older story, which has been supplemented with Jehovistic insertions; the vivacious and picturesque style of the Jehovist, far more anthropomorphic than that of the Elohist; similar phenomena found in the earlier and later writings of other religions; the scientific difficulties in Genesis of no consequence when the composition of the Book is understood; different religions become purified from within from time to time, as the Indian, the Jewish, and the Christian.

THE ELOHIST AND JEHOVIST IN GENESIS.

FOR the first time in the History of the Church of England the first three verses of the second chapter of Genesis have been publicly read for a Sunday Lesson in connection with the first chapter of that book, as the closing portion of the account of the Creation contained in that chapter. Some of you perhaps will have hardly noticed this fact—will have hardly perceived that any difference has been made in the Lesson for Septuagesima Sunday—will have taken for granted that the same words were read on that day in your ears which have been read year after year ever since you were old enough to enter a church, and centuries before you were born. But a change has really been made by the lawful authority in the Church— small in appearance, but momentous in its consequences— one which opens up the whole question of Modern Biblical Criticism before the eyes of the Laity in every congregation, and will inaugurate, I believe, a new era in the life of our Church. In the present age, as you know, three great works in reference to the Bible have been taken in hand by leading men in the Church of England, under the authority of its Bishops and Archbishops—a new Lectionary, a New Commentary, and a New Translation—all professedly based upon the latest results of learned, as well as devout, study of the sacred oracles. The Translation is slowly progressing, but lies at present hidden in the secret chamber, and not yet communicated to the world. We remember, however, that one of the most eminent of the translators said openly in Convocation when this work was begun—'I must own it is my belief that, when the Authorised Version has received all the amendments of which it is capable and which it absolutely requires, this will be found to have effected a very great change in many parts of the Bible; and I think one effect of this will be that it will deprive many of the Clergy, and perhaps still more of Dissenting ministers, of some of their most favourite texts. We ought not to conceal from ourselves that it will very materially alter the text of Scripture.'[1] The New Bible Commentary has been partially completed, but only so far as the Pentateuch is concerned; and I may draw attention to two of the most prominent facts which distinguish this Commentary from any that has ever before been published with any semblance of authority in the Church of England. These are, first, the recognition that the two versions of the Ten Commandments, which we find in Exodus and Deuteronomy, 'differ from each other in several weighty particulars,' and that neither of them represents exactly the 'Ten Words' as they were uttered by the Divine Voice on Sinai;[2] and, secondly, the not less important recognition that most of the laws in Exodus, Leviticus, and Numbers, which are usually supposed to have been orally communicated by the Divine Being to Moses—'JEHOVAH spake unto Moses'—were not so communicated at all, were merely the result of thought which arose by Divine inspiration in the mind of the human legislator,[3] and were adopted frequently 'from existing and probably very ancient and widely spread institutions.'[4] But the Lectionary is completed, and is estab-

---

[1] Bp. (THIRLWALL) of St. David's (*Guardian*, Feb. 16, 1870, p.193).
[2] *B.C.*, I. p. 335, 6.   [3] *Ib.* p. 634-6, 643.   [4] *Ib.* p. 15, 16, 670, 717.

lished already by law in the Church of England; and, though simple and unobtrusive in appearance, it will be found, on a little closer consideration, to involve principles which will tend to revolutionize the whole system of traditionary teaching, admitting light and air into the long shut up, darkened and musty, chambers.

For why is the Lesson on Septuagesima Sunday now for the first time made to end with the third verse of the second chapter of Genesis? A glance at the Bible will show at once the reason. It is because the matter contained in these verses is precisely similar in character to that contained in the whole first chapter, and quite distinct from that which follows in the rest of the second chapter and in the third. The attention of thoughtful persons is thus directed to the fact that there are *two* accounts of the Creation in the Bible, one contained in the first chapter of Genesis and the first three verses of the second, the other exhibited in the rest of the second chapter, with which the third is closely connected. In the former of these the name of the Deity is always 'God,' in Hebrew 'ELOHIM,' and hence this narrative is called the *Elohistic* story of the creation. In the latter narrative the name of the Deity is always 'LORD GOD,' in Hebrew 'JEHOVAH ELOHIM,' except where the serpent uses it, or the woman in reply to the serpent;[a] and hence this second account is called the *Jehovistic* story of the Creation. The attention, I say, of all thoughtful persons will now be called to the fact of the existence of these two separate accounts by the Lesson for Septuagesima Sunday in the New Lectionary, in which the old division of the chapters, sanctioned by the pious ignorance of past ages, which has hitherto obscured the truth for most English readers, is once for all deliberately set aside, and reason and scholarship are at last allowed their due rights even in the treatment of Holy Scripture. It is the duty of all

[a] G. iii. 1, 3, 5.

intelligent members of the Church of England to understand clearly the truth of this matter, which is now brought before them by the highest authorities, not of their Church only, but of the State also, by which that Church is governed; and it is the duty of the clergy to set that truth in a plain intelligible form before the eyes of the laity.

For not only are these two accounts of the Creation distinguished by the names of the Deity employed in them; they are marked also by very characteristic differences of style and phraseology throughout. This appears most plainly in the Hebrew original, and it requires some labour to bring it home to the apprehension of the mere English reader; nor is it possible to enter here at length into critical discussions like these. But the same peculiarities of style, which distinguish these two accounts of the Creation, are found also to pervade other portions of the Book of Genesis, except that after the third chapter we no longer observe the compound name 'LORD GOD,' or 'JEHOVAH ELOHIM,' but simply 'JEHOVAH,'[*] in the second set of passages, corresponding to the second account of the Creation; whereas in that which corresponds in style to the first account of the Creation only 'ELOHIM' still continues to be used,[†] as in that. About one-fourth of the Book belongs to the writer who uses only 'ELOHIM,' and is therefore called the 'Elohist' or 'Elohistic writer'; while the writer of the rest of the Book, or the greater part of it, who uses freely the name 'JEHOVAH,' is called the 'Jehovist.' And it is especially to be noted that when the Elohistic passages are all extracted and copied one after another, they form a complete, connected narrative; from which we infer that these must have composed the original story, and that the other passages were afterwards inserted by another writer, who wished to enlarge or supple-

---

[*] G. iv. 1, 3, 4, 6, &c.   [†] G. v. 1, 22, 24. vi. 9, 11, 12, 13, 22, &c.

ment the primary record. And he seems to have used the compound name 'JEHOVAH ELOHIM' in the first portion of his work[*] in order to impress upon the reader that 'JEHOVAH,' of whom he goes on to speak in the later portions, is the same Great Being who is called simply 'ELOHIM' by the older writer, and notably in the first account of the Creation.

It is this later writer who gives so much vivacity and spirit to the narrative in the Book of Genesis, and paints so graphically the transactions which he describes. It is only he, for instance, who uses such expressions as 'lift up the eyes and see,' 'lift up the feet and go,' 'lift up the voice and weep,' 'fall upon the neck and weep,'—who employs the words 'sin,' 'swear,' 'steal,' 'smite,' 'slay,' 'fear,' 'hate,' 'comfort,' 'embrace,' and 'love.'[*] It is his part of the story, in short, which abounds with those tender touches of human nature and expressions of emotional feeling, which for many have constituted the great charm in the narrative of Genesis; while on the other hand to him also are due the darker parts of the histories of individual life, those, for instance, which record the ill-will between Cain and Abel, the strife between Lot's herdsmen and Abraham's, Abraham's and Abimelech's, Isaac's and Abimelech's, the enmity between Sarah and Hagar, Ishmael and Isaac, Esau and Jacob, Jacob and Laban, Leah and Rachel, Joseph and his brethren, and, above all, those indecent stories which have so long been offensive to our ears when read in the public services of the Church, but are now happily removed altogether from the Sunday Lessons and most of them from the Daily Lectionary. While no stain of moral weakness is attached by the older Elohistic writer to the character of any one of the three patriarchs, in the other parts of Genesis we find each of them exhibited as grievously faulty in some particular. It is here only we meet with the

---

[*] G. ii, iii.   [*] *Pent.* V. 40.

disobedience of Adam and Eve, the drunkenness of Noah, the cowardice and insincerity of Abraham, twice repeated and again imitated by his son Isaac, the greed and selfishness and incestuous conduct of Lot, the harshness and untruthfulness of Sarah, the partiality and gross deceitfulness of Rebekah, the ready lying of Jacob, the deadly hatred of Esau, with a multitude of other similar incidents, which light up the more sober pages of the older narrative with the lurid gleams of human passion, or sometimes with the brighter beams of human affection.[10]

It is the Jehovist also who introduces strong anthropomorphic expressions, ascribing human thoughts and actions, passions and affections, to the Deity—who tells us how Jehovah 'planted a garden' and was 'heard walking in it in the cool of the day,'—how He made coats of skins and clothed the first man and woman—how He grudged the man being like Himself, and refused to let him eat of the tree of life—how He set a mark on Cain, and shut up the Ark after Noah, and came down to see the city and tower of Babel—how He ate bread and meat with Abraham.[11] We find none of these strong anthropomorphisms in the older writer. He speaks indeed of ELOHIM 'remembering' Noah, Abraham, and Rachel,[12] making a covenant and appointing a sign of it,[13] appearing and speaking to Abraham and Jacob, and 'going up' from them after the interview.[14] But these expressions are obviously very different in kind from those of the Jehovist, far less coarse and sensuous. The Elohist in short appears to have had nobler, purer, grander ideas of the nature of the Divine Being and of His paternal relations to mankind than those entertained by the later writer, as will be seen by any one who will thoughtfully read the first account of the Creation and compare it with the second. And

[10] *Pent.* V. 47, 48. [11] *Pent.* V. 43. [12] G. viii. 1, xix. 29, xxx. 22.
[13] G. ix. 8-17, xvii. 1-14 [14] G. xvii. 1, 22, xxxv. 9, 13.

this is quite in accordance with experience in other cases.
The early Vedas of the Hindoos were far higher in tone and
thought than the books which correspond to a later development of that religion : the older portions of the Zendavesta,
the sacred book of the Parsee religion, show the same superiority to the later additions. So the first days of Christianity
were brighter and purer than those which followed, when
fierce conflicts began about Creeds and Dogmas, and at last
Christianity became the religion of the Roman Empire, and
the celebration of pagan rites and mysteries, with the worship
of the Queen of Heaven under the name of the Virgin, and
the offering of the 'tremendous sacrifice' by the hands of a
celibate priesthood, took the place of that worship of the
heart and of the life, which was enjoined by Him who said to
his disciples 'Blessed are the meek—the merciful—the peacemakers—the pure in heart!'

You will perceive that I have not dwelt at length upon the
points in respect of which the accounts of the Creation and
the Deluge, and other portions of the Book of Genesis, are
contradicted by the most elementary results of Modern
Science, such as are, or should be, taught in our days in any
ordinary Village School. As soon as we know the true nature
of the composition of the narrative, and understand that it is
the production of different writers in different ages, who, however devout and truly inspired for their work, never probably
claimed for it a Divine Infallibility, nor, so far as appears,
even pretended to be writing real history, or were supposed
by their contemporaries to be doing anything more than
composing from their own imagination, with the help, perhaps, of some traditionary reminiscences, a sketch of the early
annals of their race, we are relieved at once from the necessity
of reconciling all such contradictions, or of explaining them
away by forcing the words of Scripture to mean something
else than was intended by the writers, nor are we any longer

troubled by the numerous discrepancies which are found to exist between one part of the story and another. These are only just exactly what we should expect to find under the circumstances of a multiplicity of writers and an unscientific age.

There is much more which I might say on this interesting subject. But the time will not now allow of it, though I hope to return to it on a future occasion. For the present let us fix our attention for a moment on this thought, how religions, which have been corrupted, have a tendency to purify themselves again after a time, and return to the simpler forms in which they first appeared, though with a great advance in clearness and certainty. Like the water of the Thames, which (they say) when stored on shipboard is at first to all appearance sufficiently clear for use, then becomes turbid and foul, and afterwards throws off its impurities, which were held by it in solution, unseen, in its original state, and becomes very pure and good, so has it been, in more than one notable instance, in the history of the chief religions of mankind.

In India, where the corruptions of the simple faith of primitive times had become multiplied beyond conception, till the whole land was polluted with gross sensualities, the very fruit of religious devotion, a new body of Reformers has arisen, having no connection whatever with our Missionaries, self-awakened, self-impelled—or rather awakened and impelled by the Spirit of God—who have shaken off the idolatries of their countrymen, and approach the Divine Being with prayers such as these—' O Lord, to Thee and Thee alone we look for aid, for Thou art the God of Salvation, our only hope in this world of temptation. We pray unto Thee: vouchsafe to enlighten our minds and purify our hearts with Thy Love. Teach us to love Truth, and give us a strong will that we may live according to it. With all humility we approach Thy Divine Presence, and we prostrate our souls beneath Thy feet: give us, O Lord, knowledge unto Salvation. Good God, have mercy on us."[19]

In like manner the Jewish religion, during those sad years of the Captivity, purified itself from the corruptions which prevailed before that time, and which defiled even the Temple itself with the grossest abominations. The writings of Jeremiah [20] and the Later Isaiah [21] breathe the same spirit as that of the Elohist of Genesis, who makes the Divine Being appear to Abram, and say, 'I am EL SHADDAI, ALMIGHTY GOD; walk before me and be thou perfect. And I will establish My Covenant between Me and thee and thy seed after thee in their generations for an everlasting covenant, to be a GOD unto thee and to thy seed after thee.' [22]

And when this purer faith had been again corrupted by the priests and scribes of a later day, who laid heavy burdens upon men's shoulders, of rites and ceremonies and superstitious observances, burdens too heavy to be borne, the work of Jesus, restoring the old simple faith in the Living God, as the Friend and Father of all, set free once more the human mind from thraldom, into the glorious liberty of the children of God.

And now, in this very age in which we live, Christianity itself, long obscured by vain traditions of warring churches, is cleansing itself from these corruptions, and returning to the first principles of that Blessed Gospel which was taught by Christ himself. Let us rejoice to know that in this, as in other things, humanity is progressing from age to age, so that the Divine doctrine of the Fatherhood of God and the Brotherhood of Men, as revealed in the life and death of Jesus, and in our measure in that of each of his true followers, is becoming more clear and plain, more purified from the gross

---

[19] The Brahmo Somaj (*Theol. Rev.*, April, 1867, p. 198).
[20] Jer. vii. 2), xl. 4, xxiv. 7, xxx. 22, xxxi. 1, 33, xxxii. 38.
[21] Is. xli. 10, 13, xliii. 3, xlv. 3, xlviii. 17, &c.   [22] G. xvii. 1, 7.

accretions of human dogmatic teaching, more manifestly the moral and spiritual truth which is needed for all mankind, the little grain, which has grown up already into a spreading tree, under whose branches all nations of the earth shall one day be sheltered, and find their long-desired refreshment and rest.

LECTURE II.

SUMMARY.

RECAPITULATION ; these views supported by the statements of Bp. BROWNE ; the duty of explaining such facts henceforth in the Pulpit and the Sunday-School, enforced by words of Abp. WHATELY ; the story of the Flood also a composite narrative, and recognised as such by Bp. BROWNE ; the importance of teaching the truth on these points in training children ; Bp. BROWNE'S strange explanation of the composite character of Genesis ; meaning of the expression 'the Five Books of Moses' ; the Elohistic Narrative probably written in the age, and perhaps by the hand, of Samuel, for the use of his schools ; it is the oldest part of the Bible, except perhaps some portions of the Book of Judges ; style of the Elohist, and indications of his age, which is fixed by the stress laid by him on Hebron ; the Book of Genesis deeply interesting when intelligently studied.

THE AGE OF THE ELOHIST IN GENESIS.

I HAVE drawn your attention to the fact of the existence of two separate accounts of the Creation in Genesis, as indicated in the New Lectionary by the choice made of the First Lesson for Septuagesima Sunday. That Lesson ends with G.ii.3, and contains one of these two accounts, which is at variance with the other in some important particulars, as set forth in critical works. In the one, as I observed, the expression used invariably for the name of the Deity is simply ELOHIM, the Hebrew word for GOD, meaning 'the Awful One'; in the other we find invariably the compound name, JEHOVAH ELOHIM, 'the LORD GOD,' meaning 'the Awful Living-One or Life-Giver.' In G.iii, which is closely connected with G.ii, the very same characteristic expressions recur as distinguish the second account of the Creation, and the same compound name is used for the Deity, except only in three places, where the writer apparently shrinks from employing the name JEHOVAH in the discourse between the woman and the serpent. I stated also that the hands of the same two writers, the Elohist and Jehovist, can be distinctly traced throughout the Book of Genesis, and that, when the Elohistic passages are separated, they are found to constitute a complete consistent story; from which fact it is concluded that this was the original basis of the narrative, and that the Jehovistic portions have been inserted afterwards, adding movement and life by their picturesque details to the more prosaic older story.

If all this should sound strangely in the ears of some of you, as something different from the old traditionary notions, which till very lately were taught universally in the pulpit and the Sunday School, and without the least misgiving were pressed home by learned doctors and divines innumerable upon the consciences of their hearers, young and old, as incontestable truth, which to doubt or disbelieve was the direst infidelity, enough to imperil the eternal safety of the soul, yet listen to what a Bishop of the Church of England has said in the New Bible Commentary; and, while I read his words in your hearing, consider within yourselves whether they do not substantially confirm the statements I have just made.

'In the history of the Creation, we have first, in G.i.1-ii.3, that which was very probably the *ancient primeval record* of the formation of the world. It may even have been communicated to the first man in his innocence. At all events, it very probably was *the great Semitic tradition*, handed down from Noah to Shem, from Shem to Abraham, and from Abraham through Isaac, Jacob, and Joseph, to the Israelites who dwelt in Egypt. *Without interfering with the integrity of this*, the sacred author proceeds in the same chapter to add *a supplementary history*, briefly recapitulating the history of the Creation, with some little addition, in v.4-7, and then proceeding to the history of Paradise, the Fall, the Expulsion, and the bitter fruits of disobedience. In the first part of this second or supplementary history, we meet with a signal phenomenon, viz., that from ii.4 to the end of iii. the two names of God, JEHOVAH and ELOHIM, are used continually together. There is no other instance in Scripture of this continued and repeated use of the united names. It is evident that the author, who adopted the first ancient record and stamped it with his authority, and who desired to bring his people to the worship of the great Self-existent JEHOVAH, used this method of transition from *the ancient Elohistic document* to his own more immediate narrative, in order that he might more forcibly impress upon his readers that the ELOHIM who created all things was also the JEHOVAH who had revealed Himself to Moses.'[1]

When facts like these have been stated so plainly under such high authority, surely no blame can be attached henceforth to any who may think it right to teach these things openly in the pulpit or the Sunday School. Rather, it is clearly the bounden duty of all truth-loving, truth-speaking men, of all intelligent teachers of all denominations, to study these questions earnestly and devoutly with such means as they have at their disposal, and first, as far as possible, ascertain the Truth for themselves, and then in God's Name convey it to others. For how can we serve the Living and True God, except so far as we are servants of the Truth? And how can we be servants of the Truth, if we knowingly shut our eyes to facts which we do not like, because they conflict with our preconceived notions, and if we not only do this ourselves, but attempt to close, or to keep shut, or to throw dust in, the eyes of others under our influence, that they may not be able to see the facts which God's wise Providence, in this age of the world, has made known to us for our instruction and guidance in life? Those are solemn words of a late Archbishop of our Church, well worthy to be weighed by religious as well as scientific teachers of all classes:—

'He who propagates a delusion, and he who connives at it when already existing, both alike tamper with Truth. We

[1] Dr. BROWNE, *B.C.*, I. p. 17, all.

must neither lead nor leave men to mistake falsehood for Truth. Not to undeceive, is to deceive. The giving, or not correcting, false reasons for right conclusions, false grounds for right belief, false principles for right practice,—the holding forth or fostering false consolations, false encouragements, or false sanctions, or conniving at their being held forth or believed,—are all pious frauds. This springs from, and it will foster and increase, a want of veneration for Truth: it is an affront put upon the Spirit of Truth.'[2]

The fact, then, of the existence of these two separate accounts of the Creation—one 'the ancient Elohistic document,' the other a 'a supplementary history'—will probably be recognized henceforth by well informed Christians as a matter beyond all doubt or dispute, as much so as the fact of the Earth's motion round the Sun, which was once so fiercely contested, but is now taught, as an elementary truth, in every nursery, without any fear of true Religion, true Christianity, being darkened or corrupted thereby. And the same is true, though not to the same extent, of the story of the Flood. As the writer in the New Commentary again observes—'If the basis of the history of the Flood were an ancient Elohistic document, Moses appears to have interwoven it with a further narrative of his own. The one portion may be marked with the prevalence of one name, the other by that of another name, for God; but the consistency of the one with the other is complete throughout.'[3] This fact, I repeat, of the existence of a compound authorship in Genesis must surely be taught henceforth among the first elements of Biblical knowledge by all Christian pastors and parents, at once intelligent as well as devout, and knowing that no good whatever can come in the end of 'speaking lies in the Name of the Lord'[4] —must be taught, if not in the nursery, yet at least in the

[2] Abp. WHATELY (*Bacon's Essays with Annotations*, p. 11).
[3] Bp. BROWNE, *B.C.*, I. p. 28.   [4] Zech. xiii. 3.

school-room,—the differences in style between the two narratives, their probable ages, the discrepancies between them, and the contradictions they exhibit to well-known facts of Science, being pointed out wisely beforehand, as soon as the child is able to understand such things or begins to feel an interest in them. Thus it will learn from the first to take a true view of the nature of Divine Revelation as we find it in the Bible, and escape the misery into which so many have been plunged for want of such faithfulness on the part of their religious guides—faithfulness in learning, as well as in teaching, the Truth—when it comes to mature years, in this age of searching enquiry and seething controversy, and finds out these things for the first time for itself.

I pointed out in my former Lecture some differences in style between the two writers, as much as the time and occasion allowed; and generally I noticed the stately solemn march of the one narrative and the sprightly vivacity of the other. What now shall be said about the ages in which these two accounts were written? The old traditionary notion supposes that they were both composed by Moses. The New Commentary, as you have heard, maintains that only the later Jehovistic passages are properly the work of Moses. The Elohistic story, according to this Commentary, was 'the ancient primeval record of the foundation of the world,' 'the great Semitic tradition,' which had been 'handed down from Noah to Shem, from Shem to Abraham, and from Abraham through Isaac, Jacob, and Joseph, to the Israelites in Egypt,' and from them was at last communicated to Moses. Thus the writer says :—' Some portions of the narrative do indeed present what is called an Elohistic aspect, and especially those portions which in their very nature are most likely to have existed in the traditions current of old time among the Israelites, viz., the general account of the Creation, the Flood, the covenant of Circumcision made with Abraham, and the genealogical tables. These, then, Moses appears to have adopted, much as he found them, perhaps perpetuating, word for word, in his writings what before had been floating in unwritten record.'[a] But who can believe that this 'ancient primeval record of the foundation of the world' could have been handed down unchanged by oral tradition from one person to another, 'word for word,' in the form in which Adam first delivered it, in the course of 2,500 years—who, at least, that knows how greatly a story is invariably altered by passing through the mouths of merely three or four persons?

The truth is, that it is merely assumed, without any ground of reason whatever, that Moses wrote the five Books which compose the Pentateuch. No doubt they are commonly called the five 'Books of Moses.' But so we speak of the Book of Judges or the two Books of Kings, without supposing that these were written by the Judges or the Kings, as we speak in like manner of the two Books of Samuel, without meaning to say that they were written by Samuel, who, in fact, dies and is buried in 1S.xxv.1. These expressions mean only the Books *about* the Judges, the Kings, or Samuel, respectively; and so the five Books of Moses mean the Books about Moses, the Books in which Moses is the principal agent, the prominent figure; so that we need not now consider the question whether Moses wrote the account of his own death and burial in D.xxxiv, or set down this character of himself for future ages—'Now the man Moses was very meek, above all the men that were upon the face of the earth.'[b]

It is probable that the earliest portion of the Pentateuch, the 'ancient Elohistic document,' was composed in the age, and, if so, then perhaps by the hand of Samuel. This great prophet, the last of the 'Judges' of Israel,[c] evidently laboured

---

[a] Bp. Browne, *B.C.*, I.p.27.
[b] N.xii.3. [c] 1S.vii.6,15-17.

much to improve the condition of his people, and, among other measures for that end, he appears to have instituted schools or colleges for the education of young men, who should take an active part hereafter in teaching and exhorting their brethren. These were the so-called 'schools of the prophets'; and, accordingly, we read in one place of a 'company of prophets coming down from the high-place with a psaltery and a tabret and a pipe and a harp before them, and prophesying,'[8] and in another of 'the company of prophets prophesying, and Samuel standing as appointed over them,'[9] and of the servants of Saul, and Saul himself, prophesying also, so that the proverb went abroad, 'Is Saul also among the prophets?'[10] So, again, in later days we read of the 'sons of the prophets,' who lived at Bethel, Jericho, the Gilgal, &c.[11]—young men, it is plain, who were not 'prophets' themselves in the higher sense of the word, but were trained under prophets, such as Samuel, Nathan, Gad, and probably, as I have said, with a view to their being usefully employed in their turn in giving like instruction to others. The practice of singing psalms to the sound of musical instruments evidently formed some part of their occupation; and, accordingly, in the Book of Chronicles we read of the choristers in David's time, who '*prophesied* with harps, with psalteries, and with cymbals,' 'according to the order of the king,' 'to give thanks and to praise the LORD.'[12] But they cannot always have been employed in these 'schools' in singing psalms. And there can be little doubt that for the use of such places the first attempts were made to set down in writing the early history of Israel, and, if so, then Samuel himself would most probably have taken some prominent part in this work.

Perhaps the oldest parts of the Bible are some portions of the Book of Judges, containing an account of events occurring

---

[8] 1S.x.5. [9] 1S.xix.20. [10] 1S.x.10–13, xix.20–24.
[11] 2K.ii.1,5,7,15,iv.1,38,ix.1. [12] 1Ch.xxv.1–3.

during the rude times which immediately preceded the age of Samuel. And then comes 'the ancient Elohistic document,' the older story of the patriarchal times, which we find in the Book of Genesis,—perhaps, as I have said, from the hand of Samuel himself. The style of this narrative is grave, prosaic, unadorned, abounding with repetitions, yet not without a certain grandeur and majesty, which accords well with our conceptions of a very early age, before the advance of literature and the progress of civilization had supplied the language with the more refined and picturesque expressions, which are so frequently employed by the Jehovist, but are almost wholly wanting in the older writer. In the whole Elohistic Narrative there is no instance of a story of indecency, whereas the Jehovistic additions abound with them.[13] The crimes, which the Elohist refers to as most common, are crimes of 'violence,' which in his view were the main cause of the Flood,[14] and against which he expressly provides, 'Whoso sheddeth man's blood, by man shall his blood be shed.'[15] He nowhere mentions any of the luxuries of later times; he knows nothing of golden bracelets, earrings, or necklaces; he never even mentions the sword. This last fact corresponds to the state of things in Israel in Samuel's time, when 'there was no smith found throughout the land of Israel; for the Philistines said, lest the Hebrews make them swords or spears: so it came to pass that in the day of battle there was neither sword nor spear found in the hand of any of the people that were with Saul and Jonathan; only with Saul and Jonathan his son there were found.'[16] In one place only does he name either of the precious metals; and then Abraham weighs out to Ephron 400 shekels of silver 'passing current with the merchant.'[17] His language, in short, betrays everywhere a primitive condition of society, before the arts had made progress

---

[13] G. xix. 4, 9, 30–38, xxxiv, xxxviii, xxxix. [15] G. vi. 11, 14.
[14] G. ix. 6.   [16] 1 S. xiii. 19, 22.   [17] G. xxiii. 15, 16.

THE AGE OF THE ELOHIST IN GENESIS.

in Israel. Moreover, he makes no allusion to priests or sacrifices. All that Jacob does, when he sets up his pillar and calls the place, where EL SHADDAI, 'GOD ALMIGHTY,' had appeared to him, by the name of Beth-El, that is, ' House of GOD,' is to ' pour a drink-offering and oil upon it.'[18] That priests existed and sacrifices were offered in the writer's day in Israel, as among the surrounding nations, cannot be doubted. But, it is clear, he laid no special stress on priestly matters. He lived at a time when there was no gorgeous ritual, no splendid temple, no complex system of sacrifices.

All this agrees closely with the age of Samuel, and other arguments might be produced which point very strongly in the same direction, especially the fact that the writer lays such very great stress upon Abraham's having purchased from the Hittites the 'field of Machpelah,' the site of the city of Hebron. He describes, for instance, the conveyance of this land to Abraham in terms of almost legal precision :— ' The field of Ephron, which was in Machpelah, which was east of Mamre, the field and the cave that was in it, and all the trees that were in the field, that were in all the borders round about, were confirmed to Abraham for a possession in the presence of the sons of Heth, before all that went in at the gate of the city.'[19] He evidently wished this place to be regarded as the most venerable and sacred in the whole land of Israel. He repeats, again and again,[20] that from the earliest times it had been acquired by Abraham their great forefather, not by conquest or by gift, but by friendly purchase, that he might secure for himself and his descendants for ever an incontestable right to it. It had been made the residence of each of the patriarchs,[21] and there each of them was buried

---

[18] G. xxxv. 14.   [19] G. xxiii. 17, 18.
[20] G. xxiii. 17, 18, 20, xxv. 10, xlix. 30, 32, l. 13.
[21] G. xxiii. 2, xxxv. 27, comp. also xxxvii. 14, a later insertion.

as also their wives, Sarah, Rebekah, Leah.[71] How dear, then, should Hebron be to the affections of every Israelite! How touching were all these memories connected with it!

But why so much stress laid on Hebron? If we turn to the history we read that, after Saul's death, 'David enquired of JEHOVAH saying, Shall I go up into any of the cities of Judah? And JEHOVAH said unto him, Go up, and David said, Whither shall I go up? and He said, Unto Hebron.'[72] Thus, by the authority of some priest or prophet, answering in JEHOVAH's name, David was directed to make Hebron the central seat of his government. Accordingly for seven years and a half David reigned over Judah in Hebron,[74] while Ishbosheth, Saul's son, reigned over the Ten Tribes at Mahanaim.[75] But after Ishbosheth's death 'all the elders of Israel came to the king to Hebron; and king David made a league with them in Hebron before JEHOVAH; and they anointed David king over Israel.'[76] And now, being thus strengthened, he captures at once the stronghold of Zion from its Jebusite inhabitants, and makes Jerusalem henceforth his capital;[77] after which Hebron is named no more in the history, except that David's rebel son Absalom also set up his kingdom at Hebron.[78] It seems highly improbable that so much importance would have been ascribed by the Elohist to Hebron if he wrote *after* the first seven years of David's reign, when Jerusalem had been made the royal city. It is clear, however, that David's priestly or prophetical advisers advised him at first to make Hebron his capital. And with this in view most probably the passages in question in the Book of Genesis were written—perhaps, as I have said, by Samuel himself, in accordance with advice which he had given to his young friend David,[79] whom he had long marked out as the future king.[80]

[71] G. xxiii. 19, xxv. 9, 10, xlix. 31, l. 13. [72] 2S. ii. 1.
[74] 2S. ii. 11. [75] 2S. ii. 8, 12, 29. [76] 2S. v. 3. [77] 2S. v. 6, 7, 13, 14.
[78] 2S. xv. 7, 9, 10. [79] 1S. xix. 18, 19, 22. [80] 1S. xv. 28, xvi. 1–13.

In this way light is thrown upon the origin and contents of the 'ancient Elohistic document.' And, studied in this manner, the Book of Genesis becomes most deeply interesting, not only from an historical point of view, as reflecting the colour of the times in which the different portions of it were written, but as revealing also the thoughts of our brethren, quickened by the self-same Spirit as we are, nearly three thousand years ago—as recording the first movements of higher Divine Life in the hearts of men of the Hebrew race, from which our own religious life has been to a great extent derived, the kindling of that spiritual flame, which in Israel's worst days was never suffered to be quite extinguished, but, fed from time to time with fresh supplies from the Eternal Source, beamed out at length upon the nations bright and clear, in the full glory of the Teaching of Christ.

LECTURE III.

SUMMARY.

The New Lesson for Quinquagesima Sunday; G.ix.1-17 Elohistic, and pointing to the age of Samuel; G.ix.28,29, Elohistic like G.v.; the criteria which distinguish the Elohistic passages; only these show signs of continuity; the Jehovistic accounts of the Creation and Fall, Cain and his descendants, and the race of giants; the probable origin of this legend of a giant race; the older story is sometimes merely retouched by the Jehovist, as in the notice of Noah's birth in G.v. and the account of the Flood; contradictions introduced by these insertions; final proof of the Elohist having lived in the age of Samuel; first indication of the Jehovist having lived in the age of David or Solomon; the rainbow, a true sign of God's Covenant with man.

THE JEHOVISTIC PASSAGES IN GENESIS.

THE First Lesson for Quinquagesima Sunday In the New Lectionary ends with G.ix.19. It would have ended more properly with v.17, because here ends the older passage which forms the main portion of the chapter. Throughout this section, G.ix.1-17, which relates what occurred immediately after the Flood, we find precisely the same style and phraseology as marks the first account of the Creation. Thus we read in v.1, 'And ELOHIM blessed Noah and his sons, and said unto them, Be fruitful and multiply and replenish the earth'; and so we find in G.i.28, 'And ELOHIM blessed them and ELOHIM said, Be fruitful and multiply and replenish the earth and subdue it': in the one case there follows, 'and the fear of you and the dread of you shall be upon every beast of the earth, and upon every fowl of the air, and upon all that moveth upon the ground, and upon the fish of the sea—into your hand they are delivered'; and so we read in the other passage, 'and have dominion over the fish of the sea, and over the fowl of the air, and over every living thing that moveth upon the earth.' We have evidently the same writer in both passages; and it is that older writer of the age of Samuel—very possibly Samuel himself—who uses everywhere the word ELOHIM, 'GOD,' in speaking of the Divine Being, and abstains from using the name JEHOVAH. He tells us here how after the Flood ELOHIM gave to man every living thing for food, as well as the green herb which alone had been hitherto allowed,¹ but strenuously forbad both the shedding of human blood and the eating of blood; and so in the age of Samuel we find recorded a remarkable instance—indeed the only one mentioned in the whole history—of the people eating with blood. 'And they smote the Philistines that day, and the people were very faint; and the people flew upon the spoil, and took sheep and oxen and calves and slew them on the ground, and the people did eat them with the blood. And they told Saul saying, 'Behold! the people sin against Jehovah in that they eat with the blood.'² He then tells us how ELOHIM 'established a covenant' with Noah that there 'should be no more a flood to destroy the earth,' and makes the rainbow appear for the first time as the sign of that covenant, being ignorant, of course, of the physical fact that, whenever the sunshine fell upon the shower before the Flood, the rainbow must have appeared in the sky.

To this same Elohistic writer belongs also the notice in G.ix.28,29, about Noah living 350 years after the Flood, and 950 years altogether. It is true, the name of the Deity does not occur here at all. But the style of these verses corresponds exactly with that of G.v, with its list of patriarchs before the Flood from Adam to Noah, living most of them more than 900 years; and in this we find repeatedly the name 'ELOHIM' used—'In the day that ELOHIM created man, in the likeness of ELOHIM made He him.' 'And Enoch walked with ELOHIM three hundred years and begat sons and daughters.' 'And Enoch walked with ELOHIM and he was not, for ELOHIM took him.'³

And this leads me to make a remark, the neglect of which

---

¹ G.i.29,30.   ² 1S.xiv.32,33.   ³ G.v.1,22,24.

has led many persons, only imperfectly informed upon this subject,[1] into great mistakes and a total misapprehension of the method of Modern Biblical Criticism. What I mean is this, that the Elohistic matter in Genesis is not distinguished from the rest by critics *merely* by noting the use of the Divine Name; for here we find two verses, which are clearly seen, from a comparison with G.v, to belong to the Elohist, but which do not contain 'ELOHIM' at all. On the other hand, there are passages in which ELOHIM frequently occurs, sometimes even exclusively, without any mention of the name JEHOVAH, but which are as clearly seen *not* to belong to the older writer, because their style and phraseology differ entirely from his.[2] It is the combination of *two* things—the constant use of ELOHIM, or the deliberate suppression of JEHOVAH,[3] and the agreement in thought and expression with that of the older writer—which alone can determine whether any particular passage belongs to the Elohist or not. But, by carefully attending to this principle, and closely examining every line, nay, every word of the Book of Genesis, the Elohistic matter has been separated from the rest; and these passages, as I have said, when thus extracted, are found to compose a complete, consistent narrative, with scarcely a break or interruption from beginning to end. As one has written—'Whatever may be the truth concerning the origin of the different narratives constituting the present Book of Genesis, two facts

---

[1] *e.g.*, Bp. BROWNE (*B.C.*, p. 133, 135, 137, 159), see my *Commentary on B.C.* (*Genesis*, 115, 119, 120, 133).

[2] *e.g.*, G. xx. 1-17, xxi. 8-34, xxii. 1-13, xl-xlviii.

[3] The sole exception to this is in G. xvii. 1, where JEHOVAH occurs in an Elohistic passage. But the exception in this case proves the rule. If the Elohist has used everywhere else invariably ELOHIM in his narrative (87 times), and never JEHOVAH, it is plain that its occurrence in this single instance must be ascribed either to the slip of a copyist or else to the fact of the writer himself having inadvertently broken his rule, and used JEHOVAH, a name with which he was himself familiar. In the rest of the chapter he employs only ELOHIM for the personal name of the Deity, v. 1, 3, 9, 15, 18, 22, 23.

are certain—(i) That it contains *but one set of passages*, in which anything like a continuous story of the antediluvian and patriarchal ages can be traced ; (ii) That it *does* contain *such a set* of passages, distinguished by marked peculiarities of language, which, when all the other passages (where these peculiarities do not occur) are struck out, may be read continuously without the addition or omission of a single word, except in two or three cases, where very large additions to the original story appear to have been made, and some portions of it to have been struck out. All the other parts of Genesis, though often forming continuous narratives of considerable length, require this original story as the thread to hold them together, and cannot be combined into an independent history complete in itself without arbitrary additions or transpositions.'[1]

This ancient Elohistic Narrative, then, the Jehovist had before him ; and he enlarged and enlivened it by introducing a number of passages recording additional incidents in the lives of the patriarchs before and after the Flood, and especially by inserting the second account of the Creation ii.4a–25,[2] with its description of the planting of the garden of Eden and of the four mighty rivers which watered it. One of these rivers is named as the Euphrates, and the others are identified by scholars with the Indus, the Nile, and the Tigris, which are here supposed to be derived from one common source, and to flow thence in different directions, the Indus to the East, the Nile to the South, the Tigris to the North, the Euphrates to the West, according to the vague geographical notions of those times. So even, a thousand years later, Josephus in his explanation of this passage regards the

---

[1] E. V. Neale (*Genesis Critically Examined*, p. vi).

[2] v.4a belongs to the Elohist, and was probably removed from its original position at the beginning of G.i, (*comp.* the similar expressions at the *beginning* of histories, v. 1, vi. 9, xi. 10, 27, xxv. 12, 19, xxxvi. 1, 9, xxxvii. 2a), in order to form the commencement of the Jehovistic account of the Creation.

Euphrates, Tigris, and Nile, as branches of the same river;
but, instead of the Indus, he reckons the Ganges.[9] Then
the Jehovist goes on to tell us how the man, whom JEHOVAH
had formed, was placed in the garden and charged not to eat
of the tree of knowledge of good and evil, and how the animals
of all kinds were brought to him from all parts of the earth,
from all extremes of climate, the White Bear of the Frozen
North and the Humming-bird of the Tropics, the beasts and
birds of prey and their ordinary victims, and he gave names
to them all. Finally he informs us that, while all the other
creatures had mates, the LORD GOD (JEHOVAH ELOHIM) saw
that the man had none; 'and the LORD GOD caused a deep
sleep to fall upon the man and he slept; and the rib, which
the LORD GOD had taken from the man, made He a woman
and brought her unto the man.' Thus in this second account
of the Creation the man is *apparently* created the first, and
the woman is *certainly* created the last, of all living creatures;
whereas in the older story the man and woman are created
last of all, as the crowning work of ELOHIM, and are created
together—'And ELOHIM created man in His own image, in
the image of ELOHIM created He him; male and female
created He them.'[10]

Next he describes the Temptation and the Fall,[11] the sin
and punishment of Cain,[12] and the progress of the arts of
cattle-keeping, music, and smithery among his descendants;[13]
and he tells us how the 'sons of God' took wives of the
beautiful 'daughters of men,' and from them sprung a race
of mighty heroes, 'which were of old, men of renown.'[14]
'There were giants too in the earth in those days'[15]—a tradition which is found to exist among most nations, and has
probably arisen from the discoveries of huge bones which have
been ignorantly supposed to be human. Perhaps this tradition

[9] *Ant.* I.i.3. [10] G.i.27. [11] G.iii. [12] G.iv.1-16.
[13] G.iv.17-22. [14] G.vi.1-4. [15] G.vi.4.

derived some support among the ancients from the gigantic statues and vast architectural structures of Egypt, Assyria, and Greece, and especially among the Hebrews from the massive ruins in the trans-Jordanic lands, where sarcophagi of huge size, made of the black basalt of the country, are now used as water-troughs, one of which is spoken of in D.iii.11 as the 'iron bedstead' of Og the king of Bashan; 'nine cubits was the length thereof and four cubits the breadth of it'—that is, it was 16 feet long and 7 feet broad. Even now, as travellers tell us, many of these stone coffins exist in this region, of vast dimensions.[16] But no human remains of such gigantic size have as yet been discovered. Josephus indeed says, speaking of the time of the Judges, 'At this time also remained some of the race of giants, who for bigness of body and terrible aspect were very unlike other men; the sight of them was astonishing, being a thing fearful to be told; their bones are yet to be seen, but so large as to exceed all belief.'[17] But these bones,[18] no doubt, belonged to huge extinct animals, which were mistaken by the ancients for human remains; as St. Augustine tells us of a tooth which he saw, a hundred times larger than ordinary teeth,[19] and which in all probability once belonged to an elephant. So Virgil supposed that there was not only a diminution in size of the human race from primeval times, but that this diminution would continue in the ages to come; and, speaking of the slaughter on one of the great battle-fields of his own time, he pictures the pigmy ploughman of later days going over the ground centuries afterwards, and marvelling at the huge bones turned out from the dug-up graves.[20] But in truth there is no sign of any

---

[16] Burckhardt, pp. 220, 246, Robinson, III. p. 658, Seetzen, I. pp. 355, 360, quoted by Keil, II. p. 409.   [17] *Ant.* V. ii. 3.
[18] That is, if any such bones were really to be seen in Palestine in the time of Josephus, who is not a very trustworthy authority on such points.
[19] *De Civ. Dei*, xv. 9.   [20] *Georg.*, 1. 497.

such change having taken place in the stature of the human race from the earliest times of which we have any knowledge till now. The remains found in ancient tombs and pyramids are enough to show this, since they correspond generally in stature and size to the men of our own times. As one has said—'Looking upward from the base of the Great Pyramid, we might suppose it the work of giants; but it is entered by passages admitting with difficulty a man of the present size, and we find in the centre a sarcophagus about six feet long.'[11]

The story in Genesis now passes on to the account of the Flood, which was sent, says the Elohist, because 'the earth was corrupt before ELOHIM and the earth was filled with violence';[12] which statement the Jehovist expands and emphasizes in his own peculiar style as follows: 'And ELOHIM saw that the wickedness of man was great in the earth, and that every imagination of the thoughts of his heart was only evil continually. And it repented JEHOVAH that He had made man on the earth, and JEHOVAH said, I will destroy man whom I have created from the face of the ground, both man and beast and creeping thing and fowl of the heaven: for it repenteth Me that I have made them.'[13] Thus this later writer has not only inserted whole stories of his own, but he has retouched the more ancient narrative, where it seemed to want point and force, or to need some additional feature. He has done this already in G.v, in the list of the antediluvian patriarchs, which belongs undoubtedly to the older writer, and must have originally contained an account of the birth of Noah, exactly similar in form to those of the seven preceding patriarchs; that is to say, the Elohist must have written, as in all the other instances, 'And Lamech lived 182 years and begat Noah.' But the Jehovist has retouched the passage, and it now stands thus—'And Lamech lived 182 years and

[11] KENRICK, *Prim. Hist.* p.74.   [12] G.vi.11.   [13] G.vi.5-7.

begat a son, and he called his name Noah, saying, This same shall comfort us concerning our work and toil of our hands, because of the ground which JEHOVAH hath cursed'[14]—where we have not only the name 'JEHOVAH,' but a distinct reference to the curse pronounced upon the ground after the Fall and the work and toil imposed on Adam—'Cursed is the ground for thy sake; in sorrow—that is, in toilsome labour—shalt thou eat of it all the days of thy life'[15]—all which belongs to the same hand.

Accordingly, the Jehovist does not give us a second account of the Flood, as he has done of the Creation; he merely retouches the older story, and sometimes not very felicitously. The Elohist, for instance, makes ELOHIM command Noah to bring 'of every living thing of all flesh, two of every sort, into the Ark, male and female.'[16] The Jehovist makes JEHOVAH say unto Noah, 'Of every *clean* beast thou shalt take into the Ark by *sevens*, the male and the female, and of the beasts that are *not clean* by *two*, the male and the female, of fowls also of the heaven by *sevens*, the male and the female';[17] and the reason for his doing this is plain, because he wishes to introduce a sacrifice of thanksgiving after the Flood, and he needs these seven pairs of clean beasts and birds that Noah 'may build an altar unto JEHOVAH, and take of every clean beast and every clean fowl, and offer burnt-offerings on the altar'; whereupon, he says, 'JEHOVAH smelled a sweet savour, and JEHOVAH said in his heart, I will not again curse the ground any more for man's sake.'[18] Again, in the midst of the older account of Noah and the other human and brute creatures coming out of the Ark, the Jehovist has inserted this clause, 'and Noah removed the covering of the Ark and looked, and lo! the face of the ground was dry;' and this took place on 'the first day of the *first* month.'[19] But Noah and the rest came out of the

---

[14] G. v. 28, 29. [15] G. iii. 17-19. [16] G. vi. 19, 20, comp. vii. 8, 9, 15, 16.
[17] G. vii. 2, 3. [18] G. viii. 20-22. [19] G. viii. 13.

Ark on 'the twenty-seventh day of the *second* month'[20]—from which it follows that, in consequence of this injudicious insertion, the Ark remains uncovered for nearly two months, the ground being dry, and yet none of the birds or insects flew away!

I have said that the Elohistic Narrative was probably written in the age of Samuel, and have given some reasons which lead to that conclusion,[21] and I will now add another. To this writer belongs G.xxxvi, which is for the most part a mere dry catalogue of names of the sons or descendants of Esau or Edom—in other words, a list of the principal Edomite tribes as they existed in the writer's time. To the eye of most readers this catalogue will have but an uninviting, dreary aspect, just as a list of Scottish clans and their remote ancestors would not be very attractive to an ordinary English student of history. But what if we found in such an ancient Scottish register a passage like this—'And these are the kings that reigned in Scotland, before there reigned any king over the people of England'? Should we not at once infer that, at the time when such words were written, England had already been ruled by a king, though possibly only by one? And so, when we read in G.xxxvi.31, 'These are the kings that reigned in the land of Edom, before the reigning of a king over the children of Israel,' we conclude that this passage could not have been written before the age of Saul, the first king of Israel, or, in other words, before the age of Samuel. But may it not have been written in a still later age? Let us look more closely at this list of Edomite kings. They are eight in number, and in each instance the king's death and the name of his successor are mentioned in precisely the same form—*e.g.*, 'and Bela died, and Jobab, son of Zerah of Bozrah, reigned in his stead'[22]—except in the case of the last king, Hadar or Hadad. The death of Hadad is not

[20] G. viii. 14, &c.   [21] p. 15-17   [22] G. xxxvi. 33.

mentioned: we read only, 'And Baal-hanan, son of Achbor, died, and Hadad reigned in his stead, and the name of his city was Pau, and his wife's name was Mehetabel, daughter of Matred, daughter of Mezahab.'[33] The writer evidently knew a great deal more about this king Hadad than about any of the others, since he mentions not only his city and the name of his wife, but the names also of her mother and grandfather. Now, since he does not mention his death or name his successor, as in all the other instances, it is plain that Hadad was still living when this passage was written. Therefore, since all these reigned before there was a king in Israel, it follows that Hadad must have reigned in Edom *before* Saul's time; again, as he was not dead at the time when this passage was written, he must have been reigning also *after* Saul became king over Israel; so that this list must have been composed in the age—and therefore, very probably, by the hand—of SAMUEL.

But, if the Elohist lived in Samuel's time, when did the later writer, the Jehovist, live? We have seen that G.ix. 1–17 and also v.28,29 belong to the Elohist. But between these two passages the Jehovist has inserted a section, which betrays unmistakably his style, not only by the use of the name JEHOVAH, 'Blessed be JEHOVAH, the Elohim of Shem!', but by the phraseology throughout, as may be seen in critical works.[34] It is obvious that the main object aimed at in this passage is to throw contempt and reproach upon Canaan. He is not descended from Shem, as the Hebrews were, but he is a son of Ham, and a heavy curse is laid upon his head by his grandfather Noah—'Cursed be Canaan! a *servant of servants* shall he be unto his brethren. Blessed be JEHOVAH, the Elohim of Shem! and Canaan shall be his servant. ELOHIM shall enlarge Japheth, and he shall dwell in the tents

---

[33] G. xxxvi. 39.   [34] *Pent.* V. Art. 47, 48.

of Shem, and *Canaan shall be his servant.'*[14] Why all this stress laid upon Canaan becoming a *servant*—that is, a slave to Shem and Japheth—'a servant of servants unto his brethren' —a slave of slaves? We know how modern slave-holders have wrested this curse into a reason for reducing all black races —supposed to be the children of Ham—into slavery, forgetting the fact that the curse is not pronounced upon the sons of Ham generally, but solely upon the Canaanites.

Manifestly the passage before us seeks to find a justification for the manner in which the Canaanites were subdued and subjected by the Israelites in *Solomon's* time. The history of Samuel, Saul, and David, exhibits no evidence whatever of such complete prostration of the Canaanite tribes under the feet of their Israelitish masters. On the contrary, it is noted that in Samuel's time 'there was peace between Israel and the *Amorites*';[16] while in the earlier part of David's reign the *Jebusites* possessed the stronghold of Zion and for a while defied him.[17] It is not till Solomon's time that we read— 'All the people that were left of the Amorites, Hittites, Perizzites, Hivites, and Jebusites'—in one word, all the people that were left of the Canaanites—'who were not of the children of Israel, their children that were left after them in the land, whom the children of Israel also were not able to exterminate, upon these did Solomon levy a *tribute of bond-service* unto this day.'[18] Yes! let Solomon make bondslaves of the sons of Canaan; for did not Noah say of old, 'Cursed be Canaan! a slave of slaves shall he be to his brethren'?

Thus the passage was probably written, perhaps by one of Samuel's pupils, such as Nathan the prophet, in the early part of Solomon's reign, or even somewhat earlier, in the latter part of David's reign, when the idea of exacting this bond-service from the Canaanites may have been already entertained.

---

[14] G. ix. 25, 27.
[17] 2 S. v. 6–8.
[16] 1 S. vii. 14.
[18] 1 K. ix. 20, 21.

How different from the tone of this passage—how far more grand, having the character of a true inspiration—was the thought of the Elohist, who has just before made the rainbow the sign of God's everlasting covenant of grace to man! We may fall back with a sure quiet trust on the firm ground of this unanswerable argument, that He who has made not only the rainbow, but other things around us so beautiful, and has given us eyes to see and hearts to appreciate the wisdom and goodness of His works, has surely kind and gracious thoughts towards us. He would not mock a world lying under a curse —a 'slave of slaves' to the spirit of evil—a race of whom (as some suppose) the vast majority are doomed to everlasting woe—with these bright exhibitions of His Fatherly Love. Whether Adam fell in Paradise or not, whether Noah was saved in the Ark or not, whether the cities of the plain were destroyed for their wickedness or not, yet in the minds of those who wrote those stories of old there was a deep and true conviction of the evil nature of sin and its terrible consequences. But so, too, to the minds of pious men of old it was revealed that the heaven and the earth are the work of the Great Creator, that the blessed light came forth at the word of God, and that man himself is made in his Maker's image. We feel the bonds of our common humanity drawn yet more closely around us when we see that in those days, as now, the Presence of a Heavenly Friend was realised as ever near to each faithful soul, ready to comfort, strengthen, bless, or, if need be, to correct and chasten—nay, that to their eyes, as to ours, the gracious signs of nature were witnessing of an eternal bond between the Father of spirits and His children, and the bright beauty of the rainbow after the storm—the simple fact that, notwithstanding all our provocations, God still gives us power to see and to enjoy His Goodness—was regarded as a token of the continuance of His loving care for us; an assurance and pledge of forgiveness, restoration, and peace.

LECTURE IV.

SUMMARY.

THE New Lesson for the First Sunday in Lent, G. xii. 12-29, a Jehovistic passage, except v. 29; this and other short fragments of the older story preserved with scrupulous care, which shows the respect paid to it, probably by Samuel's disciples after his death, and enables us to reconstruct it almost in its original form; the Jehovistic passages in Genesis may have been all written by one hand; G. xiv. xv., not included in these; the name 'Jehovah' used more freely in some of them than in others; all indications of time place the Jehovist in the age of David and Solomon, e.g. extended geographical knowledge, signs of progress in the arts and familiarity with the customs of courts, and especially the prophecy of Edom's throwing off the yoke of Israel; the composite character of Genesis gives a confused view of the patriarchs, especially of Abraham; the primary Elohistic account of Abraham; the patriarch's hope at Sarah's grave compared with that of the Christian.

THE AGE OF THE JEHOVIST IN GENESIS.

IN my previous Lectures I have set before you the main distinctions between the ancient Elohistic Narrative and the later insertions in the Book of Genesis. Especially I have mentioned that the older writer is distinguished everywhere, not merely by his using constantly the name 'ELOHIM' to the exclusion of 'JEHOVAH,' but by a characteristic phraseology.

Let us take, for instance, the section G.xix.12-29, appointed in the New Lectionary as the First Lesson for the First Sunday in Lent. In this whole section, except in *v.*29, the name of JEHOVAH is continually employed—'the cry of them is waxen great before JEHOVAH, and JEHOVAH hath sent us to destroy it'—'up, get you out of this place, for JEHOVAH will destroy this city'—'JEHOVAH being merciful unto him'—'then JEHOVAH rained upon Sodom and upon Gomorrah brimstone and fire from JEHOVAH out of heaven' —'and Abraham gat up early in the morning to the place where he stood before JEHOVAH.'[1] In all these places the English Bible has 'the LORD,' printed in capital letters, by which our older translators, in imitation of the Septuagint and Vulgate, have represented everywhere the name 'JEHOVAH',

[1] *v.* 13, 14, 16, 24, 27.

obscuring frequently the sense by so doing—a defect which will doubtless be amended in the New Translation. But in v.18, 'And Lot said unto them, Oh, not so, my Lord,' the word 'Lord' is printed in ordinary type; and here it means no more than it would in common English, viz., 'Master' or 'Sir,' as an expression of respect. The Lesson in this case, however, begins most abruptly, 'And the men said unto Lot, Hast thou here any besides?'; and the reason of this is, that the New Lectionary omits the offensive passage with which the chapter begins and which used to be read among the Sunday Lessons,[1] as even the former Lectionary omitted that with which it ends[2]—both of which, though they do not either of them contain the name of the Deity, belong undoubtedly to the Jehovist, since they resemble closely the other passages due to this writer, not only in expression and style, but in subject-matter, all the stories in Genesis of a similar character having come from his hand.

But in the midst of this Jehovistic matter, at the end of the account of the destruction of Sodom and Gomorrah, occur the words of v.29, 'And it came to pass, when ELOHIM destroyed the cities of the plain, that ELOHIM remembered Abraham, and sent Lot out of the midst of the overthrow, when He overthrew the cities in which Lot dwelt.' Hitherto in this story, in this and the preceding chapter, only JEHOVAH has been used, altogether seventeen times, and never once ELOHIM. How can it be supposed that the *same* writer would suddenly change his style and use only ELOHIM in one single verse as here? And how strange it would be if, after giving a long detailed account of these occurrences, of the visit of JEHOVAH to Abraham, the destruction of the cities, and the deliverance of Lot, he had added this notice at the end, just as if none of these things had been

[1] v.1-11.   [2] v.30-38.

before related at all ! This verse, in short, is part of the Elohistic Narrative, and contains all that the Elohist said upon the subject; and in that Narrative, when extracted and read by itself, it will be found to take its place very properly, though in its present position it forms but a tame and spiritless conclusion after the long and striking circumstantial story of the Jehovist. And we find here repeated the phraseology of the older writer. As before he had mentioned that 'Lot dwelt in the cities of the plain,'[a] so here he speaks of 'ELOHIM destroying the cities of the plain,' and 'overthrowing the cities in which Lot dwelt.' As before he said that 'ELOHIM remembered Noah,'[b] so here he says that 'ELOHIM remembered Abraham.' Beyond all doubt, therefore, it belongs to the Elohist; and, as it lay before the later writer in the older story, it formed the text—the *thema*, as it were—upon which the latter has composed his own vivacious narrative in these two chapters, with which he has supplemented the very brief Elohistic notice.

I have also given reasons for supposing that the Elohistic Narrative was composed in the age, and therefore probably by the hand, of the great Reformer Samuel, for the use of the students in the schools which he established, and over which indeed towards the close of his life we find him apparently presiding.[c] It is very natural that after his death it should have been retouched, embellished, and enlarged, by some one or more of his favourite disciples, in the next age, the age of David and Solomon. It would seem almost certain that this would happen. Their Master's work may have been left by his death in his pupils' hands unfinished ; they may have been advised by him or charged to complete it, or their own feelings may have

[a] G. xiii. 12.   [b] G. viii. 1.   [c] 1 S. xix. 20.

prompted them to do so. Even during his lifetime, and under his eye and direction, they may have been practised already in such labours; and we read, in fact, of the 'Book of Jashar'[1] and the 'Book of the Wars of JEHOVAH,'[2] which have altogether disappeared, but were probably composed in these schools. It is easy to believe that the reverence paid to the Master in such a case would protect as far as possible the identical words which he had written, so that the first account of the Creation was retained, with all its supposed defects, when the second was inserted; whereas, instead of the older story of the Flood being cancelled and another substituted in its place, almost every line and letter of the more ancient story has been preserved, the later writer having contented himself with merely interlining, as it were, his own additional insertions; and so, too, the short Elohistic notice has been left about the overthrow of the cities of the plain, though rendered quite unnecessary and superfluous by the long Jehovistic story which precedes it. It is this scrupulous care to preserve every word of the more ancient Narrative, which enables us to extract that Narrative from the whole Book of Genesis almost in its complete form as an unbroken history; and such scrupulosity, as I have said, would be only natural in a writer who undertook to carry on and supplement his great Master's work when he was gone.

Accordingly in my last Lecture I showed that some portion of the Jehovistic matter in Genesis was most probably composed either in the first years of Solomon's reign or the last of David's. According to the usual chronology Samuel died about four years before the death of Saul, and then David reigned for 40½ years.[3] Thus about 45 years elapsed between Samuel's death and Solomon's

---

[1] J.x.13, 2S.i.18.   [2] N.xxi.14.   [3] 2S.v.5.

accession; so that one and the same disciple of Samuel—
such as Nathan—might have made additions to the older
story at different times, and, if 20 years old at his Master's
decease, would be not older than 70, if writing in the fifth
year of Solomon. It seems possible that this is really the
case, viz., that the Jehovistic parts of Genesis were almost
all written by the same hand, as they exhibit everywhere the
same peculiar phrases and modes of thought and feeling.
G.xiv, however, is marked by a distinct phraseology of its
own, and, though belonging to the same age, was no doubt
contributed by another writer. G.xv also shows signs of
a *much later* age, and with some few other small insertions
in Genesis [10] belongs to a writer of whom I shall speak more
at length hereafter, who lived four centuries afterwards,
and who seems to have edited the story, as it had come
into his hands, with amplifications of his own. But
otherwise the supplementary portions of Genesis all betray
the same peculiarities of style, and may all perhaps be due
to one and the same hand, though written, it may be, at
different intervals in the space of half a century, during
the latter years of Saul, the whole reign of David, and the
first years of Solomon. In some of these ELOHIM is used
exclusively,[11] and not JEHOVAH at all; in others JEHOVAH
is used, but sparingly;[12] in others JEHOVAH is used
very freely;[13] but in all the same phraseology occurs entirely distinct from that of the Elohist. It would seem
as if the writer began by following the example of his
predecessor, using only ELOHIM, but in the later portions of
his work, for some reason or other, employed more familiarly
the name JEHOVAH. Perhaps we may see hereafter more

---

[10] G.vi.4, x.8-12, xv.1-21, xviii.18,19, xxii.14-18, xxiv.59,60, xxvi.4,5, xxviii.15,20-22, xxxi.13, xxxv.2-4, as shown in *Pent.* (V.66,VI.482.)

[11] *e.g.* G.xx.1-17, xxi.8 sq. [12] *e.g.* G.xxi.33,34, xxii.1-13.

[13] *e.g.* G.xviii,xix.

clearly the reason of this. Meanwhile it is possible, of course, as some eminent critics maintain, that other writers, even of different ages, may have contributed parts of the Jehovistic matter, employing a somewhat similar phraseology, especially when we remember that an oriental tongue, as, for instance, the Arabic,[14] may remain unchanged for centuries. But there is no *necessity* as yet for supposing this in the present instance, since every sign of time, which has hitherto been detected in these passages, seems to point to the age of David and Solomon, and therefore very possibly to one and the same writer.

Look, for instance, at the extended geographical knowledge displayed in these passages—the four great rivers in G.ii. 10-14, the seventy nations in G.x—a sign of that more intimate acquaintance with Phœnician commerce, which existed in the latter years of David and the first of Solomon, when 'Hiram, king of Tyre, sent his servant unto Solomon, for he had heard that they had anointed him king in the room of his father, for Hiram was ever a lover of David.'[15] It is here also that we read of Abraham being rich not only in flocks and herds, camels and he-asses,[16] but in silver and gold,[17] and of his producing out of his treasures for Rebekah, his son's bride-elect, 'a golden nose-ring and bracelets,' 'jewels of silver and jewels of gold.'[18] It is here we find mention made of 'instruments of music' and 'working in brass and iron'[19]—of the 'servants of Pharaoh,'[20] the 'servants of Abimelech,'[21] and of the large household of 'menservants and maidservants' belonging to Abraham, Isaac, and Jacob[22]—all signs of a great advance in civilization from the days of Samuel and Saul, when at one time 'there

[14] PALGRAVE (*Arabia*, I. p. 311.) [15] 1 K. v. 1. [18] G. xxiv. 35.
[15] G. xiii. 2, xxiv. 35. [16] G. xxiv. 22, 53. [19] G. iv. 21, 22.
[17] G. xl. 20, xli. 10, 37, 38, &c. [21] G. xx. 8, xxi. 25, &c.
[22] G. xxiv. 35, xxvi. 14, xxx. 43.

THE AGE OF THE JEHOVIST IN GENESIS. 49

was no smith found throughout all the land of Israel,'[13] and giving evidence of some familiarity with the customs of royalty, as in an age when the arts had made considerable progress, such as that in which first the Tabernacle of David and then the palaces and Temple of Solomon were built in Jerusalem, the last with the aid of Phœnician workmen.

It is the Jehovist again who predicts that Esau or Edom shall be subject to his younger brother Jacob or Israel in the following words addressed to their mother Rebekah :—

> 'Two nations are in thy womb,
> And two folks shall be separated from thy bowels ;
> And folk shall be stronger than folk,
> And the elder shall serve the younger.'[14]

This passage, if we regard it as merely reflecting contemporary history, refers plainly to the subjection of the Edomites to Israel in David's days, when 'David put garrisons in Edom, throughout all Edom put he garrisons; and all they of Edom became David's servants.'[15] And the bitter enmity between Edom and Israel which resulted from this assumption of sovereignty, the younger brother taking the right of pre-eminence, which belonged by the order of birth to the older people, and claiming to lord it over the neighbouring tribes—an enmity which was deepened into a deadly and inveterate hatred, by the defeat of David's forces on one occasion, and the cruel revenge which Joab took in consequence, when he 'went up to bury the slain' of Israel[16]—is strikingly shadowed forth in another Jehovistic passage, 'And Esau hated Jacob because of the blessing wherewith his father had blessed him ; and Esau said in his heart, The days of mourning for my father are at hand ; then will I slay my brother Jacob.'[17]

This prediction, therefore, of Israel's supremacy over Edom

[13] 1 S. xiii. 19. [14] G. xxv. 23. [15] 2 S. viii. 14.
[16] 1 K. xi. 16. [17] G. xxvii. 41.

E

was very probably written in David's time. But we find afterwards another prediction put into the mouth of Isaac and addressed to Esau himself, as follows:—

> 'By thy sword shalt thou live,
> And thou shalt serve thy brother;
> And it shall come to pass, when thou shalt have rule,
> That thou shalt break his yoke from off thy neck.'[39]

It is certain that Edom did remain a 'servant' to his 'younger brother' Israel during the latter part of David's reign, having been thoroughly crushed by Joab's massacre, and held in awe by David's garrisons. But the very fact that David was obliged to place 'garrisons' in the country, in order to maintain his authority in it—a fact which is repeated with special emphasis, 'throughout all Edom put he garrisons'—implies that he was not perfectly secure of his position—that there was a certain stubborn unwillingness on the part of the Edomite people to submit to his yoke. And accordingly we find that in the very beginning of Solomon's reign, as soon as ever the triumphant conqueror David and David's great captain Joab were dead, Hadad the Edomite, a fugitive prince, who had escaped when quite young from Joab's massacre,[40]—very possibly the son or grandson of that same Hadad whom the Elohist mentions last in the list of Edomite kings before there was any king in Israel,[41] and who was reigning, as we saw, in Samuel's time,[42]—raised the standard of revolt against the rule of Solomon,[43] as Rezon also did in Syria;[44] and, no doubt, both succeeded in shaking off the yoke of Israel. With respect to Rezon, indeed, our English Bible tells us, 'He was an adversary to Israel all the days of Solomon, together with the evil which Hadad did: and he abhorred Israel and reigned over Syria.'[45] But the Greek translation omits all mention of Rezon and Syria, and says,

[39] G. xxvii. 40.   [40] 1 K. xi. 14-20.   [41] G. xxxvi. 31-39.   [42] p. 37, 38.
[43] 1 K. xi. 21, 22.   [44] 1 K. xi. 23, 24.   [45] 1 K. xi. 25.

'This is the mischief which Hadad did, and he vexed Israel and reigned in the land of Edom.'[35] Thus this second prediction which says of Edom, 'Thou shalt serve thy brother Israel, but, when thou shalt have rule, thou shalt break his yoke from off thy neck,' may have been written in the early days of Solomon.

Such are some of the reasons which help us to fix the composition of the Jehovistic insertions in Genesis in the reign of David and the early part of Solomon's reign; and these may suffice for the present. I will only now draw your attention to the fact that, in consequence of the composite character of the Book of Genesis, it must necessarily follow that we obtain but a broken and distorted view of the life and character of any one of the patriarchs, as meant to be exhibited by the original writer. This is a point of very great interest, and, of course it is altogether ignored by ordinary readers and expositors of the Bible. We often hear, for instance, the character of Abraham set forth as a model of excellence for the imitation of all ages. But *what* Abraham?—*which* of the *three* or *four* Abrahams whose doings are mixed up in utter confusion by the different writers concerned in the composition of Genesis? How perplexing it is to find, in the account of the 'father of the faithful,' the record of conduct so mean and unworthy as that related of him in one place, where he prompts Sarah to say that she was his sister instead of his wife, and exposes her to injury in the Court of Pharaoh in order to screen himself from harm,[36] and then in another place to find him, at the end of twenty years, repeating the same base act in the Court of Abimelech,[37] when Sarah was already 'old and well-stricken in years,'[38] in fact ninety years old,[39] yet expected soon to be the mother of a firstborn son,[40] the child of

[35] 1 K. xi. 22 (Vat. M.S.) [36] G. xii. 10–20. [37] G. xx. 1–18.
[38] G. xviii. 11. [39] G. xvii. 17. [40] G. xviii. 14, xxi. 2.

promise, the centre of such great hopes, the reward of so many years of patient faith and expectation!

But nothing of all this appears in the original Elohistic Narrative, which in its grand simplicity represents each one of the patriarchs, as I have said, without any flaw in his character. In that Narrative Abraham migrates of his own accord, without having received any miraculous call, from Charran to Canaan,[41] carrying out in so doing the purpose of his father.[42] He dwells in the land of Canaan,[43] and there Hagar bears him a son Ishmael, 'for Sarah had no children.'[44] But many years afterwards, in his old age, the Deity appears to him saying, 'I am (EL SHADDAI) GOD ALMIGHTY,' and covenants to give to him and to his seed after him the land of his sojournings,[45] commanding the rite of circumcision to be observed as the sign and seal of the covenant,[46] and promising a son to him by Sarah.[47] Abraham obeys the command,[48] and receives the promised son, and circumcises him.[49] His wife Sarah dies, and he buys from the sons of Heth the burying-place at Hebron, where he buries Sarah,[50] and where he himself is buried by his two sons, Ishmael and Isaac, 'in a ripe old age, an old man and full of years, and he was gathered unto his people.'[51]

And this is all the genuine original story of Abraham! This is the *real* Abraham of the Bible, the Abraham of the Elohist. We have here no warlike sheikh, with his 318 trained servants all born in his house, going to do battle with five confederate kings [52]—no expulsion of Ishmael,[53] no purpose of sacrificing Isaac,[54] no marrying another wife or wives and begetting six sons,[55] either during Sarah's life-time, when Abraham was above a hundred years old,[56] or after her

---

[41] G.xii.5. [42] G.xi.31. [43] G.xiii.12a. [44] G.xvi.1,3,15,16
[45] G.xvii.1 &. [46] G.xvii.9–14. [47] G.xvii.15–22. [48] G.xvii.23–27.
[49] G.xxi.2–5. [50] G.xxiii.1–20. [51] G.xxv.7–10. [52] G.xiv.
[53] G.xxi.9–21. [54] G.xxii.1–13. [55] G.xxv.1–6. [56] G.xxi.5.

death, when he was 137 years old,[57] though it seemed to himself incredible that a son should be born to him even at 99[58]—above all, no miserable subterfuge at the Court of Pharaoh,[59] or still more reprehensible repetition of the fault at the Court of Abimelech.[60] All these additions, which have been made by later writers, are mere refractions and distortions of the older story, and mar the simple dignity of the patriarch's character as there portrayed.

Still the Elohist can touch our hearts as men when he places us beside that cave in the field of Machpelah, and describes for us the affecting scene, how 'Abraham came down to mourn for Sarah and to weep for her,'[61] and 'stood up from before his dead,' and pleaded with the sons of Heth, saying, 'I am a stranger and a sojourner with you: give me a possession of a burying place with you that I may bury my dead out of my sight.'[62] And yet we must not carry to that scene our own emotions, our own hopes, our own faith, as Christians—for whom the great Apostle of the Gentiles has made the patriarch's faith a very watchword, 'Abraham believed God, and it was counted unto him for righteousness.'[63] In the days of Abraham, or rather in the far later days of him who writes here the story of Abraham, the strongest faith was hardly able to reach out the hand and lay hold of a hope beyond the grave; the dead were buried, like Sarah in this Narrative, 'out of sight'[64] for ever and ever; and even long afterwards the good Hezekiah could say, 'The grave cannot praise Thee; death cannot celebrate Thee; they that go down into the pit cannot hope for Thy Truth.'[65]

We Christians, however, taught by the lips of Him who 'has brought life and immortality to light by the Gospel,'[66] believe that the same 'Faithful Creator,'[67] who 'is loving

---

[57] G. xxiii. 1, comp. xvii. 17. [62] G. xvii. 1. 17. [67] G. ii. 10–20.
[58] G. xx. 1–18. [63] G. xxiii. 1. [64] v. 3–16. [65] Rom. iv. 3.
[66] G. xxiii. 4, 8. [67] Is. xxxviii. 18. [65] 2 Tim. i. 10. [67] 1 Pet. iv. 19.

unto every man,' whose 'tender mercies are over all His works,'[a] is the Lord of both worlds, that the same Fatherly and Motherly Care and Wisdom and Might will order for us *there* as here. We know that the dear Son of God and all the best and noblest of our race, who have followed in his train in different paths of duty, have passed the mysterious barrier, the gate which leads out of Time into Eternity; and we feel and are sure that all these are safe under the Shadow of the Mighty Hand. But the same Love broods over all, and we can leave our dear ones, and leave ourselves, in the merciful care, to the wise disposal of Him who watches day and night, guiding the ages as they go, ordering the movements of this Mighty Universe, yet listening to the humblest prayer of the poor penitent. In our hours of saddest bereavement we may learn to bow to the will of Him who is the Lord of death as well as life, 'JEHOVAH,' the Living God, the Life-giver, 'the same yesterday, and to-day, and for ever.'[b] But, while we live, our song shall be—like that which the Jewish king poured forth from his overflowing heart when raised from sickness nigh unto death—' The living, the living, he shall praise Thee, as I do this day; the father to the children shall make known Thy Truth.'[c]

[a] Ps. cxlv. 9.   [b] Heb. xiii. 8.   [c] Is. xxxviii. 19.

LECTURE V.

SUMMARY.

The Jehovist assigned by some to a later age than Solomon's, because of the revolt of Edom in Joram's time; this conclusion unnecessary, since the Moabite Stone implies the revolt of Moab in Solomon's time; despotic acts of Solomon on his accession; revolts of subject provinces after the death of David and Joab; the statements of the vast extent and peaceful condition of Solomon's empire at variance with other Scripture statements, and written during the Captivity; signs of internal disorder in Solomon's reign, as well as of external troubles, which explain the prediction of Edom's revolt; Jacob's Blessing, Jehovistic; that on Judah points to the time of David's glory, before his great sin; that on Joseph points to the same happy time, when the Ten Tribes had acknowledged David as king; that on Levi points to the depressed condition of the priestly tribe in the same age, the golden period of David's life, about the twelfth year of his reign; the Rev. JAMES MARTINEAU on Bible-reading in Sunday Schools.

THE AGE OF THE JEHOVIST FURTHER CONSIDERED.

> ' And by thy sword shalt thou live,
> And thou shalt serve thy brother ;
> And it shall come to pass, when thou shalt have rule,
> That thou shalt break his yoke from off thy neck.'[1]

N my last lecture I quoted these words as showing that the passage in which they occur must have been written in the early part of Solomon's reign, when the Edomite prince Hadad returned from his long exile in Egypt, and raised a rebellion among his people, and they broke from off their neck the yoke of Israel. But I notice this passage again, because it has mainly influenced some eminent critics to assign a far later date to this and other Jehovistic portions of the Book of Genesis than the age of Solomon ; and indeed it is the only passage, as far as I know, that has been plausibly alleged in support of that view. We read, in fact, that more than a century after Solomon, in the days of Joram, son of Jehosaphat, king of Judah, ' Edom revolted from under the hand of Judah unto this day ' ;[2] and hence it has been concluded that the prophecy before us must have been written some time after this event. But there seems to be no necessity whatever for such a conclusion.

---

[1] G. xxvi. 40.   [2] 2 K. viii. 22.

AGE OF THE JEHOVIST FURTHER CONSIDERED.

Every other indication of time, which has been detected as yet in this part of the story in Genesis, points to the fifty years which include the last years of Saul and the first of Solomon. And, as to the passage we are now considering, the newly-found Moabite Stone brings further unexpected confirmation of the fact that the revolt of Hadad was successful, and Edom was really liberated from the yoke of Israel in Solomon's time.

For we learn from that remarkable monument that Moab, which lay adjoining Edom, must in all probability in Solomon's time have recovered its independence, though once, like Edom, fearfully crushed under David's ferocious measures, and brought under the yoke of Israel.[1] As one of the ablest commentators on this Stone has written, 'This therefore throws new light upon the Biblical history, inasmuch as it shows that the Moabites must either have taken advantage of the distracted state of Judæa [after the death of Solomon] to free themselves of the Jewish vassalage, or that they *obtained their liberty under Solomon*. We incline to the latter opinion.'[2] In short, there can be little doubt that Edom and Syria, Moab and Ammon, outlying districts which David had subdued, all threw off the yoke of Israel as soon as the conqueror was dead, when Joab, the valiant warrior, whose name had been for thirty years a terror to the foes of Israel, had been put to death by Solomon's orders in the first years of his reign.[3] You will remember the pitiful story —about the aged priest Abiathar, who had followed David's fortunes for half a century, had fled to him when hiding from fear of Saul in the wilderness, had carried the ark before him afterwards as king, in his times of gladness and of grief, 'having been afflicted in all wherein he was afflicted,'[4]—and Joab, the commander-in-chief, who had been David's right-

[1] 2 S. viii. 2.
[2] GINSBURG (*Moabite Stone*, p. 20.)
[3] 1 K. ii. 29, 34.
[4] 1 K. i. 7, ii. 26.

hand from the first, had helped to gain so many victories, and had done so much to extend his empire, and who, though undoubtedly a man of craft and blood, was surely not worse in this respect than David himself, since we know that by David's orders he placed Uriah in the front of the battle, and left him there unsupported to perish by the enemy's hand, in order that the treacherous king might carry on undisturbed his guilty intercourse with Bathsheba, Uriah's wife.[7] You will remember, I say, how these old friends and comrades of David supported the claims of his eldest son Adonijah, and how a cabal was formed, headed by Nathan the prophet and Zadok the priest, in concert with the adulteress Bathsheba, to secure the throne for her own son Solomon, a mere youth,[8] and how they prevailed upon the aged king, then in his dotage, to appoint Solomon as his successor.[9] So David died and Solomon sat on the throne; and soon, very soon, after Oriental fashion, on the first plausible pretext, Adonijah and Joab were killed by Solomon's orders[10] and Abiathar deposed from his priestly office.[11] 'And the king put Benaiah, son of Jehoiada'—the executioner of his bloody commands—'in the room of Joab, and Zadok the priest did the king put in the room of Abiathar.'[12]

Under such a change of circumstances, what wonder is it that Syria and Edom, Moab and Ammon, should have thrown off the yoke of Israel, and that no effort should have been made to suppress these rebellions! It is true, we are told, that 'Solomon reigned over all kingdoms from the River'—the great River Euphrates—'unto the land of the Philistines even unto the border of Egypt; they brought presents and served Solomon *all the days of his life*.'[13] Again we read that 'he had dominion over all across the River, from Tiphsah (or Thapsacus on the Euphrates) to Azzah (or

[7] 2S.xi.14-17. [8] 1K.i.7,8. [9] 1K.i.11-40. [10] 1K.ii.12-25,28-34.
[11] 1K.ii.26,27. [12] 1K.ii.35. [13] 1K.iv.21.

Gaza on the shores of the Mediterranean), over all the kings across the River; and *he had peace on all sides roundabout him.*'[14] But these notices are only the result of the glorifying imagination of a much later age, exaggerating the traditional splendour of Solomon's reign; just as our own poet has depicted in glowing terms the magnificence of King Arthur's Court and the glory of his times. We see at once that they are not historically true; for they contradict directly that other statement that Rezon, the rebel chief of Syria, '*was an adversary to Israel all the days of Solomon,* besides the mischief that Hadad did,'[15] so that certainly Solomon cannot have 'had peace on *all* sides roundabout him.' Moreover, the present English Version, which says that 'he had dominion over all *on this side* the River, over all the kings *on this side* the River,' beguiles the reader through a mistake of the translators. In the New Translation, no doubt, we shall find the passage rendered correctly, 'over all *beyond* or *across* the River, over all the kings *on the other, farther side* of the River'; and it will then be seen that these words must have been written not in the land of Israel, but by some one of the exiles carried captive to Babylon centuries after the time of Solomon, or by one of their descendants, living in the Babylonish territory *east* of the Euphrates, and recording with natural pride his notion of the vast Empire, which according to the fond traditions of his people was ruled under the sceptre of Solomon, including 'all the kings on the *western* side' of the Euphrates. No doubt, Solomon did receive at first such an Empire from his father's hands: but it is plain that he did not retain his hold upon it. In the land of Israel itself, from Dan to Beersheba, and even in the trans-Jordanic lands occupied by Israelites, there was probably peace and prosperity during his reign; though there are signs

[14] 1 K. iv. 24.   [15] 1 K. xi. 25.

of internal disturbances,[16] which immediately after his death broke out in the rebellion of Jeroboam and the separation of the Ten Tribes from the kingdom of Judah,—when they said to his son Rehoboam, 'Thy father made our yoke heavy, but make thou it lighter to us,'[17] and he answered, 'My father chastised you with whips, but I will chastise you with scorpions,'[18] and they shouted, 'What portion have we in David, neither have we inheritance in the son of Jesse! To your tents, O Israel!'—that is, everyone to his own home! 'Now see to thine own house, David!'[19] These heavy tributes were doubtless levied in contributions or in labour, partly for building purposes, for the Temple, his own palace, and the other edifices with which he adorned or strengthened Jerusalem,[20] but partly also, we must suppose, for supplying the wants of his large harem and luxurious Court.[21] At all events we read of no warlike exploit in the reign of Solomon under his new commander-in-chief; and Edom and Ammon, as well as Syria and Moab, most probably regained their independence without difficulty, and 'broke the yoke of Israel from off their neck.' A century afterwards, however, in the time of Jehosaphat, king of Judah, the power of Judah seems to have prevailed again over Edom, since we are told that in his days 'there was no king in Edom, a deputy was king';[22] as Moab also, according to the Moabite Stone, had been subdued by Omri, king of Israel, the father of Ahab, who reigned about fifty years after Solomon's time.

Let us now consider the very striking prediction of the future fortunes of the Twelve Tribes, put into the mouth of Jacob when near his death,[23] which also belongs to the Jehovistic passages, as appears from the ejaculation in the midst

---

[16] 1K.xi.26-28,40.   [17] 1K.xii.10.   [18] 1K.xii.14.   [19] 1K.xii.16.
[20] 1K.v.11,13-18, vii.1-12,13-51, ix.15-19, xi.27.
[21] 1K.iv.7,22,23,26,28, x.5,14-29, xi.1-3.   [22] 1K.xxii.47.   [23] G.xlix.1-27.

of it, 'I have waited for Thy Salvation, JEHOVAH!',[14] as well as from the style and phraseology throughout.[15] Some words are here addressed to each of the tribes, corresponding, no doubt, to their actual circumstances at the time when this passage was written. But we will confine our attention to the language used with reference to Judah, Joseph, and Levi.

Listen now, first, to the Blessing on Judah.

> 'JUDAH! thou—thy brethren shall praise thee;
> Thy hand is on the neck of thy foes;
> Thy father's sons shall bow down to thee.
> A lion's whelp is JUDAH,
> Ravaging the young of the sucking-ewes;
> He stooped, he crouched, as a lion,
> And as a lioness—who shall rouse him?
> The sceptre shall not depart from JUDAH,
> Nor the ruler's rod from between his feet,
> Until he come to Shiloh,
> And to him be the obedience of the peoples.'[16]

Now in what age can such words as these have been written? Is it not plain that we have here the reign of David depicted, the lion of the tribe of Judah,—that we have here the lordship of Judah over the tribes, the triumphs of David over his foes? Yet his conquests are not completed; for 'the sceptre shall not depart from Judah, nor the ruler's rod from between his feet,'—in other words, the reign of David shall endure,—'until he shall come to Shiloh, and to him be the obedience of the peoples;' where there appears to be an allusion to the fact that, when the wars of Israel on entering the Promised Land were ended, as described in the Book of Joshua, and the whole land 'was subdued before them,' Joshua and the people, according to the story, 'came to Shiloh,' and set up the sacred Tent of Meeting there.[17] So David, too, would 'come to Shiloh'

---

[14] G. xlix. 18.
[15] G. xlix. 8–10.
[16] *Prol.* V. An. 337.
[17] J. xviii. 1.

AGE OF THE JEHOVIST FURTHER CONSIDERED. 63

in a metaphorical sense, that is, he would 'come to rest,' for the word 'Shiloh' means 'rest,' and bring up the sacred ark to Mount Zion, into the Tent which he had prepared for it.[8] And, accordingly, the very first words, which follow the account of the bringing up of the ark, inform us that ' JEHOVAH had *given David rest roundabout from all his enemies,*'[9] the identical expression which is used to describe the condition of the Israelites under Joshua,[10] when 'the land was subdued before them.' It is true that war broke out again and again to disturb the peace of David,[11] and his rest was mournfully disturbed in later times by family troubles, the consequences for the most part of his own folly and sin.[12] But the words before us clearly point to the golden time of David's reign; we hear a trumpet-sound of war in them, as well as a full tone of royalty. And they were probably written not long before the time when the ark was brought up to Jerusalem in the fourteenth year of his reign—when the opposition of the Northern Tribes, who for seven years had held out against him, was at an end,[13] and 'his father's sons had bowed' to the rule of Judah—when David had already come to rest after his first great victories, and had not yet committed that great sin which embittered the latter portion of his life.[14] Think of his daughter Tamar dishonoured by her half-brother Amnon[15]—Amnon murdered by her brother Absalom[16]—David's long and mournful estrangement from Absalom[17]—the rebellion of Absalom[18]—the treason of Ahitophel,[19] explained by the fact that he was the grandfather of Bathsheba,[20]—the wretched flight of David from Jerusalem,[21] under the insulting curses of Shimei,[22]—

[8] 2S. vi. 12-19.
[11] 2S. 8, xii. 26-31.
[14] 2S. xi, xii.
[17] 2S. xiii. 37-39. xiv.
[20] 2S. xi. 3, xxiii. 34.
[15] 2S. vii. 1.
[12] 2S. xiii, &c.
[18] 2S. xiii. 1-22.
[16] 2S. xv. 1-11.
[21] 2S. xv. 13-30.
[10] J. xxi. 44, xxii. 4, xxiii. 1.
[13] 2S. v. 1-5.
[19] 2S. xiii. 23-36.
[22] 2S. xv. 12, 31, xvi. 20-23.
[9] 2S. xvi. 5-14.

AGE OF THE JEHOVIST FURTHER CONSIDERED.

Absalom's outrage upon his father's wives[43]—his miserable death,[44] and his father's broken heart[44]—the insurrection of the Benjamite Sheba[44]—the overbearing arrogance of Joab,[47] as one who had his master in his power, being cognizant of his guilty secret, and the confidential agent of his crime,[48] known or suspected probably by some, as Nathan the prophet,[49] but not perhaps generally divulged to the people ! No ! it is impossible that such grand words about Judah can have been written *after* that melancholy turning-point in David's history in the *twentieth* year of his reign.

Let us take now the Blessing pronounced on JOSEPH.

> 'A fruitful branch is JOSEPH,
> A fruitful branch by a spring ;
> The sprout mounts over the wall . . .
> Blessings of the heaven above,
> Blessings of the deep couching beneath,
> Blessings of the breast and of the womb . . .
> May they be upon the head of JOSEPH,
> And on the crown of the pre-eminent among his brethren.'[50]

A passage like this with such warm laudations of JOSEPH, that is, of the populous and powerful tribe of Ephraim, the leader of the Northern Tribes, could hardly have been written after the rupture between Judah and Ephraim in the days of Rehoboam,[51] nor even in the latter part of Solomon's reign when dissatisfaction already existed between them.[52] These words also suit best that golden period in David's reign, when the Northern Tribes had joined him after their seven years' opposition,[53] forming by their redundant population the main body of his forces, 'Ephraim the strength of his head' as 'Judah was his lawgiver,'[54] and helping him greatly in achieving his recent

---

[43] 2 S. xvi. 22. [44] 2 S. xviii. 9-17. [45] 2 S. xviii. 33, xix. 1-4. [46] 2 S. xx. 1-22.
[47] 2 S. xviii. 12-14, xix. 5-7, xx. 8-10. [48] 2 S. xi. 14-25. [49] 2 S. xii. 1-14.
[50] G. xlix. 22-26. [51] 1 K. xii. 19, 20. [52] 1 K. xii. 3, 4.
[53] 2 S. v. 1-5. [54] Ps. lx. 7.

conquests. And indeed it would be very natural that an effort should have been made to soothe in this way any feelings of mortified pride which might and, as later events showed,[25] did actually exist in the tribe of Ephraim, at the supremacy having been made over in such plain words to Judah. But the tone of tenderness, which marks this address to JOSEPH, seems almost to imply a special affection, a personal interest, for the tribe in question, as if the writer was himself an Ephraimite, though warmly attached to the house of David.

And, lastly, these are some of the words spoken of LEVI.

> 'SIMEON and LEVI are brethren;
> Instruments of wrong are their weapons.
> Into their circle let not my soul enter!
> Into their assembly let not mine honour be joined! . . .
> Cursed be their anger, for it was fierce!
> And their wrath, for it was hard!
> I will portion them out in Jacob,
> And I will scatter them in Israel.'[26]

How little indication have we here of the glory and dignity to which the Levites attained in a far later age! They are spoken of here in disparaging terms, as having no territory of their own like the other tribes, as being 'portioned out in Jacob' and 'scattered in Israel.' To whomsoever this utterance may be ascribed—whether to Jacob himself or to Moses on the traditionary view, or to some writer of David's age, as we conclude—it is clear that he had not the least anticipation of the dignity and ample prerogatives enjoyed by the Levites in later days, and specially secured to them by numerous laws in the subsequent Books of the Pentateuch. Here they are simply placed on a level with the Simeonites, the feeblest tribe of all, which was soon absorbed in Judah, to which most of its towns are reckoned,[27] and which is not even named as adhering with Judah to the

[25] 2 S. xix. 41-43. [26] G. xlix. 5-7. [27] comp. J. xix. 2-7 with xv. 26, 28-33.

house of David,[19] though its territory from its very position must have formed part of the Southern Kingdom.

The whole history of the Levites must be left for consideration on a future occasion. For the present it is enough to say that the only mention of them in the Book of Judges is in the last five chapters, where we read of one homeless vagabond of this tribe 'sojourning where he could find a place,'[20] that is, a place to act as priest—a chaplaincy, as we should say—at any one of the various high-places which in those days stood in all parts of the land, and of another who 'sojourned in Mount Ephraim,' but was 'going up to the House of Jehovah' at Shiloh, perhaps with the purpose of sacrificing or else of earning his livelihood by helping in priestly offices there. But there is no sign of any large number of Levites assisting the sons of Eli or Eli himself, when officiating as priests at Shiloh. It is even predicted that Eli's descendants should 'come and crouch' to the chief priest of their time 'for a piece of silver and a morsel of bread, saying, Put me, I pray thee, into one of the priests' offices, that I may eat a piece of bread.' From these examples it is natural to infer that even in David's time, before the Temple was built, an event which no doubt added somewhat to their dignity, little account was made comparatively of the Levites. A few probably officiated at Jerusalem, and others at the different high-places throughout the land; and for these, of course, sufficient provision was made out of the sacrifices. But the rest appear to have been dispersed about the country, at least during the first years of David's reign, before the ark was brought up to Mount Zion, getting their living as best they could, as by acting as priests in private houses, when they could not find employment at some one or other

[19] 1 K. xii. 20.   [20] Ju. xvii. 8, 9.

AGE OF THE JEHOVIST FURTHER CONSIDERED. 67

of the idolatrous altars scattered throughout the land. About the *twelfth* year of David they might well be spoken of by the writer of this prediction, as 'portioned out in Jacob and scattered in Israel.'

You will now, I trust, have some clear idea of the origin and composition of the Book of Genesis: and I hope to set before you information of a similar kind with reference to the other four Books of the Pentateuch. And, if we may judge from the signs of the times, the day is not far distant when all the more enlightened of the Clergy of different denominations will take at once the stand which in the end must assuredly be taken, will welcome heartily the facts as they are and bring them forth in their habitual teaching, so making them by degrees familiarly known to the people. In this way, without any dangerous shock to their faith, an ignorant and superstitious reverence for the mere letter of the Bible would give way to an intelligent reception of the life and spirit of its Divine Teaching, and a true appreciation of the real value of the ancient Hebrew Scriptures, as containing the records of the dawn of religious light among that people, to whom above all others have been committed of old the 'oracles of God,' the revelations of Eternal truth to the heart of man. In short, let the Bible be explained from the pulpit and taught in the Sunday School: but let the truth be told about its contents, and old and young be no longer misled by a blind enforcement of traditionary views. Those are admirable words which have lately been uttered on this point:—' I feel absolute confidence in three things. First, I shall never believe in the religiousness of falsehood; and therefore I altogether deprecate the idea of the conscious maintenance of any falsehood on the part of the teacher for the purpose of maintaining a religious effect, or, as he may think, of saving a religious effect, which otherwise might be injured or sacrificed.

The second principle is akin to the first, viz., that there can be no danger ultimately in what is clearly and plainly true. I do not say there may be no inconvenience, no particular mischief and danger for the time; but it is a danger which it is our duty to encounter if we are sure that a thing is true. The third principle is this: the basis of our Sunday School teaching must continue to be the Scriptures of the Old and New Testament. I am convinced that there can be nothing but a more religious influence derived from the Bible the better and the more thoroughly it is understood, and that the more progress is made in the clearing of it, the ascertainment of what portion of the history is true and what portion is not true, and when the books were written and when they were not written, and what the relative authority is and the value of this book or that—the more clearly and distinctly we can see this, the better will the Bible be fitted for purposes of religious instruction. The difficulties of the Bible arise all from the assumption that it is all of equal religious authority, and that every part of it can be taken and used for the purposes of producing religious impression. The moment we attempt this, we come across things which shock our moral feeling and our historical sense of what is true. If we once know the Bible critically, we know perfectly well that we can discharge those things which obstruct our religious teaching, and save the gems that remain for religious use, and that they will have more value and a greater influence in that condition than if they are mixed up with a mass of material that can serve no direct religious or spiritual purpose. We are therefore greatly indebted to those who take up our ancient Scriptures, and bring them directly face to face before the religious conscience of the present day, showing how we may clear away questionable elements, and preserve that which is to build up the faith and action of the future.'*

* MARTINEAU (*Pall-Mall Gazette*, June 14, 1872, p. 5).

LECTURE VI.

SUMMARY.

RECAPITULATION; the Elohistic Narrative in Exodus; its statement that the name JEHOVAH was not known to the patriarchs, to whom God appeared, once and again, by the name EL SHADDAI; another view of this passage shown to be erroneous; names in the Elohistic Narrative formed with ELOHIM, not JEHOVAH; obscurity caused by the Jehovist representing the name as known in primeval times; the Elohistic Narrative ends with the revelation of the Name in E. vi. 2–5; this points to the Hebrews having first become acquainted with it about the time of the Exodus; the mysterious name of the Phœnician and Syrian Sun-God; the Sun worshipped everywhere in Canaan as the Baal or Lord of the land; this evidenced by names of places; IAO used to express in Greek the Hebrew Deity, and also the Sun-God, as shown by an ancient oracle; IACCHUS and the cry at the Bacchic festival; Phœnician names formed, like Hebrew, with YAHVEH, and Hebrew, like Phœnician, with Baal; these latter not allowed to appear in the Books of Samuel; the Hebrews adopted the worship of YAHVEH the Sun-God of Canaan; YAHVEH first recognised as the God of Israel when the national life began under Saul; the Elohist, disliking this origin of the Name, composed the story of its revelation to Moses; the Name HE IS, expressing well the Living God; progressive development of Divine Truth in Israel.

THE ORIGIN OF THE NAME JEHOVAH.

IN my previous Lectures, starting from the phenomena presented by the New Lectionary, I have pointed out the existence of narratives by different writers in the Book of Genesis, a fact which is plainly betrayed by their differences of style and expression, as well as by varying and sometimes contradictory statements. Of these writers, the oldest, who uses only the name 'ELOHIM' for the Divine Being, may very possibly, I said, have been the prophet Samuel, composing here a sketch of primeval times for the use of the students of his schools. But this older narrative, the foundation of the whole story of the Exodus, has been considerably enlarged by another writer, the Jehovist, who uses also the name 'JEHOVAH,' as the personal name of the Elohim of Israel. And both sets of passages are distinguished not only by this peculiarity in the use of the Divine Name, but each by its own distinct phraseology. Indeed, as I observed, some insertions in the Book of Genesis, and they are moreover the oldest, do not contain 'JEHOVAH' at all, and yet exhibit plainly the style of the Jehovist throughout, and therefore appear to be due to his hand. We are brought, then, face to face with this singular fact, that the writer of the oldest portions of Genesis has for some reason or other deliberately abstained from using the name 'JEHOVAH,' and the writer of the oldest of the supplementary insertions follows the same rule. I purpose to consider in this Lecture the probable explanation of this peculiarity.

But first let me illustrate further the fact in question by reference to the Book of Exodus, which has not yet been touched upon in these Lectures. We find here the same phenomena precisely as in Genesis; that is to say, we find here also passages in which only ELOHIM is used, and which agree exactly in style with the Elohistic passages in Genesis, and, like those, when extracted from the rest of the Book, form a complete connected narrative ; and these are separated, as the story now stands, by a number of other passages written in a totally different style, the style in fact of the Jehovist in Genesis, which expand and enliven the more brief and sombre details of the older story.

I will now read to you that portion of the ancient Elohistic Narrative, which we are able to extract from the first six chapters of the Book of Exodus.

And these are the names of the children of Israel, who came to Egypt with Jacob, each and his house they came—Reuben. Simeon, Levi, and Judah, Issachar, Zebulun, and Benjamin, Dan and Naphtali, Gad and Asher. And all the souls that went forth out of Jacob's loins were seventy souls ; and Joseph was in Egypt.

And Joseph died and all his brethren and all that generation. And the children of Israel fructified and teemed and multiplied, and were exceedingly mighty, and the land was filled with them. And the Egyptians made the children of Israel to serve with rigour. And the children of Israel sighed because of the service, and they cried, and their wail went up to ELOHIM because of the service. And ELOHIM heard their sighing and ELOHIM remembered His covenant with Abraham, with Isaac, and with Jacob. And ELOHIM saw the children of Israel and ELOHIM knew.

THE ORIGIN OF THE NAME JEHOVAH.

And ELOHIM spake unto Moses and said unto him, I am JEHOVAH. And I appeared unto Abraham, and unto Isaac, and unto Jacob, as EL SHADDAI (GOD ALMIGHTY); but by My name JEHOVAH (I was not known, or) I did not make myself known to them. And I have also established My covenant with them, to give to them the land of Canaan, the land of their sojournings in which they sojourned. And I have also heard the sighing of the children of Israel, whom the Egyptians make-to-serve, and I have remembered My covenant.[1]

You will have noticed the frequent repetition of the name ELOHIM in these few verses; and you will have observed also the fact that the writer here states that the name JEHOVAH was not even known to the patriarchs. 'I appeared unto Abraham, and unto Isaac, and unto Jacob, as EL SHADDAI;'[1] and so the Deity appears to Abraham and to Jacob, and in each case says 'I am EL SHADDAI'[2] But the account of a like revelation to Isaac must either have been cancelled, which is not probable, or the promises made by EL SHADDAI to Abraham—'to be a God to thee and to thy seed after thee,' 'to give to thee and to thy seed after thee all the land of Canaan,' 'Sarah thy wife shall bear thee a son indeed, and thou shalt call his name Isaac, and I will establish My covenant with him and his seed after him'[3]—may have been regarded as virtually including an 'appearance' to Isaac. And this last explanation seems to be confirmed by the words ascribed to EL SHADDAI in the account of the revelation to Jacob, which seems to refer to these promises to Abraham, 'and the land which I gave to Abraham and to Isaac, to thee will I give it, and to thy seed after thee will I give the land,'[4] as also by the statement with which this latter account is introduced, 'and ELOHIM appeared to Jacob again when he came out of Padan-Aram and blessed him'[5]—not 'appeared

---

[1] E.i.1 7,13, ii.23b 25, vi.2-5. [2] G.xvii.1, xxxv.11.
[3] G.xvii.7,8,19.   [4] G.xxxv.12.   [5] G.xxxv.9.

again to *Jacob*,' as if this was the second appearance of EL SHADDAI to Jacob, in which case he would have been more highly distinguished than even Abraham himself, and no former appearance to Jacob has been recorded by this ancient writer, but '*appeared*, again—a second time—to one of the patriarchs, and in this case to Jacob,' a sign of superabundant Divine Favour towards them, since the first appearance to Abraham included them all. 'But by My name JEHOVAH I did not make-myself-known to them.' These words might indeed be explained, as they are by some commentators, to mean only this, 'I did not make myself *thoroughly* known to them—I did not reveal to them the full meaning of my name JEHOVAH, though they knew and used that name familiarly.' Thus the writer in the New Bible Commentary paraphrases the passage as follows, 'I manifested Myself to the patriarchs in the character of EL SHADDAI, the Omnipotent God, able to fulfil that which I had promised; but as to My name (*i.e.*, My character and attributes) of JEHOVAH, I was not made manifest to them.'[a] It is hard to reconcile such an explanation with the fact that JEHOVAH Himself is represented as saying to Abraham, 'I am JEHOVAH, &c.,'[b] and that Abraham is said to have 'believed in JEHOVAH;'[c] though even this might be allowed, if there were no other reason for doubting the correctness of this view. But when we know that the Elohistic Narrative can be taken out by itself from the Book of Genesis—that the writer of it has deliberately suppressed the name JEHOVAH throughout his account of the times before the Exodus—that he never puts it into the mouth of any one of the patriarchs before or after the Flood—that he gives us numerous names in Genesis compounded with ELOHIM or EL, such as Isra*el*, Ishma*el*,[d] and not one compounded with

---

[a] Bp. BROWNE (*B.C.*,I.*p.*26).   [b] G.xv.7.   [c] G.xv.6.
[d] Mahalal*el*, G.v.12; Adb*el*, G.xxv.13; Eliphaz, Reu*el*, Mehetab*el*, Magdi*el*, G.xxxvi.4,39,43; Jemu*el*, Jahle*el*, Malchi*el*, Jahze*el*, G.xlvi.10,14,17,24; besides Isra*el* and Ishma*el*.

JEHOVAH or JAH, like those which occur elsewhere so frequently in the Bible—when, I say, we take note of these facts, it is clear that the writer intended to represent the name JEHOVAH as not even known before the Exodus, as first revealed to man when 'ELOHIM spake unto Moses and said unto him, I am JEHOVAH; and I appeared unto Abraham, and unto Isaac, and unto Jacob, as EL SHADDAI; but by My name JEHOVAH I did not make-myself-known unto them.'

For some reason, then, this ancient writer regards this sacred name as not having been used at all by the patriarchs or their descendants before the time of the Exodus. It is true that no one would perceive this fact in the Bible from merely reading the Book of Genesis as it now lies before us. However surprised he might be at perceiving the difference between the first account of the Creation, which uses only ELOHIM, and the second, which uses only JEHOVAH ELOHIM, he would never suppose that the former peculiarity can be traced distinctly throughout the whole Book of Genesis, in the parts belonging to that ancient writer to whom we owe the first account of the Creation—more especially when he saw that in the greater part of Genesis no such peculiarity exists, that the name JEHOVAH is freely used by patriarchs before and after the Flood,[10] nay, even by heathen persons,[11] and we are told that, as early as the days of Adam's son Seth or his grandson Enos, 'then began men to call upon the name of JEHOVAH.'[12] This later writer, it is plain, has abandoned altogether the idea of the Elohist, and supposes the sacred name to have been known from a very early time in the history of the human race. Accordingly he puts it everywhere into the mouths of persons introduced as speaking, and repre-

---

[10] G. iv. 1, v. 29, ix. 26, xiv. 22, xv. 2,8, xvi. 5, &c.   [11] G. xxvi. 28, 29.
[12] G. iv. 26.

sents the Deity as appearing to Jacob and saying, 'I am
JEHOVAH, the Elohim of Abraham thy father and the Elohim
of Isaac.'[10] By these insertions the older story is completely
overlaid, and its Elohistic character hid from the sight of most
readers. It is only when it is extracted separately from the
Book of Genesis that we find it forming a continuous narrative
in which the name JEHOVAH is carefully suppressed.

What, now, can be the reason of this? And here I must
observe that the Elohistic Narrative in the Pentateuch ends
with the words which I have just read as the portion of it contained in the first six chapters of the Book of Exodus. We
find no trace of it after this passage. It would seem as if the
older writer—Samuel, as we suppose—having undertaken to
sketch the history of the primeval times, had completed his
work so far as to record the revelation of the name JEHOVAH
to Moses, and then had stopped—his labours having been
perhaps finished according to his original intention, when he
had brought the narrative up to this critical point in the history of Israel, or perhaps cut short by sickness or death, and
the story of the Exodus having been afterwards carried on
and completed by his disciples. What, I repeat, is the historical fact implied by this circumstance, that the oldest writer
of the Pentateuch represents the name JEHOVAH as first communicated to Moses, and through him to Israel, *at the time of
the Exodus?* Since this statement, as we have seen, is directly
at variance with the other parts of Genesis, which assume this
name to have been known from the first, we are relieved from
any necessity of regarding either view as historically true.
Nevertheless, the statement of the Elohist must mean something; it must point to some fact which that writer had before
his mind's eye, and for which he has tried to account by saying that the name was first made known to the Israelites *at*

[10] G. xxviii. 13.

THE ORIGIN OF THE NAME JEHOVAH.

the time of the Exodus. And what can that fact have been but this, that it really then first became known to them—*then*, at or about the time of the Exodus—not, indeed, in Egypt, as here supposed, before they started on their march to Canaan, nor by means of a miraculous revelation to Moses and an audible voice—but by contact with the tribes of Canaan, as soon as they had crossed the Jordan and settled down as inhabitants in that land.

Accordingly, modern researches[14] have shown that among the Canaanite tribes, especially among the Phœnicians and Syrians in the northern districts, the Sun-God was worshipped under a mysterious name almost identical with the name JEHOVAH, or, as it should be pronounced more properly, YAHVEH or YAHWEH. The Syrian word is YAHVEH, the Hebrew YAHVEH, differing only in fact by a stronger, more guttural, aspirate being heard in the former name, as the Zulu aspirate is heard more strongly north of the Tugela than south of it. All over the land of Canaan the worship of the Sun-God prevailed; as indeed it is most natural that in the first dawning of religious life the Sun should have been regarded as the most glorious symbol of the unseen Deity—should at one time have been hailed as the life-giver, the source of health and strength, the bountiful dispenser of food and plenty, to be worshipped with joyous festivals, at another have been dreaded as the life destroyer, the cause of famine, disease, and death, to be entreated with earnest supplications and appeased with gloomy rites. He was, in fact, regarded as the Baal or Lord, in the sense of Owner or Husband of the land; and accordingly we find a multitude of places mentioned in the Bible in all parts of the country, where the Sun-God was worshipped under some special appellation, as Baal-Hazor,[15] Baal-Hermon,[16] &c., 'our Lord' of this place or that,

---

[14] MOVERS (*Phönizier*, XIV. p. 539–558, translated in *Penl. V. App.* iii.).
[15] 2 S. xiii. 23.   [16] Ju. iii. 3

just as in Roman Catholic countries shrines are set up in different localities to 'our Lady' of this place or that. Besides which, the prevalence of Sun-worship among the ancient inhabitants of the land of Canaan is abundantly indicated by such names as these, Beth-Shemesh,[17] 'House of the Sun,' like Beth-El, 'House of Elohim,' En-Shemesh,[18] 'Fountain of the Sun,' Ir-Shemesh,[19] 'City of the Sun,' &c.

The mysterious name of the Syrian Sun-God, moreover, is expressed by heathen writers by the very same word IAO, by which Christian Fathers and others express the Hebrew name of the Deity. Thus CLEMENT of Alexandria says of the God of the Jews, 'He is called IAOU, which is interpreted to mean WHO IS AND WHO SHALL BE';[20] and DIODORUS tells us, 'It is said that among the Arimaspians Zathraustes professed that the Good Spirit had given him his laws, and that among the Jews Moses made a similar claim with regard to the Deity named IAO.'[21] On the other hand an ancient oracle says—'It was right that those initiated should conceal the soul-soothing mysteries. But in deceit there is little sense and a slender understanding. Take notice that IAO is the highest of all the gods; in winter Hades, Zeus in commencing spring, Helios in summer, and in the autumn IAO.'[22] Thus, as one explains this oracle, 'IAO is the highest of all the gods, because he gives life to all, and his dwelling is heaven which spreads over all. Yet in heaven he reveals Himself specially by the Sun. In winter, when the nights are longest, the god prefers to dwell in the under-world, and rules over the shades as Hades. In the spring-time, when the grain-harvest is at hand, all depends upon the weather, upon sufficient rain and sunshine; and the god is addressed as Zeus, as especially the god of

---

[17] J. xv. 10.   [18] J. xv. 7.   [19] J. xix. 41.
[20] *Strom*. V. p. 562, ed. *Par.* 1869.   [21] I. p. 105, ed. *Wessling*.
[22] MACROBIUS (*Sat.* I. 18).

heaven and of the weather. In the summer he is the scorching Sun, which burns up everything, and is tempered by no cloud. Lastly, in the autumn comes the ripeness of the fig, olive, pomegranate, above all of the grape with its mysterious life-awakening juice; and now is the god known as the tender IAO, the spring of all beauty, love, and life.'[22]

This joyous, autumn form of the Sun-God was the Deity known among the Greeks under the name of Dionysus or Iacchus, which last name clearly points to the Phœnician YAKHVEH, as do also other expressions and ejaculations used in Sun-worship, [24] *e.g.* the repeated cry of IA or YA at the triennial feast of Iacchus or Bacchus, which reminds us of the triennial feast upon the tithes among the Hebrews,[25] and of the festival cry, 'Hallelu-YAH!'[26] The Sun-God was also called 'Adonis,' *i.e.* 'Lord,' in the sense of Master, as also 'the Most High God': and the Deity is repeatedly called by both these names in the Hebrew Bible.[27] And as Hebrew names were compounded with JAH or IAH,[28] we find also Phœnician names similarly formed. Thus in Virgil, the Phœnician courtier, who 'quickly drained the foaming bowl and laved himself in the brimming gold,'[29] is called Bithias, which is merely the Hebrew Bith*iah*,[30] the same in meaning as Bethu*el*,[31] compounded with *El*; and so Josephus[32] mentions a Tyrian Abdæus, which is only the Greek form of the Hebrew Obad*iah*. Again, Phœnician names were in like manner compounded with *Baal*, as Hanni*bal*, which corresponds exactly to the Hebrew Hanni*el*, or Hanan*el*, or *El*hanan,[33] Hann*iah* or *Jo*hanan,[34] *i.e.*, John, with the Divine

[22] LAND (*Theol. Tijdschr.*, March, 1868, *p.* 161).
[24] MOVERS (as above, *Pral.* V. *App.* iii. 23-31).
[25] D. xv. 28, 29, xxvi. 12, Am. iv. 4. [26] See Ps. lxviii. 4.
[27] For 'Lord' see G. xv. 2, 8, E. iv. 10, 13, xv. 17, xxxiv. 9, &c.; for 'Most High God' see G. xiv. 18, 19, 20, 22, N. xxiv. 16, D. xxxii. 8, &c.
[28] *e.g.* Hezek*iah*, Adoni*jah*, where *jah* is properly *iah* or *yah*.
[29] Æn. l. 7.   [30] 1 Ch. iv. 18.   [31] G. xxii. 22.   [32] *c. Ap.* l. 18.
[33] N. xxxiv. 23, Neh. iii. 1, 2 S. xxi. 19.   [34] 1 Ch. iii. 19, 2 K. xxv. 23.

Name prefixed in the form *Jeho* or *Jo*,—as Asdru*bal* does to Azriel or Azar*el*,[35] *E*liezer or *El*eazar,[36] Azariah or *Jo*ezer.[37] On the other hand one of David's officers was called *Baal*-hanan,[38] which is only Hanni*bal* inverted; while the name of Saul's son was Esh*baal* and of Saul's grandson Merrib*baal*,[39] and even of David's son *Baal*yadah,[40] and one of David's warriors is called *Baaljah*,[41] meaning 'Jah is Baal.' The first three of these names, indeed—all of which may be seen in the Books of Chronicles—have been modified in the Books of Samuel, and appear there as Ish*bosheth*, Mephi*bosheth*, E*ly*adah.[42] And the reason of these changes is plain. Among pious Jews after the Captivity the more ancient and venerable Books of Samuel were more highly honoured and more commonly read than the very late Books of Chronicles. It is probable, therefore, that the Jewish Scribes, desiring to obliterate as much as possible, or at least to obscure, the traces of so close a connexion between the religion of Israel in the time of David and Solomon and the idolatrous worship of Canaan, suppressed the offensive 'Baal' in these names in those histories which were most studied by their countrymen.

But why should there be any doubt that the Hebrews adopted the Canaanitish Sun-worship? We are told repeatedly that, when settled in Canaan, they 'followed other Elohim of the Elohim of the people that were round about them.'[43] It is certain, therefore, that they *must* have adopted the worship of the Sun-God, and taken part in the lascivious or bloody rites accompanying that worship. In fact, if they wished to be regarded as possessors of the soil, it was necessary, according to the notions of those days, that they

---

[35] 1 Ch. xxvii. 19, 22. [36] Ezr. x. 23, 25. [37] 1 Ch. ix. 11, xii. 6.
[38] 1 Ch. xxvii. 28. [39] 1 Ch. ix. 39, 40. [40] 1 Ch. xiv. 7.
[41] 1 Ch. xii. 5. [42] 2 S. ii. 8, iv. 4, v. 16, comp. 1 Ch. iii. 8.
[43] Ju. ii. 12, 17, 19, iii. 6, 7, vi. 10, and see especially vi. 25-32.

should do homage to YAHVEH, the 'God of the land.'[44] And what at first was done through mere imitation of the practices of the surrounding tribes, was at last established as the law of the whole community, in the time of Samuel, under the first king Saul. Then Israel was first formed into a nation, and then, too, YAHVEH was first formally acknowledged as the National Deity of Israel; and his might and pre-eminence over the gods of the neighbouring nations were fully exhibited in the view of the people, when David's armies marched triumphantly under his auspices. 'Lift up your heads, O ye gates, and be ye lift up, ye everlasting doors, and the King of Glory shall come in! Who is this King of Glory? It is YAHVEH strong and mighty! it is YAHVEH mighty in battle.'[45]

Such, then, is the explanation, which seems to be most probable, of the singular peculiarity which characterises the Elohistic Narrative in the use of the Divine Name. The writer, it would seem, was unwilling that the Name of Israel's Deity should be traced to the worship of the tribes of Canaan. But he knew that the name was unknown to the Israelites before they entered Canaan; and he wrote this account of the revelation of it to Moses about the time of the Exodus in order to explain this fact. But what matters it whence they obtained the name, which must have been invented somewhere, by some one, at some time or other? It is enough that the great prophets of Israel, taught by the Divine Spirit, saw that it was a name well suited to express the idea of the One only True and Living God, in opposition to the dumb idols of the heathen, to the blocks and stones which some even among the Israelites ignorantly worshipped,[46] or the figure of an ox under which the Sun-God was long adored by Canaanites

---

[44] 2K. xvii. 26, 28, 33, 41, comp. 1S. xxvi. 19.   [45] Ps. xxiv. 7, 8.
[46] Jer. ii. 27.

and Israelites alike." The name YAHVEH means 'HE IS,' being derived from the Hebrew verb which means 'to be'; and so we read 'And ELHOIM said unto Moses, I AM THAT I AM; and He said, Thus shalt thou say unto the children of Israel, I AM hath sent me unto you.'⁴⁸ And the prophets seem to have eagerly seized on this idea that the God of Israel was YAHVEH, HE IS, the Living God, the Being by whom all things else had life and being. From age to age these prophets strove to raise their people to higher views of the Divine Being, of His nature and character, and His relations to man. And gradually their own minds were enlightened, their own views became more bright and clear; and they had even glimpses of the glorious truth that the Living God was not the God of Israel only, but the Father of spirits, the Faithful Creator,⁴⁹ the 'confidence of all the ends of the earth.'⁵⁰

Let us thankfully trace the progressive development of Divine Truth among Israel of old, even down to him who has revealed to us fully our Father's Love and our Father's Holiness, and has given us a name 'better than that of our sons and daughters.'⁵¹ Let us devoutly receive the revelations made to us in the past by the hands of our brethren of Jewish or other races, whom He has chosen to be His special ministers to us-ward for this great work, but be ready also to welcome joyfully the revelations of the present day, each 'good and perfect gift coming down from above from the Father of lights.'⁵²

⁴⁸ Ex. xxxii. 1-6, 1 K. xli. 28, 29.   ⁴⁹ I. iii. 14.
⁵⁰ Ps. xxii. 27, lxxxvi. 9, xcviii. 3, Is. xlii. 6, xlv. 22, 23, xlix. 6, li. 3.
⁵¹ Ps. lxv. 5.   ⁵² Is. lvi. 5.   ⁵³ Jam. i. 17.

LECTURE VII.

SUMMARY.

RECAPITULATION; in some passages of Exodus, not due to the Elohist, only ELOHIM is used, in some JEHOVAH appears, but sparingly, in others more freely; this explained by the age in which such passages were composed, as the name JEHOVAH became more familiarly employed in the reigns of David and Solomon; Ps. lxviii. belongs apparently to the age of David; its character, and the occasion for which it was probably composed; the writer knew the name JEHOVAH, but uses it rarely compared with Elohim, as if not familiar with it; identity between v. 1 of this Psalm and N. x. 35; proof that the Psalm was written first, and the words in Numbers copied from it, probably by an author of the same age; the 'Song of Deborah' composed in the prophetical schools; identity between v. 7, 8, of the Psalm, and v. 4, 5. of the Song; proof that the Psalm again was written first, and the words of the Song copied from it; Balaam's Prophecies incredible as history, possibly by the same author as Jacob's Blessing, written after David's conquests of Moab and Edom, *before* that of Ammon, and not long after Saul's overthrow of Agag and Amalek; relative extent of the original story, the Deuteronomistic matter, and the Levitical Legislation; the history of Israel now becomes intelligible and instructive, as a history of human development.

THE AGE OF THE JEHOVIST IN NUMBERS.

IN my last Lecture I read to you the final words of the Elohistic Narrative extracted from the Book of Exodus, the writer having apparently, perhaps by design or perhaps through some accident, brought his work to a close with the account of the revelation of the name of JEHOVAH or YAHVEH to Moses. And I showed that this name was probably adopted by the idolatrous Israelites from the name by which the Sun-God was known and worshipped among the tribes of Canaan; though it was gradually invested with a higher and holier meaning, as the name of the True and Living God, through the teaching of the great prophets of Israel inspired with Divine Wisdom and Truth. The Narrative, thus commenced, as we suppose, by Samuel, was carried on by his disciples, the framework of the story, as he left it, having been filled in by the labours of one or more of them, during the fifty years which followed after his death. These supplementary passages, however, though agreeing in style with each other, and differing entirely in this respect from the Elohistic Narrative, exhibit, as we saw, a noticeable variety in the use of the Divine Name. In some of them only ELOHIM is used, as in the oldest matter, or JEHOVAH is used very sparingly; and, if these occurred only in Genesis, we might suppose that the writer was merely following the lead, so to speak, of his Master, and suppressing deliberately the use of JEHOVAH until the account of its revelation had been recorded in E. vi. But it is of great importance to observe that such passages are found in Exodus also, long after that account has been given.[1] The fact of their existence, therefore, requires some further explanation. The writer may have been influenced, when making his insertions in Genesis, by the example of his predecessor; but still some reason peculiar to himself must have operated to account for his abstaining in so marked and unmistakable a manner from using freely the name JEHOVAH, when this name had been represented as fully revealed to Moses and Israel. It would seem as if he was not himself *familiar* at first with the name, and used more naturally the older name ELOHIM; as, of course, would be the case if, at the time when he wrote these passages, JEHOVAH or YAHVEH had been only recently adopted, as the name of the National Deity of Israel, during the age of Saul and Samuel. Accordingly in the rest of this series JEHOVAH is employed much more frequently,[2] and indeed so freely, that, when these were written, the name must certainly have been quite familiar both to the writer and the people. Such passages as these last may have been composed in the *middle* or *latter* part of David's reign or during the early years of Solomon's, or even, as some suppose, in a still later age.

And now let us consider for a moment what light is thrown upon this question by the Book of Psalms. These are popularly called, as we know, the Psalms of David; and yet it is certain that very many of them were composed long after the Captivity,[3] and that very few can have been written by the hand or in the age of David. There is one Psalm,

---

[1] E.I.17-22, iii, xiii.17-19, xviii, xix.16-19, xx.18-21, xxiv.9-13.
[2] E.iv,v,&c. [3] *e.g.* Ps.lxxix, lxxx.

however, Ps. lxviii, which undoubtedly appears to belong to that age. This Psalm is spoken of by different eminent critics as 'one of the most able and powerful,'[1] as 'the most spirited, lively, and powerful,'[2] as 'the grandest, most splendid, most artistic,'[3] in the whole collection, as 'one among the oldest relics of Hebrew poetry, of the highest originality,'[4] and its writer as one 'in whom we cannot but recognise a poet of remarkable genius';[4] and one of them says, 'The occasion, which most immediately presents itself for this Psalm, is the removal of the ark by David to Mount Zion, and this is adopted by most of the ancient and later interpreters. It gives incontestably the best sense.'[5] This very writer, however, with other able critics of the present day, himself assigns this Psalm to a far later date for certain reasons. But their arguments do not appear convincing;[6] and, for myself

---

[1] OLSHAUSEN, *Ps. p.* 288. [2] HUPFELD, *Ps.* III. *p.* 199.
[3] EWALD, *Ps. p.* 297. [4] DE WETTE, quoted by HUPFELD, *Ps.* III. *p.* 201.
[5] HUPFELD, *Ps.* III. *p.* 196.
[6] The arguments alleged against the Davidic origin of Ps. lxviii are as follows (KUENEN, *Hist. Krit. Ond.* III. *p.* 258):— (i) In *v.* 15-18 'the settlement of JEHOVAH on Zion is surely not described by a contemporary'— (ii) In *v.* 22 'mention is made of bringing back the captives who had been carried away E. and W. (Bashan and the Mediterranean Sea)'— (iii) In *v.* 29 'JEHOVAH'S *Palace* (Heb.), *i.e.* the Temple, is mentioned'—(iv) In *v.* 29, 31, 32, &c., 'the expectation of all mankind coming to worship on Zion could hardly have been entertained in David's time.'
Ans.—(i) *v.* 15-18 suits thoroughly the time of David, when JEHOVAH, after a series of conquests, came to 'dwell on the hill which ELOHIM desired to dwell in, yea, and would dwell on it for ever,' *v.* 16; (ii) *v.* 22 speaks only of 'bringing back' into the power of Israel for vengeance their *fugitive enemies* from all directions, E. and W., *comp.* Am. ix. 1-3, 'that their foot may be dipped in the blood of their enemies and the tongue of their dogs in the same,' *v.* 23, *comp. v.* 21, and see 2S. viii. 1, 2, xi. 31; (iii) David's Tabernacle on Mount Zion was, doubtless, not a mere common tent, but an erection of some architectural pretensions, to which the Hebrew word might be well applied, as it is to the Sanctuary at Shiloh in 1S. i. 9, iii. 3; (iv) *v.* 29, 31, 32, &c., refer rather to the princes of neighbouring countries, (*e.g.* Egypt and Ethiopia, *v.* 31, with which David was probably in amicable alliance, *comp.* 1K. iii. 1, as well as with Tyre, 1K. v. 1), showing respect and reverence for the triumphant God of Israel, by sending presents, *v.* 29, for use in the Tabernacle or in building the contemplated Temple, *comp.* 2S. viii. 10, 11, —not to their adopting JEHOVAH as their own National Deity.

I am satisfied that, if any Psalm in the whole book belongs to the age of David, it is this noble Ps. lxviii.; and I believe that it was written—perhaps, but not necessarily, by David himself—for the occasion just mentioned, when he brought up with great pomp and solemnity the sacred ark to Mount Zion.

Now observe the peculiar use of the Divine Name in this Ps. lxviii. *Four* times JEHOVAH or JAH is used,[18] and in *v.* 4 especially great stress is laid on this particular name.

'Sing unto ELOHIM, sing praises to His Name;
His name is JAH, so rejoice before Him.'

The writer then knew the name JEHOVAH; and he has not suppressed it from superstitious motives, such as those which

On the other hand, besides the points mentioned above in the text, it seems to be decisive against the post-Captivity date ascribed to this Psalm by HUPFELD, EWALD, KUENEN, LAND, &c., (i) that it has the phrases 'Sing unto ELOHIM,' *v.* 4, 32, 'Bless ye ELOHIM,' *v.* 26, 'Praise ye ADONAI,' *v.* 32, 'Blessed be ADONAI,' *v.* 18, 'Blessed be ELOHIM, *v.* 35, instead of 'Hallelu-jah,' 'Praise ye JEHOVAH,' which would certainly have been found in a very late Psalm of this character, especially at the end, as in Ps.civ.-cvi, cxiii, cxv, cxvi, cxxxv, cxlvi-cl, whereas four of these expressions occur nowhere else in the Bible, and the last only besides in Ps. lxvi. 20, and (ii) that it nowhere mentions the Priests and the Levites, who would almost certainly have been named, especially the latter, in a post-Captivity Psalm, as present on such an occasion, *comp.* 2Ch. v. 12, instead of whom we read 'before went the singers, behind were the players, in the midst of the damsels timbrelling,' *v.* 25.

The mention of 'little Benjamin their ruler,' in *v.* 27 is hardly intelligible after the Captivity, but suits well the time when Benjamin, which as Saul's tribe, had only just ceased to be, under Saul and his son Ishbosheth, the royal tribe in Israel, had now submitted itself to David, but is spoken of here, in a politic manner, as being of princely dignity. And the mention of four tribes only in *v.* 27, 'Benjamin and Judah,' 'Zebulon and Naphtali,' as representatives of all Israel, is also explained by the fact that in David's time the latter two were the chief *Northern*, as the former two were the chief *Southern*, tribes, who came up heartily—represented by their chiefs—to take part in the ceremony of installing the ark; whereas the great tribe of Ephraim, which lay between, was in all probability not at all enthusiastic in support of this new project of David, of making Jerusalem the seat of religious influence, as well as of government, for the whole land, to the depreciation of its own famous Sanctuary at Bethel, and expressed at last its long-smothered dissatisfaction at this centralizing system in Jeroboam's words, 'Ye have had enough of going up to Jerusalem,' 1 K. xii. 28. See further in *Pent.* II. 405-421.

[18] JAH, *v.* 4, 18, JEHOVAH, *v.* 16, 20.

are known to have prevailed in a very late age with regard to the utterance of this sacred name. Yet he mentions it only *four* times, while *thirty-one* times he uses ELOHIM and *seven* times also Adonai, 'Lord,' corresponding to the title of the Sun-God, Adonis. It would seem that JEHOVAH, though already adopted as the name of the National Deity of Israel, was not yet familiar in the mouth either of the writer or of the people at the time when this Psalm was composed, that is, at the time when the ark was brought up to Mount Zion, in the fourteenth year of David's reign, about eighteen years after the death of Samuel.

And now listen to the words with which the Psalm begins:—

> 'Let ELOHIM arise, let His enemies be scattered,
> And let them, that hate Him, flee before Him!'

And compare them with those which are represented in the Pentateuch as uttered by Moses at each movement of the ark in the wilderness:—

> 'Arise, JEHOVAH, and let Thine enemies be scattered,
> And let them, that hate Thee, flee before Thee!'[11]

It is plain that one of these two passages must have been copied from the other—that the writer of one of them must have had the other before him or in his memory when he wrote his own words. Which, then, was the older of these two passages? We observe that in the Psalm ELOHIM is used where in the other passage stands JEHOVAH. Now it is incredible that the Psalmist, if he had before him the story of the Exodus, of venerable antiquity, at all events, and having at least Mosaic, if not Divine, authority, would have presumed to substitute the common name ELOHIM, which might stand for any heathen deity, in place of the sacred name JEHOVAH, the personal name of the God of Israel, which had been actually used by Moses himself in the formula here supposed

[11] N.x.35.

to be copied, and used repeatedly, whenever the Camp was moved in the wilderness—more especially as it would have been the very name required in this Psalm, composed for so grand an occasion. Whereas it would be very natural that such words as these, if really first used at this memorable time, when the ark was removed 'with shouting and trumpet-sounds' by 'David and all the House of Israel' from the place where it had been long laid aside, and brought up to 'the Tent that David had pitched for it,'[13] should have been afterwards adopted by a writer of that age with the change of ELOHIM into JEHOVAH, and inserted in the story of the Exodus as fitting words to announce each removal of the ark in the wilderness. But it is plain that they can never have been so used in reality—that they have been introduced into the Pentateuch by a mere poetical fiction; and, in point of fact, as the story now stands, they would not have been fitting words to have been employed on such occasions, since there was no fighting during those marches in the wilderness, no 'enemies' of JEHOVAH and Israel to be 'scattered' before the ark during those forty years of dreary wandering. But in this Psalm they stand quite in their place, being closely connected also with the words that follow; their martial tone suits well with David's time when he had had wars on every side, and when, perhaps, the ark itself, as the symbol of the Divine Presence, was at times carried forth at the head of his armies,[14]—

'Let ELOHIM arise, let His enemies be scattered,
And let all, that hate Him, flee before Him!
As smoke is driven away, so drive Thou them away;
As wax melteth before the fire,
So perish the wicked before ELOHIM.
But let the righteous be glad and exult before ELOHIM;
Yea, let them rejoice with gladness.'[15]

And now let us consider a very similar phenomenon presented in the Song of Deborah.[16] This noble poem is evidently

[13] 2S.vi.15.19.   [14] 2S.xi.11.   [15] Ps.lxviii.1–3.   [16] Ju.v.

one of the 'Lays of Ancient Israel,' that is to say, it is an artistic composition, written by one who has thrown himself heartily into the spirit of the times portrayed in it, but who lived long after the events to which it refers—as, in fact, is plainly indicated by the statement that 'on that day Deborah and Barak the son of Abinoam sang this Song' together,[16] whether this be understood of the joint *utterance* or the joint *authorship* of it. If, indeed, such a splendid composition had really been produced in so rude and primitive an age, and had been handed down either in writing or in memory from that time, it would be reasonable to expect that we should find some remains of other like poems written in the same powerful style, and commemorating other great events of the same or subsequent ages. It is, no doubt, of very ancient date *comparatively*, that is, with reference to the oldest portions of the Bible; and it may very probably have been written in the prophetical schools, where the older portions of the Book of Judges were composed, in the same age which gave birth to those other very spirited poems which occur in the Pentateuch—in short, in that golden age of Hebrew Literature to which we owe the poetry of the 'Blessing of Jacob,'[17] the 'Song of Moses,'[18] and the 'Prophecies of Balaam.'[19]

Listen now to the following passage from this Song:—

> 'JEHOVAH, at Thy going forth from Seir,
> At Thy marching from the field of Edom,
> The earth trembled, the heavens also dropped,
> The clouds also dropped with water,
> Before JEHOVAH the mountains melted,
> That Sinai before JEHOVAH the Elohim of Israel.'[20]

And compare the following words from Ps. lxviii:—

> 'ELOHIM, at Thy going forth before Thy people,
> At Thy marching in the wilderness,
> The earth trembled, the heavens too dropped,
> Before ELOHIM,
> That Sinai before ELOHIM the Elohim of Israel.'[21]

---

[16] P.1. [17] G.xlix.1-26. [18] E.xv.18.
[19] N.xxiii,xxiv. [20] Ju.v.4,5. [21] Ps.lxviii.7,8.

Here, too, it cannot be doubted that the one passage has been directly imitated from the other. Which, again, was the oldest? I answer, the Psalm undoubtedly, for these reasons. In the Psalm the statement stands in close connexion with the following context, introducing very naturally the account of the benefits bestowed upon Israel in the wilderness,[n] and itself also very naturally introduced by the preceding context;[24] whereas in the Song the corresponding passage enters abruptly, as if derived from another source, there being not the slightest connexion between it and the verses which precede and follow it. Again, in the Song there is an appearance of an *expansion* of the words of the Psalm: thus 'from Seir, from the field of Edom' in the Song seems equivalent to the simple words 'In the wilderness' of the Psalmist; and so, too, the phrases 'the heavens also dropped, the clouds also dropped water,' 'the mountains melted,' are mere amplifications of the older language, 'the heavens also dropped' and 'that Sinai.' Moreover, 'the clouds also dropped with water' is but a feeble repetition of 'the heavens also dropped'; and the reference to 'Seir' and 'Edom' in the Song is an incorrect substitute for 'the wilderness' of the Psalm, since the whole description evidently refers to the portents at Sinai,[24] long before the Israelites reached the Edomite territory,[25] but while JEHOVAH still 'went before His people' as they 'marched in the wilderness.'[26] Above all, as before, it is most unlikely that any writer would have changed 'JEHOVAH the Elohim of Israel' of the Song into the tamer expression of the Psalm, 'ELOHIM the Elohim of Israel,' more especially as the writer of the Psalm has not suppressed the name JEHOVAH altogether; whereas it would be most natural for one who was imitating an older composition to change 'ELOHIM' into 'JEHOVAH' in such a connexion, if 'JEHOVAH' had become

[n] v.9-11.   [23] v.5,6.   [25] E.xix.16-19, xx.18
[24] N.xx.14-21.   [26] E.xiii.20-22.

familiar in men's mouths as the name of the 'Elohim of Israel,' which apparently was not the case when the Psalm was written. Once more, it seems incredible that 'a poet of remarkable genius,' the writer of a Psalm described as 'the most spirited, lively, and powerful,' 'the grandest, most splendid, most artistic,' 'one of the most beautiful and most *original*,' of the whole collection, should have borrowed two little scraps from two other ancient documents, one of them certainly *not* Mosaic. And, on the other hand, what could be more natural than that words of this Psalm, composed for so memorable an occasion and fresh in the recollection of the writers, should have been used by them in N. x. 35 and Ju. v, as appears from the quotations I have made, as well as from other minor resemblances which have been pointed out by critics?[17]

We conclude, then, that this portion of the Book of Numbers[18] was written after the fourteenth year of David's reign, when the ark was brought up to Mount Zion. Let us now consider the Prophecies of Balaam.[19] From our point of view we are not troubled here with the strange occurrence of the ass conversing as a human being with Balaam, who, however, retained his composure and replied calmly without any signs of dismay or astonishment, though no part of the conversation was heard by his servants or the princes of Moab who travelled in his company,—or with the fact that the angel was seen by Balaam and the ass, and spoke with Balaam, but, as before, was neither seen nor heard by his companions—or by the circumstance that Balaam must be supposed to have uttered his prophecies, on the impulse of the moment in prophetic rapture, in the ears—not of Moses and Israel, but of Balak king of Moab and his princes, and Moses to have secured somehow a

---

[17] *comp.* Ju. v. 3 with Ps. lxviii. 4, Ju. v. 12 with Ps. lxviii. 18.
[18] N. x. 35.

manuscript of them—or by the strange phenomenon that these prophecies are found to be written in the purest Hebrew, though Balaam was not of Hebrew birth, but summoned by Balak from his native land on the banks of the Euphrates,⁷⁷—or by his employing the name JEHOVAH repeatedly, and even saying 'JEHOVAH is my Elohim,'³⁰ and using in his utterances the identical language of the dying Jacob in the Book of Genesis, as where Jacob says in his blessing on Judah—

> 'He stooped, he crouched as a lion,
> Even as a lioness—who shall rouse him?'³¹

and Balaam says, speaking of Israel—

> 'He stooped, he lay down as a lion,
> Even as a lioness—who shall rouse him?'³²

Is it possible that Jacob's Blessing and Balaam's Prophecies may be the work of one and the selfsame hand?

I showed on a former occasion,³³ by considering especially the Blessing on Judah, that the Blessing of Jacob was probably written in the midst of David's conquests, about the twelfth year of his reign. Listen now to these words out of Balaam's final prophecy:—

> 'I see him, but not now,
> I behold him, but not near.
> A Star has appeared out of Jacob,
> And a Sceptre has arisen out of Israel,
> And has smitten the temples of Moab,
> And the crown of the head of all the sons of pride.
> And Edom shall be a possession—
> Yea, Seir shall be a possession—his enemies';
> But Israel shall be gaining force.'³⁴

Here is plainly announced, in the form of a prophecy, the conquest by Israel of Moab and Edom; and 'it is not possible to see in the illustrious king, from whom this picture is borrowed, any later one than David,'³⁵ who smote

---

⁷⁷ N. xxii. 5, see *B.C.I. p.* 734. ³⁰ N. xxii. 18. ³¹ G. xlix. 9. ³² N. xxiv. 9.
³³ *p.* 62–67. ³⁴ N. xxiv. 17, 18. ³⁵ EWALD (*Hist. of Israel*), Eng. Ed. I. *p.* 108.

both Moab and Edom, as no other king did, Moab first
and Edom afterwards, as here predicted. 'He smote Moab
and measured them with a line, casting them down to the
ground ; even with two lines measured he to put to death,
and with one full line to keep alive'—massacring, therefore, in cold blood two out of three of all his male (?)
Moabite captives; 'and so the Moabites became David's
servants and brought gifts.'[36] And he 'put garrisons in
Edom ; throughout all Edom put he garrisons ; and all
they of Edom became David's servants;'[37] though afterwards apparently, perhaps on some revolt, 'Joab went up
to bury the slain' of Israel, after he had slain every male
in Edom ; for 'six months did Joab remain there with all
Israel, until he had cut off every male in Edom.'[38] But
David smote also in an equally memorable manner the
people of Ammon. 'And David gathered all the people
together, and went to Rabbah the royal city, and fought
against it. And he brought forth the people that were
therein, and put them under saws and under harrows of
iron and under axes of iron, and made them pass through
(the brick-kiln, or rather, as it should probably be rendered,
made them pass over, i.e. in the fire) to Molech ;' in other
words, David sawed asunder, and tore with harrows, and
chopped with axes, and burnt alive, his Ammonite captives
out of Rabbah ; 'and thus did he unto all the cities of the
children of Ammon.'[39] Now Edom, Moab, and Ammon
are continually named together in the Bible, and Moab and
Ammon are coupled almost invariably.[40] And therefore it

---

[36] 2S.viii.2.   [37] 2S.viii.14.
[38] 1K.xi.15,16.   [39] 2S.xii.31.
[40] 'Edom, Moab, and Ammon,' D.ii.4,9,19, xxiii.3,7, 1S.xiv.47, 1K.xi.1, 1Ch.xviii.11, 2Ch.xx.10,22,23, Ps.lxxxiii.6,7, Is.xi.14, Jer.ix.26, xxv.21, xxvii.3, xl.11, xlviii.1-xlix.22, Ez.xxv.1-14, Dan.xi.41, Am.i.11-ii.3, comp. 'Moab and Ammon,' G.xix.37,38, Ju.iii.12,13, x.6, xi.15, 2S.viii.12, 1K.xi.7,33, 2K.xxiii.13, xxiv.2, 2Ch.xx.1,xxiv.26, Ezr.ix.1, Neh.xiii.1,23, Zeph.ii.8,9.

is most unlikely that any writer, whether predicting beforehand, as the traditional view supposes, or recounting afterwards, the triumphs of David's reign, should have mentioned only the conquest of Moab and that of Edom and said nothing whatever about the conquest of Ammon. It would seem that this prophecy must have been written in the interval of five or six years between the conquests of Moab and Edom and that of Ammon, at a time when the reigning king of Ammon was on very friendly terms with David.[11] We are thus brought to the very same date exactly for Balaam's Prophecies as for the Blessing of Jacob, *viz.*, about the twelfth year of David's reign in the midst of his conquests, when the 'lion's whelp' had 'gone-up from the prey' and had 'crouched' again for a time, and 'who should rouse him?'[12]

There are other indications of the same age in other parts of Balaam's Prophecies, as, for instance, in the words which say that Israel's king 'shall be higher than Agag,'[13] which must have been written at a time when the power of Agag, king of Amalek, was still fresh in the recollection of the Hebrew people or, at all events, had not yet passed out of the popular talk. In other words, these prophecies must have been composed *not long* after the time when Saul 'utterly destroyed' the Amalekites, and Samuel 'hewed Agag in pieces before JEHOVAH at the Gilgal,'[14] that is, they were written in the early part of David's reign. In short, as I have said, no sign of time has yet been traced in all the Jehovistic matter to the end of the Book of Joshua, which carries the age of its writer or writers certainly below the first years of Solomon's reign.[15]

But, after all, these Jehovistic amplifications of the more ancient Elohistic Narrative with that Narrative it-

[11] 2S.x.2. [13] G.xlix.9. [12] N.xxiv.7.
[14] 1S.xv.8,33. [15] *p.*57.

self, which together we may call the Older or Original Story of the Exodus, make up less than one-half of the whole work, as it now lies before us, to the end of Joshua. More than one-half, therefore, still remains to be accounted for; and of this about as much as the Elohistic matter belongs to the Deuteronomist, and about as much as the Jehovistic matter belongs to the Levitical Legislation.

I shall speak more fully hereafter about these two sets of passages. For the present I confine myself to a few closing remarks upon the general results of these criticisms. We now find that Israel was under Divine Teaching just exactly as we are. We are now able to observe in Israel, as in other nations, the signs of growth and orderly progress, the people making gradual advancement in religious truth and moral perception, under the teaching of those great men whom the Spirit of God enlightened and quickened, and whom His Providence raised up among them from time to time, for this end first, but with a further view to the education of the race, even of us among the rest. Their history now becomes rational and intelligible, being stripped—not of all that is supernatural or Divine, but—of all that is portentous, perplexing, and contradictory. It will no longer be full of marvels and prodigies, painfully staggering to an intelligent faith—as where Elisha by a word makes the iron axe-head float,[16] or his bones revive a dead man,[17] or where the Jordan, when overflowing all its banks, is suddenly stopped in its course, its waters 'rising up in a heap' till Israel had crossed its bed on dry land[18]—and these wonders being profusely lavished on a favoured people or individual, and performed oftentimes, as it seems to our reason, the guiding light which God has given us, without any adequate object or proportionate result, as where the

[16] 2K.vi.5-7.   [17] 2K.xiii.21.   [18] J.iii.15-17.

ass reproves Balaam with human voice[19] or the whale swallows Jonah.[20] It is surely strengthening and comforting to know that God, our God, is amongst us still, as He was of old, speaking to us by His Spirit in our hearts and consciences with that still small voice which is mightier far and more effective than any thunders of Sinai could be. Let us bless God that we live in an age when the mist has been cleared away which hid from those who lived before us the true history of Israel, and made the Bible to many thoughtful and devout persons a stone of stumbling and a rock of offence—ay, which veiled from us the face of our Heavenly Father, and darkened the teaching of the Gospel of Christ.

[19] N. xxii. 28-30.   [20] Jon. i. 17, ii. 10.

LECTURE VIII.

SUMMARY.

The Ten Commandments in Exx. inserted by the Deuteronomist; the New Commentary admits that these differ 'in several weighty particulars' from those in D.v, and that neither copy represents correctly those actually uttered by Jehovah on Sinai; fallacious view of the Commentary on this point; no room for the Decalogue in the Original Story; the context quoted, and shown to be an early portion of the Jehovistic matter; it contains no sign of the utterance of the Ten Commandments; a series of very different commands received by Moses in the Original Story, and made the basis of the Covenant between Jehovah and Israel; the points of resemblance between the two series show that the Decalogue did not exist in the Original Story; the Book of the Covenant belongs to a rude and primitive age; its barbarous slave-laws; impiety of our ascribing these to the Deity; fallacious view of the New Commentary on this point; these laws composed for a settled agricultural people, as in the time of Saul; perhaps a transcript of the 'manner' or common-law of the kingdom, as administered by Samuel and 'written in a book' by him for Saul; the comfort of being released from the moral difficulty of believing that such laws ever had Divine authority.

THE TEN COMMANDMENTS.

I HAVE already mentioned the Deuteronomist[1] as the writer of some portions of the story of the Exodus, as it now stands, from Genesis to Joshua. Among these, of course, is the Book of Deuteronomy itself, or the greatest part of it, which is written in a totally different style from any passages of the Original Story, and about which I shall hereafter give you some further information. The most important, however, of all the Deuteronomistic insertions is not the Book of Deuteronomy itself, however interesting and instructive that is in many respects, but the Decalogue or Ten Commandments in E.xx. The New Bible Commentary admits that these, as we now read them, recorded first in Exodus[2] and repeated in Deuteronomy,[3] but in forms 'differing from each other in several weighty particulars,'[4] cannot be in either form a genuine copy of the 'Ten Words,' as, according to the traditionary view, they were spoken by the Divine Voice on Sinai. The writer suggests that the Ten Commandments were originally uttered all in the same terse form as those which now remain, 'Thou shalt not kill,' 'Thou shalt not steal,' &c., and were afterwards —those sacred words, supposed to have been formulated by

[1] A.97. [2] E.xx.1-17. [3] D.v.6,21. [4] B.C.I.p.335.

Infinite Wisdom and delivered with solemn emphasis in the ears of all Israel 'out of the midst of the fire, of the cloud, and of the thick darkness, with a great voice'[a]—considerably amplified by Moses,[b] a supposition which is, of course, entirely subversive of the usual traditionary notion. Thus, for instance, the Fourth Commandment, as uttered by JEHOVAH on Sinai, was merely the brief injunction, 'Remember the sabbath-day to sanctify it.' It was Moses who added the further details, 'Six days shalt thou labour and do all thy work: but the seventh day is the sabbath of JEHOVAH thy Elohim; thou shalt not do any work, thou, nor thy son, nor thy daughter, thy manservant nor thy maidservant, nor thy cattle, nor thy stranger that is within thy gates;' and this addition appears—but with some variation[c]—in both forms of the Decalogue. But in Exodus he has given this as the reason for keeping the sabbath—'For in six days JEHOVAH made heaven and earth, the sea and all that in them is, and rested the seventh day; *therefore* JEHOVAH blessed the seventh day and sanctified it;' whereas in Deuteronomy he has given a totally different reason for observing it—'And remember that thou wast a servant in the land of Egypt, and that JEHOVAH thy Elohim brought thee forth from thence through a mighty hand and a stretched-out arm; *therefore* JEHOVAH thy Elohim commanded thee to keep the sabbath-day.' And similar additions are on this view supposed to have been made by Moses to the second, third, fifth, and tenth Commandments, as originally spoken by JEHOVAH. It is unfortunate for this theory that even, in their reduced forms, consisting only of a few words, the two copies of the Fourth Commandment are not identical; since in Exodus we read

---

[a] D. v. 22. [b] *B.C.* I. p. 336.
[c] D. iv. 14, has 'nor thine ox, nor thine ass' instead of 'nor thy cattle' of E. xx. 10, and adds at the end 'that thy manservant and thy maidservant may rest as well as thou.'

'*Remember* the sabbath-day to sanctify it,'[8] and in Deuteronomy, '*Observe* the sabbath-day to sanctify it;'[9] so that the words of the Commentary, written with reference to the longer statement, apply also to the shorter statement of these Commandments—'Each is said, with reiterated emphasis, to contain the words that were actually spoken by the Lord and written by him upon the stones. . . . It has been generally assumed that the whole of one or other of these copies was written on the Tables. Most commentators have supposed that the original document is in Exodus, and that the author of Deuteronomy wrote from memory, with variations suggested at the time. Others have conceived that Deuteronomy must furnish the more correct form, since the Tables must have been in actual existence when the Book was written. But neither of these views can be fairly reconciled with the statements in Exodus and Deuteronomy, to which reference has been made. If either copy, as a whole, represents what was written on the Tables, it is obvious that the other cannot do so.'[10]

But, when you have heard the Jehovistic matter extracted by itself from E.xix,xx, as you heard before the Elohistic matter in E.i-vi,[11] you will see that there is no room whatever for the Ten Commandments in the Original Story of the Exodus. For this is how that story ran:—

'And it came to pass on the third day, when it was morning, that there were voices (or thunderings) and lightnings, and a thick cloud upon the Mount, and the sound of a trumpet very loud; and all the people trembled that were in the Camp. And Moses brought forth the people to meet ELOHIM out of the Camp, and they took their stand underneath the Mount. And Mount Sinai was all of it smoke, because JEHOVAH had come down upon it in fire; and its smoke went

[8] E.xx.8.   [9] D.v.12.   [10] *B.C.*],*p*.335-6.   [11] *p*.72,73.

up as the smoke of a furnace, and the whole Mount trembled greatly. And the trumpet-sound kept going very much louder and louder: Moses spake, and ELOHIM answered him by a voice (or thunderings). And all the people were seeing the voices and the flashes and the trumpet-sound and the Mountain smoking; and, when the people saw, they shrank back and stood at a distance. And they said to Moses, "Speak thou with us, and we will hear; but let not ELOHIM speak with us, lest we die." And Moses said unto the people, "Fear ye not; for ELOHIM hath come that He may prove you and that His fear may be before you that ye sin not." So the people stood at a distance, and Moses drew near unto the thick darkness where ELOHIM was.'[13]

You will have observed in this short passage five times ELOHIM and only once JEHOVAH; in other words, it is one of the earlier additions to the Elohistic Narrative, when, as we suppose,[13] the writer had not yet come to use very freely the name JEHOVAH. It is this passage evidently which is referred to in those verses of Ps.lxviii which I quoted in my last Lecture—

> 'ELOHIM, at Thy going forth before Thy people,
> At Thy marching in the wilderness,
> The earth trembled, the heavens also dropped,
> Before ELOHIM,
> That Sinai before ELOHIM, the Elohim of Israel';[14]

where allusion is made to 'the whole mountain quaking greatly,'[15] and to the heavy rain-storm which might naturally be supposed to accompany the 'thunderings and lightnings.'[16] This portion, therefore, of the Original Story must have been already in existence at the time when Ps.lxviii was composed, and was in the hands, most probably, of the same circle of prophetical writers from which the Psalm itself proceeded.

---

[13] E.xix.16-19, xx.18-21.   [14] p.85,90.   [15] Ps.lxviii.7,8.
[13] E.xix.18.   [16] E.xix.16, xx.18.

THE TEN COMMANDMENTS.

But where now, in this passage of the Original Story, are the Ten Commandments? Or where is there any room for them? In the account, which we have now before us in the Bible, they are inserted just before the words 'and all the people were seeing the voices and flashes and the trumpet-sound and the mountain smoking;' where reference is clearly made to the previous statement that, 'when it was morning, there were voices and lightnings and a thick cloud upon the mount and the sound of a trumpet very loud, and Mount Sinai was all of it smoke, because JEHOVAH had come down upon it in fire.'[17] The people, we are told, were appalled by the mighty thunderings, the terrific flashes of lightning, the awful trumpet-sounds, and the thick smoke that covered the quaking mount and 'went up like the smoke of a furnace.'[18] But not a word is said about their having heard a tremendous Voice, uttering audibly the Ten Commandments. Rather, it is plainly implied that they had *not* heard any such utterances; for they entreat Moses saying, 'Speak thou with us and we will hear; but let not ELOHIM speak with us, lest we die.'[19] And so Moses alone draws near to ELOHIM,[20] and receives a long series of commands of a totally different character,[21] which he afterwards communicates to the people, and on the basis of which, not upon that of the Ten Commandments, a Covenant is solemnly made between JEHOVAH and Israel.[22]

Moses received, I say, on this occasion 'a long series of commands of a totally different character' from the Ten Commandments. Yet some of them are not unlike, as, for instance, the very first injunction, 'Thou shalt not make with Me ELOHIM of silver and ye shall not make you ELOHIM of gold.'[23] But then how tame would this be if the Divine Voice had been represented as having already

[17] E.xix.16,18. [18] E.xx.18. [19] E.xx.19. [20] E.xx.21.
[21] E.xx.22, &c. [22] E.xxiv.3-8. [23] E.xx.23.

uttered in the ears of all Israel the Second Commandment with all its details, 'Thou shalt not make for thyself any graven image,' &c. ?[14] In like manner the words 'Six days shalt thou do thy work, and on the seventh day thou shalt rest, that so thine ox and thine ass may repose, and the son of thy handmaid and the sojourner may be refreshed,'[15] would have been quite superfluous, if the Fourth Commandment, with its much more precise and full directions, had been previously published. Again, the words, 'ELOHIM shalt thou not revile, and the prince among thy people shalt thou not curse,'[16] correspond in some sense with the language of the Third Commandment, and 'he that curseth his father or his mother shall surely be put to death,'[17] with that of the Fifth; and so in other instances. But there is no ground for supposing that these laws are only an expansion and explanation, or a repeated enforcement, of the Ten Commandments; for these last are more full than the others, and are perfectly clear, and need no enlargement or explanation; and surely a private communication to Moses can hardly be thought of as 'enforcing' commands represented as having been uttered by GOD Himself, with awful power and majesty, in the hearing of all the people.

In short, it will be seen at once that these laws in E.xxi-xxiii are, as a whole, altogether different in tone and character from the Ten Commandments. They contain, for instance, a number of details as to matters connected with worship or with social and private life, which betray unmistakably the signs of a rude and primitive age. Thus we read 'An altar of earth shall ye make for Me; and thou shalt sacrifice upon it thy burnt-offerings and thy peace-offerings, thy sheep and thy oxen; and, if thou shalt make for me an altar of stones, thou shalt not build them of hewn stones; if

[14] E.xx.4-6.   [15] E.xxiii.12.   [16] E.xxii.28.   [17] E.xxi.17.

thou hast waved thy tool upon it, then shalt thou defile it.'[ ]
And here we find ourselves in an age when the first rude
altars of earth or rough stones were made on high-places in
all parts of the land, at Mizpah,[ ] at Ramah,[ ] at Bethel,[ ] at
the Gilgal,[ ] and were allowed or even encouraged by these
laws to be made, 'in *every* place where I record My name
I will come unto thee and I will bless thee,'[ ] before any
splendid Temple had been built with its *one* brazen altar,[ ]
upon which all sacrifices were to be offered, 'in the place
which Jehovah had chosen,'[ ]—in other words, before the time
of Solomon or even of David's Tabernacle on Mount Zion,
where probably stood also a more elaborate altar than was
allowed by these ordinances.[ ]

But we find here other laws ascribed to JEHOVAH, which, so
long as they are believed to have Divine authority, might be
justly appealed to, and no doubt have been appealed to, as
sanctioning the worst evils of slavery. 'When a man shall
smite his servant or his handmaid with a rod and he die under
his hand, he shall certainly be punished. Only, if he shall
stand a day or two days, he shall not be punished; for he is
his money.'[ ] Let us thank God that we are no longer
required to ascribe to the Most Holy and Merciful Creator,
'the God of the spirits of all flesh,'[ ] our Heavenly Father,
this horrible command, which an orthodox German commentator very honestly explains as follows:—'Through his
remaining in life, if only for one or two days [N.B. however
mangled or maimed], it became evident that the master did
not wish to kill him; if, however, after this he died, *the loss
of the slave was punishment enough for his master.'*[ ] And,
strange to say, the same language is repeated in the New
Bible Commentary—'The master was permitted to retain the

[ ] E.xx.24,25.	[ ] 1S.vii.5,9.	[ ] 1S.vii.17.
[ ] 1S.x.3.	[ ] 1S.xi.15.	[ ] E.xx.24.
[ ] 1K.ix.25.	[ ] D.xii.5,6.	[ ] 1K.i.50,51,53,iL.28,29.
[ ] E.xxi.20,21.	[ ] N.xvi.22,xxvii.6.	[ ] Keil,I.p.472.

power of chastising his slave with a rod; but the indulgence of unbridled temper was so far kept in check by his incurring punishment if the slave died under his hand. If, however, the slave survived the castigation a day or two, it was assumed that the offence of the master had not been so heinous, and he did not become amenable to the law, because *the loss of the slave*, who by old custom was recognized as his property, *was accounted, under the circumstances, as a punishment.*'[40] Why, what could a Legree have wished more than this, except the addition of the previous command, 'If his master have given him a wife and she have borne him sons or daughters, the wife and her children shall be her master's, and he shall go out by himself'[41]—'go out,' either 'free for nothing,' as this law prescribes,[42] after six years' service, or else, I suppose, 'go out free' by death, even death under a brutal castigation, 'if he shall stand a day or two'—which, says the same candid German writer, 'may appear hard, but it was rightly grounded in the nature of slavery. In order, however, to soften the hardship of separation from wife or children, it is allowed to the slave to remain in the service of his master, provided he will for ever renounce his freedom.'[43] In other words, the poor wretch — a Hebrew slave — is here tempted to buy his own freedom by abandoning his wife and children? Slaves they were already—and so a Hebrew might sell his own daughter into slavery by another of these laws[44]—and slaves they are to remain; they have only been bred, it seems, for the master's use. But they will be deprived of the little comfort of living together, unless the husband and the father will consent to become a slave for ever!'[45] And the New Bible Commentary says—'The protection here afforded to the life of a slave may seem to us but a slight one. But it is the very earliest trace of such protection in legislation, and it stands in

[40] R.C.I.A.345.
[41] Keil, I.A.469.
[42] Exi.4.
[43] Exi.7.
[44] Exi.2.
[45] Exi.5,6.

strong and favourable contrast with the old laws of Greece, Rome, and other nations. These regulations were most likely *as much as was feasible at the time*, to mitigate the cruelty of ancient practice; they were as much as the hardness of the hearts of the people would bear.'[46] Such remarks might be just if these laws were merely *Mosaic* laws, that is, laws adopted or originated by Moses and ascribed by him to the Deity. But to say that the Divine Being ever really sanctioned or enforced, much less originated, such laws as these—that for the Great God, the 'Faithful Creator,'[47] this was 'as much as was feasible at the time,' that He could not do more in the cause of humanity 'because of the hardness of heart' of his chosen people—is simply to blaspheme the Holy Name of our Father in Heaven. Even the text appealed to says, '*Moses* because of the hardness of your hearts suffered you to put away your wives.'[48] Verily, those of the clergy, of all ranks and denominations, will have much to answer for, who will shut their eyes obstinately to the light of Modern Criticism, and allow their flocks still to believe that the slaveholder may draw support for his practices from the actual utterances of the Living God. Either these words are God's, as the Bible says,[49] or they are not. Let us not any longer blink the question, but tell the plain truth to our people, and trust God with the consequences.

I have said that these laws show signs of having been written in a rude and primitive age, and, I may add, for an agricultural people. 'They imply that the people of Israel were not only settled in Palestine, but were in peaceful and undisturbed possession of the land. They betray not a trace of the disturbance of the conquest and the struggle for possession, but rather are employed in giving careful prescriptions for the moral and judicial cases likely to occur among a

---

[46] *B.C.I. p.* 346.
[47] 1 Pet. iv. 19.
[48] Mt. xix. 8, Mk. x. 3-5.
[49] E. xx. 22, xxi. 1, xxiv. 3, 4, 7, 8.

people employed in agriculture and living in regular intercourse with themselves and with strangers. That others also, besides Israelites, possessed fields or vineyards or olive-gardens, is nowhere implied: rather a humane and mild treatment of non-Israelites remaining in the land is enjoined,[40] just in the same way as that of widows and orphans.[41] This remark hardly allows us, even if we regard this law-book as the oldest handed down in the Pentateuch, to carry back its composition to the time of the Judges; it seems rather to belong to the time of the Kings.'[42]

Rather, it seems to belong to the time of the *first* king, Saul. We read that, when Saul was made king, 'Samuel told the people the *manner of the kingdom*, and wrote it in a book, and laid it up before JEHOVAH.'[43] What was this 'manner or custom of the kingdom' which Samuel 'told the people'? Apparently it was the system by which they were to be ruled under Saul,—the *common-law*, as it were, which he himself had hitherto administered in his yearly circuits to judge the people; for as we are told, 'Samuel judged Israel all the days of his life; and he went from year to year in circuit to Bethel and the Gilgal and Mizpah, and judged Israel in all those places; and his return was to Ramah, for there was his house, and there he built an altar unto JEHOVAH.'[44] The phrase used repeatedly in these laws with reference to a dispute or trespass, 'bring unto ELOHIM,' 'come unto ELOHIM,'[45] implies just such an age as this, when Samuel 'went in circuit' to different sacred places and judged the people 'before JEHOVAH,'[46] that is, before the altar or within the chapel of the high-place, deciding the lighter cases himself, but having recourse in doubtful matters to some

---

[40] E. xxii. 21, xxiii. 9.   [41] E. xxii. 22-24.   [42] GRAF, *Gesch. Büch.*, p. 29.
[43] 1 S. x. 25.   [44] 1 S. vii. 15-17.
[45] E. xxi. 6, xxii. 8, 9, where the E. V. has 'judges,' but the Heb. 'ELOHIM.'
[46] 1 S. vii. 6.

sacred 'ephod'⁵⁷ or other mode of divination, by which the Divine sentence was supposed to be obtained, as Jethro advises Moses, 'Be thou for the people towards ELOHIM, that thou mayest bring the causes unto ELOHIM.'⁵⁸ It would hardly have been used in the later time when David or Solomon administered justice either in their own persons⁵⁹ or by means of their officers.⁶⁰ May we not, in short, have in these very laws of Exodus a *copy* of that ' common-law of the kingdom,' which Samuel had hitherto administered and by which the new king was henceforth to be guided? We are told that Samuel 'wrote it in a book and laid it up before Jehovah.'⁶¹ And so we are also told that the laws we are now considering were 'written' in a 'book' by Moses;⁶² and these laws too, as we shall see, and not the Ten Commandments, are said in the Original Story to have been written by the Finger of ELOHIM on two tables of stone, which were put into the Ark and laid up before JEHOVAH, as the laws by which the people were to be governed, and on the basis of which the Covenant was made between JEHOVAH and Israel.

However this may be, it seems clear that these laws must have been written in the age of Samuel, except the last twelve verses⁶³ and one or two other small insertions,⁶⁴ which are due to the later Deuteronomist. Let us rejoice to know that the Divine Spirit is no longer to be held responsible, as the traditionary view supposes, not only for the innumerable contradictions of scientific fact and discrepancies in statement, which are observed in the story of the Pentateuch, but for moral delinquencies, like that which we have been considering, and many others of a similar kind. For myself, I repeat, what I have publicly stated, that it was not the scientific difficulties in the accounts of the Creation and the Flood,

---

⁵⁷ 1 S. xxi.9, xxiii.6,9, xxx.7, and xiv.18 (LXX).   ⁶⁰ E. xviii.19.
⁵⁸ 1.K.iii.28, vii.7.   ⁶² 2 S. viii.15, xv.2–6.   ⁶¹ 1 S. x.25.
⁵⁹ E. xxiv.4,7.   ⁶³ E. xxiii.22–33.   ⁶⁴ E. xxiii.13, 15bc, 19.

which brought my own mind to a stand, and compelled me to seek a satisfactory solution of them. Those difficulties I met, as they are met now by many, by supposing that they were mere reflections of ancient myths—not, of course, to be received as infallibly or even historically true, but such as a good and true man might write for the edification of an ignorant age. But the fact that such barbarous commands, as those we have heard to-day, were here attributed to the Fountain of all Goodness, was painfully forced upon my mind while engaged in translating the Book of Exodus into Zulu. I felt that it was absolutely impossible to believe this, without abandoning all trust in a righteous and perfect Being, whose children we are, and whose moral excellencies are faintly reflected in our own. From that time I resolved that, cost what it might in time and labour, ay, and in other things which men hold dear, I would, God helping me, search into the mystery, and master, if possible, the history of the composition of the Pentateuch. I thank God that I have finished my work, at least sufficiently for all practical purposes, and am now able to lay before you the ripe results of my labours. And, if I have helped in any way to relieve your minds and the minds of others, as well as my own, from the misery of finding such laws as I have quoted, and other like laws, ascribed to the God of Truth and Love, the Father of our Lord Jesus Christ, in a Book which traditionary teaching represents as Divinely infallible, I feel that I shall not have lived in vain.

LECTURE IX.

SUMMARY.

RECAPITULATION ; the Book of the Covenant, with its laws on slave holding, retaliation, cattle-stealing, grass-burning, witchcraft ; its three agricultural Feasts, in Spring, Summer, and Autumn ; its words apparently enjoining human sacrifices ; plain evidence in Scripture of human sacrifices being common in Israel, derived from the practice of the Canaanites ; example in the case of Jephthah ; the story of Abraham's sacrifice written to check the practice, but not condemning it ; human sacrifices general among other ancient nations ; the practice lasting among the Hebrews to Josiah's time ; signs in Jeremiah and Ezekiel that the Original Story was appealed to as enjoining such sacrifices ; in Micah's days they were regarded as acts of piety ; human sacrifices in Christendom ; 'giving up witchcraft' in what sense 'giving up the Bible.'

HUMAN SACRIFICES IN ISRAEL.

IN my last Lecture I directed your attention to the series of laws in E.xxi-xxiii, which are represented as having been imparted by JEHOVAH to Moses at the foot of Mount Sinai, while the people in terror stood afar off, and Moses alone 'drew near unto the thick darkness where ELOHIM was.' These laws, as I showed, bear the marks of having been composed in a rude age and for an agricultural people—in short, of having been written in Samuel's time, before the arts of civilised life had made any progress in Israel, as they did soon afterwards during the martial age of David and the luxurious reign of Solomon. Among these were the oppressive slave-laws which we noticed, and that law of retaliation which our Saviour expressly set aside by His own gracious teaching, 'life for life, eye for eye, tooth for tooth, hand for hand, foot for foot, burning for burning, wound for wound, stripe for stripe.'[1]

But there are other regulations, the reasons for which we can well understand, and the good sense of which we can thoroughly appreciate, from our own experience in a land like this. Thus we read 'When a man shall steal an ox or a sheep, and slaughter it or sell it, five oxen shall he repay for the ox and *four* sheep for the sheep';[2] and we

[1] E.xxi.23-25, Mt.v.38,39.   [2] E.xxii.1.

remember how, when Nathan the prophet brought home to David his guilt in the case of Bathsheba, by relating the parable of the poor man's ewe-lamb which the rich man had seized and slaughtered for his guest, the king replied, before he recognised the prophet's meaning, 'he shall restore the lamb *four*fold,'[1] in exact accordance with this law, which was still apparently in force as part of the law of the realm, administered formerly as common-law by Samuel, but reduced, as we suppose, to a written statute in the law-book before us at the time when Saul, the first king, was chosen to reign over Israel.[2] So, too, we have here the very reasonable ordinance, 'When a man shall eat-off a field or a vineyard, yea, shall let loose his beast that it eat-off in the field of another, the best of his field and the best of his vineyard shall he repay,'[3] and again, 'If fire go-forth and catch dry grass, so that stack or standing-corn or field be devoured, he that kindled the conflagration shall certainly repay.'[4] We find here also the command, 'A witch thou shalt not let live,'[5] and we remember how the witch of Endor said to Saul, when he went in his despair to consult her before his last fatal fight with the Philistines, 'Behold! thou knowest what Saul hath done, how he hath cut off those that have familiar spirits and the wizards out of the land; wherefore then layest thou a snare for my life to cause me to die?'[6] But Saul, from all that we know about him, was not a man to have set his face so sternly against witchcraft from his own mere motion. It is probable that, in his early days as king, he had exhibited this zeal against witchcraft in obedience to this very law, and under the direct influence of Samuel himself.

So in these laws we have three agricultural feasts established,[7] at which the Israelites are enjoined to 'appear before

[1] 2 S. xii. 6. [2] p. 110, 111. [3] E. xxii. 5. [4] E. xxii. 6.
[5] E. xxii. 18. [6] 1 S. xxviii. 9. [7] E. xxiii. 14-16.

JEHOVAH,'[10] probably it is meant at the nearest highplace, and 'not to appear empty,'[11] that is, to bring gifts and sacrifices,—namely, the 'Feast of Mazzoth' (or unleavened cakes), the Spring festival, the 'Feast of Harvest, the firstfruits of their labours,' the Summer festival, and the 'Feast of Ingathering at the end of the year,' the joyous Autumn festival, when thank-offerings were made for the blessings of the year. Naturally this last—afterwards called the 'Feast of Tabernacles'[12]—was the favourite festival, when the weather would be fine and the roads dry, and all things conspired to heighten the universal gladness and mirth. It is this feast which is probably referred to in the Book of Judges as held to JEHOVAH in Shiloh yearly, when 'the daughters of Shiloh would come out to dance in dances.'[13] And so in the days of Elkanah the father of Samuel it seems to have been the only festival regularly observed by pious Israelites; for we are told how he went up, he and all his house, 'to offer the *yearly* sacrifice' at Shiloh.[14] In Solomon's time, however, the custom of celebrating all three feasts was fully established; 'and three times in the year did Solomon offer burnt-offerings and peace-offerings upon the altar which he had built unto JEHOVAH.'[15] Hence we may conclude that it had been previously enjoined, as we suppose, in this law-book of Samuel's time.

Once more, we read 'Thy fullness and thy tears '—in other words, the firstfruits of thy threshing-floor and of thy presses for wine and oil—' thou shalt not delay; the firstborn of thy children thou shalt give to Me. So shalt thou do with thine ox, with thy sheep; seven days shall it be with its dam; on the eighth day thou shalt give it to Me.'[16] These words *sound* as if they directly enjoined the practice of human sacrifice—'the firstborn of thy children thou shalt give to Me'; and nothing whatever is said about the way in which these firstborn children were to be 'given to JEHOVAH'; only it is added, '*so* shalt thou do with thine ox, with thy sheep; on the eighth day thou shalt give it to Me.' To all appearance, then, the firstborn children were to be given to JEHOVAH just in the very same way as the firstling of an ox or a sheep, and therefore, though probably not before the eighth day, they were to be sacrificed. This, I repeat, is the direct and obvious meaning of the passage; and I cannot undertake to say that it was not the meaning actually intended by the writer in Exodus. It is true that, as the story now stands, these firstborns of men 'given to JEHOVAH' are elsewhere in the Pentateuch ordered to be 'redeemed.'[17] But there is no such direction in the Original Story, of which this law-book forms a part; it only occurs in later passages, either inserted by the Deuteronomist or belonging to the Levitical Legislation, and reflecting therefore, as we shall see hereafter, the views entertained in Israel centuries after the age of Saul and Samuel. We must remember that in those more ancient times there was, apparently, nothing horrible or revolting in the thought of human firstborns being sacrificed to JEHOVAH or YAHVEH, first killed and then burnt upon the altar; and it is very certain that pious—or, as we should say, superstitious Israelites did sacrifice their firstborn children, male and female, in this way, following the practice of the tribes of Canaan in their worship of the Sun-God; as we read of the king of Moab, when sore pressed in battle by Israel, 'taking his eldest son who should have reigned in his stead, and offering him as a burnt-offering upon the wall,'[18] or as we are told generally of the Canaanite tribes, 'even their sons and their daughters they have burnt in the fire to their Elohim.'[19]

[17] E. xiii. 13, xxxiv. 20, N. iii. 46, 47, xviii. 15, 16.   [18] 2 K. iii. 27.   [19] D. xii. 31.

This is so distinctly stated in the Bible itself that there can be no room for any doubt on this point. Thus we are expressly told that the kings Ahaz and Manasseh made each his son to 'pass-over in fire,'[20] and again that the people generally 'made their sons and their daughters to pass-over in the fire.'[21] And that this expression 'make to pass-over in the fire' does not mean, as some have supposed, a merely harmless ceremony, by which these children were dedicated to the Sun-God without any bodily injury, but is employed as an euphemism for actual slaying and burning, is abundantly plain from such passages as these—'They have built the high-places of Tophet which is in the valley of the son of Hinnom, to burn their sons and their daughters in the fire,'[22] —'They have built also the high-places of the Baal, to burn their children with fire as burnt-offerings unto the Baal,'[23]— 'Moreover thou hast taken thy sons and thy daughters whom thou hast borne unto Me, and these hast thou sacrificed unto them to be devoured,'[24]—'Is this of thy whoredoms a small matter that thou hast slain My children and delivered them to cause them to pass-over in the fire for them?'[25]—'For, when they had slain their children to their idols, then they came the same day into My sanctuary to profane it,'[26]—in other words, they considered these human sacrifices to be not at all incongruous with the worship of JEHOVAH, but regarded them rather as an evidence of their piety, a proof of their intense devotion to that worship—and yet once more, 'Yea, they sacrificed their sons and their daughters unto devils, and shed innocent blood, even the blood of their sons and their daughters, whom they sacrificed unto the idols of Canaan, and the land was polluted with blood.'[27]

There can be no doubt, then, that the sacrificing of first-born children was a common practice throughout the whole

---

[20] 2 K. xvi. 3, xxi. 6. [21] 2 K. xvii. 17. [22] Jer. vii. 31. [23] Jer. xix. 5.
[24] Ez. xvi. 20. [25] Ez. xvi. 21. [26] Ez. xxiii. 39. [27] Ps. cvi. 37, 38.

land of Israel, at least from the time of King Ahaz downwards. But, if from the time of Ahaz, then assuredly from a much earlier date; for, when that king reigned, three centuries after the death of Saul, the Canaanite tribes had long ceased to exist, as distinct from the Israelites and likely to corrupt them by their idolatries. They had either been exterminated, or had been reduced to the condition of bondmen in Solomon's time,[*] or, having lived among the Israelites on friendly terms, as Araunah the Jebusite king under David,[*] had intermarried and mingled in family relations with them.[*] In short, if they learned these practices from the tribes of Canaan, it must have been in the very earliest period, immediately after the conquest, as the result of these very intermarriages, and the free intercourse which was maintained between the new-comers and those who survived of the older inhabitants,—just exactly as the Norman invaders mingled freely and intermarried with the Saxon population of England, when the first fierce strife of the conflict was over.

Accordingly the Bible tells us of human sacrifices being offered to YAHVEH in those early times,—not merely in the case of Agag, king of Amalek, whom Samuel 'hewed in pieces before YAHVEH,'[*] or in that of Saul's seven sons and grandsons, whom David 'delivered into the hands of the Gibeonites, and they hanged'—or, rather, impaled or crucified —'them before YAHVEH,'[*]—but especially in that of Jephthah the Gileadite, who offered his daughter, his only child, as a burnt-offering to YAHVEH;[*] and it is very noticeable that the account of this sacrifice is given, by a writer who probably lived in the age of Samuel, without one word of censure or expression of abhorrence at the action. So, again, the story of Abraham's sacrifice in G.xxii, a Jehovistic narrative which

[*] 1 K. ix. 20, 21.   [*] 2 S. xxiv. 18–24.   [*] D. vii. 3, J. xxiii. 12.
[*] 1 S. xv. 33.   [*] 2 S. xxi. 9.   [*] Ju. xi. 31.

uses frequently ELOHIM, and which was probably written in the early part of David's reign, appears to have been composed for the express purpose of helping to abolish such sacrifices, by substituting for them animal sacrifices, 'redeeming' them, in fact, as Isaac is redeemed with a ram.[M] But the writer expresses no horror whatever at the purpose of Abraham. On the contrary, he represents the patriarch as having had the thought suggested to him by God himself, and as concluding that it was a pious duty to sacrifice 'his son, his only son Isaac, whom he loved';[M] and the lesson which he is taught, that God will be satisfied with his willingness of mind, his readiness to give up the dearest treasure of his heart at the Divine command,[M] would have been joyfully welcomed, we may well believe, by many a pious Israelite, who was 'tempted,' after the example of others round him, to show his fear of the unseen Deity by making his firstborn son or daughter to 'pass-over in the fire' to YAHVEH. But the fact that this writer expresses no condemnation of Abraham's conduct, but on the contrary commends it, implies that in his time the custom in question actually existed, and was practised habitually by pious persons, as it was, we have seen, at a somewhat earlier period in Jephthah's days. He desires apparently to check the practice and to encourage that of 'redeeming' the firstborns of men. But he does not denounce it as utterly impious and abominable; and it may be that his own views were not yet sufficiently clear and decided to enable him to do so. The same might be said of similar reforms being made in a country where infanticide now prevails, or the regular practice of human sacrifice, as in Dahomey or among certain tribes of British India. An European Christian, going fresh from our lands of light, would feel and express intense horror and disgust at such

[M] G.xxii.13. [M] G.xxii.2. [M] G.xxii.12.

proceedings. But a native reformer, if any such arose, would not feel this so strongly; he might object to them and desire to abolish them, and yet would be able to find some excuse for them. Inured to such superstitions from his childhood, it would be difficult for him at first to inveigh severely against customs, which were so manifestly founded on pious motives, and the evil of which, brought up in the midst of such associations, he perhaps only imperfectly realized.

It seems very possible, therefore—nay, rather, highly probable—that this early law-book really meant to enjoin the duty of sacrificing human firstborns, male and female, as well as the firstlings of sheep and oxen, as a token of gratitude and devotion to YAHVEH the Life-giver. And we know that the custom of offering human sacrifices has prevailed extensively—far more extensively than is commonly supposed—not only among the Canaanites and Hebrews, but amongst almost all ancient nations, civilized and uncivilized, even down to the birth of Christianity and after it. Pages, indeed, might be filled with an account of the various forms of human sacrifices which were practised in older times, and so universally, that it is difficult to find a people who were wholly free from this dire superstition. Egyptians, Phœnicians, Syrians, Arabians, Athenians, Spartans, Etrurians, Romans—the Hindoo in the East, the Mexican in the West—Thracians and Syrians, Gauls and Teutons, Saxons and Swedes, Danes and Pomeranians—all have taken part in the celebration of these bloody rites. And they were practised down to a comparatively late age, and in the midst of the highest civilization, as well as among the most barbarous tribes. In fact, as one has said, 'in every generation of the four centuries, from the fall of the Republic to the establishment of Christianity, human victims were sacrificed by the Roman Emperors';[7]

---

[7] Sir JOHN ACTON (quoted by KALISCH, *Lev.* Part I. p. 349.)

while the old Prussians and Goths adhered to the custom for centuries after their nominal adoption of Christianity.[38]

Yet among the Hebrews, in a very early age, as we learn by the story of Abraham's sacrifice, the spirit of some great prophet was moved by Divine inspiration to raise a first mild protest against the continuance of this practice of offering human sacrifices, or at least to point out a 'better way' of showing forth that singleness and sincerity of heart which God, the Living God, desires in his worshippers. And with some, no doubt, the lesson took effect as time went on; and yet it is clear that so late as the days of Jeremiah and Ezekiel, just before the Captivity, if not even later still,[39] the practice still prevailed extensively; and king Josiah, in his great Reformation, in the eighteenth year of his reign,[40] 'defiled Topheth, which is in the valley of the children of Hinnom, that no man might make his son or his daughter to pass-over in the fire to Molech.'[41] Four centuries, however, had passed since the time when the story of Abraham's sacrifice was written; and during that period there had been a growth in spiritual things in Israel, and a great advance had been made in the knowledge of religious and moral truth. And now the prophets, supported, no doubt, by the better feeling of many of their contemporaries, denounced the practice as utterly horrible and detestable. Yet, when Jeremiah repeats again and again so earnestly, with reference to these sacrifices of firstborn sons and daughters, the words 'which I commanded them not nor spake it, neither came it up into my heart,'[42] he must surely have had in view some passage such as that of the Original Story of the Exodus, which we are now considering, and which the people urged as implying a Divine command for the immolation of their firstborns. Ezekiel also seems to be referring to a similar direction when

---

[38] Kalisch (*Lev.* Part I. p. 323-351.)   [39] Is. lvii. 5.   [40] 2 K. xxii. 3.
[41] 2 K. xxiii. 10.   [42] Jer. vii. 31, xix. 5, xxxii. 35.

he says, 'Wherefore I also—*I gave them statutes not good, and judgments whereby they should not live*, and I defiled them in their gifts, in their making to pass-over all that openeth the womb.'[42] And a century previously Micah had taught his people thus:—

> ' Wherewithal shall I come before JEHOVAH,
> And bow myself before the High God?
> Shall I come before Him with burnt-offerings,
> With calves of a year old?
> Will JEHOVAH be pleased with thousands of rams,
> With ten thousands of rivers of oil?
> Shall I give my firstborn for my transgression,
> The fruit of my body for the sin of my soul?
> He hath shewed thee, O man, what is good :
> And what doth JEHOVAH require of thee,
> But to do justly, and to love mercy,
> And to walk humbly with thy God?'[44]

Alas! we know that Christianity too has had its human sacrifices—not only in that cloister-system which immures for life in monasteries and convents young men and women, who have hardly yet begun to taste the gift of life, shuts them out in their prime from the cares and joys and trials of their family and of their kind, and bars them from all rational development of their mental powers, and preparation for those social and domestic duties for which God created them, a life which has too often been death, or worse than death, for many of the victims—but also in the frightful 'acts of faith,' as they were called, when human beings, male and female, frequently some of the best and noblest of our race, were burnt alive as heretics, for the glory of God and in the name of the blessed Jesus, the loving, compassionate Son of Man. And witches, too, have been burnt innumerable in Christian lands, under the sanction of such laws as that recorded in this ancient Hebrew law-book, supposed to have a paramount,

[42] Ez. xx. 25, 26.   [44] Mic. vi. 6-8.

Divine authority. 'Thousands of victims were sometimes burnt alive in a few years; and it was not until a considerable portion of the eighteenth century had passed away that the executions had finally ceased.'[46] In England, in the time of Elizabeth, new laws against witchcraft were made, which were executed with severity; and the good Bishop JEWELL, 'when preaching before the Queen, expressed a hope that the penalties might be still more rigidly enforced.'[46] In the following reign of James I. 'a law was enacted which subjected witches to death on the first conviction, even though they should have inflicted no injury upon their neighbours; and twelve Bishops sat upon the Commission to which it was referred.'[47] Sir MATTHEW HALE, in sentencing two women to be hung for witchcraft, took the opportunity of declaring that the reality of witchcraft was unquestionable, for the Scriptures had affirmed so much.'[48] Sir THOMAS BROWNE asserted that 'those who denied the existence of witchcraft were not only infidels but atheists.'[49] And only about a century ago (1768) JOHN WESLEY declared that 'the giving up witchcraft is in effect giving up the Bible.'[50]

To such an extent, but a few generations ago, were the minds of truly pious men, though living in the full light of the Gospel of Christ, possessed by this frightful superstition, the result of prevailing traditionary views respecting the origin and authority of the Hebrew Scriptures; yet the Hebrew law condemns the witch only to die; it was a refinement of so-called Christian legislators to burn alive both witches and heretics. No doubt, it is true that in 'giving up witchcraft' we do 'give up the Bible,' as a record in every line and letter of Divine, Infallible Truth. But we restore it to its true place—its place Divinely intended—for the education of the

[46] LECKY (*Rise and Influence of Rationalism in Europe*, I. p. 51.) [47] Ib. p. 111.
[48] Ib. p. 114. [49] Ib. p. 120. [50] Ib. p. 120. [51] Ib. p. 115.

race. And once more I say, let us bless God devoutly for the gift of Modern Science, which has not only swept away these abominable superstitions, but has enabled us to read the Bible also with an intelligent faith, and to find in it Divine utterances, bringing life and health and spiritual strength and consolation to the soul of man.

LECTURE X.

SUMMARY.

The laws in the Book of the Covenant were not the Ten Commandments; the Vision of JEHOVAH by Moses, Aaron, and the Elders; Moses in the Mount for forty days; what became during this time of Joshua? Moses receives the two tables of stone, which he dashes in pieces on seeing the Golden Calf; he is summoned to come up again, and receives two other tables, inscribed with the words of the 'Book of the Covenant' or 'Testimony'; two such stone tables very probably placed in the Ark in David's time, which by their weight may have caused the death of Uzzah; their size compared with the laws to be engraved on them and the sacrificial table of Marseilles; the Ten Words in E. xxxiv. 28, shown to be a later interpolation; the Deuteronomist, though he abridged the laws of the Book of the Covenant, would hesitate to cancel them; he afterwards wrote the Ten Words, as if these had been engraved on the tables; this explains the variations in the two copies of the Decalogue; the plain facts to be stated about the Ten Commandments; they do not include all Christian duties.

THE LAWS ON THE STONE TABLES.

N the last two Lectures we have been considering the very ancient code of laws contained in E.xx. 23-xxiii.19. It is important to notice that it was this old law-book, with all its quaint prescriptions, chiefly on agricultural matters, its portentous slave-laws, its antiquated injunctions,—and not the Ten Commandments,— which was accepted by the people and recorded by Moses, as the Law by which they were hereafter to be governed—the Law as it existed in the Original Story of the Exodus. This is plain from the following chapter, where we read—'And Moses came and told the people all the words of JEHOVAH and all the judgments; and all the people answered with one voice and said, All the words which JEHOVAH hath said will we do. And Moses wrote all the words of JEHOVAH, and arose early in the morning, and builded an altar under the hill, and twelve pillars according to the twelve tribes of Israel. And he sent young men of the children of Israel, who offered burnt-offerings and sacrificed peace-offerings of oxen unto JEHOVAH. And Moses took half of the blood and put it in basons, and half of the blood he sprinkled on the altar, And he took the book of the Covenant and read it in the ears of the people, and they said, All that JEHOVAH hath said will

we do and be obedient. And Moses took the blood and sprinkled it on the people and said, Behold the blood of the Covenant which JEHOVAH hath made with you concerning all these words.'[1]

But this is not all. These 'words of the Covenant' were not merely to be recorded in the perishable pages of a written book; they were to be registered as a lasting deposit for all future ages, in tables of stone, by the 'Finger of God.' So we are told that, after ratifying this covenant between JEHOVAH and his people, 'Moses went up, and Aaron, Nadab, and Abihu, and seventy of the Elders of Israel. And they saw the Elohim of Israel, and under His feet like a work of transparent sapphire, and as the body of heaven for clearness. And upon the nobles of the children of Israel He put not forth His hand; and they beheld ELOHIM and they ate and drank.'[2] It seems to be meant that they saw some actual manifestation of the Deity, and yet they still lived on, still 'ate and drank' as living men might do; He 'put not forth his hand upon them' to destroy them, as might have been expected in accordance with the view of those and indeed of far later times, that no mortal could survive after seeing God's face[3] or hearing God's word.[4] And, in fact, when afterwards Moses himself desired to see the 'glory' of God,[5] JEHOVAH answers, 'Thou canst not see My face; for man shall not see Me and live. But it shall be that, when My glory passeth by I will place thee in a cleft of the rock, and I will cover My palm upon thee until I have passed by; and I will take My hand away, and thou shalt see My back, but My face shall not be seen.'[6] We are reminded here of the apostle's words. 'Who only hath immortality, dwelling in the light which no man can approach unto, Whom no man hath seen nor can

---

[1] E. xxiv. 3-8. [2] E. xxiv. 9-11.
[3] G. xvi. 13, xxxii. 30, E. xxxiii. 20, Ju. vi. 22, xiii. 22, Is. vi. 5. E. xx. 19, D. iv. 33, v. 26. [4] E. xxxiii. 18. [5] E. xxxiii. 20-23.

see,'[7] and of that central truth of Christianity that in the face of Jesus Christ and of all the good and true of all ages— in the beauty of holiness revealed in human lives—is revealed the glory of the Invisible Godhead, the goodness and truth of the Eternal Father, with Whose spirit they are filled. But those seventy-three who went up with Moses, can hardly have been supposed to have seen on this occasion what Moses alone, at his earnest entreaty, is some time afterwards permitted to see. Perhaps the writer meant that they saw on the far-off summit of Sinai a fiery splendour, the symbol of JEHOVAH'S presence, and, underneath it, the clear deep blue of the sky like a sapphire throne. They were not, in fact, allowed to go up to the top of the Mount and come nigh to JEHOVAH: only Moses was to do this.[8] They 'went up' merely to its foot, and were not even permitted to enter the 'cloud' which enveloped the whole Mount— the 'thick darkness where ELOHIM was,' which Moses entered before[9] and now again enters with his servant Joshua.[10] For after this glorious vision, we are told, 'Moses arose and his servant Joshua, and Moses went up into the Mount of GOD. And unto the Elders he said, Stay for us here, until we return unto you; and lo! Aaron and Hur are with you; whoever has matters of business, let him draw near unto them. And Moses went up into the Mount, and Moses was in the Mount forty days and forty nights.'[11]

But where during these forty days was Joshua? The careless manner in which this narrative is commonly read and interpreted, is sufficiently shown by the fact that, whereas great stress is laid upon the circumstance of Moses having fasted forty days and nights on this occasion, no notice whatever is taken of Joshua his servant having done the same;[12] nor does the writer himself seem to have considered that, if

[7] 1 Tim. vi. 16.   [8] E. xxiv. 2.   [9] E. xx. 21.
[10] E. xxiv. 15, 18.   [11] E. xxiv. 13, 14, 18.   [12] E. xxxiii. 17.

Joshua followed the steps of Moses, he too must have not only shared in the vision of God, vouchsafed to Moses and his companions,[13] but must have gone up also to the top of the Mount, and been present at the Divine communications made to his master, a privilege denied to Aaron and the rest, who were still in contact with the people at the foot of the Mount.[14]

At the end of those forty days, we read, JEHOVAH 'gave unto Moses, when He had ceased to speak with him on Mount Sinai, two tables of the Testimony, tables of stone written with the Finger of ELOHIM.'[15]

Now we shall not be troubled with the question, which has perplexed an 'orthodox' Commentator, as to the possibility of Moses carrying these two tables of stone, as large as the inside of the Ark in which they were afterwards placed and proportionally thick, which (he says) 'Moses, without the strength of a Samson, could not have carried down from the Mount in one hand or even in both.'[16] Nay, it is probable that a pair of stone-tablets of much smaller dimensions, such as this Commentator himself supposes,[17] viz., each nearly three feet long and two feet broad and some inches thick, about the size of an ordinary gravestone, would have taxed the strength of Moses considerably to carry *up* to the top of Sinai, as he afterwards does,[18] as well as down. Nor does it exactly appear what Joshua was about, the 'minister' or servant of Moses,[19]—at least, on the first occasion of Moses coming down from the Mount, when he is expressly said to have been present[20]—that he did not carry one at least of these stones. The Hebrew writer evidently paid little regard to considerations of this kind: he was writing an imaginary, not an historical, narrative. It is of more consequence to enquire

[13] E. xxiv. 9-11.   [14] E. xxiv. 14, xxxii. 1-6.   [15] E. xxxi. 18.
[16] Keil (*Comm.* l. p. 356.)   [17] Keil, *l.c.*   [18] E. xxxiv. 4.
[19] E. xxiv. 13.   [20] E. xxxii. 17.

what he meant to be inscribed on these stone-tables, which he calls 'tables of the Testimony, written with the Finger of ELOHIM.' And this we shall see more clearly if we advance a step or two further in the story.

As Moses, attended by his servant Joshua, was descending from the Mount with the two tables in his hand,[21] they heard (we are told) the cries of the people, who were dancing and shouting around a Golden Calf,[22] the image of the Sun-God, which Aaron had made at their request,[23] when, weary of the long absence of their leader, and not knowing what was become of him, they begged that Aaron would make them an Elohim to go before them.[24] So Aaron made a molten calf, 'and they said, This is thy ELOHIM, O Israel, who brought thee forth out of the land of Egypt! And Aaron saw it, and built an altar before it, and Aaron made proclamation and said, To-morrow is a Feast to JEHOVAH!'[25] It is plain that the writer intends to represent Aaron as identifying the Sun-God, symbolised by this calf, with JEHOVAH or YAHVEH, the ELOHIM of Israel. When Moses, then, drew near to the Camp and saw the calf and the dancing, we are told that, in horror and indignation at the sight, he dashed the tables out of his hands, and brake them in pieces beneath the Mount.[26] You all know the story and will remember how Aaron makes a pitiful excuse for his conduct,[27] and how the Levites come forward at the summons of Moses and massacre three thousand of the people,[28] and Moses then intercedes for them,[29] and so they are merely plagued, instead of being utterly cut off for their sin.[30]

After this the command is issued to go forward on the march to the Promised Land,[31] and Moses, before he starts, desires to see the glory of JEHOVAH,[32] and receives that

[21] v. 15.	[23] v. 17-19.	[25] v. 2-4.	[27] v. 1.
[22] v. 4, 5.	[24] v. 19.	[26] v. 21-24.	[28] v. 26-28.
[29] v. 30-32.	[30] v. 33-35.	[31] E. xxxiii. 1, 2.	[32] v. 18.

promise, 'Thou shalt see My back, but My face shall not be seen.'[33] Then follows the direction—'And JEHOVAH said unto Moses, Hew thee two tables of stone like unto the first, and I will write upon these tables the words that were in the first tables which thou brakest. And be ready in the morning, and come up in the morning unto Mount Sinai, and present thyself there to Me in the top of the Mount.'[34] And Moses does this, and climbs the Mount once more with the two stone-tables in his hand,[35] and there JEHOVAH proclaims His awful Name.[36] 'And Moses made haste and bowed his head to the earth and worshipped.'[37] Then follow nineteen verses[38] which formed no portion of the Original Story, but have been inserted by the later Deuteronomist; after which the Original Story is resumed—'And he was there with JEHOVAH forty days and forty nights; bread he ate not, and water he drank not: and He (JEHOVAH) wrote upon the tables the words of the Covenant.'[39]

The words, which were written on these tables, are here called 'the words of the Covenant.' But they were also to be the very same words which were written on the first tables which Moses brake,[40] and which were called 'tables of the Testimony.'[41] What 'Covenant,' then, can this be but that which was made so solemnly between JEHOVAH and Israel, based upon that ancient law-book,[42] the words of which are represented as first written in a book by Moses[43] and then engraved upon the stones by the Finger of God,[43] as a 'Testimony' or witness of what obedience was due from Israel to its Divine King? So, when Joash was crowned in after days, we are told that they put into his hands the 'Testimony'[44]—that is, most probably a roll, on which was copied this code of laws, engraved on the stone-tables which were preserved in

[33] v. 23 [35] E. xxxiv. 1, 2. [38] v. 4. [41] v. 5–7.
[34] v. 8. [36] v. 9–27. [39] v. 28. [42] E. xxxiv. 1.
[37] E. xxxi. 18. [37] E. xxxiv. 3–8. [40] v. 4, 7. [44] 2 K. xi. 12.

the ark—perhaps the identical roll or book which Samuel himself wrote for the first king Saul and 'laid up before JEHOVAH.'[43] I repeat, the two tables contained, according to the Original Story, the 'words of *this* Covenant'; there is not a shadow of real ground for supposing that they contained, as is commonly imagined, the Ten Commandments.

It might, perhaps, be thought that the two stone-tables here described could have hardly contained, in characters large enough for ordinary purposes, the numerous prescriptions of this ancient code. And it is not enough to say in reply that this is only an imaginary story, and the two stone-tables may never have really existed; because it is possible that this portion of the narrative may not be altogether imaginary, but may be based on a real historical fact. For we are told in the account of the dedication of Solomon's Temple that 'the priests brought in the Ark of the Covenant of JEHOVAH into its place'[44] and that 'there was nothing in the Ark save the two tables of stone.'[47] Assuming this to be historically true, it is most probable that they were first prepared and placed in the Ark on that memorable occasion in David's reign, when he brought up the Ark to Mount Zion,[48] after it had been long laid aside in the house of Abinadab;[49] and very possibly their weight may have caused the accident by which Uzzah died on David's first attempt to bring up the Ark, when he tried to support the cart in which it was being carried, at some bad part of the road.[50] But, if the two tables were engraved in the early part of David's reign, they would probably contain—not the Ten Commandments, which are the work of the Deuteronomist, and were written, as we shall see, in a much later age, but—a transcript of the 'manner of the kingdom,' which Samuel 'wrote in a book' in the days of Saul, and which was, perhaps almost identical with

[43] 1 S. x. 25.
[45] 2 S. vi. 2, 3.
[44] 1 K. viii. 6.
[46] 1 S. vii. 1, 2.
[47] v. 9.
[48] 2 S. vi. 6, 7.

the 'Book of the Covenant' in E.xx.22–xxiii.21. It becomes important, therefore, to consider within what space this section, containing about 1,100 Hebrew words, could be legibly inscribed. Now at Marseilles there was found not long ago a stone-tablet of great antiquity, inscribed with Phœnician characters, which were almost identical with the ancient Hebrew; the whole surface of this stone contained 1⅓ sq. ft.; and on this were engraved distinctly for public uses 94 words.[41] But the stone-tables of Sinai, if their size may be conjectured from the dimensions given for the Ark,[42] would be nearly 3 ft. long and 2 ft. broad,[17] and would have had on their four faces an area of about 24 sq. ft., large enough to have held 1,500 such words, and so might have very well contained the code in question, the 'words of the Covenant.'

It is true, we now read in our Bibles, 'And He wrote upon the tables the words of the Covenant, *the Ten Commandments*,'[43] or rather, as it should be rendered, 'the Ten Words.' But this last expression, 'the Ten Words,' is plainly a later addition to the original passage, which stands complete without it—'He wrote upon the tables the words of the Covenant.' There are some who suppose that the 'Ten Words' here meant are ten separate commands which they find in the nineteen verses just preceding, and which end, in fact, with the direction, 'And JEHOVAH said unto Moses, Write thou these words; for after the tenor of these words I have made a Covenant with thee and with Israel.'[44] But it would be easy to find more than ten commands in these verses. And these nineteen verses have been, as I have said, inserted by a later hand, that of the Deuteronomist; and it is easy to see the object with which the insertion has been made. In my next Lecture I shall show that the Deuteronomist was a prophet of a very much later age, the age of Josiah. Let us assume

[41] MOVERS (*Off. d. Karth.*)
[42] E.xxxv.28.
[43] E.xxv.10, xxxvii.1.
[44] E.xxxiv.9-27.

this for the present, and suppose that such a prophet had
before him in the Original Story of the Exodus the series of
laws which we have been considering in E.xxi–xxiii. He
would find very many of them antiquated and inapplicable in
the present more advanced state of his nation ; and with his
own higher and more spiritual views they would have seemed
to him very unfit to be made in this form the basis of the
Covenant between JEHOVAH and Israel. Accordingly, he
extracted from them those injunctions which he deemed most
important to be maintained in the future ; and, upon carefully
comparing these nineteen verses with the more ancient code,
it will be seen that almost all the laws contained in them have
been simply copied from the older record,[85] sometimes in the
very same words and in the very same order. Of course, it
is incredible that the *same* writer, after describing the solemn
ratification of a Covenant between JEHOVAH and Israel upon
the basis of certain 'words' expressly revealed by JEHOVAH
to Moses, would immediately go on to describe a *second*
Covenant based upon a different set of words, as having
been made between JEHOVAH and Israel within only a few
weeks of the first. But the Deuteronomist, having merely condensed the original code, by omitting the civil laws, many of
which had in his time become obsolete, and retaining only the
commands more expressly connected with religion, is thus
able to say at the end, 'After the tenor of these words I have
made a Covenant with thee and with Israel,'[86] without doing
any great violence to the Original Story, since ' these words '
may be regarded as an abstract or summary of those upon
which the Covenant was really based. Very probably he intended to suppress the older passages[87] and to replace them
by his own more condensed matter. But it is easy to understand that it would cost him a much greater pang, if he lived

---
[85] v. 19, 20a = E. xiii. 12, 13, which also belongs to D., and v. 24 is added.
[86] E. xxxiv. 27.   [87] E. xx. 22–xxiii. 33, xxiv. 3–8.

some centuries after the older writer, actually to cancel a portion of his work however antiquated, than if he had lived only in the next age, and had been perhaps his disciple and a sharer in his plan and in his labour. He may have composed his own abstract and, as he considered, improvement of the original, with a view to supersede it, and yet may have hesitated to remove and destroy the older and now venerable record.

But he was not content, it would seem, with this. These laws, even in their reduced form, are occupied chiefly with matters of outward rite and ceremony—the keeping of festivals, the sacrificing of firstlings, the redemption of firstborns. And such laws as these, however proper in themselves, did not touch the more important questions of public and private life—did not provide solemn warnings against murder, adultery, and theft. Accordingly the Deuteronomist composed the Ten Commandments—marked clearly as his by his own peculiar style[58]—the germs of which may in most cases be found indeed in the older code, but in a less impressive form and mixed up with a mass of miscellaneous ordinances. And these he has inserted in the Book of Exodus, as we saw in a former Lecture,[59] in a place where they could not possibly have existed in the Original Story, as having been pronounced aloud by the Divine Voice on Sinai. To these 'Ten Commandments,' no doubt, the reference was meant to be made by the phrase 'the Ten Words,' which some one—perhaps the Deuteronomist himself or a later writer—has added to the original passage in the place which we have just been considering,[60] so conveying the idea that *these* were engraved on the stone-tables as the 'Words of the Covenant' which JEHOVAH had made with Israel. But the copy of these Ten Words, as given in Deuteronomy itself,

[58] See *Pent.* VI. *App.* 107.   [59] *Lect.* VIII.   [60] E. xxxiv. 28.

(as the New Bible Commentary admits,[*]) differs considerably in some respects from that in the Book of Exodus—a fact which is utterly inconceivable if the Decalogue, as first given in Exodus, was regarded as the record of the actual utterances of the Divine Lawgiver, but is easily intelligible if the same later writer was the author of both versions, and took the opportunity in his later work of altering and amending his own earlier form.

It is natural that many who may have noticed this striking difference in the two versions of the Decalogue, should shrink from examining very closely into a matter which interferes so seriously with long-established traditional views, or, if they do, from speaking of what they find. But how right and good would it be if the truth were openly taught in the pulpit as well as in the school, that in these Commandments we have only embodied the main points of human duty towards God and Man, as they were conceived in the mind of a pious Jewish writer in the seventh century before Christ. But then we must remember that there are also other points of Christian duty for which these 'Ten Words' have not provided, unless some strange and unnatural interpretation be put upon them—as, for instance, the duty of abstaining from lying and drunkenness, the duty of 'doing justly' and 'loving mercy' as well as of 'walking humbly with God,' the duty of self-sacrifice, of laying down one's life, or what makes life sweet, for the brethren, all which the Master has summed up for us in the duty of 'loving God and Man.'

[*] p.71.

الجزء الأول

LECTURE XI.

SUMMARY.

THE reign of the good king Josiah; the high-priest Hilkiah probably Jeremiah's father; the discovery, and private and public reading, of the Book of the Law; the Covenant made in consequence, and the Reformation of Religion throughout Judah and Israel; the prophetess Huldah consulted on this occasion, not Jeremiah, who never mentions this Book of the Law; her language is identical with Jeremiah's, but strongly resembles that of Deuteronomy, as also does Jeremiah's language in his prophecies and in the Books of Kings; Jeremiah himself the writer of Deuteronomy, a portion of which was the Book found in the Temple; Jeremiah has retouched the Original Story throughout; circumstances which probably led to his writing Deuteronomy; what is true in the Bible is true in itself, not because it is found in the Bible.

THE BOOK FOUND IN THE TEMPLE.

IN the year 624 B.C. there was a great commotion in Jerusalem. It was the eighteenth year of king Josiah,[1] who was only eight years old when he began to reign,[2] and was therefore naturally from the first greatly under the influence of the high-priest and leading prophets of that time, and seems to have been a thoroughly well-disposed and pious prince, so that the character given of him in the Book of Kings is this—' He did the right in the sight of JEHOVAH, and walked in all the ways of David his father, and turned not aside to the right-hand or to the left.'[3] Jeremiah began to prophesy in the thirteenth year of Josiah;[4] and he had therefore been in full activity as a prophet for four or five years, when the events occurred to which I am now referring. The high-priest at the time in question was Hilkiah,[5] and, as Jeremiah is described as the son of Hilkiah,[6] it is very possible that he was the son of this very same Hilkiah the high-priest. It is true Jeremiah's father is not distinctly called the *high*-priest; but then the high-priest Hilkiah is repeatedly styled simply 'the priest' in this very narrative which we are now considering,[7] composed pro-

---

[1] 2K.xxii.3,&c. [3] v.1. [5] v.2. [6] Jer.l.2,xxv.3.
[2] 2K.xxii.4. [4] Jer.l.1. [7] 2K.xxii.10,12,14,xxiii.24.

bably by Jeremiah himself, who is generally believed to have been the writer of the two Books of Kings;[8] and in those days the high-priest, though, no doubt, a more important person under Josiah than he was in former times,[9] seems to have had little of the grandeur and pre-eminent dignity which was attached to the office in a later age.

On a certain day, then, in this eighteenth year of King Josiah, the king sent his secretary Shaphan with a message to Hilkiah the high-priest in the Temple. 'And Hilkiah the high-priest said unto Shaphan the scribe, I have found the Book of the Law in the House of JEHOVAH. And Hilkiah gave the Book to Shaphan and he read it.' So, when Shaphan returned to the king, he 'shewed the king saying, Hilkiah the priest hath given me a Book. And Shaphan read it before the king. And, when the king had heard the words of the Book of the Law, he rent his clothes. And the king commanded Hilkiah the priest,' and four others, 'saying, Go ye, enquire of JEHOVAH for me and for the people and for all Judah, concerning the words of this book that is found; for great is the wrath of JEHOVAH that is kindled against us because our fathers have not hearkened unto the words of this Book.' So they went to 'Huldah the prophetess, the wife of Shallum, and they communed with her; and she said unto them, Tell ye the man who sent you unto me, Thus saith JEHOVAH, Behold! I am bringing evil on this place and on its inhabitants, even all the words of the Book which the King of Judah hath read. Because they have forsaken Me and have sacrificed unto other gods, that they might provoke Me with all the works of their hands, therefore My wrath shall be kindled against this place and shall not be quenched. . . . So they brought the king word again.'[10] And the king sent and they gathered unto him all the elders of Judah and of Jerusalem.

---

[8] Bp. Lord HERVEY, *Dict. of the Bible*, II. p. 28.
[9] *comp.* 1 K. iv. 2-4, 2 K. xii. 2.   [10] 2 K. xxii. 3-20.

And the king went up into the House of JEHOVAH, and all the men of Judah and all the inhabitants of Jerusalem with him, and the priests and the prophets and all the people, both small and great ; and he read in their ears all the words of the Book of the Covenant which was found in the House of JEHOVAH. And the king stood by the pillar and made a Covenant before JEHOVAH ... to perform the words of this Covenant that were written in this Book ; and all the people stood to the Covenant.'[11]

And now Josiah takes in hand a most energetic and sweeping Reformation. He begins at Jerusalem, and orders Hilkiah to remove from the Temple—observe, from the Temple itself where Hilkiah was in authority as high-priest, and ought not to have allowed such abominations—'the vessels made for the Baal and for the Ashera and for all the host of heaven,' and he burns them without Jerusalem and scatters their ashes.[12] He puts-down the idolatrous priests, who had sacrificed in the cities of Judah, and in the high-places roundabout Jerusalem, 'to the Sun and to the Moon and to the Twelve Signs and to all the host of heaven.'[13] He brings forth the Ashera—an obscene symbol of Sun-worship —from the House of JEHOVAH, and burns it, and stamps it small to powder, and casts the powder upon the graves of the people.[14] He breaks-down the houses, by the House of JEHOVAH, where foul impurities were practised in honour of the Sun-God.[15] He defiles the idolatrous high-places throughout the whole land of Judah, as well as those within the walls of the city, and brings their priests to Jerusalem, degrading them into a sort of lower priesthood.[16] He defiles the Topheth in the valley of Hinnom, close to Jerusalem, where up to that time the people had slain and sacrificed their firstborn children to Molech 'the king,' in other words, to

[11] 2K. xxiii. 1-3. [12] 2K. xxiii. 4. [14] v. 5.
[13] v. 6. [15] v. 7. [16] v. b. 9.

YAHVEH, the Sun-God.[17] He removes the 'horses of the Sun' and burns the 'chariots of the Sun,' which the kings of Judah had placed at the entrance of the Temple, and demolishes the idolatrous altars which Manasseh had built in the two courts of the Temple.[18] He defiles the high-places which Solomon had made on the right of the Mount of Olives for Ashtoreth and Chemosh and Milcom or Molech.[19] And then, beyond the boundaries of Judah, he carries the Reformation into the land of Samaria, whose Israelitish inhabitants had mostly been carried captive into Assyria about a century previously,[20] their places having been filled by foreigners,[21] and over which district Josiah seems to have exercised authority, perhaps as a vassal or ally of the Assyrian king.[22] Here he destroys the ancient altar and high-place which Jeroboam had made at Bethel,[23] when the Ten Tribes separated from Judah,[24] and destroys the 'houses' or chapels of the high-places in the cities of Samaria, and slays ruthlessly the priests beside their altars, 'and he burned men's bones upon them and returned to Jerusalem.'[25] 'And the king commanded all the people saying, Keep the Passover unto JEHOVAH your Elohim, as it is written in the Book of the Covenant. Surely there was not holden such a Passover from the days of the Judges that judged Israel, nor in all the days of the kings of Israel nor of the kings of Judah. Moreover, the familiar spirits and the wizards and the teraphim and the idols and all the abominations that were spied in the land of Judah and in Jerusalem, did Josiah put away, that he might perform the words of the Law which were written in the Book that Hilkiah the priest found in the House of JEHOVAH.'[26]

Such is Jeremiah's account in the Book of Kings of the Great Reformation carried out by Josiah in the eighteenth

[17] v. 10.   [18] v. 11, 12.   [19] v. 13, 14.   [20] 2 K. xvii. 6.
[21] v. 24.   [22] comp. 2 K. xxiii. 19.   [23] v. 15.   [24] 1 K. xii. 34.
[25] 2 K. xxiii. 19, 20.   [26] 2 K. xxiii. 21-24.

year of his reign. From the full details which he gives of these proceedings it is plain that he took a very deep interest in them. And the question must naturally arise, Where was Jeremiah himself all the while? In five years he had been known as a prophet in Jerusalem. And yet the deputation, sent by the king to 'enquire of JEHOVAH,' go and consult—not Jeremiah, but—a woman, 'the prophetess Huldah, the wife of Shallum,' perhaps Jeremiah's aunt, since Shallum was the name of his uncle.[17] It is strange that Jeremiah himself was not consulted on this occasion, if present at the time in Jerusalem; or, if he lived at Anathoth his native place,[18] where his family possessed some property,[19] it was only about an hour's distance, and the report of the great event would soon have reached him, and would have brought him at once, we may be sure, to the City. He was present, at all events, we must suppose, among the 'priests and prophets,' in whose ears Josiah read the contents of the Book,[20] perhaps on the day after the discovery; and assuredly, as I have said, he must have been not only aware of that event, but intensely concerned in it, and in the measures which followed it. How is it, then, that in the whole of Jeremiah's very copious prophecies this 'Book of the Law,' this 'Book of the Covenant,' is never once mentioned, although he does apparently refer to the Covenant made by Josiah,[21] as also to the Covenant made by Moses as recorded in this Book of Deuteronomy,[22] and although he certainly knew the Book well, inasmuch as more than once he quotes the identical words of it?[24] How is it also that the prophecy of Huldah, when carefully examined, betrays in its language a very close resemblance not only to Jeremiah's prophecies, but to the Book of Deuteronomy,[24]

[17] Jer. xxxii. 7.   [18] Jer. i. 1.   [19] Jer. xxxii. 7, 8.   [20] 2 K. xxiii. 2.
[21] Jer. lii. 10, xi. 1–6, xxiv. 15, 18, 19.   [22] Jer. xxxiv. 13, 14, comp. D. xv. 12.
[23] comp. xxxiv. 14 with D. xv. 12—vii. 23 with D. v. 33—vii. 33, xvi. 4, xxxiv. 20, with D. xxviii. 26— xi. 4 with D. iv. 20—xxii. 8, 9 with xxix. 24-26, &c.
[24] See Pent. III. 574. v.

supposed to have been lost, and only then, to the astonishment of all, accidentally found in the Temple, so that its contents would have been utterly unknown to her? How is it above all that Jeremiah's language throughout his prophecies and throughout the two Books of Kings agrees in a most singular manner with that of Deuteronomy? Thus the New Commentary says—'The writings of Jeremiah often strikingly recall passages of Deuteronomy. The prophet repeatedly employs words and phrases which are characteristic of Deuteronomy, and there is also at times a remarkable similarity of general style and treatment. These resemblances are neither few nor insignificant. It is needless in this place to demonstrate their existence and importance, which are now admitted on all hands.'[35] And then the writer tries to account for this similarity by supposing that the prophet had so closely studied—not the whole Pentateuch, but—this particular Book of the Pentateuch, that he had become thoroughly imbued with its spirit and had made its very language his own.

Rather, the true explanation of the matter is simply this, that Jeremiah himself wrote the prophecy which he has put into the mouth of Huldah, and wrote also the Book of Deuteronomy, and that this, or some portion of it, was the 'Book of the Law' or 'Book of the Covenant,' which was found by Hilkiah in the Temple, having been placed there with the knowledge and connivance of Hilkiah, and probably also with that of Huldah, to be found at this time. It cannot be supposed that Josiah 'read in the ears of the people' all the stories in Genesis, all the minute details about the Ark and Tabernacle in Exodus, all the ritualistic prescriptions in Leviticus and Numbers, the numberings of the Camps[36] and the list of the marchings and stations in the wilderness[37]—that

---

[35] *B C* I, p. 794.   [36] N. i.–iv.   [37] N. xxxiii.

THE BOOK FOUND IN THE TEMPLE.

these would have produced such a mighty effect upon the king and people, or that all this could have been read at one time. It was evidently the Book of Deuteronomy which was found in the Temple, to which Huldah's words refer, ' I will bring evil upon this place and upon the inhabitants thereof, all the words of the Book which the king of Judah hath read,'[34] and which is called repeatedly the 'Book of the Law' in Deuteronomy itself;[39] or rather it was the *original* part of this Book, the part of it which was first written, *viz.*, Ch.v-xxviii, except ch.xxvii, which a glance will show to have been inserted afterwards, since it breaks the connexion where it now stands. This portion consists of a long address of Moses, beginning with the Ten Commandments, which vary here considerably, as we have seen,[40] from those in E.xx, and ending with an awful denunciation of Divine Judgment, the closing words of which may well have rung long in Josiah's ears—' If thou wilt not observe to do all the words of this Law that are written in this Book . . . then JEHOVAH will make thy plagues wonderful and the plagues of thy seed, even great plagues of long continuance, and sore sicknesses and of long continuance. . . . Also every sickness and every plague which is not written in the Book of this Law, them will JEHOVAH bring upon thee until thou be destroyed. . . . And JEHOVAH shall scatter thee among all people, from the one end of the earth even unto the other. . . . And among these nations shalt thou find no ease, neither shall the sole of thy foot have rest; but JEHOVAH shall give thee a trembling heart and failing of eyes and sorrow of mind. And thy life shall hang in doubt before thee, and thou shalt fear day and night, and thou shalt have none assurance of thy life. In the morning thou shalt say, Would God it were even! and at even thou shalt say, Would God it were morning! for the fear of thine

[34] 2K.xxii.16, *comp.* D.xxix.27. [39] D.xxviii.61,xxix.21,xxx.10,xxxi.26.
[40] *p.*101.

heart wherewith thou shalt fear, and for the sight of thine
eyes which thou shalt see. And JEHOVAH shall bring thee
into Egypt again with ships by the way whereof I spake unto
thee, Thou shalt see it no more again ; and there ye shall be
sold unto your enemies for bondmen and bondwomen, and no
man shall buy you.'[41]

After this it is added, 'These are the words of the
Covenant, which JEHOVAH commanded Moses to make with
the children of Israel in the land of Moab, beside the Covenant
which He made with them in Horeb.'[42] You will remember
that older Covenant supposed to have been made at Sinai or
Horeb, as the Deuteronomist always calls it,[43] based upon a
number of ordinances recorded in E.xxi–xxiii, respecting
agricultural and other matters, of which many were totally
unsuited to a more advanced stage of civilized life,[44] and how
(as I explained in my last Lecture[45]) the Deuteronomist—
Jeremiah, as we have now seen reason to conclude—first
abridged these, retaining only the more important laws
relating to religion, and represented this abridgment or
summary, which in fact contained the substance of the
original code, as the basis of that Covenant, 'Write thou
these words, for after the tenor of these words I have made a
Covenant with thee and with Israel,' and how, not content
with this, he further composed the 'Ten Words' of the
Decalogue, as more fully and forcibly expressing the basis of
such a Covenant as JEHOVAH might be supposed to have
made with Israel, and inserted these in E.xx as having been
uttered with a loud voice on Sinai, amidst thunderings and
lightnings, in the ears of all the people, and as having been
engraved on the two Tables of Stone.[46] But, further, it
appears upon a close examination that he has retouched also

---

[41] D.xxviii.15–68.
[43] D.L.2,6,19,iv.10,15,v.2,ix.8,xviii.16,xxix.1.
[45] p.136.
[42] D.xxix.1.
[44] p.106,115,116.
[46] p.138.

the Original Story as it had come into his hands, inserting shorter[7] or longer[8] passages, which breathe his own prophetical spirit and exhibit unmistakeably his well-known style. But even this, it seems, did not satisfy him. The work in its present form was not likely to make any strong impression upon a people so sunk in gross idolatries as the people of Judah and Jerusalem in his time. You have heard the long list of abominations practised even in the Temple itself during the first seventeen years of the pious king Josiah, surrounded by priests and prophets, and advised by the high-priest Hilkiah and for five years past by Jeremiah himself. The prophet saw that something more was needed to rouse the king and people from their deadly lethargy; he felt that even his own stirring words, introduced here and there into the Original Story, were too much overlaid by historical and other matter to answer the needs of the present time. He must discharge the solemn duty to which he knew God's Spirit had called him, of warning his people of their doom if they persisted in their wickedness. But he was young at the time when the call had reached him and he felt his spirit first stirred for this work; and in the sense of his weakness and inexperience he cried, 'Ah Lord God! behold! I cannot speak, for I am a mere youth.'[9] What wonder is it that, even when reassured by promises of Divine support, he shrank from facing the angry crowd, and feared that rebukes, poured out from his lips against the idolatrous practices of the age, encouraged by priests and prophets[10] and even permitted by the king, would fall unheeded and be spoken to the winds? Perhaps he had found this already by experience to be true; and so he resolves to speak to them in the name of Moses—

[7] G. vi. 4, x. 8-12, xviii. 18, 19, xvii. 14-18, xxiv. 59,60, xxvi. 4, 5, xxviii. 15, 20-22, xxxi. 13, xxxv. 2-4, E. iii. 1, '10 Horeb,' xv. 25b, 26, xvii. 6, 'in Horeb,' 14, xix. 3b-8, 9b, xxiii. 13, 15bc, 19, xxiv. 12, xxiii. 7-14, 34, xxxiii. 3-6.
[8] G. xv, E. xiii. 3-16, xx. 1-17, xxiii. 22-33, xxxiv. 9-27. [9] Jer. i. 6.
[10] Jer. i. 18, ii. 8, 26, v. 31, vi. 13, viii. 1, 2, &c.

to embody his own earnest lessons and warnings in the form of a last discourse, supposed to have been delivered by the great lawgiver to his people immediately before his death, including the Ten Commandments and such laws of the older Covenant as still seemed suited for his people, and making the whole the basis of a second Covenant made by JEHOVAH with Israel at the end of the wanderings, as the former was made at the beginning of them.[61]

This, then, in all probability was the 'Book of the Law' or 'Book of the Covenant' which was found by Hilkiah in the Temple, and the reading of which produced such a mighty effect at the time in Jerusalem. In my next Lecture I shall return to this subject. For the present I will only ask, Are such words as these, 'Man doth not live by bread alone, but by all that proceedeth out of the mouth of JEHOVAH doth man live'[62]—are such words as these less true because they occur in Deuteronomy, and were written by a later prophet, not by Moses? Are they not rather true in themselves, by whomsoever spoken or written, and as such come home at once with power to the hearts and consciences of men? 'Truly the light is sweet and a pleasant thing it is for the eyes to behold the Sun.'[63] But is the light sweet to our eyes only because this statement is found in the Bible? Is not the light sweet because our gracious God and Father has made the Sun and given us our visual powers, that we may open our eyes, and we shall behold the glory and beauty of the Universe? And is the light of Truth sweet to us only because we find the bright reflexion of it in the Bible? Rather, we rejoice to know that God's Truth exists for us eternally, shining like the Sun in the spiritual heavens, and that we, His children, have spiritual senses wherewith to behold it —a spiritual eyesight, to which this light of the inner man is

---

[61] D. xxix. 1.   [62] D. viii. 3.   [63] Ecc. xi. 7.

sweet, by which we can enjoy its brightness,—a spiritual hearing, by which we can hear and receive Divine Truth, wherever and by whomsoever spoken to us, whether in the Bible or out of the Bible, whether in the Church of Christ or out of it—a spiritual appetite, by which we can 'taste the good word of God and the powers of the world to come,'[63] by which we can feed upon the living bread—can 'eat the flesh' and 'drink the blood' of Christ's Divine Teaching[64] and live.

[63] Heb. vi. 5.   [64] John vi. 53-63.

LECTURE XII.

SUMMARY.

THE Book of Deuteronomy the main cause of Moses being regarded as a great lawgiver; it breathes the true prophetical spirit; ch. i–iv, xxix, xxx, added after the Captivity, and ch. xxvii also inserted into the original address of Moses; the Book found in the Temple not the autograph of Moses; such impersonations often employed for pious ends by Christian and Jewish writers, as in the Books of Enoch, Daniel, Ezra, Nehemiah, and the Chronicles; Jeremiah in the Books of Kings records fictitious prophecies and other utterances; such fictions no more dishonest than similar instances in Thucydides or Tacitus; the effect of reading the book in Josiah's time may have been greater than was anticipated; the real facts perhaps afterwards disclosed to the King; the Deuteronomist orders the three great feasts to be kept at Jerusalem; this would have been impracticable in the days of David and Solomon, but points to the diminished kingdom under Josiah; the hope of Jeremiah in writing Deuteronomy painfully frustrated; the lesson for our own times.

JEREMIAH THE DEUTERONOMIST.

IN my last Lecture I set before you what appears to be the true account of the origin of the Book of Deuteronomy. Of course, traditional theologians find it very difficult to allow this, since out of the whole Pentateuch it is Deuteronomy which really attracts most forcibly the reader's attention, and has helped mainly to establish the reputation of Moses as a great lawgiver. The legislation in the other books, except a few passages inserted by the Deuteronomist himself, is comparatively dry and uninteresting, and has no prophetical ring about it. Two-thirds of Exodus, Leviticus, and Numbers are almost wholly occupied with prescriptions about the different kinds of sacrifices, the duties and prerogatives of the Priests and Levites, the ceremonies of purification, the construction of the Tabernacle and its vessels. Even the code of laws on which the Covenant is based in the Original Story, in E. xxi-xxiii, has hardly been much studied, I imagine, by the majority of Christians. On the other hand, almost every line of Deuteronomy breathes the true prophetical spirit, and is 'profitable for doctrine, for reproof, for correction, for instruction in righteousness.'[1] In the last four chapters, indeed,

[1] 2 Tim. iii. 16.

there are still retained one or two fragments of the Original Story,* as well as some insertions of a very late date,* of which I shall have to speak hereafter, mixed up with words of the Deuteronomist, to whom especially we owe the grand 'Song of Moses' in D.xxxii, whereas the 'Blessing of Moses' in D.xxxiii belongs apparently to the same age, but not to the same hand. But the first thirty chapters, with the exception of two verses,* are wholly Jeremiah's, four chapters having been subsequently prefixed by him by way of introduction, and two appended, to the book as found in the Temple, besides ch.xxvii, inserted awkwardly, as we have seen,* in the place where it now stands. These introductory and concluding chapters must have been added at least twenty-five years afterwards, when the woes of the Babylonish Captivity had at last overwhelmed the land ; as appears from the fact that, whereas in the original address of Moses there is only a *threatening* of the misery which would assuredly befall his countrymen if they continued in their impenitence,* these additional chapters refer distinctly to that calamity as having already fallen upon Judah. 'When all these things are come upon thee ... and thou shalt recall them to thine heart among all the nations whither JEHOVAH thy Elohim hath driven thee, and shalt return unto JEHOVAH thy Elohim ... with all thine heart and with all thy soul, then JEHOVAH thy Elohim will bring back thy captivity, and have compassion upon thee, and will return and gather thee from all the nations whither JEHOVAH thy Elohim hath scattered thee.'* These words were probably written after the *beginning* of the Captivity, when Josiah's grandson, Jehoiachin or Jechoniah, was carried away to Babylon, with all the nobles, warriors, and craftsmen, so that 'none remained, save the poorest sort of the people of the

---
* D.xxxi.14,15,23,xxxiv.5,6,10.
* D.xxxi.16,22,xxxiii.44.48-52,xxxiv.1 4,7-9.   * D.x.6,7.
* p.149.   * D.xxviii.15-68.   * D.xxx.1-3, comp.iv.29-31.

land,'⁸—eleven years after which event the rebellion of his uncle Zedekiah, whom Nebuchadnezzar had made king in his room, brought about the final catastrophe,⁹ in which all the rest of the people were carried captive and Jerusalem was burnt to the ground.¹⁰ It is the main address of Moses, therefore, in D.v-xxvi,xxviii, which is, strictly speaking, the 'Book of the Law,' the 'Book of the Covenant,' on the basis of which the second Covenant was supposed to have been made between JEHOVAH and Israel.¹¹ And it is this which is blindly received as the work of Moses—if (as one has said ¹²) 'that which is little better than passivity can be called receiving' —received merely because 'presented by tradition, or assertion, or authority,' in that state of 'dull, lifeless, irreceptive torpor, in which the intellect has been hitherto entranced'— and has won for Moses mainly the reputation of a lawgiver. There are some, indeed, who would still keep the intellect drugged with sophistries, and drowned in that 'dull, lifeless torpor,' so forcibly described, under the influence of traditionary teaching. And even the New Commentary leans to the view that the book found by Hilkiah was 'the original copy of the Pentateuch deposited by order of Moses;' ¹³ while a living prelate of our Church has written, 'Though the copy cannot be proved to have been Moses' autograph, it seems probable that it was from the place where it was found, viz. in the Temple, and from its not having been discovered before, but being only brought to light on the occasion of the repairs which were necessary; and from the discoverer being the high-priest himself it seems natural to conclude that the particular part of the Temple where it was found was one not usually frequented, or ever, by any but the high-priest. Such a place exactly was the one where we *know* the original copy

⁸ 2K.xxiv.10–16. ⁹ 2K.xxiv.17-20. ¹⁰ 2K.xxv.8-21
¹¹ D.xxix.1. ¹² Bp. WILBERFORCE (*Guardian*, Oct. 26, 1870.)
¹³ *B.C.I.p.*794.

of the Law was deposited by command of Moses.'[14] We '*know*' this, says the writer, because the order is given in this very Book of Deuteronomy to put it 'by the side of the ark'[15] —as if this could not have been part of the plan pre-arranged by Jeremiah himself and his friends, that it should be placed there, where of course it was found! But how is it that, if it lay all along where Moses ordered it to be placed, not *in* the ark but 'by the side' of it, it was never seen by Hilkiah or any other high-priest during the first seventeen years of Josiah's reign? And how is it that when the ark was brought up to David's Tent, and afterwards removed to Solomon's Temple, no mention is made of this venerable 'Book of the Law,' the very 'autograph of Moses,' though placed each time (it is supposed) 'by the side of the ark'?

Yet some one perhaps will say, How can we ascribe such a proceeding as that here supposed to good men, such as Hilkiah and Jeremiah, or believe that they can ever have sanctioned, much less contrived, such a 'pious fraud'? In the first place, we must not judge of those times by the higher morality of our own, enlightened, as we have been, by eighteen centuries of Christian teaching; though we know that even in the Christian Church 'pious frauds' have been not uncommon— that Gospels and Epistles and other works innumerable have been ascribed to apostles and others who never wrote them, and that a prophecy is actually quoted in the canonical epistle ascribed to St. Jude, as having been really uttered by 'Enoch the seventh from Adam.'[16] In the Jewish Church, however, such impersonations were often employed for pious ends. We have, for instance, the prophecies ascribed to Daniel, which were written in the time of the Maccabees, B.C. 165, to comfort the godly Jews under the tyrannical oppressions of the Greek Prince, Antiochus Epiphanes, and strengthen

---

[14] Bp. Lord HARVEY (*Dict. of the Bible*, I. *p*. 814). [15] D. xxxi. 9, 26.
[16] Jude 14, 15.

JEREMIAH THE DEUTERONOMIST.

them to resist the fiery temptations to which they were exposed from the heathen influences around them, represented under a figure by Nebuchadnezzar, Belshazzar, and Darius. In the Books of Chronicles, Ezra, and Nehemiah, we have numerous fictitious speeches and prophecies, royal decrees and letters—for instance, a letter from the prophet Elijah to king Joram seven years at least after Elijah (according to the story) was taken up into heaven;[17] and accordingly the English Bible tells us in the margin that it was 'writ before Elijah's death,' or rather, it should have said, 'before his translation.' Again, the Books of Kings, composed by Jeremiah himself, contain utterances by various prophets, Ahijah,[18] Shemaiah,[19] Jehu,[20] the prophetess Huldah,[21] which are all written in Jeremiah's own style. The prophets in question may, no doubt, have delivered solemn warnings on the occasions referred to; but, if so, no record of their words was kept; the historian has put into their mouth his own language, embodying the thoughts with which, as he conceived, their minds would most probably be filled at such times. So the long prayer of Solomon at the dedication of the Temple [22] and his previous words [23] are entirely Jeremiah's. And in like manner in the Book of Deuteronomy the writer puts his own words into the mouth of Moses, ascribing to him such feelings as he might naturally be supposed to have when taking leave of his people—doing here, in fact, what the writer of the Original Story had done before him, in composing the 'Blessing of Jacob'[24] or the 'Song of Moses'[25] or the 'prophecies of Balaam,'[26] and no more than the greatest writers of all ages have done without being charged with bad faith or dishonesty, as when Thucydides ascribes a grand funeral oration to the great Athenian statesman

---

[17] 2Ch. xxi. 12–15. [19] 1K. xi. 31–39, xiv. 6–16. [21] 1K. xii. 22–24.
[18] 1K. xvi. 1–4. [20] 2K. xxii. 15–20. [22] 1K. viii. 23–61.
[23] v. 12, 13, 15–21. [24] G. xlix. 1–27. [25] E. xv. 1–18. [26] N. xxiii, xxiv.

Pericles,[n] or when Tacitus records a long address, as spoken by the Highland Chieftain Galgacus—who spoke, of course, if he spoke at all, in Gaelic to his own warriors—before the decisive battle with the Roman invaders.[o]

Moreover, the effect of reading this 'Book of the Law,' may have been far greater than had even been anticipated, and may have taken by surprise Jeremiah himself and the other parties to the design. Their intention was probably merely to produce this new work, a prophecy in disguise, in the hope that it might startle the drowsy king and people, and strengthen the hands of those who were labouring in the same spirit with Jeremiah himself to reform the state of religion in Judah. At the moment of the discovery Jeremiah seems very naturally to have kept himself out of the way, and to have subsequently taken no prominent part in the proceedings. Perhaps in the first hours of excitement it was felt to be difficult or undesirable to say or do anything which might act as a check upon the zeal and energy exhibited by the king, and in which, as it seems, he was supported by the people, in putting down by force the gross idolatries which polluted the land. That impulsive effort, which followed immediately upon the reading of the book, would most probably have been arrested, if he had been told at once the true origin of those awful words which had made so strong an impression on him. They were not less awful, it is true, because uttered in the name of Moses by such a prophet as Jeremiah. But their effect would be infinitely greater, we may be sure, if they were regarded as the dying instructions and warnings of Moses himself, than if they had been heard as the denunciations of a youthful prophet actually living in their midst. But we seem to have an indication that the real facts of the case became afterwards known to the king, at all events,

---

[n] Thuc. II. xxxv-xlvi.   [o] Tac. Vit. Agric. xxx-xxxii

though not perhaps to the people generally, in the circumstance that he does not appear to have kept any other Passover, or the other two great Feasts in this very same year, with the like solemnity, as the law of this Book required —'Thrice in the year shall all thy males appear before JEHOVAH thy Elohim in the place which He shall choose, in the Feast of Mazzoth, and in the Feast of Weeks, and in the Feast of Tabernacles.'[29]

This command is merely copied from the older code,[30] but with one important difference, that in *that* no mention is made of all male Israelites appearing at these Feasts, 'in the place which JEHOVAH would choose.' The original command is simply this—'Thrice in the year shall all thy males appear before the Lord JEHOVAH';[31] and they would doubtless go to the nearest Sanctuary, the worship not having been confined to one place only in that ancient law-book written in the days of Samuel.[32] How indeed was it possible that from all parts of the original land of Israel, from the distant Dan, from the regions across the Jordan, all the males should present themselves for these three Feasts at some one place? The Feast of Mazzoth[33] or Unleavened Bread, with which the Passover was connected, occurred in the very midst of the rainy season; and the weather in Palestine at this part of the year is described by travellers as follows—'Much rain falls, sometimes in torrents, by day and night, but chiefly by night; and all that has been said before about inundated plains and hollows is strictly applicable to this month, as well as that the streams are in many cases swollen to deep and rapid rivers dangerous to pass.'[34] Imagine all the males being required to travel in such weather—mostly, we must suppose, on foot—a distance of a hundred miles or more from the more distant localities, whose inhabitants would therefore consume about a

---

[29] D. xvi. 16.   [30] E. xxiii. 14-17.   [31] v. 17.   [32] p. 78.
[33] E. xxiii. 15, xxxiv. 18, D. xvi. 16.   [34] KITTO (*Phys. Hist. of Palestine*, p. 220.)

week at least on the journey each way! But, having lost three weeks thus about the beginning of the barley-harvest, during which they would have left their farming operations, their cattle and flocks, in the charge of women, children, and slaves, the men would then remain a month at home, before being required to start again, in the midst of the wheat-harvest, to keep the Feast of Weeks,[42] called in older times the Feast of Harvest.[44] But how can we conceive of all the males of the Trans-Jordanic tribes, or any considerable number of them, crossing the river at this season, when Jordan, we are told, 'overfloweth all its banks all the time of harvest,'[47] and travellers inform us that 'the current is then so strong that many of the pilgrims are swept away by it, and a year seldom passes in which some of them are not drowned'?[48] No doubt, in David's time, when the ark had been brought up to Mount Zion, and in Solomon's, when David's Tent had been replaced by the Temple, it was desired to draw the affections of the people towards the royal city, as the centre of the civil and religious life of the community. Here Solomon kept the three Feasts,[49] and many would be encouraged by the king's example and by other influences to 'go up to offer sacrifices in the House of Jehovah at Jerusalem.'[40] In that age, too, some pressure may have been put upon the people to induce them to celebrate at Jerusalem 'the Feast that is in Judah' in the seventh month,[41] that is, the joyous Autumn festival, called in the older law-book the 'Feast of Ingathering'[42] and afterwards the 'Feast of Tabernacles'[43]—the only Feast which seems to have been generally kept in early times.[44] And Jeroboam therefore said to the Ten Tribes with great significance, 'Ye have had

_{42 E. xxxiv. 22, D. xvi. 16.   43 E. xxiii. 16.   47 J. iii. 15.}
_{48 Kitto (Phys. Hist. of Palestine, p. 173.)   49 1 K. ix. 25.}
_{40 1 K. xii. 27.   41 1 K. xii. 32.   42 E. xxiii. 16, copied in xxxiv. 22.}
_{43 L. xxiii. 34, D. xvi. 16, xxxi. 10, Ezr. iii. 4, Zech. xiv. 16.}
_{44 Ju. ix. 27, xxi. 19, 1 S. i. 3, 21, ii. 19.}

enough of going up to Jerusalem!'[45] and established accordingly a *single* Feast also in his kingdom, on the same day of the *eighth* month,[46] which time probably suited better the seasons in the north of Palestine. But such a direction as that before us, requiring on Divine authority the attendance of all male Israelites thrice a year at 'the place which JEHOVAH would choose'—in other words, in the Temple at Jerusalem—could only have been imagined in such an age as that of Josiah, when the Ten Tribes had been already carried into captivity, and the petty kingdom of Judah alone remained of the wide territories once ruled over by David and Solomon, so that almost all the people lived within a day's journey of the capital.

I shall have yet something more to say about this Book of Deuteronomy. But let us consider for a moment what object the prophet must have had in view in laying down such an injunction as this. He hoped, no doubt, that, if the idolatrous altars were destroyed and the idolatrous symbols once swept out of the land, and if the people were required to worship three times a year in the Temple at the three great festivals, and so were brought under the more direct influence of the pious priests and prophets who would surely be gathered around the Sanctuary, all would go well; his countrymen would no longer be able to indulge unrestrained their evil propensities at the different high-places; they would no longer desire to do so, being fed with Divine Truth from the central source—more especially if, according to one provision of this very Book, each king at his accession wrote for himself with his own hand a copy of this Law, 'that it might be with him and he might read in it all the days of his life,'[47] while another enjoins that every seventh year, in the solemnity of the Feast of Tabernacles, 'when all Israel is come to appear

---

[45] 1 K. xii. 28.   [46] v. 32, 33.   [47] D. xvii. 19.

before JEHOVAH in the place which He shall choose, thou shalt read this Law before Israel in their hearing.'[48] There is no sign that this direction was carried out even in Josiah's reign. And alas! Jeremiah must have been soon undeceived in his fond expectation. Priests and prophets, indeed, abounded in Jerusalem; but they did not forward earnestly the work on which his own heart was set, the work of 'JEHOVAH, the Elohim of Israel.' It is probable that the grosser forms of idolatry were not set up again in Judah after Josiah's Reformation. But the heart of the nation was still as foul as ever in the sight of their Heavenly King. Again and again Jeremiah says in his prophecies, 'From the least of them even unto the greatest of them everyone is given to covetousness; and from the prophet even unto the priest everyone dealeth falsely.'[49] He cries 'I have seen filthiness in the prophets of Jerusalem; they commit adultery and walk in lies; they strengthen also the hands of evildoers, that none doth return from his wickedness; they are all of them unto me as Sodom, and its inhabitants as Gomorrah.'[50] And he sums up all in one exceeding bitter cry—'The prophets prophesy falsely, and the priests bear rule by their means, and My people love to have it so; and what will ye do in the end thereof?'[51] It is plain that the whole nation was but as a whited sepulchre, made fair without by Josiah's cleansing, but inwardly still full of 'dead men's bones and of all uncleanness.'[52]

And the lesson surely for our own times is this—that it is not an outward show of religion which God desires of us, whether in the profession of creeds, the maintenance of dogmas, or the observance of ritual, but that singleness and sincerity of heart and faithfulness of daily life, which becomes the children of God, 'sons and daughters of the Lord

---

[48] D. xxxi. 10-13. [49] Jer. vi. 13, viii. 10, comp. ii. 8, xxiii. 11.
[50] Jer. xxiii. 14. [51] Jer. v. 31.   [52] Matt. xxiii. 27.

Almighty.'⁵⁰ There was ritual enough in our Saviour's time in Jerusalem, multitudinous sacrifices, cleansings, and washings—many and long prayers, punctiliously performed in the Temple and at the corners of the streets—frequent fastings, solemn faces, phylacteries or portions of the Law fastened upon the forehead in literal fulfilment of the Deuteronomist's injunction.⁵¹ There was plenty of orthodoxy—'Behold! thou art called a Jew, and restest in the Law, and makest thy boast of God, and knowest His Will, and approvest the things that are more excellent, being instructed out of the Law, and art confident that thou thyself art a guide of the blind, a light to them that are in darkness, an Instructor of the foolish, a teacher of babes, who hast the form of knowledge and of the truth in the Law.'⁵² There was a grand outcry against blasphemers and heretics—above all against the holy Jesus and afterwards against his follower Paul. But the first says to them, 'Ye serpents; ye generation of vipers! how can you escape the damnation of hell?';⁵³ and the last charges them with causing the name of God to be blasphemed among the heathen by their impieties and immoralities.⁵⁴ Let us remember that daily and hourly 'the true worshippers may worship the Father in spirit and in truth,'⁵⁵ amidst the duties of common life, as well as on Sundays and in the Sanctuary. Let us not be judging each his brother, but judge each himself, knowing that the watchwords of our faith are these—'The Lord knoweth them that are His,' and 'Let all that name the name of Christ depart from iniquity.'⁵⁶

⁵⁰ 2 Cor. vi. 18. ⁵¹ D. vi. 8, xi. 18, comp. E. xiii. 9, 16, due also to D.
⁵² Rom. ii. 17-20. ⁵³ Matt. xxiii. 33. ⁵⁴ Rom. ii. 21-24.
⁵⁵ John iv. 23. ⁵⁶ 2 Tim. ii. 19.

LECTURE XIII.

SUMMARY.

MISTAKEN notions about the Pentateuch may poison all our views of the Divine character; the Ten Commandments, by whomsoever written, come to us at once with Divine authority, because in accordance with our moral and spiritual nature, all except that enjoining the observance of the Sabbath; but the weekly rest also is Divinely indicated by the changes of the Moon, as yearly festivals, and especially the nightly rest, by the course of the Sun; the Sabbath among the Hebrews, as among other nations, originated with observing the Moon's phases; the New Moon, as the first Sabbath of the month, honoured with larger sacrifices than the other Sabbaths, and always named first before the Captivity; the fourth week in each month probably of uncertain length; other commands in Deuteronomy repulsive to us as men and Christians, e.g. those which exclude mutilated persons and others from the Sanctuary, or enjoin perpetual hostility against the Moabites and Ammonites; the stoning of a rebellious son, the utter destruction of the Canaanites; these last express only Jeremiah's strong feelings against his idolatrous countrymen; in other passages he teaches the Fatherly Love of God.

THE CONTENTS OF DEUTERONOMY.

AN eminent living statesman has said—'Every one truth is connected with every other truth in this great Universe of God. . . . Therefore to accept as a truth that which is not a truth . . . . is an evil having consequences which are indeed incalculable. There are subjects on which one mistake of this kind will poison all the wells of Truth, and affect with fatal error the whole circle of our thoughts.'[1] Nothing can be more true or can be more clearly and forcibly expressed. Mistaken notions, for instance, respecting the Mosaic origin and Divine authority of the Pentateuch may darken or confuse men's views of the Divine Character, and issue consequently in very serious faults and aberrations of the life—in bigotry, harshness, and uncharitableness on the one hand, and on the other hand in laxity, irreverence, and immorality. The same writer adds, 'This is among the most certain of all the laws of man's nature, that his conduct will in the main be guided by his moral and intellectual opinions.'[2] And the fact of the existence of this law in human nature is, in truth, the very justification of the work in which I am now engaged, which aims at the clearing away of much which has long been

[1] Duke of ARGYLL (*Reign of Law*, p. 54, 55).   [2] *Ib.*, p. 432.

mistaken for Truth, but is no longer tenable as such, from the ground on which the 'moral and intellectual opinions' of multitudes have been formed.

For let us consider some of the phenomena presented by the laws in Deuteronomy. The address of Moses begins, as I have said, with the Ten Commandments.[3] We may assume that these, as they now lie before us, in two different copies varying from each other in some important particulars, especially in respect of the Fourth Commandment,[4] were not really uttered by the Divine Voice on Sinai, since this is distinctly stated in the New Commentary, which may be fairly regarded as expressing the present views of the English Archbishops and Bishops on this point. Yet we feel at once that such commands as these 'Honour thy father and thy mother,' 'Thou shalt do no murder,' 'Thou shalt not commit adultery,' 'Thou shalt not steal,' 'Thou shalt not bear false witness,' 'Thou shalt not covet,' *are* Divine laws, grounded in the very nature of our being, and, as such, they are approved by the noblest and best of all nations and religions, without any reference to the supposed revelation at Sinai. And so, too, wherever the religious life has made any considerable progress, the first three Commands, which enjoin a spiritual and reverential worship of the One True God, commend themselves to the conscience of each of us, as living words which God has spoken, not indeed amidst lightnings and thunderings, out of the thick darkness, but with the still small voice of His Spirit, and engraved—not upon stones, but— upon the tables of man's heart, where in the light vouchsafed by that Divine Spirit our spirits may plainly read them. And in like manner a little consideration will satisfy us that a Divine Sanction clearly enjoins the observance of a sabbath, of one day in seven, as a day of recreation, refreshment, and

---

[3] p. 149.   [4] p. 101, 102.

rest, for the supply of our physical, moral, social, and religious needs as human beings.

Thus we can no longer believe that the world was created in six days, with successive outward Divine utterances, as described in the first chapter of Genesis. Yet, for all this, and although the Hebrew writer had, no doubt, mistaken notions about the nature, magnitudes, and distances of the Sun, Moon, and Stars, he discerned the eternal, underlying truth, when he wrote, 'and God said'—said, not with audible voice on the fourth day, but said in the depth of the Divine Mind—' Let there be lights in the firmament of heaven to divide the day from the night,'[1] and so He made the Sun to rule by day and the Moon the night,[2] or, as the Psalmist says—

> 'He appointed the Moon for seasons,
> The Sun knoweth his going down.
> Man goeth forth unto his work,
> And to his labour until the evening."[3]

As a rule, then, there is a law laid upon us by our Wise and Good Creator, that we should wake and work by day, and rest and sleep at night—a law not meant to be enforced with rigid severity, as if we might never work by night or sleep by day—a law made known by a Gracious Father to intelligent children—a law made for man, not man for the law. The same Almighty Being, who ages ago, before man existed, prepared gigantic growths of vegetable matter, which, deposited through millions of years in primæval swamps, have formed the coal-beds for the use of man—who provided the stores of lime and slate and stone, and the mineral wealth that lies deep buried in the bowels of the earth, with an express view to the wants of just such a creature as man—has ordered also the grateful interchange of light and darkness, of day and night—I say not, for man alone, but for the benefit of man among the rest. The law of daily toil and nightly rest

---

[1] G.i.14. [2] v. 16. [3] Ps. civ. 19, 23.

is to be our rule, our general guide; though we are free, whenever we see sufficient reason for it, to depart from that law. We know, however, that, if we do depart from it constantly—if we turn day into night and night into day habitually, without something to compensate this breach of Nature's law—we shall suffer the evil consequences; and those amusements or occupations, which compel to any great extent a persistence in such habits, are almost sure to injure health and shorten the duration of life. 'God has spoken' this word to our reason, as plainly as if He had uttered it with a loud voice in our hearing, that the day time shall, as a rule, be the time for labour, not only for individuals, but for social common work, for those employments which concern the whole community.

And so it is with regard to the week and the weekly rest. We know by experience that men cannot go on for ever, day after day, wearied and worn by toil and the cares of business and the labours of public life—that they need intervals of rest besides the nightly sleep, by means of which the body may be restored and reinvigorated, and the mind recover its tone, and both may be ready to spring on cheerfully again to the work suspended. Nature herself points out to us certain annual seasons of more extended holiday, as at Mid-summer or Mid-winter, in the Spring, or after Harvest. Thus the Jews had their three annual festivals, in Spring, Summer, and Autumn; and we find that among almost all nations, even the most barbarous, some such seasons are observed as times of very general relaxation from anxious thought and care, as well as of social meeting and enjoyment.

But besides these greater annual festivals, marked out by the Sun, we need also—at all events in civilised communities, where there is such continual tension of the brain and drainage of the nervous power—the recurrence of days of rest at shorter intervals, for bodily or mental recreation, for family meetings and friendly greetings, and, above all, for common worship—rest, not enforced by positive law, but commended to us by the wise provisions of our Great Creator, and approved by experience as the source of infinite good to the whole community—the right of the poor man as well as the rich—as needful, in fact, for the wants of our complex nature as the rest by night after the daily toil. 'God has spoken' to us this word also, that every seventh day shall be kept as a day of rest, not from the burning summit of Sinai, but, in His Fatherly Wisdom and Goodness, by the mere fact of ordering the changes of the moon for us, so that she completes each phase in seven days. I do not say that this is *the* reason—the only or the main reason—why this has been ordered thus. But I do say that we may thankfully believe that the changes of the Moon exist for this reason among others. As one has said, 'The phases of the Moon supply a familiar mark of time to the simplest and rudest nations—the phenomena of the New and Full Moon especially being such that men cannot fail to notice and employ them as the natural rule of their calendar. And, if a twofold division of the month is thus a matter of necessity to an ordinary observation, a fourfold division is, at least, inevitably suggested by the Moon's intermediate phases. Thus we have the week of seven days.'[1]

That this was really the object of the weekly Sabbath among the Hebrews is plain from the fact that the New Moon was—at least in the older times—regarded by them as a more important day than the ordinary Sabbath; and, accordingly, in addition to the usual daily sacrifice, the Levitical Law provides a 'burnt-offering' on the New Moon of 'two bullocks, one ram, and seven lambs,' with a kid for a sin-offering, whereas on the Sabbath the additional sacrifice was only a burnt-offering of 'two lambs.'[2] The New Moon, in short,

---

[1] *Ed. Review*, cxiv. p. 545; see *Natal Sermons*, I. p. 272, 3, where passages are quoted from HESSEY's *Bampton Lectures* & COX's *Literature of the Sabbath Question*.
[2] N. xxviii. 9, 11, 15.

was the first Sabbath of the month, which was specially announced by trumpet sounds,[10] and gave the law, as it were, for the rest, the first,[11] eighth, fifteenth,[12] and twenty-second,[13] days of every month being kept as days of rest, and the next Sabbath being the first of the following month; though, as the lunar changes are completed—not in 28, but—in $29\frac{1}{2}$ days, it would seem that the last week of the month must have contained sometimes eight and sometimes nine days, and probably lasted until the New Moon was seen. Hence the New Moon is always named *first* in connection with the Sabbath by the prophets before the Captivity, as where Isaiah says, 'The New Moons and Sabbaths I cannot endure,'[14] or Hosea prophesies, 'I will cause all her mirth to cease, her Feast-days, her New Moons, and her Sabbaths,'[15] or Amos hears the people asking, 'When will the New Moon be gone, that we may sell corn, and the Sabbath that we may set forth wheat?'[16] or the Shunammite's husband says to her, 'Wherefore wilt thou go to the prophet to-day? It is neither New Moon nor Sabbath!'[17] It was only about the time of the Captivity[18] that greater stress was laid upon the observance of the Sabbath, as bringing the people together for religious instruction and binding them in common worship, and especially after it,[19] when their City and Temple lay in ruins and they lived as exiles in a heathen land; and then we begin to find the Sabbath sometimes named first,[20] as it always is in the still later days of the second Temple.[21]

It is not, then, because according to the traditionary

---

[10] N. x. 10.   [14] comp. E. xl. 2, 17, L. xxiii. 24.
[11] comp. L. xxiii. 6, 7, 34, 35.   [15] comp. L. xxiii. 8, 36, 2 Ch. vii. 10,
[12] Is. i. 13.   [13] Hos. ii. 11.   [16] Am. viii. 5.   [17] 2 K. iv. 23.
[18] Jer. xvii. 19–27.   [19] Ez. xx. 12, 13, 16, 24, xxii. 8, 23, 26, xxiii. 38, xliv. 24. Is. lvi. 2, 4, lviii. 13.
[20] Ez. xlvi. 1, 3, but see Ez. xlv. 17, Is. lxvi. 23.
[21] 1 Ch. xxiii. 31, 2 Ch. ii. 4, viii. 13, xxxi. 3, Neh. x. 33.

teaching these Ten Commandments are supposed to have been spoken by the Divine Voice on Sinai, that men's views of the Divine Character are in danger of being darkened—except so far as such teaching requires them also to believe that the sole recipient of these awful revelations and of a multitude of others, attested and enforced by a series of stupendous miracles which produce very little or no effect, was one insignificant, rebellious, idolatrous tribe, as being God's 'peculiar treasure above all people,'[77] whom JEHOVAH 'had chosen to be a special people for Himself above all peoples that are upon the face of the earth.'[52] We can recognise these Ten Words as Divine laws, by whomsoever spoken or written. But there are other commands in this Book of the Law which we instinctively reject, because they are at variance with the laws of our moral being, because they conflict at once with the plain lessons of Christ's Gospel, and with those eternal principles of right and wrong, which the Creator Himself has planted within us, in respect of which we are made 'In His image, after His likeness.'[76]

For instance, that Law of Justice and Equity, which God has written with His own Finger upon our hearts, contradicts such commands as that which excludes from the congregation of JEHOVAH one mutilated, perhaps in helpless infancy,[16] while those who had done the deed were allowed free access to the Sanctuary, or which excludes in like manner an innocent base-born child,[78] but takes no account of the vicious parents, or which bars all approach to the Temple against the Ammonites and Moabites for ever, because of some real or supposed unkindness on the part of their forefathers towards the ancestors of the Israelites when they came out of Egypt nearly a thousand years previously, and orders, 'Thou shalt not seek their peace nor their prosperity all thy days for

[76] Exix 5.   [77] D.vii.6.   [78] G.i.26.   [79] D.xxiii.1.   [80] D.xxiii.2.

ever,'⁷⁷—with other laws of a kindred nature. We feel that these cannot be regarded as utterances of the blessed Will of God—that the writer of them, though an inspired man, cannot certainly have written thus by Divine Inspiration; and it is a relief to our consciences to be no longer compelled to receive such commands as proceeding from Infinite Goodness and Wisdom, as guaranteed by Supreme Authority, as Divinely perfect, infallibly true. How much more when we find another law which orders that a 'stubborn and rebellious son' shall be stoned to death," though no punishment is denounced against the parents, who perhaps by their own vicious example had corrupted, or by their weak and faulty training had ruined, their child, and others which enjoin, 'When JEHOVAH thy Elohim shall deliver these nations before thee, thou shalt smite them and utterly destroy them; thou shalt make no covenant with them, nor show mercy unto them,' ⁰ 'thou shalt save alive nothing that breatheth, but thou shalt utterly destroy them.' ⁵⁰ When these ferocious commands and others like them are ascribed to the Fountain of all loving-kindness, 'the God of the spirits of all flesh,' ⁸¹ the Father of our Lord Jesus Christ, our Father in Heaven, or to Moses speaking in His Name to His chosen people, we shudder and shrink away from the painful thought of such words revealing the Divine character to man. Were the Cananites idolaters? and what were the Israelites? Were they any better than the Canaanites? Were they not worse, as they sinned against clearer light and knowledge,—if not amidst the Divine revelations supposed to have been imparted in the wilderness,⁸² yet certainly amidst the warnings of those great prophets whom God had raised up from time to time among them? And does not this book of Deuteronomy say of them, 'JEHOVAH hath not given you an heart to perceive, and eyes

⁷⁷ D. xxiii. 3-6.   ⁷⁸ D. xxi. 18-21.   ⁷⁹ D. vii. 2.   ⁸⁰ D. xx. 16, 17.
⁸¹ N. xvi. 22, xxvii. 16, Heb. xii. 9.   ⁸² E. xxxii. 1-6, N. xxv. 1-5.

to see, and ears to hear, unto this day'?[33] Was it to protect a people like this from being corrupted by intermarrying with the heathen tribes around them, that the Holy One uttered such commands as these? Or shall the All-Wise be charged with such a shortsighted policy which was utterly frustrated in the result? No! our reason and conscience, our whole being, revolts from them; we feel that we cannot worship with our whole heart and soul, we cannot adore and love, we can only fear and distrust, a Deity whose character is thus exhibited. And we turn with comfort and life-inspiring hope to him who said—'Love your enemies, bless them that curse you, do good to them that hate you, and pray for them which despitefully use you, and persecute you, that ye may be the children of your Father which is in Heaven.'[34]

But, again, what a relief it is to know that here we have only the prophet Jeremiah, one of the most tender-hearted of men, making use of the tribes of Canaan as a warning for his own idolatrous countrymen, at a time when those tribes had for centuries ceased to exist, and setting forth the *figure* of them, driven out from their old abode, and ruthlessly exterminated, as a sign of the doom which they deserved, and which most surely awaited them, if they too practised the like abominations. And so the rebellious son is only a type of that rebellious people of whom he says in JEHOVAH's Name, 'I am a Father unto Israel and Ephraim is My firstborn,'[35] yet who had 'said to a stock, Thou art my Father, and to a stone, Thou hast brought me forth,'[36] but whom he longed to bring back to the footstool of Divine Mercy, saying henceforth, 'My Father, Thou art the guide of my youth.'[37]

When, therefore, we hear such words as these, 'Thou shalt also consider in thine heart that, as a man chasteneth his son, so the Living God, thy God, doth chasten thee,'[38] we shall

---

[33] D. xxix 4. [34] Matt. v. 44, 45. [35] Jer. xxxi. 9. [36] Jer. ii. 27.
[37] Jer. iii. 4. [38] D. viii. 5.

joyfully welcome them as words of truth, not merely because we find them in the Bible, but because they are true, eternally true. For it is true that God loves us as dear children, and that we may go to Him at all times with a childlike trust and love, as with a childlike reverence and fear. Rather we must go to Him thus if we would please Him, acting upon the words of that dear Son who has taught us all to say 'Our Father.' We must 'consider in our hearts' that He who has planted in our breast, as human beings, dear love to our children, a love stronger than death, does by that very love of ours shadow forth to us His own Fatherly Love. *Our* love can take in every child of the family; *our* hearts can find a place for all; yes, and our love embraces the far-off prodigal in his miserable wanderings, no less surely and no less tenderly than the dear obedient child, that sits by our side, rejoicing in the sweet delights of home. He who has taught us to love our children thus, how shall He not also love His children, with the Love in which the separate loves of earthly parents are blessed and find their full infinite expression—the Father's wisdom and firmness, to guide and counsel, or, if need be, to chasten—the Mother's tender pity and compassion, that will draw near with sweet consolations in each hour of sorrow and suffering, will sympathise with every grief and trial, will bow down to hear each shame-stricken confession, will be ready to receive the first broken words of penitence, and whisper the promise of forgiveness and peace.

Ah! truly the little one may cling to its mother's neck, and the mother's love will feel the gentle pressure, and will delight to feel it: but it is not the feeble clinging of the child that holds it up to its mother's breast; it is the strong arm of love that embraces it. And we, in our most earnest prayers and aspirations, in our cleaving unto God, in our longing and striving after Truth, in our 'feeling after Him' who 'is not far from anyone of us,'[b] are but as babes 'stretching out weak hands of faith' to lay hold of Him 'whom no man hath seen or can see,'[c] but who, unseen, is ever near us, whose faithful Love embraces all His children, those that are far off as well as those that are near, the heathen and the Christian, the sinner as well as the saint. But it is not our knowledge, however clear, nor our faith, however firm and orthodox, nor our charity, however bright and pure, that holds us up daily and binds us to the bosom of our God. 'Our Father' will delight in all the sacred confidences of His children—their clingings of faith and hope—their longings of pure desire for a closer sense of His Presence—their holy aspirations and penitential confessions. But it is not our prayer that will hold us up. It is His Love alone that does this.

'The Eternal God is our refuge,
And underneath are the Everlasting Arms.'[d]

[b] Acts xvii. 27.   [c] 1 Tim. vi. 16.   [d] D. xxxiii. 27.

LECTURE XIV.

SUMMARY.

RECAPITULATION ; the very late age of the Levitical Legislation only recently ascertained ; innocent fictions of heathen and older Hebrew historians, including the Deuteronomist ; dishonest fictions of the priestly writers of the Pentateuch ; the Deuteronomist refers repeatedly to the Original Story, but nowhere to the Levitical Legislation ; he differs materially from that Legislation by never speaking of the priests as sons of 'Aaron,' by making no distinction between the priests and the Levites, by making a much smaller provision out of the sacrifices for the Levites officiating as priests, by classing the Levites generally with the needy and destitute, and not assigning to them the tithes and firstlings ; hence the Levitical Legislation was not known to the Deuteronomist (Jeremiah) ; some portions of it, apparently, were composed by Ezekiel, who has followed Jeremiah's example, and like him knows nothing of an Aaronic priesthood, but speaks of the priests as 'Levites, sons of Zadok ;' petty ritualism enforced by still later priestly writers ; meaning of the desire of man's heart for the priestly office ; the priesthood of Christ and his true followers.

THE LATER OR LEVITICAL LEGISLATION.

E have now considered the composition of the Pentateuch, so far as concerns, first, the oldest portions in Genesis and Exodus, the foundation of the whole story, written probably in the age of Samuel, in which the name 'ELOHIM,' GOD, is used always for the Deity to the exclusion of 'JEHOVAH,' and which, when taken out by themselves, are found to form a continuous narrative—then the copious additions and amplifications in the days of David and Solomon, in which the name JEHOVAH is used, and which together with the former made up the Original Story, as it came into the hands of the Deuteronomist,—and, lastly, the Deuteronomistic passages and the greater part of Deuteronomy itself, introduced about four centuries afterwards, in the age, and most probably by the hand, of Jeremiah. There still remains, however, the Levitical Legislation, filling about one half of the Pentateuch, which has had so important a part in establishing the priestly system, first in the Jewish and then in the Christian Church. It has been the special work of the last few years to have solved the question as to when this portion of the Pentateuch was written; and the result is one of the utmost interest and importance, not only as regards the history of religious

development in Israel, but in its bearing upon the ritualistic movement of our own times.

In the historical passages of the Original Story we find only the result of an innocent and praiseworthy attempt to dress up in a pleasing and instructive style the early traditions of the Hebrew people, with all the aid of poety and fiction, such as have been employed abundantly by the greatest writers of Greece and Rome, by Homer and Herodotus, Virgil and Livy, in their histories of primitive times. Their works are the delight and admiration of all ages, and they have never brought upon the writers the reproach of dishonesty, however inconsistent with the actual facts we are very sure their statements must often be. But, in putting forth such statements, they had no intention to deceive; they were ignorant themselves of the real course of events, and they were known to be so: they did but collect and embellish the ancient myths and legends which existed in their days, expanding these scanty data out of their own imaginations, and so building up a circumstantial narrative, with events, addresses, conversations, Divine and human, accompanied at times with sage remarks, according to their light, upon the moral bearing of the incidents recorded.

Just so with the early writers of Hebrew History. They knew nothing certainly about those ancient times of their forefathers, except the great facts that their nation had once been in a servile condition in Egypt, and had escaped from that slavery and after painful wanderings had found their way to Canaan, and there by degrees had made themselves masters of the land—which facts, with others like them, had come down by tradition from sire to son through the two or three centuries which had elapsed from the Exodus to Samuel's time. In the course of a very few generations the details of this march and of the conquest must have been lost among a people who were living in a rude state as separate tribes, and were probably little exercised in writing before the age of Samuel and his schools. But for the arts of writing and printing what should *we* know, as Englishmen, about the details of Queen Elizabeth's reign, about the part, for instance, which this or that hero took in the defeat of the Great Armada, unless perhaps some song or ballad had preserved the memory of the gallant deed for future ages? Upon such data, however, Samuel and his immediate followers—very probably students in his schools—appear to have built up the Original Story of the Exodus very much out of their own imaginations, with the help of ancient myths, such as those of the Creation, the Fall, and the Deluge, and legends attached to the names of famous persons and places or to those of sacred stones and trees, which legends, however, seem for the most part to have originated with the writers themselves, suggested by the mere existence of the names in question. Still, in all this there was no dishonesty or deceit: we have no reason whatever to suppose that they even pretended that what they wrote was veracious history: they may have put forth their narrative from the first as a mere work of the imagination. It is the men of later days who have insisted upon regarding these stories as actual history, with all their astounding contradictions of the plainest facts of Natural Science and their agglomeration of stupendous miracles.

So, too, the attempt of Jeremiah, as we suppose, to infuse a more religious character into the Older Story, by the insertion of passages written in his own spirited, prophetical style, and by the addition of almost the whole Book of Deuteronomy as a kind of commentary on the older law, can be perfectly reconciled, as we have seen, with good faith on his part, and with a high and noble motive, more especially when we take into account the habits of his people. In our days few pious persons would presume to ascribe directly to the Supreme Being the thoughts with which their own bosoms were stirred, though fully believing themselves to be under the influence of the Divine Teacher of men. But a Jewish prophet like Jeremiah would have said at once, 'Thus saith JEHOVAH,' if any idea presented itself to his mind with overpowering force as unquestionably right and good and true. Hitherto, therefore, we have had nothing to which the terms 'forger' and 'forgery' can be justly applied, which have been freely used by some defenders of traditional views,[1] to raise a prejudice in their readers' minds against the conclusions of Modern Criticism.

But hitherto we have only had to deal with *prophetical* writers, or with men, like Jeremiah, in whom the prophetical entirely overpowered the priestly element. We come now upon the domain of the priest. And here, if anywhere, such words may with some justice be applied; for there can be little room for doubt, with any who will take the pains to study thoroughly the subject, that the whole of the Levitical Legislation of the Pentateuch was written by priestly writers during or after the Captivity, and written, most of it, with the direct purpose of magnifying their own office and asserting their own special rights and prerogatives. The first clear hint which we get of this fact is derived from a close consideration of the Address of Moses, which formed the Book of the Law as found in the Temple by Hilkiah. In this, or rather in D.i–xxx, we find numerous allusions to the Original Story of the Exodus—to Jacob's going down into Egypt 'a Syrian ready to perish,' with only 'a few,'[2] *i.e.* seventy persons,[3]— where Israel became 'a nation, great, mighty, and populous'[4] — to the Egyptians afflicting the Israelites,[5] who cried unto JEHOVAH, and He 'looked upon their affliction,'[6]—to the

---

[1] *e.g.* Bp. BROWNE, *New Bible Commentary*, 'a *forger*,' p. 12, 17, 20, 196, 227, 229, 232, 'any skilful *forger*,' 'who have been fixed upon as probable *forgers* of the Pentateuch, such as Samuel or Jeremiah,' p. 18, &c.

[2] xxvi. 5, *comp.* E. i. 1.   [3] x. 22, *comp.* E. i. 5.

[4] i. 10, x. 22, xxvi. 5, xxviii. 62, *comp.* E. i. 7, 9, 12, 20.

[5] xxvi. 6, *comp.* E. i. 11, 13, 14, vi. 9.   [6] xxvi. 7, *comp.* E. ii. 23–25, iii. 7, 9, iv. 31.

THE LATER OR LEVITICAL LEGISLATION. 189

promise made to their fathers of the land of Canaan,[7] and the 'deliverance of Israel out of Egypt with signs and wonders' wrought upon 'Pharaoh and all his house,'[8]—to the flight out of Egypt 'in haste,'[9] 'by night in the month of Abib,'[10] and the drowning of the Egyptians in the Red Sea,[11]—to the provocations of JEHOVAH in the wilderness,[12] the murmurings,[13] the rebellion,[14]—to the manna,[15] the Golden Calf,[16] the fiery serpents,[17]—to the attack of Amalek,[18] the leprosy of Miriam,[19] the destruction of Dathan and Abiram,[20] the prophecies of Balaam,[21]—in short, to a multitude of incidents which show that the writer must have been well acquainted with the Original Story very much in its present form. It may have been preserved in the Temple, or in the hands of some of the priests, from the time of Solomon downwards, and may have thus been seen and studied by Jeremiah, as being himself a priest, perhaps the son of the high-priest of Josiah's time. However this may be, certain it is that the Original Story must have existed in his time, and that he must have been familiar with it.

How, then, can we account for the fact that, amidst all these numerous references, there does not occur in D.i-xxx one single allusion to any of the historical incidents or precepts specially recorded in the Levitical Legislation? He mentions the Ark indeed,[22] but that is mentioned in the Original Story:[23] he does not mention the splendid Tabernacle, built (it is supposed) by express Divine instructions, after the model which was shown to Moses in the Mount.[24]

---

[7] vi. 10, 18, &c., comp. E. vi. 2-4, &c.
[8] xvi. 3, comp. E. xli. 33, 39.
[9] xi. 4, comp. E. xiv. 27, 28.
[10] ix. 22, comp. N. xi. 1-3, 31-34.
[13] viii. 3, 16, comp. N. xi. 4-9.
[14] viii. 15, comp. N. xxi. 6.
[16] xxiv. 9, comp. N. xii.
[17] xxiii. 4, 5, comp. N. xxii-xxiv.
[19] D. ii. 1-5, 8, xxxi. 9, 25, 26.

[11] vi. 21, 22, &c., comp. E. vii, &c.
[12] xvi. 1, comp. E. xiii. 4, xxxiv. 18.
[15] ix. 7, comp. E. xiv. 11, xvii. 3, &c.
[18] ix. 23, comp. N. xiv. 1, &c.
[20] ix. 8-21, 25-29, comp. E. xxxii.
[21] xxv. 17-19, comp. E. xvii. 8, 16.
[22] xi. 6, comp. N. xvi. 25-33.
[23] N. x. 33, 35, xiv. 44.
[24] E. xxvi. 30.

He mentions Aaron,[15] but only in connexion with his scandalous conduct, as related in the Original Story,[16] in respect of the Golden Calf, the symbol of the Sun-God, which Aaron had made for Israel to worship. He never speaks of him as 'priest' and the head of the priesthood: he never calls the priests the 'sons of Aaron,' as they are invariably called in the Levitical Law; he calls the priests always 'Levites'[17] or 'sons of Levi.'[18] But the Levitical Legislation everywhere sharply distinguishes between the 'priests, the Sons of Aaron,' and the 'Levites,'[19] and makes Moses rebuke indignantly the 'sons of Levi' for aspiring to act as priests, saying, 'Seek ye the priesthood also?'[20] and it lays down the law that no one, 'who was not of the seed of Aaron, should come near to offer incense before JEHOVAH, that he be not as Korah the Levite and his company,'[21] who were struck dead by lightning for having presumed to do so.[22] Accordingly, whereas the Deuteronomist says that 'the *whole tribe* of Levi' was 'separated *to stand before* JEHOVAH *to minister unto Him,* and to bless in His Name,'[23] the Levitical Law reserves these offices exclusively for the priests,[24] and orders that the Levites shall be only the *servants of the priests,* shall '*stand before Aaron the priest that they may minister unto him,*'[25]—that Aaron and his sons shall keep their priesthood, and any stranger that cometh near, whether layman or Levite, shall be put to death,'[26]—that the Levites shall not even 'go in to see when the holy things are covered by the priests,'[27] or

---

[15] D. ix. 20. N.B. x. 6,7, is probably a fragment of the O.S., out of its proper place, except the last clause of v. 6, which belongs to the Levitical Legislation (L.L.), as does also D. xxxii. 48–52.   [16] E. xxxii. 1–6, 21–25.
[17] D. xvii. 9, 18, xviii. 1, xxiv. 8, xxvii. 9, *comp.* xviii. 6, 7, xxvii. 14, xxxi. 25, where also 'Levite' = 'priest.'   [18] D. xxi. 5, xxxi. 9.
[19] E. xxxviii. 21, xxxix. 41, L. i. 5, 7, 8, &c., viii. 2, &c., N. iii. 3, 4, 9, 10, &c.
[20] N. xvi. 10.   [21] v. 40.   [22] p. 35.   [23] D. x. 8.
[24] E. xxviii. 1, 3, 35, 43, N. vi. 27.   [25] N. iii. 5–10, viii. 19, xviii. 1–6.
[26] N. iii. 10, 38, xviii. 7.   [27] N. iv. 15, 19, 20.

'come near to the holy vessels and the altar,'[38] 'lest they die.'

Moreover, the Deuteronomist makes certain provisions for the maintenance of these 'priests the sons of Levi': but these are entirely at variance with those in the Levitical Law. Thus he directs that *all* the Levites—'the *whole tribe* of Levi' —shall eat the 'fire-offerings of JEHOVAH,'[39] and that *any Levite*, coming 'with all the desire of his mind' to minister at the Sanctuary, should 'have like portions with the rest of his brethren, who stood there before JEHOVAH to minister,'[40] that is, should 'have like portions' with the other Levites who officiated there as *priests*. But in the Levitical Law these 'fire-offerings' are expressly assigned to the 'sons of Aaron the priests';[41] whereas the Levites were to receive merely the tithes of corn, wine, and oil,[42] and of these they were to give a tithe to the priests.[43] Also the Deuteronomist defines these 'fire-offerings'—that is to say, the portions which the priests might claim of the sacrifices—as the shoulder, the two checks (or head), and the maw (or tripe-stomach);[44] whereas the Levitical Law makes a much more sumptuous provision, namely, the breast and hind-leg of every victim,[45] together with all the firstfruits of corn, and wine, and oil,[46] and all the firstlings of sheep and oxen.[47] Once more the Deuteronomist classes the Levites repeatedly, not only with 'the manservant and the maidservant,' but, as being generally poor and needy, with 'the stranger, the widow, and the fatherless,'[48] who should be charitably invited to share in the feasts which pious Israelites were commanded to make for their families annually at the Sanctuary,[49] upon the *tithes* of corn, and wine, and oil, and the

---

[38] N. xviii. 3.   [39] D. xviii. 1.   [40] v. 6-8.
[41] L. ii. 3, 10, vi. 17, 18, vii. 5, &c., 31-35, x. 14, 15, xxiv. 9.   [42] N. xviii. 21, 24.
[43] v. 25-28.   [44] D. xviii. 3.
[45] E. xxix. 26, 28, L. vii. 31, 34, N. xviii. 18.   [46] N. xvii. 12, 13.
[47] v. 15-18.   [48] xii. 12, 18, xiv. 29, xvi. 11, 14, xxvi. 11, 12, 13.
[49] xii. 11, 12, 17-19, xiv. 22-27, xxvi. 12, 13.

firstlings of sheep and oxen,⁵⁰ and once in three years upon the tithes at home⁵¹—'and the Levite that is within thy gates, thou shalt not forsake him,' 'the Levite and the stranger and the fatherless and the widow, that are within thy gates, shall come and shall eat and be satisfied.'⁵² But the Levitical Law, as we have just seen, assigns these very tithes wholly to the Levites and these firstlings wholly to the priests; and, though the New Bible Commentary invents a 'second' set of 'tithes' to explain these contradictions, which should be expressly used for such feasts, the 'first' tithes' having been duly paid to the Levites,⁵³ it does not venture to suggest a second set of 'firstlings.' From all this it is plain that the Deuteronomist could never have had before him the Levitical Law, as part of a Mosaic and Divine dispensation, prefaced everywhere by the announcement 'And JEHOVAH said to Moses'⁵⁴—that, in other words, no such Levitical Law existed at all in his time. It must have been inserted in later days, after the time of Jeremiah, that is, during or after the Captivity.

Accordingly it is found that some portions of the Book of Leviticus, as L.xviii–xx, and especially L.xxvi, betray unmistakably the hand of Ezekiel, who was one of the priests carried captive to Babylon with Josiah's grandson Jehoiachin.⁵⁵ The captive Jews in the district of Babylon had perhaps referred to the priest Ezekiel for instruction on certain points; or he may have thought it good to lay down a number of precepts, partly ceremonial, partly moral and religious, as necessary to be observed by them, if they would still remain in that far-off land true servants of their Heavenly King; and accordingly he does this in L.xviii–xx. But Ezekiel was a prophet as well as a priest, and in L.xxvi he gives a grand prophetical warning, containing a number of his own peculiar

---

⁵⁰ xli.6,17,xiv.23. ⁵¹ xiv.28,29,xxvi.12,13. ⁵² xiv.27,29. ⁵³ I.p.797.
⁵⁴ E.xxv.1,xxx.11,17,22,34,&c. ⁵⁵ Ez.i.2,3.

expressions, which all occur again in Ezekiel's prophecies, but of which eighteen are found nowhere else in the Pentateuch.[16] It has been said indeed that Ezekiel may have derived these phrases from the Book of Leviticus, which he had devoutly read. But it is idle to suppose that a writer so profuse and so peculiar, as this prophet is on all hands acknowledged to be, should have studied so closely—not the whole Book of Leviticus, but—this *one particular chapter* out of the whole Pentateuch (L.xxvi), as to have become thoroughly imbued with its style and to have made its very language his own. Rather, he had before him the grand words of his brother prophet Jeremiah in D.xxviii, xxxii, from which, in fact, he quotes some expressions in this chapter,[17] as he does also in his prophecies;[18] and after Jeremiah's example, though not with the same rhetorical power, he launches against his countrymen threats of Divine vengeance if they persist in their idolatry and disobedience, mingled with promises of good if they are faithful, and ending with a pledge of final restoration. And it is very noticeable that Ezekiel the priest, like Jeremiah the priest, never speaks in his prophecies of the priests as 'sons of Aaron,' nor even once mentions Aaron as the supposed head of his own priestly order; from which it is clear that in their time this title did not exist—much less

---
[16] *Pent.* VI. 5.
[17] v. 16, 'consumption, fever,' *comp.* D. xxviii. 22; v. 16, 'consuming the eyes and causing sorrow of heart,' *comp.* D. xxviii. 65; v. 16, 'and ye shall sow your seed in vain and your enemies shall eat it,' *comp.* D. xxviii. 33, 51; 'and ye shall be smitten before your enemies,' *comp.* D. xxviii. 7, 28; v. 19, 'and I will make your heaven as iron and your land as brass,' *comp.* D. xxviii. 23; v. 21, 'and I will add plagues upon thee,' *comp.* D. xxviii. 59, 61; v. 29, 'and ye shall eat the flesh of your sons and the flesh of your daughters shall ye eat,' *comp.* D. xxviii. 53, &c.; v. 8, 'and five of you shall chase an hundred, and an hundred of you shall chase ten thousand,' *comp.* D. xxxii. 30.
[18] *comp.* Ez. v. 10 with D. xxviii. 53-57—Ez. v. 12, xx. 23, xxii. 15, with D. xxviii. 64—Ez. v. 14, 15, with D. xxviii. 37—Ez. xiv. 8, 'and I will make him a sign and a proverb,' xxii. 4, xxxvi. 3, with D. xxviii. 37—Ez. v. 16, 17, with D. xxii. 23, 24—Ez. vii. 15 with D. xxxii. 25—Ez. vii. 26 with D. xxxii. 23—Ez. viii. 3, 'which provoketh to jealousy,' with D. xxxii. 16, 21—Ez. xvi. 13, 15, with D. xxxii. 13-15.

exist as one Divinely originated. They both speak of the priests as 'Levites' or 'sons of Levi'; [59] and, when Ezekiel wishes to distinguish between the great body of the Levites who had taken part in idolatrous rites before the Captivity and those who had adhered to the pure worship of JEHOVAH, he calls the latter 'the priests the sons of *Zadok* among the sons of Levi,' 'the priests the Levites who are of the seed of *Zadok*,' 'the priests the Levites the sons of *Zadok*,' 'the priests who are sanctified of the sons of *Zadok*, who kept My charge, who went not astray when the children of Israel went astray, as the Levites went astray' [60]—from which also we see that the idea of the Aaronic priesthood, as laid down in the Levitical Law, must have been of a later date than the days of Ezekiel.

But the example thus set was followed in a very different spirit by those who composed the great mass of the Levitical Law, abounding with minute directions for ritualistic and ceremonial observances, and enjoining the utmost reverence for the Sanctuary, and also for the priest as alone privileged to enter the holy place and draw near to the symbol of JEHOVAH'S presence. And so they 'bound heavy burdens and grievous to be borne, and laid them on men's shoulders,' while the weightier matters of the Law, on which such stress is laid in the Book of Deuteronomy, justice, mercy, and truth, are almost wholly passed by in this priestly Legislation. In this Law, for instance, mere natural occurrences are classed as offences for which a sacrifice must be offered—always, of course, to the advantage of the priest who had his share of it —such as child-birth,[61] leprosy,[62] &c., or trivial acts of inadvertence by which some ceremonial defilement may have been incurred,[63] it being ordained, for instance, that anyone who

---

[59] Jer. xxxiii. 18, 21, 22, Ez. xl. 46, xliii. 19, xliv. 15, xlviii. 13.
[60] Ez. xl. 46, xliii. 19, xliv. 15, xlviii. 11.
[61] L. xii. 8.   [62] L. xiv. 19.   [63] L. xv. 14, 29.

touched, without even knowing it, a dead mouse, lizard, mole, or snail, should be 'unclean until the evening,'[44] that anyone who ate turtle should be an 'abomination,'[45] that any vessel of wood, raiment, skin, or sack, over which a snail had crossed or a mouse had run, should be unclean,[46] and every earthen vessel so defiled should be broken.[47] It need hardly be said that all distinctions between right and wrong must have been confounded in the writer's mind and in that of his fellow-priests who enforced or tried to enforce such teaching, and in that of the laity who received it as the Word of the Living God.

Yet in all ages, wherever this priestly power, with its claim to discharge the office of mediator between God and man, has become the supposed possession of a class of men, who could use it to admit their fellows to religious privileges or else to debar them from them, whether those of the Jewish Church or of the Christian, 'casting out,' as they of old cast out the man who confessed that Jesus was the Christ,[48] or rejecting for doctrinal differences the true in heart and life from the common feast of Christians,—who claimed not only to receive into the number of God's children, but to exclude from the care and love of the Universal Father,—the real profaneness of the assumption has not prevented the power thus arrogated being allowed by very many, and the supposition that it can exist elsewhere than in the imagination of the priest himself and his disciples has been a heavy chain upon the progress of humanity.

Still the thirst of man's heart for the office of the priest, which has been exhibited, more or less, in all times, in all places, under all religions, must have some real meaning. And indeed that office derives its significance and power from the deepest of all the instincts of humanity, the craving to

[44] L. xi. 29–31.   [45] v. 29, 43.   [47] v. 32.
[46] v. 33.   [48] John ix. 22–34.

know something about Him who is exalted above all blessing and praise, to be brought into the fuller consciousness of His Presence, to have some sure hope of His Favour, at least, of His Pity, to be able to believe that the utterance of our hearts reaches His Ear, our song of adoration and thanksgiving, or our moan of regret and self-abhorrence. The voice of a fellow-mortal, who claims to have some assurance of these things to offer, is too welcome to the longing spirit or to the sick and weary soul, not to be welcomed. It is not for us to judge our brother who may find the priestly office a stay and support for his tottering steps along the way of life. It is enough if we remember for ourselves that this is the true priestly function, when one who is more spiritually minded than his brethren, more pure in heart, more faithful in life, who has thus been brought more near to God than they, confirms their faith and quickens their love and holy fear by sympathy with his own—even as he, the great high-priest of our profession,[9] by his blessed teaching has brought us all near to God,[10] and by the ministrations of his Father's Love in life and death has opened for us the way of access with boldness to His Presence[11]—even as we too, in our different relations, may day by day reveal the Father to each other, by the spirit of Christ which abides in us, the filial spirit of trust and loving obedience, and help to bring one another near to His Footstool, in accordance with that word, 'One is your Father, even God; one is your Master, even Christ; and all ye are brethren.'[12]

[9] Heb. iii. 1.
[11] Heb. xii. 19-22.
[10] Rom. v. 2, Eph. ii. 18, iii. 12.
[12] Matt. xxiii. 8, 9.

LECTURE XV.

SUMMARY.

THE account of the Mosaic Tabernacle, &c., part of the priestly legislation; in the O.S. the Tent of Meeting is set up for religious purposes *outside* the Camp, under the charge of a layman, Joshua; in the L.L. the Tabernacle is set up in the *centre* of the Camp, under the charge of the whole body of priests and Levites; in the O.S. Jehovah descends in the pillar of cloud, and speaks with Moses at the entrance of the Tent; in the L.L. JEHOVAH speaks from off the mercy-seat in the innermost recess of the Tabernacle; in the O.S. the Ark goes *before* the people; in the L.L. it is carried in the middle of the host; these differences occur in various parts of the O.S., which forms by itself a connected story from Exodus to Joshua; the L.L. brings forward into special prominence Aaron and his priesthood; the O.S. nowhere speaks of him as priest, but treats him merely as a colleague of Moses, as does also the prophet Micah, whereas the very late Books of Chronicles, &c., follow the lead of the L.L.; the priestly interpolations in the story of Dathan and Abiram, which contained originally no mention of Korah and his rebellion against Aaron, as appears from Deuteronomy; the probable historical meaning of this narrative in its older and later forms; the tendency to take refuge in ritualism from the power of truth exemplified in Israel after the Captivity and in our own times.

THE LATER LEGISLATION COMPARED WITH THE ORIGINAL STORY.

WE have been considering the evidence afforded of the very late origin of the Levitical Law, by the mode in which the Deuteronomist treats the question of the priesthood, showing that that Law with its phrase, 'the sons of Aaron' instead of 'the sons of Levi,' and its far more liberal provision for the support of the priests and Levites, could not have been known to him, or, in other words, could not have been composed till after his time, during or after the Captivity.[1]

Let us turn now to another no less convincing proof of this fact. You will remember the account in the Book of Exodus of Moses going up into the Mount with Joshua,[2] and remaining there in communion with JEHOVAH for forty days and forty nights [3]—at the end of which it is added, 'And He gave unto Moses, when He had made an end of communing with him on Mount Sinai, two tables of stone, tables of the Testimony, written with the finger of ELOHIM.'[4] And this notice is immediately preceded by six chapters, which contain minute directions, said to have been communicated by JEHOVAH to Moses, for the construction of the Tabernacle

[1] p. 191-4.   [2] E. xxiv. 13-15.   [3] v. 18.   [4] E. xxxi. 18.

and its vessels.⁵ Was this a portion of the Original Story, or was it introduced as part of these later insertions? That Tabernacle was to be a gorgeous Tent, with magnificent curtains,⁶ golden taches,⁷ silver sockets,⁸ and bars overlaid with gold,⁹ and a hanging for the door of 'blue and purple and scarlet and fine twined linen, wrought with needlework.'¹⁰ But, if this was to be the case, how was it that in Eli's time the House of God at Shiloh, supposed to have been this very same Mosaic Tent, which had been set up at that place by Joshua,¹¹ when 'the land had rest' after the conquest of Canaan,¹² had 'doorposts'¹³ and 'doors'?¹⁴ Or how was it, if this splendid Tabernacle was still in existence, that the Ark, when brought back by the Philistines after the death of Eli, was not restored at once to it, as the place expressly provided by JEHOVAH Himself for its reception, but was allowed to remain for twenty years or more in the house of a private individual, whose son was 'sanctified to keep it'¹⁵—apparently a mere layman, or, if a Levite, as some suppose, yet as such strictly forbidden by the Levitical Law to touch or even to look upon the Ark on pain of death?¹⁶ How was it again that when David brought up the Ark to Jerusalem, instead of bringing with it the gorgeous Tabernacle, he himself erected a Tent for it on Mount Zion?¹⁷ All these phenomena make it plain that no such Tabernacle ever really existed, and that this portion also of Exodus is no part of the Original Story, but has been inserted by later writers; and accordingly we find that two of these six chapters are mainly employed in describing the dresses of the priests and the ceremonies to be used at their consecration.¹⁸

A further consideration will leave no doubt on this point. We are told that, as Moses came down from the Mount with

---

⁵ E.xxv–xxxi.17.   ⁶ E.xxvi.   ⁷ v.1–5.   ⁸ v.6.   ⁹ v.19–25.
¹⁰ v.29.   ¹¹ v.31.   ¹² J.xviii.1.   ¹³ 1S.i.9.   ¹⁴ 1S.iii.15.
¹⁵ 1S.vii.1,2.   ¹⁶ N.iv.15,20.   ¹⁷ 2S.vi.17.   ¹⁸ E.xxviii,xxix.

the two stone-tables in his hand, he beheld the Golden Calf and the people dancing around it, and in anger and horror at the sight he dashed the tables out of his hands and broke them in pieces.[19] Then the Levites at his summons—that is, the men of his own tribe [20]—rush through the Camp of Israel from one end to the other, slaughtering all they meet. 'And there fell of the people that day about three thousand men. For Moses had said, Consecrate yourselves to-day to JEHOVAH, even every man upon his son and upon his brother, that He may bestow upon you a blessing this day.'[21] What that blessing most probably was we shall consider hereafter.[22] But now Moses intercedes for the people, and after being plagued they are forgiven;[23] at all events, the order is issued for the forward march to Canaan.[24] Then follows this remarkable passage:—'And Moses took the tent, and pitched it outside the Camp, a little way off from the Camp, and it was called [the Tabernacle of the Congregation, or rather, as it should be more properly rendered,[25]] the Tent of Meeting. And it came to pass that everyone seeking JEHOVAH went out unto the Tent of Meeting which was outside the Camp. And it came to pass, when Moses went out of the Camp, that all the people arose, and they stood each at the opening of his tent, and they looked after Moses until he went into the Tent. And it came to pass, when Moses had gone into the Tent, that the pillar of cloud came down and stood at the opening of the Tent, and He spake with Moses. And all the people saw the pillar of cloud standing at the entrance of the Tent; and all the people arose and worshipped, each at the entrance of his tent. And JEHOVAH spake unto Moses face unto face, as a man speaketh unto his friend; and he returned unto the Camp, and his servant Joshua, a young man, departed not out of the Tent.'[26]

[19] E. xxxii. 15-19.   [20] E. ii. 1-10.   [21] E. xxxii. 26-29.   [22] Lect. XVII.
[23] E. xxxii. 30-35.   [24] E. xxxiii. 1.   [25] B.C. I. p. 382, 410, 432.   [26] E. xxxiii. 7-11.

Now here we have several things to notice. This tent, which Moses pitched outside the Camp, was, of course, not the Tabernacle, which (according to the story as it now lies before us) he had only just been instructed to make, and which, in fact, he makes in a subsequent chapter.[87] But it is here called '*the* tent,' as if it were a tent well known to the people, that is, as the New Commentary explains it, 'very probably the one in which Moses was accustomed to dwell,'[78] and to which the people may be supposed to have resorted before, for judicious and religious purposes.'[79] This tent he now sets apart for sacred uses, and calls it the 'Tent of Meeting,' the very name by which, in those preceding chapters the splendid Tabernacle, presently to be built, is called repeatedly by JEHOVAH Himself,[80] expressly because there He would 'meet with Israel.'[81] It would be strange if Moses in the Original Story had taken upon himself to anticipate thus the erection of this Divinely-ordered Tabernacle, and had given this very same name to an ordinary tent. Plainly the fact is, that in those six chapters the later writer has merely copied the name already used in the passage just quoted from the Original Story.

But where is Aaron? or where is there any sign of the existence of priests in this passage? True, Aaron and his sons had not yet been consecrated.[82] But they had been already designated for the sacred office;[83] and we might have expected that they would have been overshadowed, as it were, with their coming glory, so that Aaron or one of his four sons, or, at least, a body of Levites, would have been appointed to keep continual watch in this sacred tent, rather than Joshua, a mere *layman*,[84] 'a young man, the servant of Moses.'[85]

---

[77] E. xxxvi.   [78] B.C.I. p.410.   [79] E. xviii. 7, 12, 13.
[80] E. xxvii. 21, xxviii. 43, xxix. 4, 10, 11, 30, 32, 42, 44, xxx. 16, 18, 20, 36, xxxi. 7.
[81] E. xxix. 42, 43, xxx. 36.   [82] L. viii.   [83] E. xxviii. 1.
[84] N. xiii. 8.   [85] E. xxxiii. 11.

But here also we have the Original Story, which knew nothing of any such extraordinary dignity now or hereafter to be attached to Aaron or to the priests 'the sons of Aaron.'

Again, this tent is set up *outside* the Camp, and all who desired to enquire of JEHOVAH went out to it. But the splendid Tabernacle was to be set up in the *very middle* of the Camp, the three Levite families being posted on three sides of it, on the north, south, and west,[36] and Moses himself, with Aaron and his sons, on the east,[37] and outside these the twelve tribes ranged in four great camps,[38] the whole forming apparently one immense square, with the Tabernacle in the centre.

Once more, in this passage JEHOVAH descends in the pillar of cloud and stands at the opening of the Tent, and there speaks with Moses. But in the preceding chapters JEHOVAH promises that He will commune with Moses 'from above the mercy-seat, from between the two cherubs which are upon the Ark of the Testimony'[39]—that is, from the Holy of Holies, in the innermost part of the Tabernacle, and not at the entrance. Accordingly, the Book of Leviticus begins, 'And JEHOVAH called unto Moses and spake unto him out of the Tent of Meeting';[40] and elsewhere we read, 'I will appear in the cloud upon the mercy-seat,'[41] and again, 'And Moses went into the Tent of Meeting to speak with JEHOVAH, and one heard the voice of one speaking unto him from off the mercy-seat that was upon the Ark of the Testimony.'[42] The two ideas, it is plain, are totally different.

Lastly, in the Levitical Law the 'cloud by day' or the 'appearance of fire by night' rests always upon the Tabernacle in the centre of the Camp when they are at rest;[43] and, when they are to be moved forward, it is 'taken up from the

[36] N.i.53,iii.23,29,35.
[37] E.xxv.22.
[38] N.vii.89.
[39] N.iii.38.
[40] L.i.1.
[41] N.ix.15,16,18,19,20,22.
[42] N.ii.2,3,10,18,25.
[43] L.xvi.2.

Tent,'⁴⁴ and is meant apparently to float over it still, as it is carried in advance of the Ark in the *middle* of the host,⁴⁵ until the next resting-place is reached, when it drops again upon the Tabernacle. But in the Original Story the pillar of cloud descends when JEHOVAH will speak with Moses;⁴⁶ and the pillar 'of cloud by day' or 'fire by night' goes *before* them when they march,⁴⁷ and the Ark itself leads the way, 'to search out a resting-place for them.'⁴⁸

To a thoughtful reader of the Bible these contradictory statements must often have seemed very perplexing, especially if he had observed that, long after the Tabernacle has been duly set in the centre of the Camp, once and again in the Book of Numbers, the 'Tent of Meeting' is spoken of as pitched *outside* the Camp, as here, and it is necessary to *go out* to it;⁴⁹ while in each of these two passages, as well as in another towards the end of Deuteronomy, JEHOVAH comes down in the pillar of cloud, as here, and stands at the entrance of the Tent, and speaks with Moses.⁵⁰ Of course, the explanation is, that these three passages are all portions of the Original Story, as appears plainly enough when it is taken out by itself, like the Elohistic Narrative, and then is found to form a connected whole, from the beginning of Exodus to the end of Deuteronomy, or rather, to the end of the Book of Joshua.⁵¹ For the Pentateuch and Book of Joshua form parts of one work, and in this last-named Book, as well as the rest, we find portions of the Original Story, retouched by the Deuteronomist in his marked prophetical style,⁵² and afterwards filled up by the priestly writers of the Levitical Law.⁵³

---

⁴⁴ v. 17.
⁴⁵ E. xxxiii. 9.
⁴⁶ N. x. 33.
⁵⁰ N. xii. 17, 25, xii. 5, 10, D. xxxi. 15.
⁴⁸ N. x. 17, 21.
⁴⁷ E. xiii. 21, 22, xiv. 19, 24, N. x. 34.
⁴⁹ N. xi. 26, 30, xii. 4.
⁵¹ *App.* II.
⁵² i. 3–18, iii. 2–4, 10, iv. 24, v. 2–8, vii. 7–9, viii. 30–35, x. 12–14, xxi. 43–45, xxii. 1–6, xxiii, xxiv. 1–25, 31.
⁵³ iv. 13, 19, v. 10–12, vi. 19, 24b, vii. 1, 25c, ix. 15b, 17–21, 27b, xi. 21–23, xii. 1–24, xiii. 21b, 22, 23, xiv. 1–15, xvii. 3–6, xix. 51, xxi. 1–42, xxii. 8–34, xxiv. 26, 27, 33.

I have thus tried to give you some idea of the Later or Levitical Legislation, which takes up so large a space in the Pentateuch, no less than two-thirds of Exodus, Leviticus, and Numbers, and which is plainly to be distinguished from the other parts of those books by its own peculiar phraseology, as well as by the subjects it treats of. The consideration of the style belongs, of course, to critical works:[34] but it may interest you if I draw your attention more closely to some of the contents.

We saw in the last Lecture that the priesthood, with its rights, duties, and prerogatives,—the paramount sanctity and dignity of the priests above that of their servants, the Levites, for whom a more moderate provision is made,—and the exaltation of both these orders of clergy above the laity,—engross a very large portion of this Levitical Law. The effort to bring into greater prominence the activity of Aaron, as the head of the future Aaronic priesthood, is strikingly exhibited in the account of the ten plagues, where several insertions are made,[35] apparently with this express object in view. In the Original Story it is Moses who invariably takes the leading part, who is to be 'as God to *Aaron*,'[36] who performs miracles with *his* rod.[37] But in these later insertions Moses is to be 'as God to *Pharaoh*,'[38] and JEHOVAH orders Moses, 'Say unto Aaron, Take *thy* rod and it shall become a [serpent or] crocodile,'[39] and so in other instances.[40] In the Original Story JEHOVAH speaks to Moses only;[41] in the later insertions JEHOVAH speaks to Moses and *Aaron*.[42] In the Original Story JEHOVAH summons Aaron and his two

---

[34] See *Pent*. VI.
[35] E. vi. 6–8, 10–30, vii. 1–13, 19, xxx, 22, viii. 5–7, 15–19, ix. 8–12, 35, xi. 9, 10, xii. 1–28, 40–51, xlv. 8, xvi. 1b, 2–36, xix. 1, 20–25, xxiv. 16, 17, xxv. 1–xxxi. 17, xxxiv. 28, 'the Ten Words,' 33–35, xxxv–xl.
[36] E. iv. 16.   [37] E. iv. 2, 3, vii. 15, 17, 20b, ix. 22, 23, x. 12, 13, 21, 22.
[38] E. vii. 1.   [39] E. vii. 9, 10, 12.   [40] E. viii. 5, 6, 16, 17.
[41] E. vii. 14, viii. 1, 20, ix. 1, 13, 22, x. 1, 12, 21, xi. 1, xiii. 1, xiv. 1, &c.
[42] E. vi. 13, vii. 8, ix. 8, xii. 1, 43, *comp*. L. xi. 1, xiii. 1, xiv. 33, xv. 1, N. ii. 1, iv. 1, 17, xiv. 26, xvi. 20, xix. 1, xx. 12, xxvi. 1.

sons with seventy of the elders of Israel, to come to the foot of the Mount with Moses,⁶³ where the privilege in question is made common to all these seventy-three persons. But the priestly writer inserts a command for *Aaron* alone to go up with Moses,⁶⁴ a command, however, which is nowhere carried out. In the Original Story Aaron figures conspicuously only on two occasions, and then not at all with credit to himself— first, in the affair of the Golden Calf,⁶⁵ next on the occasion where Aaron and Miriam 'speak against Moses,' saying, 'Hath JEHOVAH indeed spoken only by Moses? Hath He not spoken also by us?' and both are severely rebuked by JEHOVAH, and Miriam is smitten with leprosy.⁶⁶ In the later insertions once indeed Moses and Aaron together provoke JEHOVAH by a fit of impatience,⁶⁷ for which they are doomed never to set their feet upon the soil of Canaan.⁶⁸ But everywhere Aaron stands in the foreground of the picture almost as much as Moses, and himself receives Divine communications without the intervention or even the presence of Moses.⁶⁹ In short, in the Original Story Aaron throughout appears not as a priest at all, but merely as a subordinate colleague of Moses,⁷⁰ apparently a fellow-leader with Moses and Miriam.⁷¹ And so says the prophet Micah, 'I brought thee out of the land of Egypt, and redeemed thee out of the house of servants, and I sent before thee Moses, Aaron, and Miriam';⁷² and this is the only passage in all the prophetical books in which Aaron is even mentioned. It may be noticed also that in the priestly insertions, though Aaron indeed, as also Eleazar, his son and successor, is ranked after Moses, yet Eleazar is always placed before Joshua, the ecclesiastical before the civil chief.⁷³

---

⁶³ E. xxiv. 1, 9. ⁶⁴ E. xix. 24. ⁶⁵ E. xxxii. 1-5, 21-25.
⁶⁶ N. xii. ⁶⁷ N. xx. 10.
⁶⁸ N. xx. 12, 24, xxvii. 12-14, D. xxxii. 48-52. ⁶⁹ N. xviii. 1, 8, 20.
⁷⁰ E. iv. 14-16, 27-30, v. 1, 4, 20, viii. 8, 12, 25, ix. 27, x. 3, 8, 16, xviii. 12, xxiv. 1, 9, 14, xxxii. 1, 5, N. xiii. 26. ⁷¹ E. xv. 20, N. xii. ⁷² Mic. vi. 4.
⁷³ N. xxxii. 28, xxxiv. 17, J. xiv. 1, xvii. 4, xix. 51, xxi. 1.

It would seem therefore, as I have said, that Aaron owes
his fame as a priest entirely to his priestly Legislation, written
during or after the Captivity. Accordingly he is never even
named in the two Books of Kings, composed by Jeremiah,
himself a priest, before the Captivity; and it is mentioned that
Jeroboam 'made priests from all parts of the people, who
were not of the sons of *Levi*'[14]—it is not said, 'who were not
of the sons of *Aaron*.' So, too, in his prophecies, as observed
in the last Lecture,[15] Jeremiah speaks only of 'the priests the
Levites,' as does his brother priest Ezekiel, the latter also
calling the faithful priests 'the sons of Zadok.' On the other
hand, in the Books of Chronicles, Ezra, and Nehemiah,
written long after the Captivity, when the Levitical Law had
become a recognized part of the Pentateuch, Aaron takes his
place of honour as the head of the priesthood,[16] and the
Levites are everywhere distinguished from the priests,[17] and
stand in due subordination to the 'sons of Aaron.'[18]

But perhaps the most striking instance of the manner in
which these later priestly writers have modified the older
narrative in order to support the claims of the priesthood, is
afforded by the account of the rebellion of Korah, Dathan, and
Abiram, as it now lies before us in N.xvi, xvii. The story is
familiar to you all, as having been annually read in the
Sunday Lessons. It tells us how 'Korah son of Izhar, son of
Kohath, son of Levi,' and Dathan and Abiram, sons of
Reuben,[19] 'gathered themselves together against Moses and
against Aaron,' being supported by a formidable band of

---

[14] 1 K. xii. 31.   [15] p. 193.

[16] 1 Ch. vi. 3, 49, 50, xii. 27, xv. 4, xxiii. 13, 28, 32, xxiv. 1, 19, 31, xxvii. 17. 2 Ch. xiii. 9,
10, xxvi. 18, xxix. 21, xxxi. 19, xxxv. 14, Ezr. vii. 5, Neh. x. 38, xii. 47.

[17] *e.g.* 1 Ch. ix. 2, 2 Ch. v. 12, Ezr. vi. 18, viii. 15, Neh. x. 38, xiii. 5.

[18] 1 Ch. vi. 48, 49, xxiii. 27, 28, 2 Ch. viii. 14, xxix. 16, xxxv. 11, Neh. xii. 47.

[19] N. xvi. 1 : as nothing more is said about 'On son of Peleth' in this story or
in any of the other places where this rebellion is mentioned (N. xxvi. 9, D. xi. 6,
Ps. cvi. 17), it is probable that there has been here some mistake in copying, and
that 'Peleth' is a corruption for 'Pallu,' so that the passage should run 'Dathan
and Abiram, sons of Eliab, son of Pallu, son of Reuben.'

Levites and laymen [60]—how Moses uttered an indignant rebuke to the ambitious Levites, 'Hear, I pray you, ye sons of Levi! Is it little for you that the God of Israel has separated you from the congregation of Israel to bring you near to Himself, to do the service of the Tabernacle of JEHOVAH, and to stand before the Congregation to minister unto them? Yea, he hath brought thee near and all thy brethren the sons of Levi with thee: and seek ye the priesthood also?' [61]—how in the end the earth opened her mouth and swallowed up Dathan and Abiram and their families,[62] while Korah and his company of incense-bearers were struck dead by lightning,[63] and then the warning is given that none but those of the seed of Aaron should presume to offer incense on pain of similar destruction [64]—how the people murmured against Moses and Aaron for the doom which had overtaken their fellows,[65] and a plague broke out, which was stopped by the act of Aaron, who 'ran and put on incense and made an atonement for the people, and he stood between the dead and the living, and the plague was stayed' [66]—how after this Moses by Divine Command took twelve rods for the twelve tribes, and laid them up before JEHOVAH in the Tabernacle, and in the morning 'lo! the rod of Aaron for the House of Levi' budded and blossomed [67]—and how this 'rod of Aaron that budded' was ordered to be kept as a token against the rebels,[68] and the terrified people exclaimed, 'Lo! we die! we perish! we all perish! whosoever cometh at all near unto the Tabernacle of JEHOVAH shall die: shall we be consumed with dying?' [69] Then in the next chapter the priests and Levites are introduced as bearing in their different degrees this awful burden of approaching the Sanctuary on behalf of their lay brethren,[70] 'that there be no more wrath

[60] v. 2, 7.   [61] v. 8-10.   [62] v. 32-34.   [67] v. 35.
[64] v. 40.   [65] v. 41.   [66] v. 47, 48.   [68] N. xvii. 1-8.
[63] N. xvi. 10.   [69] v. 12, 13.   [70] N. xviii. 1-7.

upon the children of Israel,' 'and the stranger that cometh nigh shall be put to death.'[91] And after this abundant supplies are secured for the priests and Levites from the sacrifices, firstlings, firstfruits, and vows and tithes;[92] and so the priesthood, with its servants the Levites, is not only established, but richly endowed in Israel, not by human laws, but on the direct authority of JEHOVAH Himself!

Now out of all this legislation in the interest of the priests not one word belongs to the Original Story, which spoke only of the rebellion of Dathan and Abiram against Moses, and made no mention at all of Korah, or of Aaron and the rights of the priesthood. This appears at once from the manner in which the Deuteronomist refers to this affair—'and what He did unto Dathan and Abiram, sons of Eliab, son of Reuben, how the earth opened her mouth and swallowed them up, and their households and their tents, and all the substance that was in their possession in the midst of all Israel.'[93] You see that nothing is here said about Korah, or the two hundred and fifty men, 'princes of the Assembly, famous in the Congregation, men of renown,'[94] who were burnt with 'fire from JEHOVAH.'[95] In fact, the Original Story records a *lay* rebellion against Moses, the leader and ruler chosen by JEHOVAH, the idea of which was perhaps suggested by the rebellious feelings entertained by the Ten Tribes towards the House of David and the supremacy of Judah from the first, especially in the time of David himself,[96] during which this passage was probably written. And this story, as it lay before the eyes of the Deuteronomist, can still be taken out as a complete consistent narrative,[97] leaving behind Korah, and Aaron, and all the priestly elements, which have been added in a totally different style and phraseology, *viz.* that which marks throughout the Later Legislation. And, no doubt, these in-

[91] v. 3, 4, 5, 7.   [92] v. 8–32.   [93] D. xi. 6.   [94] N. xvi. 2.   [95] v. 35.
[96] 2 S. ii. 8, 9, iii. 1, xix. 43, xx. 1, 2, 1 K. xii. 16–20, 26.   [97] See *App.* II.

sertions tell us indirectly of some fierce struggle of the leading Levitical families against the claims of the priesthood to lord it over them, on the return from the Captivity.

Thus the driest details of the Levitical Law, rightly understood, become invested with real historical interest and meaning for us, though they reveal to us the history of times far later than those of Moses and the Exodus. But certainly the result of these enquiries makes the patent peculiarity of the Jewish history, the cessation of the prophetical spirit after the Captivity, intelligible and highly instructive, instead of its being, as it used to appear, while it was supposed that the Levitical system had all along coexisted with the prophets, an unaccountable mystery. That the free utterance of the Spirit of God should have been stifled beneath the mass of minute ritualism imposed by the Later Legislation in the name of God, is very conceivable. But how remarkable is this phenomenon, and how instructive! For centuries we find the great prophets of Israel struggling to deliver their countrymen from slavery to the Sun-Gods and other 'Lords' with their bloody and licentious rites; they succeed at last with the aid of the Babylonish Captivity: a race of pure JEHOVAH-worshippers returns to Jerusalem: and lo! their first act is to enslave the minds of their descendants beneath the yoke of priestly ordinances, from which it required the teaching of Jesus, and the irruption of the Gentile world into the fold of the Church through the breach which St. Paul made in the name of Jesus, to save men's minds: and the seed of the rescued have employed their freedom in erecting a new set of prison-walls for the spirit of man under the sanction of the Church! And now, when our martyred Reformers have laid down their lives to secure for us the enjoyment of that liberty wherewith Christ has made us free as children of God, the priestly spirit is at work again, to quench, if possible, the light of Science, to suppress the Truth, and to bring back the pernicious system which we thought had been banished from our Church for ever!

The truth is, that the ritualistic system is for not a few of its votaries, clergy and laity, but a means of escaping from the duty which is laid upon us of pondering solemnly those great questions which occupy—and in God's good Providence were *meant* to occupy—the present age. It may avail as a temporary expedient, in a time of transition like this, to block out anxious thought upon such questions, and may help to fill up in some measure the vacuum which would otherwise exist in the minds of many, who live in ignorance of the grand results of scientific enquiry on this and other domains, and who are content to do so, rather than be troubled with 'doubts' which they have been taught by their religious directors to regard as 'sins'—as sparks of hellish fire, to be stamped out as if proceeding from the fuse of a 'loaded shell shot into the fortress of the soul'[*] by the Great Enemy, when in reality they were signs of a Divine Fire, which has been kindled in our midst in these days by the Spirit of God, as in the days of the First Reformation. But this state of things can only last for a while. By degrees the light and life, which are God's precious gifts to the present age, will penetrate into every corner of Society. And, as surely as the Earth's motion around the Sun, though once condemned as heretical and blasphemous, is now recognised as a fact to be taught as elementary knowledge in the commonest village-school, so before long will the non-Mosaic origin and the unhistorical character of the whole Pentateuchal story, together with the very late date of the Levitical Legislation, be regarded as established facts in Biblical Instruction, in the Pulpit and the Sunday-school—through the very touch of which the whole foundation of the priestly and ritualistic system crumbles at once into dust.

[*] Bp. Wilberforce.

LECTURE XVI.

SUMMARY.

THE L. L. enforces with like severity the paramount sanctity of the priesthood and a minute ritualism, and especially enjoins the observance of the sabbath before any sabbath-law had been given; this severity more apparent than real, as shown in the account of the slaughter of the Midianites; the L. L. repeats incidents of the O.S.; it makes a pretence of strict historical accuracy, as in the numberings of the people; it makes an absurdly extravagant provision for the three priests and their families, as also for the Levites; the Levitical cities never existed; the Day of Atonement was unknown before the Captivity; the Sabbatical year, as prescribed in the L. L., a mistaken perversion of the original institution, was not observed till after the Captivity, and the Jubilee never at all; the New Bible Commentary evades the difficulty by ascribing such laws to Moses, not to Jehovah.

THE LATE DATE OF THE LEVITICAL LEGISLATION.

WE have seen that the priestly writers of the Levitical Law were very zealous in advancing the interests of their order, and never hesitate to secure their dignity and their emoluments by appeals to Divine injunctions, and Divine judgments for neglect or disregard of them. Now and then, indeed, a warning is given to the priests themselves, as when Nadab and Abihu, the eldest sons of Aaron, are struck by lightning for offering incense with unhallowed fire,[1] when apparently in a state of intoxication, since it follows immediately—'And JEHOVAH spake unto Aaron saying, Drink no wine nor strong drink, thou nor thy sons with thee, when ye go into the Tent of Meeting, lest ye die.'[2] But elsewhere these same threats are used to enforce the sanctity of the priests above the Levites,[3] and of both above the laity,[4] or else to punish a number of most trivial, as well as more serious, offences against the ritual law. Thus the doom of death or of excommunication is pronounced against any who should 'compound any ointment like the holy ointment, or put any of it upon a stranger,'[5] or 'make any scent like the holy perfume,'[6] or eat

[1] L. x. 1, 2.   [2] v. 8, 9.   [3] N. iii. 10, 38, xvi. 40.
[4] N. i. 51, xviii. 22.   [5] E. xxx. 33.   [6] v. 38.

of the sacrifices being unclean,⁷ as by touching for instance a dead snail.⁸ In this Law also the Sabbath is enforced with very strict injunctions,⁹ and in one place before any Sabbath-law had been given;¹⁰ just as Aaron is said to have 'laid up a pot of manna before the Testimony,'¹¹ when as yet no Ark or Testimony existed, and no hint had been given about Aaron's priesthood, or just as Moses under Sinai is made to order the 'priests that come near to JEHOVAH' to 'sanctify themselves, lest JEHOVAH break forth upon them,'¹² when as yet there were no such priests, but 'young men of the children of Israel' offered sacrifices,¹³ and a 'young man, Joshua, the servant of Moses,' kept watch and slept in the Tent of Meeting.¹⁴ Moreover, the violation of the Sabbath by doing any kind of work, such as lighting a fire, was by this Law to be punished with death;¹⁵ and the decree in this case is enforced by the example of a man being stoned, by express command of JEHOVAH, for 'gathering sticks on the Sabbath-day.'¹⁶ This passage, however, is shown to be one of the very latest insertions in the Pentateuch, not merely by its general agreement in style and language with the other portions of this Levitical Legislation, but expressly by its close resemblance to another passage, where a man is in like manner stoned for blaspheming 'the Name'¹⁷—not 'the name of JEHOVAH,' but simply 'the Name'.¹⁸—an expression used by superstitious Jews in later times to avoid mention of the Divine Name; as the Greek translators always substitute for JEHOVAH the expression 'the Lord,' which has been copied in the later Vulgate, and unfortunately retained in our English Version. But it is plain that all this severity, like that in Deuteronomy against the nations in Canaan,¹⁹ is more appa-

---

⁷ L. vii. 20.   ⁸ L. xi. 29-31.   ⁹ E. xxxi. 12-17.
¹⁰ E. xvi. 22-30.   ¹¹ v. 34.   ¹² E. xix. 22, 24.
¹³ E. xxiv. 5.   ¹⁴ E. xxxiii. 11.   ¹⁵ E. xxxv. 1-3.
¹⁶ N. xv. 32-36.   ¹⁷ L. xxiv. 10-16.   ¹⁸ v. 12, 16.   ¹⁹ p. 178-9.

rent than real, and is intended merely to deter from the commission of such offences—with this difference, however, that the Deuteronomist, in the true spirit of a prophet, wishes to prevent the Israelites from taking part in the debasing idolatries of heathen worship, which militated with inward purity of heart, whereas the Levitical Law denounces chiefly breaches of mere ceremonial law, which, according to priestly notions, interfered with the observance of the command 'Be ye holy, for I am holy.'[m]

For instance, when the priestly writer tells us that 12,000 Israelites 'avenged JEHOVAH on Midian'[n] by killing in battle 88,000 warriors, and then butchering in cold blood 88,000 women and girls and 32,000 boys, carrying off also as slaves 32,000 young female children,[o] he apparently feels no horror or compunction at recording these facts, but coolly describes the deliberate massacre of so many thousand defenceless persons as a religious act. He is anxious, however, that the booty taken in cattle and slaves shall be properly divided, the priests and Levites getting, of course, their shares,[p] including 'JEHOVAH's tribute' of 32 young female slaves for the priests,[q] as also that the chief actors in the affair shall be duly 'cleansed'—' Abide ye in the Camp seven days; whosoever hath killed any person, and whosoever hath touched any slain, purify both yourselves and your captives on the third day and on the seventh day; and ye shall wash your clothes on the seventh day and be clean, and afterwards ye shall come into the Camp.'[r] Happily, this frightful butchery, exceeding infinitely in atrocity the tragedy at Cawnpore, has been carried out only on paper. Still it shows how the writer's mind must have been warped and corrupted, that he

---

[m] L. xi. 44, 45.   [n] N. xxxi. 3.
[o] v. 7, 17, 18, 35 : 32,000 young girls—say under 15 years—imply at least 8,000 females under 20, and 80,000 over 20, that is, 88,000 women and full-grown girls, and consequently 88,000 men and full-grown youths, and 32,000 boys.
[p] N. xxxi. 25–30.   [q] v. 40, 41.   [r] v. 19, 24.

could even compose such a narrative as this, without being sensible of the violence done by it to our best feelings as men, unless indeed our own minds, as the result of long-continued traditionary teaching, have been warped and corrupted also. But he further assures us, in utter defiance of reason and common-sense, that all this was done, and 800,000 head of cattle carried off, by 12,000 Israelites without the loss of a single man [56]—not one of the 80,000 warriors having struck a death-blow in defence of his life and all he held dear on earth —not one even of the 88,000 women and girls or 32,000 boys having struck down one of the murderers, who had killed their parents and children, husbands and brothers and sisters, and were now about to butcher themselves. And he tells us that the captains brought, as a thank-offering for this immunity, a magnificent present for the Sanctuary, 'jewels of gold, chains and bracelets, rings, earrings, and tablets,' 'to make atonement for their souls.'[57] It is surely time in this age of the world that the true account of this matter should be clearly given, instead of attempting to defend this narrative as real history, as the New Commentary does by saying—' No doubt, a general license to slay at pleasure could hardly have been given without demoralising those employed. But the commission of the Israelites in the text must not be so conceived. They had no discretion to kill or spare. They were bidden to exterminate without mercy, and brought back to their task when they showed signs of flinching.'[58]

Whenever, in fact, the priestly writer steps out of his favourite beaten track of mere ritualistic legislation and passes into narrative, his stories have often a gloomy—even at times a savage—character,[59] very different from the life-like spirited sketches of the Jehovist; and they show, moreover, great sameness and poverty of invention. Thus, instead of intro-

[56] v. 5, 49.   [57] v. 50–54.   [58] B.C., I. p. 766.
[59] L. x. 1, 2, xxiv. 10–16, N. xv. 32–36, xvi. 35–50, xxv. 6–15, xxxi.

ducing new incidents, he merely repeats before the arrival at Sinai the accounts of the manna and the quails,[30] using sometimes the very words of the older writer at a later point of the wanderings,[31] and introducing here, as I have said, the Ark and the priesthood of Aaron out of their proper place,[32] so betraying at once the unhistorical character of his additions. And in other instances his own statements help very much to betray this, and thus to undo in some measure the evil of his work, as we have just seen in the case of the exaggerated account of the slaughter of the Midianites. But so, too, in numbering the people, the priestly writer shows a deliberate purpose to give to his statements an *appearance* of strict historical accuracy. The Original Story had spoken of the host of Israel as consisting of 'about 600,000 men besides women and children'[33]—an enormous number truly, which implies an entire population of about three millions; and since there were in the wilderness no upper and lower stories, no garrets or underground cellars, none of the appliances for crowding which a great city provides, but all lived upon the ground in tents, the whole encampment would have covered about the same area as LONDON. And, of course, the question would immediately arise as to how such a vast population could have found wood and water in the barren waste, or pasture for their innumerable flocks and herds, if they themselves were fed all along on manna—though the story seems not to have contemplated this, but only to mean that manna was afforded on two separate occasions.[34] Above all, after the well-known experience of only 20,000 at the Diamond Fields, with a splendid river within their reach, we might well ask how this immense Camp, without any sewage arrangements and with very scanty supplies of water, could have kept free from pollution and fever. In short, a multitude of such

[30] E. xvi. [32] v. 13b, 14, 31, comp. N. xi. 7, 8b, 9.
[31] v. 33, 34. [33] E. xii. 37, N. xi. 21. [34] E. xvi, N. xi. 4-9.

questions might be asked, and have been asked, and the difficulty of replying to them has been so great that one Commentator has been driven to the necessity of suggesting that for 600,000 we should read 60,000, when 'all would be clear, every numerical difficulty worth thinking of would vanish at once'; though he adds in a note on the very same page, 'Notwithstanding the admitted difficulty of the large numbers, it is very questionable whether the difficulties would not be greater on the supposition that the number were very much less'?[36]

But it may be fairly assumed that this sum-total of 600,000 warriors was only set down hastily, without due consideration of the consequences, by one who was recording an imaginary story, but had probably no idea of teaching it as actual historical fact. It is very different when we turn to the priestly writer, and find that, not content with the number as originally given, 'about 600,000', he has defined the total accurately as 603,550,[36] dividing it carefully among the twelve tribes; though, strangely enough, the number for each tribe is given as so many *round hundreds*,[37] except one with an odd fifty,[38] and, still more strangely, the number of the whole host is identically the same as he represents it to have been six months previously,[39] as if the number of warriors who had become full-grown in the interval had exactly equalled the number of those who had passed beyond the military age or died! But he is not even content with this. He records another numbering thirty-eight years afterwards, at the end of the wanderings, where the separate numbers for the different tribes are all, as before, *round hundreds*,[40] except one with an odd thirty,[41] and are most artificially constructed, six tribes having more than 50,000 at each numbering, and six less,

---

[36] Bp. Browne (*Elak. Psalms*, p. 26.)
[37] N.i.21,23,27,&c.
[38] N.xxvi.14,18,22,&c.
[39] v.25.
[40] v.7.
[41] N.i.46,ii.32.
[42] E.xxxviii.26.

some being increased in the interval and some diminished, but so that the total is nearly the same on the second occasion as on the first, *viz.* 601,730,[40] implying that, through a Divine Judgment for their offences, the population, instead of increasing, had slightly diminished in the wilderness.

So, again, the prodigious provision made for the support of the priesthood—the breast and the hind-leg of all the peace-offerings, the whole of the sin-offerings and trespass-offerings, except the suet burnt upon the altar, all of the meal-offerings except a handful burnt as a memorial, all the firstfruits, all the firstlings, all the votive offerings, and one-tenth of all the tithes,[42] from a population like that of LONDON, having vast multitudes of sheep and oxen,[44] is made—for whom?—for just *three* priests, Aaron and his sons,[45] Eleazar and Ithamar, and their families, these two having been introduced by the priestly writer,[46] apparently to supply the place of Nadab and Abihu killed (according to him), by lightning,[47] Aaron having only these two sons in the Original Story,[48] as Moses also had only two sons.[49] For instance, the 'sin-offerings' were to be eaten only by the males 'in the most holy place';[50] and the pigeons or turtle-doves alone, to be brought as sin-offerings for the birth of children[51] for three millions of people, would have averaged about 250 a day,[53] or more than 96,000 annually, and all to be eaten by three priests 'in the most holy place'!—to say nothing about the possibility of such numbers of pigeons or turtle-doves having been obtained in the wilderness. It might be supposed that these provisions were intended for after-time, when the people would be settled in Canaan, and the number of priests would be increased, though indeed there would

---

[40] v. 51. [42] N. xviii. 8–19, 25–28. [44] N. xxxi. 32–34, xxxii. 1.
[45] N. xviii. 8, E. vi. 23. [46] E. xxviii. 1.
[47] L. i. 1, 2, 6, 12, 16, N. iii. 2, 4, xxvi. 60, 61. [48] E. xxiv. 1, 9.
[49] E. xviii. 3, 4. [50] N. xviii. 9, 10. [51] L. xii. 6.
[53] The births in LONDON for a week (*Times*, Sept. 3, 1862) were 1,852.

seem to have been only three at Shiloh in Eli's time.⁵⁵ But not a trace of such intention really appears in the narrative. On the contrary some of the Levitical Laws are introduced with the words 'When ye be come into the land of Canaan,'⁵⁶ and are thus expressly distinguished from the rest of that legislation; while in others the 'Camp' is mentioned,⁵⁵ implying therefore that they were meant to be put in force in the wilderness. In short, the unhistorical character of these laws is self-evident: they are merely insertions of later priestly writers.

So, too, the Levites, numbered as 22,000 males of all ages,⁵⁶ implying about 12,000 adults, are to have the tithes of 600,000 Israelites;⁵⁷ so that each single Levite, without his own labour or that of his family, was to receive as much as *five* Israelites obtained by their daily toil!—except a tenth which was to go to the three priests,⁵⁸ each of whom, therefore, was to receive as much as four hundred Levites, or two thousand Israelites!! Here, again, the unhistorical character of this legislation is obvious, in spite of the argument which has been urged that 'tithes are never paid punctiliously, and were then without doubt paid with just as little conscientiousness as now, when the tithe-owners often scarcely receive the twentieth.'⁵⁹ But this is represented not as a *human* law, but as a Divine Command, which was meant to be religiously obeyed.

Once more, in the Levitical Law, forty-eight cities with their suburbs are assigned to the Levites,⁶⁰ of which thirteen —that is, about a fourth of the whole—are given to the 'sons of Aaron the priests'⁶¹—out of all proportion, of course, to their relative numbers, which were as one to 4,000; nor is it

---

⁵⁵ 1 S. ii. 12–17, 34. ⁵⁶ L. xiv. 34, xix. 23, xxiii. 10, xxv. 2, N. xv. 2, 18, xxxiv. 2.
⁵⁷ L. iv. 12, 21, vi. 11, xiii. 46, xiv. 3, 8, xvi. 26, 27, 28, xvii. 3, N. xix. 3, 7, 9.
⁵⁸ N. iii. 39.   ⁵⁹ N. xviii. 21–24.   ⁶⁰ N. xviii. v. 25–28.
⁶¹ Keil, II. p. 266.   ⁶² N. xxxv. 1–7.   ⁶³ J. xxi. 13–19.

easy to see what two priests and their children and grandchildren—for Eleazar was still living[10]—would have done with thirteen cities. But, very singularly, these thirteen priestly cities are all fixed in the territories of Judah and Benjamin, that is, close to the site of the future Temple, conveniently for the future priests; and this is supposed to be done at a time when the Temple was not even thought of, and Mount Zion was still, and remained for centuries afterwards, in the hands of the Jebusites, the original inhabitants of the land![42] Moreover, we find in Deuteronomy a merciful provision that there shall be six 'cities of refuge,' to which one who had killed another accidentally might flee and be safe from the avenger of blood. In his main address Moses merely directs the people to sever three cities in Canaan itself for this purpose, and, if their land be enlarged, to add three more,[43] which, however, in the four chapters afterwards prefixed, the writer inadvertently makes Moses do himself.[44] It need hardly be said that these six 'cities of refuge,' three on each side of the Jordan, are included by the priestly legislator among the Levitical cities.[45] These cities, however, are mentioned long before,[46] but most abruptly, before a word has been said to explain the reason for which they were to be set apart. It is possible that the writer really expected this arrangement to be carried out, at least to some extent, after the return from the Captivity. But, however this may be, there is no sign in the history that any such cities were ever at any time recognized in Israel; and Nob, the 'city of the priests' which Saul ravaged, was not one of the Levitical cities.

Nor is there any sign before the Captivity of the Day of Atonement having been kept, the observance of which as a day of fasting, on *the tenth day of the seventh month*, is strictly

[a] v. 1. [b] aS.v.6-9. [c] D.xix.1-7,8-10.
[d] D.v.41-43. [e] N.xxxv.6. [f] L.xxv.32,33.

required in the Levitical Law under pain of death.[68] The Deuteronomist does not mention it, and it is plain that Ezekiel knew nothing about it, since, while giving special directions for the Passover, the Feast of Unleavened Bread, and the Feast of Tabernacles,[69] he appoints an atonement to be made annually for the Sanctuary and people, very similar to that ordered for the Day of Atonement, and perhaps the original type of the latter, on *the first and seventh days of the first month*.[70] But *after the Captivity* we find this fasting-day strictly observed, so as to be called simply 'the day.'[71]

The Sabbatical year is also enjoined in this Law, JEHOVAH being introduced as saying, 'in the seventh year there shall be a sabbath of rest for the land, a sabbath for JEHOVAH: thou shalt neither sow thy field nor prune thy vineyard; that which groweth of its own accord of thy harvest thou shalt not reap, neither gather of thy undressed vine : it is a year of rest for the land.'[72] What a dreary injunction must this have been for the active husbandman, who for a whole year would be thus compelled to absolute idleness, when all his fellow-men in cities and towns were as busy as ever ! But how would the vine prosper, if left unpruned ? Or would the land have had a 'year of rest' from producing weeds ? The fact is that the more ancient law, on which this is based, says nothing about the *land* resting. It says only 'Six years thou shalt sow thy land and gather its produce. And the seventh year thou shalt let *it* rest and lie still '—*it*, that is, the *produce*, not the land —'that the poor of thy people may eat, and *what they leave*'—which of itself implies a plentiful yield, not the scanty gleanings of untilled land—' the beasts of the field shall eat. So shalt thou do to thy vineyard, to thine oliveyard.'[73] This law, however, which meant that the farmer

---

[68] L. xvi. 29-34, xxiii. 26-32, N. xxix. 7-11.   [69] E. xlv. 21-25.
[70] v. 18-20.   [71] JOSEPH. *Ant.* XIV. xvi. 4, III. x. 3, Acts, xxvii. 9.
[72] L. xxv. 4, 5.   [73] E. xxiii. 10, 11.

should cultivate his land as usual in the seventh year, but for the benefit of the poor and needy, seems to have been wholly neglected in actual practice, as well as that other law which orders that, after six years' service, every Hebrew slave shall go free, if he will.[14] And so at last the Deuteronomist directs that every seventh year shall be a 'year of release' for all Hebrew debtors and slaves;[15] and, instead of repeating the older law about the crops being left in the seventh year for the use of the poor, he prescribes that *every* year the tithes shall be employed for feasting, in which the poor and the Levite shall be allowed to share.[16] This command for the liberation of Hebrew slaves was once actually carried out in Zedekiah's reign,[17] very probably under Jeremiah (the Deuteronomist)'s influence; though he bitterly reproaches and terribly threatens the king, the princes, and the people, for retracing the step, and bringing back their manumitted slaves into servitude again.[18] Perhaps they had come to understand that the provision in Deuteronomy had no real Mosaic authority; though surely it was a humane and merciful law, from whatever pen it proceeded. But the later priestly writer changes the whole character of the original command. 'That which groweth of itself' in the Sabbatical year, from the untilled lands and unpruned vines, is not here to be left wholly to the poor and the beasts, as before, but is to be food for the owner and his family, and the 'sojourner,' the cattle, and the beasts;[19] and it is further promised that in the sixth year the land 'shall bring forth fruit for three years.'[20] Thus the benevolent purpose of the original institution is turned into a mere empty show of reverence for God, the result being that no *charity* whatever is here enjoined; for the farmer is only to give away, and that partially, the scantier produce of the seventh year, and is to keep for himself the

---

[14] Exd. 2-6. [15] D. xv. 1-18. [16] D. xiv. 22-29. [17] Jer. xxxiv. 8-11.
[18] v. 11-22. [19] L. xxv. 6, 7. [20] v. 20-22.

threefold produce of the sixth year, spending the seventh in idleness unpleasing to God and unprofitable to man! We learn from Josephus [a] that the Sabbatical Year was kept in this way, but only *after the Captivity*.

The Levitical Law institutes also the 'Year of Jubilee,' that is, the fiftieth year was also to be kept as a Sabbatical Year ; [b] and, perhaps, the threefold crops in every sixth year may have been provided with a view to the Jubilee being kept immediately after the forty-ninth year, that is, the seventh Sabbatical Year, so that *two* Sabbatical Years would come together. But there is no trace of the Jubilee having ever been kept, before or after the Captivity.

It is painful to mark these proceedings of the later priesthood. But, at all events, it is a blessing to have our minds relieved from the burden of receiving such laws as the express utterances of the Most High. The New Commentary evades the difficulty by speaking continually as if it was only *Moses* who enacted them—*e.g.* 'The Jubilee, as *instituted by Moses*, is without a parallel in the history of the world ' [c]—or again ' It is assumed that *Moses could not have foreseen* that the Sabbatical Year would be neglected ' [d]—or again, ' *Moses knew the human heart*, and he was acquainted with the temper and disposition of the people. . . . *The legislator knew that his words would be but imperfectly obeyed.*' [e] But this is to heap one delusion on another. These laws are represented as Divinely given: throughout it is JEHOVAH 'speaking unto Moses and saying.' [f] And our duty is to look the truth in the face, and so relieve both our own consciences from infinite pain and perplexity, and the character of Moses himself from the reproach which the work of these priestly writers would otherwise fasten upon him. We now know that the whole

---

[a] JOSEPH. *Ant.*XI.viii.6,XIV.x.6,xvi.2,XV.i.2, *comp.* 1 Macc. vi. 49, 53.
[b] L. xxv. 8–12. [c] *B.C.* I. p. 636. [d] *Ib.* p. 640.
[e] *Ib.* p. 643. [f] L. i. 1, iv. 1, v. 14, &c.

THE LEVITICAL LEGISLATION. 227

ritualistic legislation, with its multiplied ordinances, 'Touch not, taste not, handle not,'[87] is but the 'commandment and doctrine of men,'[88] of fallible men, like ourselves, but of men possessed by the priestly spirit, which has always been antagonistic to the free Gospel of the Grace of God—that Gospel which makes the sign of a Christian's faithfulness to consist, not in the performance of rites and ceremonies or the maintenance of dogmas and creeds, but in 'putting on Christ,'[89] in practising love to God and Man after Christ's example[90]— which tells us that 'Now abideth faith, hope, charity, these three: but the greatest of these is charity.'[91]

[87] Col. ii. 21. [89] Matt. xv. 9. [91] Rom. xiii. 14.
[88] Matt. xxii. 35-40. [90] 1 Cor. xiii. 13.

LECTURE XVII.

SUMMARY.

Signs of progress in the legislation of different ages; the Mosaic Tabernacle specially related to the Second Temple; indications that the splendid Mosaic Ark never existed; the real ark of the Exodus; the original account of its construction suppressed, and the 'ark of the covenant' of the O.S. replaced in the L.L. by the 'Ark of the Testimony'; the original notice of the separation of the tribe of Levi as the priestly caste suppressed to make room for the later account of the institution of the Priests and the Levites; the Bible, though taken from us as an idol, restored to us as the work of living men; contrast between its priestly and prophetical portions.

THE ARK AND THE PRIESTHOOD IN THE ORIGINAL STORY.

IN my last Lecture I drew your attention to certain institutions of the Priestly Legislation of the Pentateuch, some of which, as the Year of Jubilee and the Levitical Cities, appear never to have been carried out at all in practice, while others, as the Day of Atonement and the Sabbatical Year, were observed only in later days, after the return from the Babylonish Captivity, giving thus a plain indication of the later age which gave birth to them. The last of these, we saw, was merely an injudicious rendering of a much older law, which had first passed through the hands of the Deuteronomist, and by him had been already modified in accordance with the needs of his own time.[1] And so in other instances it is interesting to trace the progress of legislation from the earlier to the later age. Thus the oldest writer in Genesis records the command, as given to Noah after the Flood, 'not to eat flesh with its soul, its blood';[2] the later Deuteronomist repeats this, but adds thrice the injunction to 'pour the blood upon the ground as water';[3] the still later priestly writer orders the blood not only to be poured out, but to be 'covered with dust,' and

---

[1] p. 224.   [2] G. ix. 4.   [3] D. xii. 16, 24, xv. 23.

extends the law to sojourners as well as home-born Israelites. Again, the Deuteronomist gives a list of unclean animals, whose flesh was not to be eaten, and among these he reckons 'every swarming-thing that flieth.'[6] The later priestly legislator corrects this too hasty generalisation, by permitting the use of four forms of the locust.[4] So with respect to an animal 'dying of itself or torn,' the Original Story says 'ye shall not eat it, to the dogs ye shall cast it';[7] the Deuteronomist also forbids such flesh being eaten by any Israelite, but adds—'to the sojourner that is in thy gates shalt thou give it that he may eat it, or sell it to a stranger';[8] the priestly writer assumes that Israelites generally may freely eat of such meat, but provides that 'every soul that shall eat anything dying of itself or torn, whether homeborn or sojourner, shall wash his clothes and bathe with water, and be unclean until the evening, and then he shall be clean.'[9] He forbids only the *priests* to eat anything 'fallen or torn.'[10] It is plain that this law, which allows all Israelites except the priests to eat such flesh, cannot possibly have been issued, as would appear from its present position in the Pentateuch, *between* the other two laws, each of which forbids such food to all Israelites. So, too, it cannot be supposed that the laws in the Book of Numbers,[11] which secure to the priests and Levites such a sumptuous maintenance on the authority of JEHOVAH Himself, giving the firstlings wholly to the priests and the tithes to the Levites,[12] should have been *afterwards* modified by Moses in Deuteronomy, assigning much smaller perquisites from the sacrifices,[13] and expressly enjoining the householder to feast with his family and servants upon these very same firstlings and tithes,[14] only not to forget the stranger, and the

---

[4] L. xvii. 13, comp. Ez. xxiv. 7, 8.   [5] D. xiv. 19.
[6] L. xi. 20-23.   [7] E. xxii. 31.   [8] D. xiv. 21.
[9] L. xvii. 15.   [10] L. xxii. 8, comp. Ez. xliv. 31, iv. 14.
[11] N. xviii. 8, &c.   [12] v. 17, 18, 24.   [13] D. xvii. 3, comp. N. xviii. 18.
[14] D. xiv. 23-29.

orphan, and the widow, and the *Levite*.[15] It is plain that the more bountiful provision was the latest of the two; and, indeed, we may be sure that the priests and Levites would never have abandoned such ample rights secured to them, it is supposed, by the Divine Lawgiver.

Further, the description in Exodus of the Tabernacle and its vessels betrays a singular relation to the Second Temple, built after the return from the Captivity. It has been ascertained that the dimensions of every part of the Tabernacle were exactly half those of the First or Solomon's Temple; and from this it has been inferred that 'the form of the Temple was copied from the Tabernacle.'[16] But how is it that not the least allusion is made to so important a fact in the account of the building of that Temple? Or how came it to pass that Solomon made for his Temple a golden altar of incense, a golden table of shewbread, golden candlesticks and bowls and snuffers and basons and spoons,[17] if these vessels existed already, made by Divine Command after a heavenly model shown to Moses in the Mount?[18] Rather, the arrangements of the Tabernacle do indeed generally correspond with those of the First Temple, as well as the Second, since the latter was, no doubt, copied in most respects from the former; but on some points they vary from those of the First Temple, and here they are found to agree with the Second. Thus in Solomon's Temple there were folding-doors, which closed the entrance to the Holy of Holies;[19] but in the Second Temple there was merely a vail,[20] as there was also to be in the Tabernacle.[21] In Solomon's Temple there stood *ten* golden candlesticks, five on the right hand and five on the left.[22] But in the Tabernacle there was to be only *one* seven-branched golden candlestick,[23] and so

[15] v. 27, 29. [16] *Dict. of the Bible*, III. p. 1455-6.
[17] 1 K. vii. 48-50. [18] E. xxx. 1-6, xxv. 23-40. [19] 1 K. vi. 31, 32, vii. 50.
[20] Matt. xxvii. 51, Heb. vi. 19. [21] E. xxvi. 31, &c. [22] 1 K. vii. 49.
[23] E. xxv. 31, &c.

there was only one in the Second Temple,[24] which was represented, as carried in triumphal procession, on the Arch of Titus at Rome.

In the Second Temple, of course, there was no Ark, since that was lost at the Captivity, having probably been destroyed in the conflagration of the City and the Temple. But that the Ark then lost was not the splendid Ark of Exodus —'overlaid within and without with pure gold,' with 'a golden crown, golden rings, and staves overlaid with gold,' and a 'mercy-seat' above it of pure gold, and two golden cherubs on the ends of it'[25]—we may safely conclude, not only from the consideration that so precious an object would hardly have been left to lie neglected in a private house, for many years and that under Samuel's rule,[26] but especially from the fact that no mention is made of its being carried off as spoil by Nebuchadnezzar. The brazen pillars of the Temple are named, the bases, and the brazen sea; 'the pots, and the shovels, and the snuffers, and the spoons, and all the brazen vessels, and the fire-pans, and the bowls, such things as were of gold, in gold, and of silver, in silver, did the captain of the guard take away.'[27] Could the precious golden Ark of Exodus have been omitted in this enumeration, if it really formed part of the plunder? The real ark was probably a mere wooden chest, such as the Egyptians and other nations used for carrying about in procession their sacred mysteries. Accordingly the Original Story speaks of the ark as going before the people in the wilderness 'to search out a resting-place for them,'[28] and again, in the Book of Joshua, as being carried by the priests in procession when they crossed the Jordan on dry ground,[29] and when they marched around the walls of Jericho.[30] In that case such an

[24] 1 Macc. i. 21, iv. 49, 50.
[26] 1 S. vii. 1, 2, comp. 2 S. vi. 2.
[28] N. x. 33.
[29] J. iii. 6.
[25] E. xxv. 11, 13, 17, 18.
[27] 2 K. xxv. 14–16.
[30] J. vi. 8, 9.

ark, however rudely made, would have been venerable for them as the sacred symbol of their religion; but in the eyes of Nebuchadnezzar's captain of the guard it would probably have seemed to be worthless, and would have been left to perish amidst the ruins of the Temple.

But when was this ark made in the Original Story? At present there is no record of its construction: it is suddenly introduced as the 'ark of the Covenant of JEHOVAH.'[31] Now we remember that Moses after breaking the two stone-tables is ordered to make two tables like the first, and to come with them up to the top of the Mount;[32] and at the end of forty days he receives these two tables on which had been inscribed by the Finger of GOD the 'words of the Covenant,'[33] that is, the words in E.xxi-xxiii, 'which were on the first tables which he brake.'[34] And then he comes down 'with the two tables of the Testimony in his hand.'[35] What now did he do with these august tables? There was as yet no proper receptacle for them, as the story now stands; for the Tabernacle was not begun to be made; and six months passed before it was set up,[36] and then, we are told, Moses 'took and put the Testimony—that is, the two stone-tables—into the Ark.'[37] Nor were there even at this later time any priests or Levites as yet consecrated,[38] to take charge of the precious deposit, but Moses himself has to burn the incense and offer the sacrifices on that occasion.[39] It can hardly be meant that these sacred tables were merely to be placed loosely in the tent of Moses, which he had set up outside the Camp, under the charge of 'the young man his servant Joshua.'[40] How then did he dispose of these tables of stone in a manner worthy of their awful character, as containing the words of the

[31] N.x.23.
[32] v.1, see p. 134.
[33] v.20.
[34] E.xxxiii.7-11.
[35] E.xxxiv.1,2.
[36] v.29.
[37] L.viii, N.viii.5-22.
[38] v.28.
[39] E.xl.17.
[40] E.xl.27,29.

Covenant made between JEHOVAH and Israel, engraved by
the very Finger of God?

The Deuteronomist will help us to answer this question.
He had, as we know, the Original Story in his hands, and
can tell us what its contents were before the priestly writers
meddled with it. And this is what he says upon this point:
—'At that time JEHOVAH said unto me, Hew thee two
tables of stone like the first, and come-up unto Me into the
Mount, *and make thee an ark of wood*. And I will write upon
the tables the words that were on the first tables which thou
brakest, *and thou shalt place them in the ark*. *So I made an
ark of shittim-wood*, and I hewed two tables of stone like the
first; and I went up into the Mount, and the two tables were
in my hand. And He wrote upon the tables according to
the first writing, the Ten Words.'[41] Now all this is copied
almost word for word from the account in Exodus,[42] which it
is plain the writer must have had before him; only instead of
'the words of the Covenant,' as it stood in that narrative, he
writes here 'the Ten Words,' referring, of course, to the Ten
Commandments, which he himself had inserted, as having
been spoken by JEHOVAH 'in the Mount out of the midst of
the fire in the day of the Assembly,'[43] but inserted in a place
where (as we have seen [44]) there is really no room for them in
the Original Story. Otherwise this statement is an exact
transcript, as from the mouth of Moses in the first person, of
what is there related of him in the third, except that the
Deuteronomist has here three short clauses, which do not now
appear in the Original Story—'*and make thee an ark of
wood*,' '*and thou shalt place them in the ark*,' '*so I made an
ark of shittim-wood*.' It is plain that he must have had before
him, in the copy which he so closely follows, corresponding
clauses, which were of necessity struck out by the priestly

[41] D. x. 1, 4.   [42] E. xxxiv. 1, 2, 4, 28b.   [43] D. x. 4.   [44] p. 105.

writer when he introduced his own account of the making of the splendid Ark of the Later Legislation.[46] And, of course, when the Deuteronomist makes Moses say in addition, 'And JEHOVAH gave them unto me, and I turned and came-down from the Mount, and put the tables in the ark which I had made, and there they are, as JEHOVAH commanded me,'[46] it is reasonable to believe that corresponding words existed also in his time in the Original Story, which must have been likewise of necessity removed when the priestly writer inserted his own account of the tables being placed in the Ark by Moses half-a-year afterwards.[47]

Thus, then, according to the Original Story, Moses made by Divine Command a simple ark of wood—of shittim-wood, he tells us—as a receptacle for the stone-tables at the same time that he made the tables themselves, and it stood therefore ready to receive them as soon as he came down with them, and it did receive them—'he put the tables in the ark which he had made, as JEHOVAH commanded him.'[48] Henceforth it is always called 'the ark of the covenant of JEHOVAH' in the Original Story of the Pentateuch, as it is also in Deuteronomy,[49] as containing the two tables of the Covenant; whereas throughout the priestly Legislation it is always called 'the Ark of the Testimony.'[50]

But who were to be the guardians of this treasure? The Deuteronomist, with his knowledge of the Original Story in its primitive form, undisturbed by the work of the later priestly legislators, will help us here also. The passage which I have just been quoting from the Book of Deuteronomy is followed by two verses which are quite unintelligible: as one eminent writer notes in his well-known Commentary, 'They so break in upon the connexion of Moses' discourse, and give

---

[45] E. xxv. 16, 22, xxxvii. 1–9.   [46] D. x. 4b, 5.   [47] E. xl. 20.
[48] N. x. 33, xiv. 44.   [49] D. x. 8, xxxi. 9, 25, 26.
[50] E. xxv. 22, xxvi. 33, 34, xxx. 6, 26, xxxi. 7, xxxix. 35, xl. 3, 5, 21, N. iv. 5, vii. 89.

such an account of the names of places, that they perplex commentators';[81] while the New Commentary says, 'It is possible that these two verses may be, as some other notices of a like character, a gloss.'[82] These two verses, in fact, are probably a later priestly insertion, consisting mainly of a fragment belonging to the list of stations in the wilderness in N.xxi of the Original Story, which contained also the statement with reference to one of them, 'there Aaron died and there he was buried'—just exactly as in the same narrative we find it said with reference to Kadesh, 'there Miriam died and there she was buried'[83]—but without any allusion to Aaron's priesthood. To this notice, however, the priestly writer has added 'and Eleazar his son acted-as-priest in his stead'; and by some mistake or accident the whole has been introduced at a point of the story where it is utterly unmeaning, since Moses in the previous context is speaking of their being under Sinai in the *first* year after the march out of Egypt, and Aaron's death occurred, as the story now stands, nearly forty years afterwards.[84]

Passing by, therefore, these two verses we read as follows: —'*At that time* JEHOVAH separated the tribe of Levi to bear the ark of the Covenant of JEHOVAH, to stand before JEHOVAH to minister and to bless in His Name, unto this day. Wherefore Levi hath no part nor inheritance with his brethren: JEHOVAH is his inheritance, as JEHOVAH thy ELOHIM promised him.'[85] Let us mark well what the Deuteronomist here says, who had before him the Original Story in its primitive form. '*At that time*'—which words, says the New Commentary, 'certainly connect themselves with *v.*5, and not with *v.*7'[86]—that is, 'connect themselves' with the passage we have just been considering with reference to the making of the ark under Sinai. 'At that time,' then—*viz.*, at the

---

[81] Rev. Thomas Scott on D.x.6,7. [82] I.p.836. [85] N.xx.1.
[83] N.xxxiii.38. [84] D.x.8,9. [86] I.p.836.

time when Moses came-down from the Mount and put the
tables in the ark which he had made—'JEHOVAH separated
the tribe of Levi'—the *whole tribe*—for the sacred duties of
the priesthood. And now we remember that, only just before,
when Moses had dashed the first pair of tables in pieces at
sight of the Golden Calf, the Levites are said to have come
forward zealously at his summons, as if they also, his fellow-
tribesmen, shared in his abhorrence of this idolatry, and to
have massacred 3,000 of the people, sparing neither kith nor
kin—'for Moses had said, *Consecrate yourselves to-day to*
JEHOVAH, *even every man upon his son and upon his
brother, that He may bestow a blessing upon you this day.*'[57]
What 'blessing' can here be meant except this priesthood
bestowed upon the whole tribe of Levi, so that henceforth
they should have no landed estate in Israel, but 'JEHOVAH
should be their inheritance'[58]—that is, they should have
JEHOVAH'S share in the sacrifices and offerings of the whole
community? Not a word, however, is here said about *Aaron*
and the *sons of Aaron* being chosen exclusively to be priests,
whereas the *Levites* were not to 'come nigh' the priestly
office, 'lest they die,' according to the later priestly law.[59]
How, indeed, could Aaron have deserved any special 'blessing'
on this occasion—Aaron, the very head and front of the
transgression in the matter of the Golden Calf[60]—much less
to have the priesthood confined to himself and his sons, to
the exclusion of the faithful Levites who had so zealously
avenged it? But, in fact, as I have said before, there is no
sign whatever that in the Original Story Aaron ever acted as
a priest at all, any more than his brother Moses; though in
that narrative the tribe, to which Moses and Aaron belonged,
seems to have been marked out from the first as the priestly
caste, but without any of the exorbitant pretensions of the

[57] E. xxxii. 25-29. [58] D. x. 9.
[59] N. iii. 10, 38, xvi. 40, xviii. 7. [60] E. xxxii. 1-5, 21-25.

later priesthood, or any special privileges attached to them, unless they were actually officiating as priests.⁶¹ Thus in Jeremiah's time the ordinary Levites are reckoned with the poor and needy of the land;⁶² and in the list of David's officers, the chief officiating priests, Zadok and Abiathar, are ranked low down in the scale of dignity,⁶³ while in Solomon's time they are placed still lower.⁶⁴

There can be little doubt, therefore, that when in the Original Story Moses comes down with the second set of tables in his hands and places them in the ark, *then* in that Story—'at that time'—'JEHOVAH separated the tribe of Levi' for the priesthood, and assigned to the whole body of Levites 'the fire-offerings of JEHOVAH, JEHOVAH'S inheritance,'⁶⁵ or, as it stands, 'JEHOVAH' Himself,⁶⁶ as their inheritance. Of course, any such passage must also of necessity have been cancelled by the later priestly writer, when inserting his own account of Aaron and his sons being called to the priesthood⁶⁷ and of the Levites being taken instead of the firstborns of Israel and given to the priests as servants.⁶⁸ But the passage in question, which the Deuteronomist must have had before him, is evidently referred to in a part of the Original Story in the Book of Joshua—'Only unto the tribe of Levi He gave no inheritance: the fire-offerings of JEHOVAH, the ELOHIM of Israel, they are his inheritance, as He spake to him';⁶⁹ and there is no place in the whole Pentateuch where JEHOVAH 'spake' such things of the 'tribe of Levi,' unless in the passage in question, now missing, which we suppose to have existed at one time in the Original Story.

Thus GOD Himself, the 'Father of lights,' by means of the facts which He has enabled us first clearly to ascertain in the

⁴⁰ D.xviii.1-8. ⁴⁵ D.xii.19,27,29, xxvi.12. ⁴⁸ 2S.viii.16,17
⁴¹ 1K.iv.2-4. ⁴⁶ D.xviii.1. ⁴⁴ D.x.9, xviii.2.
⁴⁷ E.xxviii, N.iii.3,4. ⁴⁷ N.iii.5,13. ⁴⁹ J.xiii.14.

present age, takes from us the Bible as an *idol* which men have set up in their ignorance, to bow down to it and worship it. But He restores it to us to be reverenced as the work of men in whose hearts the same human thoughts were stirring, the same hopes and fears were dwelling, the same gracious Spirit was operating, thousands of years ago, as now. It is true, the priestly portions of the Pentateuch are rather of use to us as a foil to the rest, at least to the Book of Deuteronomy. They show how the thirst for spiritual power and pre-eminence, the desire to secure for themselves dignity and influence, not to speak of other worldly advantages, as the only authorised dispensers of the Divine favour and blessing for the soul of man, which in all ages and under all forms of religion have more or less distinctly characterised the priesthood, played a very conspicuous part in Jewish affairs after the return from the Captivity. GOD only knows, who has suffered it, how dark a page in human history the history of the priesthood has been, from the *isanusi* of the Zulu to the Jesuit of Christendom—how 'the fine gold has become dim,' the finest and brightest specimens of man have been corrupted and distorted by the false and poisonous notion that one man, or, rather, that one order of men, is nearer to GOD than others, not by virtue of their goodness, but merely as the prerogative of their class—that one order of men has been invested with this prerogative, and made the channel of Divine grace and communication to their fellows in some supernatural, magical way. Mysterious, doubtless, are all Divine communications —though not more or otherwise mysterious than human nature and its Divinely-appointed relationships. But this notion of the priesthood is specially antagonistic to human relationships, and tends ever to interfere with them in the most *ungodly*, because *inhuman*, manner. And it is altogether alien to the spirit of Christianity, of which the leading features are the Fatherhood of God and the Brotherhood of Man.

'Ye are,' says St. Peter, 'a royal priesthood'; [70] 'ye are built up a spiritual house, a holy priesthood, to offer up spiritual sacrifices, acceptable to GOD by Jesus Christ.'[71] The idea expressed in these words, the true Christian idea, is that all Christians as such are brought into the immediate presence of GOD, and have access to His mercy-seat, to pour forth their prayers and 'the fruit of their lips giving thanks to His Name.'

But there were prophets also in those days, 'preachers of righteousness,' according to their lights, as well as priests; and one of these it is who says to the people in JEHOVAH'S Name, 'Now, therefore, if ye will obey My voice indeed and keep My Covenant ... then ye shall be unto Me a kingdom of priests and an holy people.'[72] There is nothing of the priestly spirit here, though he had not been blessed with the light of Christianity and still restricts the privileges of GOD'S children to the 'House of Jacob,' the 'children of Israel.' And there are prophets still among us, raised up in this as in every age, to speak God's word, the word of truth, to their brethren, whether in the pulpit or out of it. And that Living Word, which is the Light and Life of men, is speaking now to us in all those words of our fellow-men, which have brought us in any degree to the clearer knowledge of Him 'whom no man hath seen or can see.' But let us be sure that, as it is GOD who teaches us by means of our fellow-men, we may expect that He will speak to us so that we can hear and understand—that He will speak to our hearts and carry inward demonstration to our spiritual being—that, when He speaks, His words will come home to us, and will be their own evidence.

[70] 1 Pet. ii. 9.   [71] v. 5.   [72] E. xix. 5, 6.

LECTURE XVIII.

SUMMARY.

The Ark and Phinehas mentioned in an interpolated passage of Judges; the stories of two Levites, as told in that Book, considered; no signs of any special dignity having been attached to the tribe in that age; the story of Samuel and Eli considered; the meaning of the 'faithful priest,' who should be raised up in Eli's place; the notices of Levites in the Books of Samuel and Kings examined; no distinction made between Priests and Levites before the Captivity; any Levite might act as Priest, though, perhaps, in some subordinate office, as 'doorkeeper'; the Gibeonites and other menials of the Sanctuary in the time of David and Solomon; the germ of the idea of distinguishing between Priests and Levites to be found in the act of Josiah, who degraded the idolatrous priests of Judah; this fructified in the mind of Ezekiel, who sharply separates the faithful Levites, the 'sons of Zadok,' from those Levites who had ministered at idolatrous altars; the idea carried out after the Captivity, though few of those degraded priests seem to have returned; the priestly legislation easily introduced after the Captivity by reason of the enormous preponderance of priests in the new community.

THE PRIESTS AND THE LEVITES.

WHAT is the real meaning of the line being drawn so sharply in the Levitical Law between the Priests and the Levites? Let us first see what is told us about them in the history from the earliest days down to the time of the Captivity, beginning with the Book of Judges. In one passage of this Book we read as follows:—'And the children of Israel enquired of JEHOVAH; for the Ark of the Covenant of ELOHIM was there in those days, and Phinehas the son of Eleazar the son of Aaron stood before it in those days.'[1] But this statement about the Ark and Phinehas is clearly a later insertion, as is suggested at once by the fact that already in the very same chapter the children of Israel have twice before 'gone up and asked counsel of JEHOVAH,'[2] without any mention being made of the Ark or Phinehas. It has manifestly been inserted by some priestly writer, who could not endure that the people should 'ask counsel of JEHOVAH' except through the intervention of a 'priest the son of Aaron.' Otherwise in the whole Book of Judges there is not the least allusion to Ark or Tabernacle, Priest or Levite—not even in the Song of the prophetess Deborah,[3] in which nine tribes are named, but not

[1] Ju. xx. 27, 28.   [2] v. 16, 23.   [3] Ju. v.

the tribe of Levi—except that two Levites figure as principal characters in the last five chapters under peculiar circumstances.

For who are these two Levites? I have made some allusion to them in a former Lecture;[1] but we must now consider their stories somewhat more at length. The first is a homeless vagrant, a Levite by birth, who, after living for a time at Bethlehem, goes to 'sojourn where he might find a place,' and makes his way to Mount Ephraim, where he comes to the house of a man called Micah, who had made for himself a 'House of ELOHIM,' a sort of private chapel, which he had fitted up with the usual accessories of worship in those days, 'a graven image, and a molten image, an ephod, and teraphim,' and 'had consecrated one of his sons to be priest.' Micah says to the Levite, 'Dwell with me and be unto me a father and a priest, and I will give thee ten pieces of silver a year, and a suit of clothes and thy food.' And the Levite consents, and so 'Micah consecrated the Levite, and the young man became his priest and was in the house of Micah. And Micah said, Now know I that JEHOVAH will do me good, seeing that I have a Levite to be my priest.'[2] This satisfaction of Micah, at have secured 'a Levite for his priest,' seems to imply that the Levites had really been separated as a priestly caste, as they were (according to our view[3]) in the Original Story at the time of the Exodus. And so in the somewhat later time of Eli we read, 'There came a man of God unto Eli and said unto him, Thus saith JEHOVAH, Did I plainly appear unto thy father's house, when they were in Egypt in Pharaoh's house?'—that is, to Moses and Aaron, as representatives of the house of Levi. 'And did I choose them out of all the tribes of Israel,'—that is, the whole tribe of Levi, —'to be My priest, to offer upon Mine altar, to burn incense, to wear an ephod before me? And did I give unto thy father's house all the fire-offerings of the children of Israel?'[4]

[1] p. 66.   [2] Ju. xvii. 5-13.   [3] p. 240.   [4] 1 S. ii. 27, 28.

THE PRIESTS AND THE LEVITES. 247

The Levite in the case before us was seeking to be employed as a priest at one of the numerous high-places of the land; and he finds such employment in Micah's chapel, ministering there for Micah himself and 'the men that were in the houses near to Micah's house.'[8] Micah, we see, himself consecrates this Levite, as he had consecrated his own son, and as afterwards Jeroboam consecrated priests from all parts of the people.[9] This priest, however, with the ephod, teraphim, and graven image, was carried off by a troop of Danites, who passed by the house on their way to 'seek an inheritance to dwell in,' and overcame his remonstrances by saying, 'Hold thy peace! lay thine hand upon thy mouth, and go with us, and be to us a father and priest. Is it better for thee to be a priest unto the house of one man, or that thou be a priest unto a tribe and a family in Israel?'[10] And so they marched northward and fell suddenly upon Laish at the extremity of the land of Canaan, whose inhabitants they killed, and seized and rebuilt the town, which they called Dan; and there they set up their graven image;[11] and there also, at Dan, as also at Bethel, the two extremities of his kingdom, Jeroboam set up in after days two calves, the symbols of the Sun-God, and bade his people go to one of these for their great annual festivals, for they had had enough of going up to the Temple at Jerusalem.[12]

Then follows an account of another Levite, who also lived in no Levitical city, but on the side of Mount Ephraim.[13] In his time Jerusalem was still in the hands of the Jebusites, the 'city of a stranger,' and he fears to enter it;[14] the events therefore occurred before the time of David,[15] and, in fact, it is expressly stated that both this story and the former belong to a time 'when there was no king in Israel,'[16] that

[8] Ju. xviii. 22. [9] 1 K. xii. 31. [10] Ju. xviii. 1-31. [11] v. 27, 29, 31.
[12] 1 K. xii. 28, 30. [13] Ju. xix. 1. [14] v. 10, 12.
[15] 2 S. v. 6, 9. [16] Ju. xvii. 6, xviii. 1, xix. 1, xxi. 25.

is, before the reign of Saul. This Levite was 'going through' the House of JEHOVAH,[17] probably Bethel, or perhaps was going *to* it, in order to become a priest there, when 'men of Belial,' Benjamites, beset him at Gibeah and ill-used his concubine to death;[19] and the narrative so closely resembles in its main features and its phraseology the story of Lot and the Sodomites,[19] that it seems probable that the account of the destruction of Sodom for the wickedness of its inhabitants was based on this very occurrence, which may have been still keenly remembered, with its sorrowful consequences to Israel as here detailed,[20] at the time when the writer in Genesis lived, that is, as we suppose, in the days of Saul or David.

As yet we have no sign of the grandeur of the priesthood, or of the dignity of the priests compared with the Levites. And now we come to the Books of Samuel. Here Samuel's father, Elkanah, was apparently not a Levite, but 'a man of Mount Ephraim, an Ephrathite'[21] or Ephraimite, like Jeroboam.[22] Yet Samuel his son slept in the Tabernacle at Shiloh,[23] and acted throughout his life as a priest.[24] Moreover, according to the priestly law, all Levites belonged to JEHOVAH from their birth,[25] though they were not to minister till thirty years of age,[26] which in another place is strangely altered to twenty-five.[27] But Samuel is here 'given' or 'lent' to JEHOVAH by his mother Hannah,[28] and he ministers before JEHOVAH in the Tabernacle as a child, 'girded with a linen ephod,'[29] that is, dressed as a priest.

Eli and his two sons appear to have been the only priests

---

[17] Ju. xii. 18.   [18] v. 22–28.
[19] *comp.* v. 5 with G. xviii. 5—v. 20 with G. xix. 2—v. 22 with G. xix. 4, 5—v. 23, 24, with G. xix. 6–8.
[20] Ju. xx, xxi.   [21] 1 S. i. 1.   [22] 1 K. xi. 26.
[23] 1 S. iii. 3, which should be translated, 'And ere the lamp of ELOHIM went out, and Samuel lying down in the Temple of JEHOVAH, where the ark of ELOHIM was,' and not as in the E.V.
[24] 1 S. vii. 9, ix. 13, x. 8, xvi. 1–5.   [25] N. iii. 12, 13.   [26] N. iv. 3.
[27] N. viii. 24.   [28] 1 S. i. 28, ii. 20.   [29] 1 S. ii. 11, 18, iii. 1.

at Shiloh;[30] and there is no hint of any multitude of Levites assisting at the Sanctuary; we read only of the priest's servant, who, instead of waiting for the fat to be burnt reverently upon the altar, and then taking the priest's portion from the sacrifice, comes with violence, and dashes his three-pronged fork into the boiler, and brings up for the priest whatever he can thus lay hold of.[31] It is plain that in those days there was no law like that of the Deuteronomist,[32] assigning the parts to be given to the priests,—much less the larger provision of the later priestly law, the breast and the hind-leg,[33] far surpassing any perquisite which the most dexterous servant would be likely to secure for his master in this way. For the sins of his sons, however, and his own sin in not restraining them, Eli's judgment is pronounced as follows:—'I said indeed that thy house and thy father's house should walk before Me for ever: but now JEHOVAH saith, Be it far from Me! for them that honour Me I will honour, and they that despise Me shall be lightly esteemed. ... And I will raise Me up a faithful priest, who shall do according to that which is in My heart and in My mind; and I will build him a sure house, and he shall walk before Mine anointed'—that is, the king—'for ever. And it shall come to pass that everyone that is left in thine house shall come and crouch to him for a piece of silver and a morsel of bread, and shall say, Put me, I pray thee, into one of the priest's offices that I may eat a piece of bread.'[34]

It might seem at first sight that, according to these words, the whole House of Levi, to which the promise had been made, was to be set aside. But the 'faithful priest,' whom JEHOVAH would raise up in the place of Eli, is evidently to be placed in a position of authority, to whom other priests might 'crouch' for bread: that is, the words refer to the *chief-*

---
[30] 1 S. i. 9, ii. 12-17, iv. 4.   [32] 1 S. ii. 13-17, 29.   [33] D. xviii. 3.
[31] N. xviii. 18.   [34] 1 S. ii. 30, 35, 36.

priesthood, and the writer probably means to say, 'the chief-priesthood shall not be continued in thy line,' Eli having come in regular descent from the chief officiating priest at the time of the Exodus. You remember how upon the death of David the old priest Abiathar, Eli's great-great-grandson,[35] who for nearly fifty years had followed faithfully the fortunes of David,[36] and 'had been afflicted in all wherein David was afflicted,'[37] together with Joab the commander-in-chief, supported the claims of Adonijah, David's eldest son, to succeed to the throne,[38] and how 'Zadok the priest and Benaiah the son of Jehoiada and Nathan the prophet were not with Adonijah,'[39] but espoused the cause of his youngest son, Solomon,[40] taking into their counsel his mother Bathsheba,[41] the guilty wife of Uriah the Hittite, with whom David had carried on an adulterous intercourse, and then had had her husband murdered, to conceal, if possible, the sin.[42] The aged king, now in his dotage, is persuaded to recognise publicly Solomon as his successor;[43] and one of the first acts of Solomon's reign is to put to death his brother Adonijah,[44] and the next to depose the old chief-priest Abiathar,[45] and the next to have Joab killed,[46] in accordance with David's dying suggestion[47]—'and the king put Benaiah'—his own supporter—'in Joab's room over the host, and Zadok the priest did the king put in the room of Abiathar.'[48] And so, says the writer, 'Solomon thrust out Abiathar from being priest unto JEHOVAH, that he might fulfil the word of JEHOVAH which he spake concerning the house of Eli in Shiloh,'[49]—this very 'word' spoken of Eli having been in all probability suggested to the writer in Solomon's days by the wish to account in some way for this outrageous act. It is very plain, however,

---

[35] 1 S. xiv. 3, xxii. 20. [38] 1 S. xxii. 20, 21. [41] 1 K. ii. 26. [45] 1 K. l. 7.
[36] v. 8. [39] v. 38. [42] v. 11, &c. [46] 2 S. xi. 2-17.
[37] 1 K. i. 28-35. [40] 1 K. ii. 13-25. [43] v. 26, 27. [47] v. 28-34.
[38] v. 5, 6. [44] v. 35. [44] v. 27.

that we have only an ordinary Court-cabal, and all the well-known features of Oriental despotism. But how incongruous with the ideas of the later priestly legislation is this act, by which a young prince ejects summarily on his own authority one high-priest and puts another in his room! How opposed to them also is the notion of there being *two* chief priests during the latter part of David's reign,[50] and those not father and son, so that one, according to the priestly law,[51] might duly succeed to the other! Zadok, however, was most probably also of Levite descent, and he may have been even related to Abiathar in some way, and so may have been appointed to assist him in his duties, when these were, no doubt, increased by the erection of the Tabernacle on Mount Zion and the bringing up of the Ark. It would seem that, aided by his more active age, and perhaps by the greater vigour of his character, he took the lead of his aged colleague, since he is always named first of the two, 'Zadok and Abiathar.'[52]

In the two Books of Samuel, Moses and Aaron are spoken of together in one passage,[53] as co-leaders of the people: but nothing is said about Aaron's priesthood, nor is he named again either in these or in the two Books of Kings. The Levites are mentioned twice in the Books of Samuel. In one place they take down the ark from the cart,[54] on which it had been brought back by the Philistines: in the other they carry the ark with Zadok, when David flees from Jerusalem before the coming of Absalom [55]—which agrees with the examples in the Original Story of 'the priests the Levites' carrying the ark across the Jordan and around the walls of Jericho.[56] In the Books of Kings also the Levites are twice mentioned. In one place Jeroboam is reproached for making priests 'from all parts of the people who were not of the sons of

---

[50] 2 S. viii. 17.   [51] E. xxiii. 29, 30, comp. N. xx. 26, 28.
[52] 2 S. viii. 17, xv. 24, 27, 29, 35, 36, xvii. 15, xix. 11, xx. 25, 1 K. iv. 4.
[53] 1 S. xii. 6, 8.   [54] 1 S. vi. 15.   [55] 2 S. xv. 24.   [56] J. iii. 6, 14, 17, vi. 12.

Levi;'[57] and this, of course, implies that the Levites were regarded, in Judah at all events, as the priestly caste, in accordance with the view maintained by the writer of the Original Story;[58] but it is also plain that the writer, Jeremiah, laid no stress upon their being 'sons of Aaron.' And they are mentioned again in the account of the dedication of Solomon's Temple, where, after the statement that 'all the elders of Israel came and *the priests* took up the ark,' it is added, 'and they brought up the ark of JEHOVAH and the Tent of Meeting and all the holy vessels that were in the Tent, even those did *the priests and the Levites* bring up.'[59] But this verse will be seen to break the thread of the story, which also before and after speaks only about 'the ark,' not 'the ark of JEHOVAH,' as here. If these 'holy vessels,' made by express Divine command by Moses, were actually 'in the Tent' at this time—for instance, the golden altar of incense, the golden table of shewbread, the golden seven-branched candlestick, with its flowers and lamps and tongs of pure gold—what became of them, these most august and precious memorials of the march through the wilderness, when Solomon made the corresponding vessels for the Temple?[60] Were they placed in the 'Tent of Meeting,' set up inside the Temple, or were the Tent and its vessels laid aside and forgotten? At all events we hear no more of them: the grand Mosaic Tabernacle disappears silently henceforth from the history. The fact is that we have here another priestly insertion of a later age, with the phrase 'priests *and* Levites,' as if they were different orders like 'priests and deacons,' a phrase which never occurs elsewhere in any book written *before* the Captivity, but appears very frequently in those written *after* it.[61]

[57] 1 K. xii. 31. [58] p. 165. [59] 1 K. viii. 4. [60] 1 K. vii. 48-50.
[61] 1 Ch. xiii. 2, xv. 4, &c., 2 Ch. vii. 6, viii. 14, 15, &c., Ezr. i. 5, ii. 70, &c., Neh. vii. 73, viii. 13, &c.

In short, the priests and the Levites were identical before the Captivity, or, rather, any Levite could act as priest,[61] though he may have had to go through some form of consecration before actually entering upon the office. In older times, as we have seen,[62] there were high-places all over the land in both kingdoms, at which such priests were needed, besides the Central Sanctuaries, at Jerusalem in the southern, and at Bethel and Dan in the northern, kingdom. Jeroboam, it seems, did not employ *exclusively* the tribe of Levi: though it is not said that he allowed *no* Levites to be priests in his kingdom. But he probably attached no weight to the statement of the Original Story which restricted the priesthood on Divine authority to that tribe, and he employed for it men of all tribes indiscriminately. In Judah, however, and especially in Jerusalem, where most probably that story was written, the Levites were regarded as the only lawful priests all along, down to the time of the Captivity. There was no distinction of 'orders' as yet between the priests and the Levites, though there was, of course, a chief-priest who had the oversight of the Sanctuary,[64] and to whom a needy Levite would have recourse when seeking employment, to whom he might even have humbly to 'crouch,' praying to be put into one or other of the priests' offices, that he might eat a piece of bread,—for instance, into that of a 'doorkeeper,' which before the Captivity was filled by priests.[65] And it may have been with a view to prevent such haughtiness that the Deuteronomist provides that, if *any* Levites chose to come to Jerusalem, 'with all the desire of their mind,' to officiate as priests there, they should have 'like portions to eat' with all the rest of their brethren who 'stood there before JEHOVAH.'[66]

---

[61] D. xviii. 6–8.
[62] 2 K. xi. 4 &c., xii. 2, 7, 9, xvi. 10, 11, xxii. 4, 8, xxv. 18.
[64] 2 K. xii. 9, *comp.* xxii. 4, xxv. 18.
[63] p. 107.
[66] D. xviii. 6–8.

For still lower work connected with the Sanctuary there were probably attached to the Temple, as servants to the priesthood, the persons spoken of in later books as 'Nethinim'[17] and 'Solomon's servants.'[18] The word 'Nethinim' means 'given,' and we read in the Original Story that the Gibeonites, whose ambassadors had beguiled Israel into making peace with Joshua on the pretence of having come from a far-distant land,[19] were 'given' by him for the work of hewing wood and drawing water for the 'House of his Elohim,' for the 'altar of JEHOVAH.'[70] But Saul, we are told, slew the Gibeonites,[71] who perhaps were servants to the priests at Nob when he massacred there 'eighty-five persons wearing the ephod,'[78] and may even be reckoned among this number as connected with the Sanctuary, since there is no sign in the history of so many *priests* existing at that time. Thus there remained only a few of the original 'Nethinim,' by whomsoever these were really first employed for such work: and there would consequently be a lack of servants, as well as priests, for the greater demands of David's Tabernacle and, at all events, for those of Solomon's Temple. Hence, most probably, Solomon assigned additional servants for these menial offices[19] from the remnant of the Canaanites, upon whom he 'levied a tribute of bondservice.'[74]

During the Captivity, however, the idea seems to have been developed of distinguishing between those Levites who had taken part in idolatrous practices, themselves or their parents, and the faithful Levites who had adhered to the pure worship of JEHOVAH. We find the germ of this idea in the account of Josiah's Reformation, where we read—'And he brought all the priests out of the cities of Judah, and defiled

---

[67] 1 Ch. ix. 2, Ezr. ii. 43, 58, 70, vii. 7, viii. 17, 20, Neh. iii. 26, 31, vii. 46, 60, 73, x. 28, xi. 3, 21.
[68] Ezr. ii. 55, 58, Neh. vii. 57, 60, xi. 3.   [72] J. ix. 3–16.
[69] v. 23, 27.   [71] 2 S. xxi. 2.   [73] 1 S. xxii. 18, 19.
[70] Ezr. viii. 20.   [74] 1 K. ix. 21.

the high-places where the priests had burned incense. . . . Nevertheless the priests of the high-places came not up to the altar of JEHOVAH at Jerusalem, but they did eat of the unleavened bread among their brethren.'[78] Thus, whereas Josiah killed without mercy the idolatrous priests in the cities of Samaria—'he slew all the priests of the high-places that were there before the altars,'[16]—he only *degraded* the idolatrous Levites of Judah: they were not to officiate henceforth at the altar, but they were still allowed to 'eat unleavened bread'—that is, probably, to keep the Feast of Unleavened Bread, with its special rite, the Passover,—'among their brethren,' and in this way they took part, we may believe, in the great Passover which was presently kept at Jerusalem.[77] This was probably done by the advice of the chief-priest Hilkiah, who could not endure that these idolatrous priests should be admitted at once to the full privileges of the Temple. And the idea, thus thrown out, seems to have fructified in the mind of Ezekiel. For in Ez. xl–xlviii, written 'in the fourteenth year after that the city was smitten,'[78] he has visions of God,[79] and plans out a scheme for the rebuilding of the City and the Temple, and the re-establishment of worship at Jerusalem; and he strongly distinguishes in his new community between those Levites 'who had kept JEHOVAH'S charge and had not gone astray when the children of Israel went astray'[80] and the other Levites who had done this.[81] These faithful priests he calls 'the sons of Zadok,' though certainly not as lineal descendants of Zadok; since those very abominations, which Josiah cleared out of the Temple, must have accumulated under high-priests of Zadok's line, from the time of Solomon downwards. Perhaps he had in his mind the words addressed to Eli and pointing to Zadok, 'I will raise Me up a faithful priest, that

[75] 2 K. xxiii. 8, 9. [76] v. 20. [77] v. 21–23. [78] Ez. xl. 1.
[79] v. 2, &c. [80] Ez. xlviii. 11. [81] Ez. xliv. 10.

'shall do according to that which is in Mine heart and in My mind,'[2] and speaks of these as being 'sons of Zadok' in spirit, according to this description of him. However this may be, he draws a strong line of demarcation between these two classes of priests, though he calls them both Levites— saying of the one, 'The priests the *Levites*, the sons of Zadok, who kept the charge of My Sanctuary when the children of Israel went astray from Me, they shall come near to Me to minister unto Me, and they shall stand before Me to offer unto Me the fat and the blood, saith the Lord JEHOVAH; they shall enter into My Sanctuary, and they shall come near to My Table to minister unto Me, and they shall keep My charge:'[3] whereas of the other class he says, 'But the *Levites*, who went far from Me when Israel went astray, who went astray from Me after their idols, let them bear their iniquity; and let them be in My Dwelling ministers appointed at the gates of the House, and ministering in the House; let them slay the burnt-offering and the sacrifice for the people and stand before them to minister to them; because they ministered to them before their idols, and became to the House of Israel a stumbling-block of iniquity, therefore have I lifted up My hand against them, saith the Lord JEHOVAH, and they shall bear their iniquity. And *they shall not draw-near to Me to act as priests unto Me*, and to draw-near beside any of My holy things unto the Holy of Holies, and they shall bear their shame and their abominations which they have done. And I have given them as *keepers of the charge of the House* for all its service and for all which shall be done in it.'[4]

He still, however, calls this latter class of Levites 'priests,' speaking of 'the *priests* the keepers of the charge of the House';[5] but he never speaks anywhere of 'the priests the

[2] 1S.ii.35, comp. 1K.ii.27.   [4] Ez.xliv.15,16.
[3] v.10-14.   [5] Ez.xl.45.

sons of Aaron.' In short, as I have said, these Levites were but degraded priests. And there can be little doubt that, on the return from the Captivity, Ezekiel's ideal view was actually carried out, and those Levites, who had been faithful to the purer worship of JEHOVAH, themselves or their parents, were henceforth dignified exclusively with the name and office of 'priest,' and very probably themselves insisted tenaciously on this distinction being maintained; while the children of those who had ministered at idolatrous altars were allowed to officiate still, but only as a class inferior to the priesthood. They were not indeed to be 'hewers of wood and drawers of water,' for which and other merely menial offices the Nethinim and Solomon's servants were, no doubt, employed. But they were to act as gatekeepers and choristers, and to slay the burnt-offerings for the people, and generally to 'stand before them, to minister unto them,'[56] whereas 'the priests the Levites the sons of Zadok' were to 'stand before JEHOVAH, to minister unto JEHOVAH.'[57] Probably very few were willing to 'bear their shame' in this way; at all events, though more than 4,000 priests returned from the Captivity,[58] in the proportion of one priest to ten laymen,[59] only 341 Levites are said to have accompanied them.[60] This enormous preponderance of sacerdotal power in the new community explains the ease with which the priestly legislation was imposed, as if revealed by JEHOVAH to Moses, upon an ignorant laity, who, returning under such circumstances, would probably for the most part be credulous devotees, the very people to be priest-ridden. Things did not go altogether smoothly even thus; and Nehemiah tells us how a son of the high-priest in his time had married the daughter of the heathen Sanballat and he 'chased him from him'[61]—besides

[56] Ez. xl. 44, xliv. 1. [57] Ez. xliv. 15, 16. [58] Ezr. ii. 36-39.
[59] v. 64. [60] v. 40-42. [61] Neh. xiii. 28.

other Jews, who had married wives of Ashdod, Ammon, and Moab, and with whom he contended."¹ But the priestly spirit triumphed in the main after the Captitity, even down to the time when they 'sought how they might kill' the blasphemer, as they called him, whose voice had sternly denounced their practices, and published the Fatherly Love of God to Man.

¹ v. 23-27.

LECTURE XIX.

SUMMARY.

RECAPITULATION ; the Pesach kept in Josiah's days as never before, in strict accordance with the rules prescribed by the Deuteronomist in the Book of the Covenant ; these rules differ strikingly from those in Exodus, and seem to connect the Pesach with the sacrifice of firstlings ; the Deuteronomist enjoins that human firstlings shall be redeemed ; in earlier times they were undoubtedly sacrificed, down to Josiah's Reformation ; such sacrifices are apparently enjoined in more than one passage of the O.S.; in the primitive age human firstborns were probably 'made to pass-over' to the Sun-God, on the eve of the Full Moon, at the Spring Festival ; the practice may have been dying out, though it was not extinct in Jeremiah's time ; points of difference between the rules for observance of the Pesach in D. and in L.L. ; the latter falsely derives the name from Jehovah's 'passing-over' by the Israelites when He slew the Egyptians ; it further claims for Jehovah the Levites and their cattle in place of the firstborns and firstlings of Israel, and then, inconsistently, claims afterwards the firstlings for the priests, as it has previously introduced the Levites as attached to the Sanctuary under the priests, and used the term 'holy shekel' before there was any sanctuary or priesthood ; the half-shekel tax in Exodus related to the post-Captivity Temple-tax ; the Christian Passover.

THE ORIGIN OF THE PESACH OR PASSOVER.

THE first germ of that practice of later times in Israel, which drew a sharp line of distinction between the priests and the Levites, lay, as we have seen,[1] in the fact that in Josiah's Reformation those priests who had ministered at idolatrous altars, were degraded from their office, and were no longer allowed to officiate at the altar of JEHOVAH—a germ which grew and sprouted in the mind of Ezekiel, who strongly distinguished between the faithful Levites, the 'sons of Zadok,' and their idolatrous brethren, and which during the exile produced the ripe fruit of the priestly system, as set forth in the Levitical Legislation of the Pentateuch, and carried out in the Jewish Church after the return from the Captivity. But these deprived priests were not excommunicated: they were allowed to 'eat the *mazzoth* among their brethren'[2]—that is, to celebrate with the other priests the Feast of Mazzoth or Unleavened Bread, the most remarkable feature of which was the Passover or Pesach, as it is called in Hebrew, from which is derived the Greek Pascha, and our own expression, the Paschal Feast. I propose to consider in this Lecture the real meaning and significance of this rite as practised among the Hebrews in primitive times.

[1] p. 256-7. [2] 2K. xxiii. 9.

his 'heart was tender,'[10] and for five of those years he had Jeremiah by his side,[11] was evidently just as faulty as the rest. Only 'in the eighteenth year of King Josiah' was this famous Passover kept in Jerusalem as it had never been kept before.

It is not said that the *numbers* then present were greater than on any former occasion; and the writer can hardly have meant this, since the Ten Tribes had long been carried captive,[12] and only the petty kingdom of Judah remained, with some scanty remnants of the northern tribes. Supposing, however, that Josiah's zeal had roused a kindred enthusiasm among his people, so that even from this diminished population more people came to keep the Passover at Jerusalem than had ever come before, yet the stress is here laid upon the fact that it was now for the first time kept *in the proper manner*, as enjoined in the Book of the Law just found in the Temple; for 'the king commanded all the people saying, Keep the Passover unto JEHOVAH your Elohim, as it is written in the Book of this Covenant.' That 'Book of the Covenant,' as we have seen,[13] was the main address of Moses in the Book of Deuteronomy, the work, as we suppose,[14] of the prophet Jeremiah, and by him probably placed in the Temple, where in due time it was found by his father Hilkiah, the reading of which produced that powerful impression on the mind of the king, which led to his great Reformation. We must examine, then, this address of Moses, and see what it enjoins about the Passover, since in this way it was kept in the days of Josiah.

Now, what the Deuteronomist says upon this subject is this:—'Observe the month of Abib and celebrate the Pesach to JEHOVAH thy Elohim; for in the month of Abib JEHOVAH thy Elohim brought thee forth out of Egypt by night. And

[10] 2K.xxii.19.   [11] Jer.i.2,xxv.3.   [12] 2K.xvii.6.
[13] p.149.   [14] p.148.

thou shalt slay the Pesach to JEHOVAH thy Elohim, of the flock and of the herd, in the place which JEHOVAH shall choose to make His Name to dwell there. Thou shalt not eat with it anything leavened: seven days thou shalt eat it with Mazzoth, bread of affliction,—for in haste thou camest-forth out of the land of Egypt,—that so thou mayest remember the day of thy coming-forth out of the land of Egypt all the days of thy life. And no leaven shall be seen with thee in all thy coast seven days; neither shall aught of the flesh, which thou slayest the first day at even, remain all night until the morning. Thou mayest not slay the Pesach in any of thy gates which JEHOVAH thy Elohim giveth thee: but at the place which JEHOVAH thy Elohim shall choose, to make His Name to dwell there, thou shalt slay the Pesach at even, at the going-down of the sun, at the season of thy going-forth out of Egypt. And thou shalt boil and eat it in the place which JEHOVAH thy Elohim shall choose, and thou shalt turn in the morning and go unto thy tents. Six days shalt thou eat Mazzoth, and on the seventh day shall be a restraint to JEHOVAH thy Elohim, thou shalt do no work.'[15]

This is the Deuteronomist's account of the Pesach or Passover. There were to be seven days for the Feast of Mazzoth, on which no leavened bread was to be eaten,[16] the seventh day being kept as a solemn day of 'restraint,' on which no work was to be done.[17] But 'on the first day at even'[18]— the Jewish day, you will remember, began with the evening— the whole assembled people was to slay the Pesach and boil[19] its flesh, and eat it during the night 'in the place which JEHOVAH would choose,' and in the morning they were to disperse to their 'tents' or dwellings. I shall point out presently in what respects these directions differ from those of the Later Legislation in Exodus. But one striking

[15] D. xvi. 1–8. [16] D. xvi. 3, 4. [17] v. 8.
[18] v. 4, 6. [19] v. 7—not 'roast,' as in the E.V.

difference is obvious at once, *viz.* that here, in Deuteronomy, the whole assembled people are to eat the Pesach *together* in the Temple Courts during the night, and in the morning to go each to his home; whereas in Exodus they are to eat it each with his family *separately* in his own house,[20] and it is added, 'none of you shall go out at the door of his house until the morning.'[21]

We observe, however, that this older law in Deuteronomy enjoins them to 'slay the Pesach *of the flock and of the herd*,'[22] and that, immediately before this, the writer has ordered that 'all the firstling males *of the herd and of the flock*' shall be 'sanctified to JEHOVAH' and 'eaten before JEHOVAH yearly in the place which He would choose.'[23] It would seem, then, that he is here specifying the time at which these firstlings of sheep and oxen should be eaten at a sacrificial feast, *viz.* at the annual celebration of the Passover in the month of Abib or 'Green-Ears,' that is, in the early Spring. So too, when the Deuteronomist, as we have seen,[24] abridges the laws of the older Covenant supposed to have been made between JEHOVAH and the people under Sinai, he writes, 'The Feast of Mazzoth shalt thou observe: seven days shalt thou eat Mazzoth as I commanded thee, at the season of the month Abib, for in the month of Abib thou camest-forth out of Egypt.'[25] And then follows immediately, as if in close connexion with this Feast, 'All that openeth the womb is Mine, and every male firstling among thy cattle, ox or sheep. But the firstling of an ass thou shalt redeem with a lamb, and, if thou redeem it not, thou shalt break its neck. All the firstborns of thy sons shalt thou redeem.'[26]

But these, as I have said, are words of the Deuteronomist, writing in Josiah's time. Were the firstborns *always* 'redeemed' in Israel? We have already seen abundantly,[27] by

---

[20] E.xii.7,13.   [22] v.22.   [24] v.2.   [26] D.xv.19,20.
[21] p.136–8.   [23] E.xxiv.18.   [25] E.xxiv.19,20.   [27] p.119.

many quotations from the Bible itself, that the practice of offering human sacrifices—of first slaying and then burning their firstborn sons and daughters in honour of the Sun-God—prevailed extensively among the Hebrew people, not only in the northern kingdom,[a] but in the kingdom of Judah,[b] in the neighbourhood of the ark and the Temple, in the presence of pious kings and zealous prophets, and in the very face of, or rather, doubtless, often with the willing help of, 'the priests the sons of Levi.' 'Yea, they sacrificed their sons and their daughters unto devils, and shed innocent blood, even the blood of their sons and of their daughters, whom they sacrificed unto the idols of Canaan, and the land was polluted with blood.'[c] Thus even Josiah, as part of the Reformation in the eighteenth year of his reign, 'defiled the Topheth, which is in the valley of the sons of Hinnom, that no man might make his son or his daughter pass-over in the fire to Molech,'[d]—that is, 'pass-over' as a sacrificial offering to 'the King,' the Sun-God; so that even down to this time the practice of offering human-sacrifices must have been continued in Jerusalem, under the good king Josiah, and in the presence of the prophet Jeremiah and the high-priest Hilkiah.

Moreover, we saw in a former Lecture[e] that in the oldest code of laws, in the Book of Exodus, dating probably from the age of Samuel, there is an ordinance which seems actually to prescribe such sacrifices:—'Thy fulness and thy tears'—that is, the firstfruits of thy threshing-floor and wine-press—'thou shalt not delay: the firstborn of thy children shalt thou give unto Me: so shalt thou do with thine ox, with thy sheep: seven days shall it be with its dam; on the eighth day thou shalt give it to Me.'[f] These firstlings of the herd and of the flock were, of course, to be *sacrificed*; and there is

---

[a] 2K. xvii. 17.   [b] 2K. xvi. 3, xxi. 6.   [c] Ps. cvi. 37, 38.
[d] 2K. xxiii. 10.   [e] p. 117.   [f] E. xxii. 29, 30.

THE ORIGIN OF THE PESACH OR PASSOVER.

no intimation whatever that the firstborns of man were to be 'given to JEHOVAH' in any other way than that in which the other firstlings were to be 'given' to Him, that is, by fire.

So, again, in the Original Story, when the Israelites had been let go out of their bondage under the terrible effect of the last plague, which smote the firstborns of Egypt, both man and beast, we read—'And JEHOVAH spake unto Moses saying, Sanctify to Me all the firstborn that openeth the womb among the children of Israel, of men and cattle—it is Mine.'[34] And then, most probably, a few more words enjoined the celebration of the Feast of Mazzoth in memory of the unleavened bread which they ate in their hurried flight, when 'they took their dough before it was leavened.'[35] But the Deuteronomist has removed this, and inserted instead of it his own more copious account of the Feast of Mazzoth,[36] at the end of which he repeats the command about 'making to pass-over to JEHOVAH' all firstborns and firstlings.[37] But here he adds 'all the firstborns of men among thy children shalt thou redeem,'[38] thus softening and in fact explaining away the abrupt words of the Original Story just quoted, which, as they read, would also seem to imply that the firstlings of man and beast were to be dealt with in like manner, and 'sanctified to JEHOVAH' by being sacrificed.

It is probable that in the primitive times in Israel, that is, before and during the age of Samuel, or even after it—in days when Jephthah could sacrifice his only daughter as 'a burnt-offering to JEHOVAH,'[39] and Samuel could hew in pieces 'before JEHOVAH' the captive Agag, king of Amalek,[40] and David could make his Ammonite captives 'pass-over' in the fire to Molech,[41] and could give up the seven sons and grandsons of Saul to be impaled or crucified 'before JEHO-

---

[34] E. xiii. 1,2.   [35] E. xii. 34, 39.   [36] v. 3–10.
[37] v. 13, instead of E.V. 'set apart,' see marg.   [38] v. 13.
[39] Ju. xi. 30-40.   [40] 1 S. xv. 33.
[41] 2 S. xi. 31, instead of E.V. 'saw through the brick-kiln.'

VAII,' [a] or even in the still later age, when such facts as these could be recorded without one word of censure,—the Spring Festival was kept in Israel, after the example of the tribes of Canaan, with human as well as animal sacrifices, the firstborns both of man and beast being made to 'pass-over to JEHOVAH' on the fourteenth day of the month at even,[b] that is, on the eve of the Full Moon. This ceremony was called the Pesach or 'Passing-over,' and the Feast lasted for seven days, with the custom, handed down perhaps from great antiquity, when the use of leaven was unknown, of eating bread unleavened. It is true, the Original Story, though it enjoins the 'giving or sanctifying' to JEHOVAH all firstlings both of man and beast, does not mention the Pesach by name. It says, however, in its ancient code, 'Thou shalt not slay with aught leavened the blood of *My* Sacrifice, neither shall the fat of *My* Feast remain all night until the morning,'[c]—as if there was some special 'Sacrifice' and special 'Feast' peculiarly dear to JEHOVAH. And, accordingly, the Deuteronomist, when copying these words, instead of 'the Fat of My Feast,' writes plainly 'the Sacrifice of the Feast of the Pesach,'[d] showing that this gloomy solemnity was the annual festival deemed of most importance, though doubtless the joyous Autumn Feast was most in favour with the people; and so the words 'blood of My Sacrifice,' which the Deuteronomist here merely repeats, were probably meant to have a similar reference to the great Spring Sacrifice of firstborns and firstlings, which was designed especially to propitiate the Sun-God and bring down a blessing on the crops of the year.

At some time or other, no doubt, the practice was introduced of 'redeeming' the firstborns of men, perhaps about the age of David, when the Story of Abraham's sacrifice was

[a] N.xxi.8,9.   [b] E.xii.6.   [c] E.xxiii.18.   [d] E.xxxiv.25.

THE ORIGIN OF THE PESACH OR PASSOVER. 269

probably written,[46] in which Isaac is 'redeemed' with a ram.[47] Probably the older custom died out gradually, and in Jeremiah's time was only observed at last by superstitious devotees. But it still, we find, existed in Israel down to the eighteenth year of king Josiah, when for the first time the Pesach was kept, 'as it was written in the Book of the Covenant,' that is, only with sacrifices of sheep and oxen, probably the firstlings of the flock and of the herd, which were slain at evening, and feasted on during the night in the Temple Courts by the offerers and their families, not forsaking the needy Levite,[48] and in the morning they went to their homes.

Very different are the directions for the observance of this Passover laid down in the Later Levitical Law. Here, too, it is represented as a memorial of the deliverance of Israel out of Egypt.[49] But instead of the firstlings 'of the flock and of the herd,' the priestly legislator, having elsewhere assigned these exclusively to the use of the priests,[50] orders a lamb or kid, 'a male of the first year,' to be slain by each householder on this occasion, the flesh to be expressly *roasted*, not boiled, and to be eaten with bitter herbs, not by the whole body of worshippers assembled together in the Temple Court, but by each offerer with his family and friends in his own house, the lintel and side-posts of which were to be smeared with the blood,—to be eaten by him hurriedly, with 'his loins girded, his shoes on his feet, and his staff in his hand.'[51] Again, the Deuteronomist orders that the seventh day of the Feast of Mazzoth shall be kept as a day of restraint, on which no work should be done;[52] so that, on returning to their homes from the Temple in the morning of the first day of the Feast, they would be at liberty to do what they liked for the rest of the day, and until the seventh

[46] p. 120-1. [47] G. xxii. 13. [48] D. xii. 17, 18. [49] E. xii. 24-27.
[50] N. xviii. 15-18. [51] E. xii. 5, 11. [52] D. xvi. 8.

day began at evening. But the Levitical Law orders the first day to be kept, as well as the seventh, as a day of 'holy Convocation'—'no manner of work shall be done in them.'[45] Both writers explained the custom that only unleavened bread was eaten on this occasion by reference to the hasty march out of Egypt.[44] But the Deuteronomist makes no allusion whatever to the sparing of the firstborns of Israel as the ground of this rite: whereas the Levitical Law derives the name Pesach from the verb *pasach*, 'pass-over,' not because the firstborns and firstlings were made to 'pass-over to JEHOVAH,' but in memory of the fact that JEHOVAH had 'passed-over by the houses of the Israelites,[46] when he slew the Egyptian firstborns and firstlings. Moreover, it represents the Levites and their cattle as taken to be JEHOVAH'S, about a year afterwards, in place of all the firstborns and firstlings in Israel:—'thou shalt take the Levites for Me instead of all the firstborns among the children of Israel, and the cattle of the Levites instead of all the firstlings among the cattle of the children of Israel.'[46] And then, in another place,[47] with strange inconsistency, he claims in JEHOVAH'S Name these very same firstborns and firstlings from all Israel for the use of the priests, the former to be redeemed with money and the latter to be eaten. This last fact is enough by itself to show that we have here no history properly so called: though indirectly we read here the history of later times, and see how it was sought after the Captivity to account for the Levites being separated as servants of the Sanctuary, in subordination to the 'priests the sons of Aaron,' and at the same time to secure for these latter a plentiful supply of fees and of food.

Long before this, however, in the priestly Legislation, the Levites have been introduced inadvertently as connected

[43] E.xii.16. [44] D.xvi.3, E.xii.11. [46] E.xii.27.
[45] N.iii.45. [47] N.xviii.15-18.

with the Sanctuary and subordinated to the priests,[38] though, as the story now stands, not a word had yet been said about their being set apart for sacred duties. So the priestly Legislator speaks repeatedly of the 'shekel of the Sanctuary,' or holy shekel, when no Sanctuary, according to the story, was in existence [39]—a designation which is used in other passages of these later laws,[40] and with which the writer in his own days was, no doubt, familiar, though it occurs nowhere else in the Bible. Thus in one place of Exodus JEHOVAH lays a tax upon the people of half a shekel for each male adult, 'according to the holy shekel;'[41] and the amount of silver thus received is carefully accounted for as expended in making different parts of the Tabernacle.[42] But here we have light thrown at once upon the age in which this passage was written. For we find it stated that in the time of Ezra and Nehemiah, long after the Captivity, the people laid upon themselves a yearly Temple-tax of a third of a shekel for defraying the expenses of public worship,[43] a tribute which must have been raised at some *later* day to half a shekel, as it existed, we know, in our Saviour's time.[44] No reference, however, is here made to any legislative direction already existing for such a tribute being levied; but the people voluntarily bind themselves to contribute annually the sum in question—one-*third* of a shekel. From this it is plain that the Law, which Ezra is represented as at this very time enforcing with all his might,[45] contained no such command as yet, fixing *half* a shekel for the Temple-tax. In other words, it must have been inserted after the time of Ezra and Nehemiah, as one of the very latest portions of the Levitical Law, which appears to have been composed by priestly writers at

[38] E. xxxviii. 21. [39] E. xxx. 13, 24, xxxviii. 24–26.
[40] L. v. 15, xxvii. 3, 25, N. iii. 47, 50, vii. 13, 19, &c. (fourteen times), xviii. 16.
[41] E. xxx. 11–16. [42] E. xxxviii. 25–28. [43] Neh. x. 32.
[44] Matt. xvii. 24, Gr. *didrachmon* = half a shekel. [45] Neh. viii.

different periods, partly in Babylonia, partly at Jerusalem, between the years 600 and 450 B.C.

I have now explained what appears to have been the true origin of the rite of the Pesach, which the Israelites adopted from the Canaanite tribes, but which comes to us in the Bible disguised under the modifications introduced in later times. The sacrifice in question was supposed to be pleasing to the Deity, one that would propitiate His Favour and secure His Blessing. And as such it was regarded by St. Paul as the type of him who was the true paschal lamb, whose offering of himself in life and in death is the standing exemplar for all ages of that living sacrifice which we ourselves are daily to be offering, 'holy, acceptable unto God, which is our reasonable service.'[66] 'Christ our Passover is sacrificed for us: therefore let us keep the Feast, not with the old leaven of malice and wickedness, but with the unleavened bread of sincerity and truth.'[67] This is the lesson for us to learn, that the lives of all true-hearted men of all times, of all countries, classes, religions, acting faithfully according to the light which God has given them, help to 'fill up,' as the same apostle says, 'that which is behind of the afflictions of Christ,'[68] and are parts of that great Sacrifice, offered by God's dear children on behalf of the whole human race, with which the Father is well-pleased.

[66] Rom. xii. 1.   [67] 1 Cor. v. 7, 8.   [68] Col. i. 24.

LECTURE XX.

SUMMARY.

DIFFICULTIES felt by different classes of readers in respect of the contents of the Pentateuch; some of these may be got rid of by rationalising processes, as in the New Commentary; there remains the impossibility of reconciling the later history of Israel with the Levitical Legislation, supposed to be Mosaic and Divine; some real movement out of Egypt must lie at the basis of the story of the Exodus; Manetho's accounts of the Shepherd-Kings and the Leprous People; the latter probably to be identified with the Israelites, the former with kindred tribes of Eastern origin, who had previously settled on the confines of Egypt and Canaan; probable oppression of the Israelites under Rameses II., and date of the Exodus; the O.S. does not imply that forty years were spent in the wilderness; this term, expressing merely an indefinite long time, first applied to the wanderings in popular talk, and used in this sense by Amos, was introduced by the Deuteronomist into the story of the Exodus, though in the original address of Moses only as a time of probation, not of judgment, as in his later insertions; our language full of allusions to the Exodus; mistakes often made in drawing such comparisons.

THE REAL HISTORY OF THE EXODUS OF ISRAEL.

E have now examined the Pentateuch sufficiently to be able to form some clear idea of the manner in which it has been composed, by writers of different ages, whose contributions betray the spirit of the times in which they lived, and reveal to us the secret history and movements mainly of those times, and not of the Mosaic age, as is commonly supposed. We are thus relieved at once from the burden of maintaining that all the miraculous stories of these Books are historically true—a burden which many in the present age of general enlightenment have found too heavy to be borne. But, if the faith of some is staggered by these things, there are others who have schooled themselves into the habit of looking upon such stories as no *essential* part of the Mosaic narrative, and who are ready to ascribe them to the processes which would be actively at work in a primitive age, adorning simple facts with marvellous adjuncts. It is true, it is not so easy to dispose of all the wonderful incidents in the Pentateuch in this way. The ten plagues may be explained as mere exaggerations of natural occurrences; for travellers tell us how at certain seasons the waters of the Nile are red as blood, how dense the gloom is sometimes at midday, how destructive are the hailstorms, how painful the boils,

how deadly the murrains and pestilences. 'The miracle at the Red Sea,' it may be said, 'may have been only the crossing an arm of that Sea, when the waters are very low, as they sometimes are now under the influence of certain winds, the cessation of which, with the springing up of a contrary wind, makes the waves return violently where shortly before had been dry land.' Of course, we are not to suppose that JEHOVAH Himself ranked the 'hare' among ruminant animals because of the quivering movement of its lips, though the Bible distinctly says so,[1] or that the Creator classed the 'mouse' and the 'mole' in the same category of 'creeping things' with the 'snail' and the 'lizard,' as again in the Bible he is represented to have done.[2] It was *Moses* who really made these statements and desired to secure Divine authority for his own laws by ascribing them to JEHOVAH. This, in fact, is exactly what the New Commentary does, which says, 'It was not *the object of the legislator* to give a scientific classification of animals;'[3] and again, 'The distinction of animals *laid down by Moses* agrees in the main with that recognized by other nations than the Hebrews;'[4] and again, 'The *ordinance of Moses* was for the whole nation.'[5] In this way many will be able to rationalize away to their own satisfaction most of the stupendous narratives of miraculous interference in the Pentateuch; though there will be some of these still, as the utterance of the Ten Commandments in two different forms in Exodus and Deuteronomy, which would still present a difficulty.[6]

But there are those again who seem able to pass over, or at least to pass by, the stumbling-blocks caused even by those miracles which appear to be interwoven into the very texture of the Mosaic story. For such persons the difficulty is felt to be much greater to reconcile the *later* portion of the Jewish

---

[1] L.xi.1-6. [2] v.29,30. [3] B.C.l.p.546.
[4] B.C.l.p.557. [5] Ib. [6] p.101-3.

History, as it lies before us in the Bible, with the earliest portion of it, assuming this to have been substantially in accordance with the story told in the middle three Books of the Pentateuch. If the account given in those books of the priestly and sacrificial system be true in the main—that is, if these institutions and practices did really originate in that early age, under Mosaic, at all events, if not under direct Divine, authority,—how is it possible, they feel, to explain the extraordinary contradictions to this supposed fact, which meet us everywhere in the records of the history, from the Book of Judges to the very end of the Second Book of Kings, where we find not a trace of these priestly laws being duly observed under the best of kings, or of any distinction being made between the priests and the Levites? Here and there, by the ingenuity of traditionary writers, some faint reference may be imagined to the observance of one or other of those laws. But the whole labour of such writers is painfully spent, not in accumulating clear and overwhelming proofs of these laws having been recognized as authoritative and Divine, at least by the most devout princes and priests and prophets, and in Israel's best days, but in trying to extract some faint evidence of this from words which do not really yield it, and explaining away the stubborn facts of a contrary character which appear in every page of the history.

Let us now see if it is possible to reconstruct to some extent the actual history of the Hebrew people, and to sketch some more rational account of their early doings than the traditionary view affords.

Upon consideration of the whole question, it can scarcely be doubted that some real movement out of Egypt in former days must underlie the story of the Exodus. It is inconceivable that such a narrative should have been written by any Hebrew without some real tradition giving the hint for it. What motive, for instance, could he have had for taking his own people into Egypt, representing them as having lived there as miserable slaves, and bringing them out of Egypt into Canaan, unless he had derived it from reminiscences of some former residence of the Hebrews in Egypt, under painful and humiliating circumstances, and of some great deliverance?

Thus, then, it is by no means necessary to suppose that the narrative in question is from beginning to end a pure fiction. It is probable that there may have been floating about in the memories of the Hebrew tribes many legendary stories of former striking events in their history—how they once were oppressed for many years in Egypt—how they fled in a large body out of that 'house of servants' under some eminent leader such as Moses—how they had crossed the shallow extremity of the Red Sea when the waters were low, and had been led through that 'great and terrible wilderness,' and had encamped under the dreadful Mount, with its blackened peaks and precipices, as if they had been burnt with fire—how they had lost themselves in the dreary waste, and struggled on through great sufferings, and many died, but the rest found their way at last into the land of Canaan, and made good their footing among the tribes settled there, and by whom they were called 'Hebrews,' or 'people who had crossed,' that is, had crossed the Euphrates, just as by the natives of Natal the refugees from Zululand are spoken of as *abawelayo*, 'people who have crossed' the Tugela. It is natural that the recollections of such a march should have left indelible traces upon the minds of the people, and the real facts may thus have been exaggerated and distorted in the popular talk, as is the case with legends generally, while circulated from one to another and passed on by word of mouth, from sire to son, in the intervening age. In this way natural occurrences may have been magnified into prodigies, some weary months or years into forty years of wandering, and many thousands multiplied into two or three millions of people. And, if so, it is difficult to avoid the conviction that the story quoted by Josephus from the Egyptian writer Manetho, who lived about B.C. 250, and declares that he translated it out of the sacred books of Egypt, must have some connexion with this movement.

This, then, somewhat abridged, is what Manetho records:—
'There was a king of ours named Timæus, under whom it came to pass that for some reason or other the Deity was averse to us. And strangely there came ignoble men out of the eastern regions who were bold enough to invade our land, and easily subdued it by force, without our risking a battle with them. So they seized our rulers and burnt down our cities, and demolished the temples of the gods, and treated barbarously all the inhabitants, slaying some and enslaving their wives and children. At length they made one of themselves king, by name Salatis, who lived at Memphis, and made Upper and Lower Egypt pay tribute, and established garrisons, securing chiefly the eastern parts, for fear of the Assyrians. He rebuilt also the city of Avaris, and made it very strong with walls and a garrison of 240,000 armed men. After him reigned five other kings, the six ruling 254 years, and all along making war with the Egyptians. These were called the Hyksôs or Shepherd-Kings, and some say that these people were Arabians. They held Egypt 511 years, when the Egyptian kings waged a long and terrible war with them, at the end of which they were driven into Avaris, from which they were allowed, on condition of leaving Egypt, to go uninjured wherever they liked. Accordingly, they went with all their families, in number 240,000, and marched through the wilderness for Syria; but, fearing the Assyrians, they built a city in that country, which is now called Judæa, and named it Jerusalem.'[7]

[7] *adv. Ap.* I. 14, 15.

Thus far, says Josephus, Manetho has followed the sacred records, and he has no doubt that these 'Shepherd-Kings' were the people of Israel. But here he has manifestly been misled by his national vanity to claim these great achievements to be placed to the credit of his own forefathers. For, if Israel had really lorded it over Egypt for a considerable period in this manner, we should surely have found some trace of this fact in the Scripture story, and the sojourning in Goshen would not have been represented as a time at best of insignificance, and at last of abject misery. But Josephus then further tells us that, besides this account taken from the sacred records, Manetho has also introduced, out of his own head or from mere rumour, 'incredible narratives,'—such as follows :—

'Long after the expulsion of the Shepherd-Kings, king Amenophis wished to see the gods, and was told that he might see them if he would clear the whole land of the lepers and other unclean people. Accordingly, he collected these people out of all Egypt, to the number of 80,000, and sent them to work in the quarries on the East of the Nile. After a while they petitioned for relief from that hard labour, and the king assigned to them the city of Avaris, which had once belonged to the Shepherds, but was now uninhabited. Here they chose one Osarsiph, priest of On or Heliopolis, the city of the Sun, for their leader, and swore to obey him in all things. He first made a law that they were not to worship the gods of Egypt, that they were to kill the animals held sacred in Egypt, and not associate with the Egyptians. Then he rebuilt their walls, and sent a message to the "Shepherds" in Jerusalem to come and help them. So they came to Avaris in great numbers, and for thirteen years the "lepers" lorded it in Lower Egypt. Meanwhile these "lepers," with their allies the "Shepherds," had committed dreadful outrages, burning towns and cities, breaking the images of the gods, and eating the flesh of the sacred animals, which they compelled the priests to kill; and all this was done by direction of Osarsiph, the priest of Osiris the Sun-God, an Egyptian by birth, who, on going over to this people, changed his name to Moses. At last Amenophis the king came against them from the south with a great army, and his son Rameses with another, and together they fought with the "lepers" and "Shepherds," and after a great slaughter chased them as far as the frontiers of Syria.'[1]

Josephus, who adopts the first legend completely, is very angry at the notion of this Leprous People being supposed to be the Hebrews, and has, of course, no difficulty in showing that, as it now stands, this narrative cannot be historically true. Yet it is probable that we have here the Egyptian version of the exodus of Israel. The Egyptians regarded all foreigners as unclean, and would be likely enough to call these nomadic tribes, who like the Shepherd-Kings before them had made their way from the far East beyond the Euphrates, to settle in the fertile land of Egypt, a 'leprous' people. According to this account also, the harsh measures of the Egyptians, and in particular the slavish service imposed by them, gave occasion to the rebellion of those oppressed, and ultimately led to their being driven out of Egypt and pursued as far as the Syrian frontier. All this, as well as the violence done to the gods of Egypt, agrees sufficiently with the Hebrew account of the Exodus to make it very probable that we have here only another version of that event from a different point of view. And Amenophis, the Egyptian king, is identified by Egyptologists with Menoptha, son of Rameses II., so that this Rameses may have been the oppressor who reduced the Israelites to slavery. This fully agrees with the character of that monarch, who during the last fifty-six years

---

[1] *adv. Ap.* I.26,27.

of his long reign was occupied exclusively with home-enterprises, *e.g.* with building temples and palaces, whose ruins are still the astonishment of travellers. It is confirmed also by the circumstance that one of the cities said to have been built by the Israelites was called Rameses,⁹ and its remains now discovered show that it was Rameses II. under whom it was built. According to this view, the Exodus of the Israelites out of Egypt took place about B.C. 1320, nearly two centuries after the date usually assigned to it.

Such, then, was very probably the basis upon which the Scripture story of the Exodus has been founded. No doubt, as I have said, the Israelites on their march to Canaan endured great hardships and encountered formidable difficulties, the memory of which, handed down from age to age during two or three centuries, may have given rise to some of the wonderful stories in the narrative, while others are merely the result of the natural growth of legendary matter, or are due to the inventive imagination of the writer or writers. It must be observed, however, that in the Original Story there is no sign of any *very long* period, such as forty years, having been consumed in the wanderings. On the contrary, in that Story the people are carried on at once from Sinai till they reach the southern boundary of Canaan,[10] when Moses sends out spies to search the land,[11] upon whose return the people murmur because of the formidable enemies they will have to encounter,[12] and, as a punishment for this, instead of being allowed to enter Canaan at once from the south, they are ordered to turn and go back again into the wilderness towards the Red Sea;[13] and, accordingly, being refused a passage across the Edomite territory,[14] they march southward until they reach its southern extremity, when they turn again towards the north coast, along its eastern border, and reach

---

⁹ E.i.11.   [10] E.xxxiii.1,2, N.x.29-33,xl.34,35,xii.16.
[11] N.xiii.1-3.   [12] N.xiv.1.   [13] v.25.   [14] N.xx.14-21.

the plains of Moab,[15] and so at last they enter Canaan from the east across the Jordan.[16] For all this a comparatively short time would have sufficed, except that they are spoken of as 'dwelling' at Kadesh[17] or Petra, perhaps for a few months only, as afterwards they are said to have 'dwelt' at Shittim,[18] where, according to the story as it now stands, they can only have remained three or four months at the most.[19] But they came to Kadesh, we are told, 'in the first month'[20] —it is not said *in what year* of the wanderings; but it is natural to suppose that the *second* year must be meant, since the movements hitherto in the Original Story have been towards the end of the first year.[21] If, however, this datum of 'forty years' had belonged to the Original Story, we should have to suppose either here or somewhere else in this chapter before the account of the death of Aaron,[22] which occurred in the fortieth year,[23] a sudden leap of thirty-eight years in the narrative—a circumstance which has greatly perplexed the most eminent commentators. Thus the New Commentary tells us that we must understand the words to mean 'in the first month of the fortieth year of the Exodus.'[24]

The fact is, as I have said, that the Original Story said nothing about these 'forty years,' though it implied a long and tedious wandering in the wilderness. This vexatious delay

---

[15] N.xxi.4, 10–20. [16] J.iii.14–17.
[17] N.xx.1,16, comp. D.i.46, Ju.xi.17, near Mount Hor, N.xxxiii.36,37, most probably the famous rock-city of Petra, to be carefully distinguished from Kadesh, = Kadesh-Barnea, in the wilderness of Paran, to which the spies returned, N.xiii.26, D.i.19, xxxii.8, J.xiv.6.
[18] N.xxv.1. [19] B.C.I.p.650. [20] N.xx.1.
[21] The dates in E.xvi.1b,xix.1, N.i.1,ix.1,xxxiii.38, all belong to the L.l. But, according to the O.S., the Exodus took place in the Spring, E.xxiii.15, after which are mentioned 'forty days' twice, E.xxiv.18,xxxiv.28, 'three days,' N.x.33, 'a month' (?), N.xi.20, 'seven days,' N.xii.15, that is, about four months altogether; so that, allowing for the march to Sinai, the searching of the south of Canaan, N.xiii.22–24, the murmuring, N.xiv, and the rebellion, N.xvi, the first year may be supposed to have come to an end.
[22] N.xx.23–29. [23] N.xxxiii.38. [24] B.C.I.p.721.

became at length spoken of in the common talk as extending over 'forty years,' this being a very common formula among the Hebrews for expressing an indefinitely long period;[*] as where Ezekiel says of the desolation of Egypt 'No foot of man shall pass through it, nor foot of beast shall pass through it, neither shall it be inhabited *forty years*; and I will make the land of Egypt desolate in the midst of the lands that are desolate, and her cities, among the cities that are laid waste, shall be desolate *forty years*.'[*] Hence the prophet Amos, about two centuries and a half after the story of the Exodus was written, already adopts the idea of 'forty years' of wandering, and writes 'I brought you up from the land of Egypt, and led you forty years through the wilderness, to possess the land of the Amorite;'[*] and again, 'Was it sacrifices and offerings that ye brought near to me in the wilderness forty years, O House of Israel?'[*] A century and a half later still the Deuteronomist first introduces it into the story as told in the Pentateuch,[*] and from him the still later Levitical Legislator has copied it.[*] Amos, however, speaks merely of JEHOVAH'S leading Israel through the wilderness, and gives no hint that during those forty years 'all the men of war' perished out of the host, as the Deuteronomist says,[*] and after him the Levitical Legislator.[*] Nor does the Deuteronomist give any hint of this in his *original* work, the address of Moses in D.v, &c., in which the forty years are spoken of, not as a time of punishment, but as a time of probation, during which they enjoyed JEHOVAH'S watchful care and guidance, while He was 'proving' them and training them as children by chastisement. 'And thou shalt remember all the way which JEHOVAH thy Elohim led thee these

---

[*] Ju. iii. 11, viii. 28, xiii. 1, 1 S. iv. 18, xvii. 16, 1 K. xix. 8, Jon. iii. 4, &c.
[*] E. xxix. 11, 12.   [*] Am. ii. 10.   [*] Am. v. 25.
[*] D. i. 3, ii. 7, viii. 2, xxix. 5. J. v. 6.
[*] N. xiv. 33, 34, xxxiii. 38—also E. vi. 7, *comp.* D. xxxi. 2, xxxiv. 7, N. xxxiii. 39.
[*] D. ii. 14, 15.   [*] N. xiv. 29-35, xxvi. 64, 65.

forty years in the wilderness, to humble thee, to prove thee, to know what was in thy heart, whether thou wouldst keep His commandments or no.'[33] 'And I have led you forty years in the wilderness; your clothes are not waxen old upon you, and thy shoe is not waxen old upon thy foot.'[34] In short, the Deuteronomist is here merely following the lead of the Original Story, which sends back the Israelites 'by the way of the Red Sea' to wander yet awhile in the wilderness, until 'those who had despised JEHOVAH'—not the whole body of warriors—should perish.[85] It is only in his later insertions that he speaks of this time as a time of judgment for all that doomed generation;[86] though even here he says, 'JEHOVAH thy Elohim hath blessed thee in all the works of thy hands; He knoweth thy walking through this great wilderness; these forty years JEHOVAH thy Elohim hath been with thee; thou hast lacked nothing.'.[87]

So thoroughly, however, have we all from our childhood been imbued with this story, so thoroughly has it penetrated our everyday language, that pious persons will often speak or sing of their weary wanderings in this wilderness-life, of the manna which has fed them by the way, of the water by which they have been refreshed from time to time, of the swelling Jordan-flood, through which they expect to pass to their rest in the Promised Land—though, in point of fact, the main struggles of the Israelites with their foes took place in Canaan itself, *after*—not before—they had crossed the Jordan.[88] For many, doubtless, whose lives have been heavily burdened with care and sorrow, there will seem to be great meaning in such resemblances, and we can all understand the force of those words, 'Verily, verily, I say unto you, Moses gave you not that bread from heaven'—that is, it was my Father who gave it then, who gave food for the body and

---

[33] D. viii. 2.   [34] D. xxix. 5.   [85] N. xiv. 22, 23.
[86] D. i. 34, 35, ii. 14, 15, J. v. 4–6.   [87] D. ii. 7.   [88] J. vi, viii. 1–29, ix. 1, 2, x–xii.

soul to the men of old; 'it is my Father also who giveth you
now the true bread from heaven—my Father and your
Father, my God and your God. For the bread of God is
that which cometh down from heaven and giveth life unto the
world'[39]—the living bread, the 'flesh and blood' of Christ's
Divine Doctrine, which we eat and drink, whenever we approach
in a right spirit the Holy Table. For, as CLEMENT
of Alexandria says, 'In saying, Eat ye my flesh and drink ye
my blood, he was manifestly speaking by an allegory of the
drink of faith and of the promise'[40]—as TERTULLIAN says,
'While describing the word as life-giving, because the word
was spirit and life, he called the same also his flesh, because
the word also was made flesh, something forsooth to be
hungered after for life's sake, to be devoured by hearing,
ruminated upon by the understanding, digested by faith'[41]—
as ORIGEN explains it, 'We are said to drink the blood of
Christ, when we receive his discourses; his flesh is meat indeed
and his blood is drink indeed, inasmuch as he supplies and refreshes
the whole race of men with the flesh and with the
blood of his word, as with pure meat and drink; ... in the
second place, after his flesh, Peter and Paul and all the
apostles are clean meat; in the third place, their disciples;
and thus everyone, in proportion to his excellencies or the
purity of his sentiments, is made clean meat to his neighbour'[42]
—as EUSEBIUS tells us, 'His words and his discourses are
the flesh and the blood, of which he who partakes, ever
nourished, as it were, with heavenly bread, will partake of
heavenly life'[43]—or JEROME, 'The body of Jesus I take to be
the Gospel, the Holy Scriptures; I take it to be his doctrine.
If, then, we hear the word, and both the word of God and the
flesh and blood of Christ is poured into our ears, while we

---

[39] John vi. 32.   [40] *Pæd.* I. vi.   [41] *de Res. Carn.* xxxvii.
[42] *Hom. vii. in Lev.*   [43] *de Eccl. Theol.* III. xii.

are thinking of something else, into how great danger do we run!'⁴⁴

But perhaps men and women have thought sometimes too much of life as a wilderness, in which they were to travel painfully on, or, rather, to wander purposely about, so long as it pleased God to keep them there, instead of regarding it as a blessed working-time, a time in which God is best to be glorified by working for the good of man, and remembering our Saviour's own words, which he has left for the guidance and encouragement of his followers, 'My Father worketh hitherto, and therefore I work'⁴⁵— 'My meat is to do the will of Him that sent me and to finish His work.'⁴⁶

⁴⁴ *in Ps. cxliii.*   ⁴⁵ John v. 17.   ⁴⁶ John iv. 34.

LECTURE XXI.

SUMMARY.

EDOM, Moab, and Ammon, perhaps belonged to the shepherd kings of Manetho's story; the conquest of Canaan by the Israelites slow and gradual, like the Anglo-Saxon conquest of England; the time of the Judges to Saul the first king; the name YAHVEH first heard by them at the time of the Exodus as the name of the Sun-God; they adopted the practices of the Canaanite tribes, and worshipped YAHVEH with heathen rites, as the Baal or Lord of the land; hence Israelitish, as well as Phœnician, names were compounded indifferently with Baal or Yahveh; distinction, though no substantial difference, between the *Tyrian* and the *Syrian* Baal; Yahveh, in other words, Iacchus or Bacchus, may have been worshipped from the first by the Israelites after their settlement in Canaan, especially by the northern tribes; in Saul's time YAHVEH was first recognised as the National Deity of Israel under the influence of Samuel; the Cross worn as symbol of the Sun-God in very ancient times.

THE WORSHIP OF THE BAAL IN ISRAEL.

WE have seen that the Israelites, according to their own tradition, entered Canaan from the eastern border, having passed by the kindred tribes of Edom, Moab, and Ammon, without a conflict, though as regards Edom and Moab perhaps not altogether in a friendly manner, since the Original Story represents these two peoples as refusing to allow the Israelites to pass through their territory.[1] These tribes were all of *Hebrew* origin, that is, like Israel, they had crossed the Euphrates, having migrated from the further East in search of richer or less crowded pastures. Accordingly, they are all reckoned as descendants of Terah the father of Abraham,[2] who 'dwelt across the flood in the olden time';[3] and, as they must have been already long settled in these parts when the Israelites arrived on their borders, they may very possibly have belonged to the Shepherd-Kings of Manetho's story.[4] And so the Deuteronomist represents Moses as saying that JEHOVAH *had given* their respective countries to Edom, Moab, and Ammon,[5] as He now would give to Israel the land of Canaan,[6] and therefore commanded Israel not to molest them. And this fact, that

---

[1] N. xx. 14-21, Ju. xi. 16, 17. [2] G. xi. 27, xix. 36-38, xxv. 19-30. [3] J. xxiv. 2.
[4] p. 279.   [5] D. ii. 5, 9, 19.   [6] D. i. 8.

the Israelites did certainly abstain from disturbing those nations, while they did not spare the Amorites, who had invaded and permanently occupied a portion of the land of Moab,[7] suggests the existence of a special relation between them, such as that which Manetho's story implies between the 'Shepherd-Kings' and the 'Leprous People.'

Having first made the conquest of the trans-Jordanic lands, the Israelites in due time must have crossed the Jordan, though in some natural way, and without the help of that stupendous miracle recorded in the Book of Joshua—far more stupendous even than the crossing of the Red Sea—when the waters of that river in a state of flood, and overflowing all its banks, 'stood as they came down from above' and 'rose up upon an heap,' while three millions of men, women, and children, with all their herds and flocks, passed over on dry ground.[8] Here they made good their footing in the land, partly by fighting, partly by intriguing, partly by intermarrying with the old inhabitants, just exactly as the Anglo-Saxon conquest of England was effected. How many the Israelites were at this time it is impossible to say: but assuredly they were not the mighty host stated in the Pentateuch, and probably they were not one-tenth of that number, or even one-hundredth. That the Canaanites, however, were not utterly destroyed, but lived on in the land, mixing probably for the most part on friendly terms with the Israelites, and gradually blending with them and disappearing, is plain from express statements in the Book of Judges,[9] as well as from David's friendship with the Phœnicians,[10] who are reckoned among the tribes to be extirpated,[11] and from Solomon's marrying women of the Hittites,[12] and levying a tribute of bondservice upon the remnant of the Amorites, Hittites,

---

[7] N. xxi. 24-26, Ju. xi. 12-23.   [8] J. III. 15-17.
[9] Ju. i. 21, 27-36, xix. 10-12, comp. 1 S. vii. 14, 2 S. v. 6-9, xxiv. 16, 18.
[10] 2 S. v. 11, 1 K. v. 1.   [11] J. xiii. 6, xix. 28, 29.   [12] 1 K. xi. 1, comp. x. 29.

Perizzites, Hivites, and Jebusites, still existing in his days,[13] three centuries after the Exodus. We learn also, from the history contained in the Book of Judges, that the tribes of Israel did not for some considerable time exist as one *nation*, but either acted independently of each other,[14] or else combined in larger or smaller bodies,[15] as circumstances required. In short, the mighty conquests, which are ascribed to the leadership of Moses and Joshua, and are represented as the achievements of a few weeks, were most probably effected in a much longer period, and by much more gradual and every-day processes.

Hence about 120 years seem to have passed after the entrance into Canaan, during the time commonly known as the time of the Judges, till the days when 'the words of Samuel came to all Israel,'[16] during the greater part of which Eli must have lived, if he was really 98 years old at his death soon afterwards.[17] Probably Eli, like the other Judges, only judged a portion of 'all Israel,' and some of them may have been contemporary with others, 'judging' or ruling in different parts of the land at the same time. But even Samuel, in the discharge of his office, seems to have confined his personal administration of justice to a very small circuit in Judah and Benjamin, viz. Bethel, Gilgal, and Mizpeh, sacred places which he visited in turn around his birthplace and dwelling-place at Ramah;[18] and he afterwards made his sons judges at Beersheba in the south of Judah,[19] on the frontier of Egypt. In short, the life of Israel as a *nation* had not yet begun; and, though the attempt had been made at some time to set up a

---

[13] 1K.ix.20,21. [14] 'Ephraim,' Ju.iii.27, 'Gilead' or 'Gad,' xi.11, comp. xii.1-6.

[15] Ju.v.15-17, where complaint is made that Reuben, Gad, Dan, and Asher took no part in the fight, while Judah, Simeon, and Levi are not even mentioned —vi.35,vii.23, comp. viii.1-3, where Gideon summons only Manasseh, Asher, Zebulun, and Napthali—xx,xxi, where 'all Israel' fight with Benjamin.

[16] 1S.iv.1. [17] v.15. [18] 1S.vii.15-17. [19] 1S.viii.1,2.

king in the person of Gideon,[9] and in that of his son Abimelech,[11] it had altogether failed. Only at last, when Samuel grew old, and his sons 'turned aside after lucre, and took bribes, and perverted judgment,' we read that 'all the elders of Israel gathered themselves together, and came to Samuel unto Ramah and said unto him, Lo! thou art old, and thy sons walk not in thy way : now make us a king to judge us like all the nations.'[12] And Samuel complied with their request,[13] and thus the nation was united for the first time under SAUL, who, after gaining as leader of the Hebrew forces a decisive victory over the Ammonites, was 'made king before JEHOVAH at the Gilgal.'[14]

'Before JEHOVAH,' says the text just quoted, and we must now look back once more upon the religious history of Israel. We have already seen in a former Lecture[15] that, according to the most ancient writer in the Pentateuch, the people had never heard this name until the time of the Exodus, when it is stated to have been specially revealed to Moses; before which time, in Egypt and previous to their arrival there, they had only used the name 'ELOHIM,' GOD, or 'EL SHADDAI,' GOD ALMIGHTY, as the personal name of the Deity. And this, as I observed, when translated into real historical fact, can mean only this, that *the Israelites first heard the name* JEHOVAH *about the time of the Exodus*. In Egypt and previously they had probably used the name ELOHIM or EL SHADDAI ; and either in Egypt itself or on their way to Canaan they may have made an ark of 'shittim' or acacia wood for sacred purposes from the trees which grew, as they still do, in the wilderness, as also in certain parts of Egypt, in which ark was carried some symbol of the Deity, after the example of those which are exhibited on Egyptian monuments as carried about by the priests in religious processions,[16] and

---

[9] Ju. viii. 22.   [11] Ju. ix. 1-6.   [12] 1 S. viii. 1-5.   [13] 1 S. i. 24, 25.
[14] 1 S. xi. 15.   [15] p. 75, 76.   [16] *Dict. of the Bible*, I. p. 106-7.

with which, of course, the enslaved Hebrews had long been familiar. Moreover, as we have seen,[17] the tribe of Levi, the leader's own tribe, seems from the first to have been specially set apart, again after Egyptian fashion, as a sacred caste for the work of the priesthood. But they heard the name JEHOVAH or YAHVEH first, not just *before* the Exodus, as the story represents it, but just *after* it, as soon as they had reached the land of Canaan. For there, in the worship of the Syrian tribes in the northern district, the mysterious name of the Sun-God, the Baal or Lord, 'the God of the land,'[18] was YAHIVEH, or, as pronounced by the more southern tribes, YAHVEH, 'Living-One,' or 'Life-Giver';[19] from whom it came gradually into use among the Israelites, as they became settled in their new abodes, and wished to be protected by the local Deity whose land they had possessed. Thus David says, 'They have driven me out this day from cleaving to the inheritance of YAHVEH, saying, Go, serve another ELOHIM,'[20] and Naaman asks, 'Shall there not now be given to thy servant two mules' load of earth? for thy servant will henceforth offer neither burnt-offering nor sacrifice to another ELOHIM, but only unto YAHVEH'[21]—from which we see how intimately connected, in the views of that age, was the worship of YAHVEH with the very soil of the land of Canaan. Of course, the prophets of Israel would be very unwilling to allow that the name was derived from the idolatrous Canaanites; and hence they tried to account for its becoming known to Israel by the supposition of a direct revelation to Moses. And so, too, 'the Gilgal' or 'Circle,' near Jericho on the banks of the Jordan, was in all probability merely a circle of twelve large stones,—the number perhaps referring to the twelve months of the year or the twelve Signs of the Zodiac —which the Hebrews found already set up in the primeval

---

[17] p. 240.   [19] 2 K. xvii. 26-28.   [20] p. 77.
[18] 1 S. xxvi. 19.   [21] 2 K. v. 17.

times for Sun-worship, like our own famous circle at Stonehenge; and it would be as easy for an active imagination to devise some incident in ancient British history, to account for the erection of these stones, as it was for the Hebrew writer to represent the twelve stones as having been set up at the Gilgal in memory of the miraculous passage of the Jordan by the twelve tribes,[42] as well as other twelve which 'Joshua set up in the midst of the Jordan, in the place where the feet of the priests who bare the ark of the covenant, stood—and they are there unto this day.'[43]

Accordingly, we find many features of the Israelitish worship derived from that of the Canaanites, as, for instance, from that of the Phœnicians, by whose help the Temple of Solomon was built.[44] Thus the 'gourds,' 'lilies,' 'palm-trees,' 'open flowers,' 'pomegranates,' which ornamented the Temple,[45] and the 'two brazen pillars' which were placed at the entrance of it,[46] all appear in Phœnician temples, and belong mostly to the worship of the Sun-God, being used to symbolise in various ways the life awakened by the Sun's influence in nature. And so Solomon built high-places on the Mount of Olives, close to Jerusalem, for 'Molech' and 'Chemosh,'[47] the names under which the Sun-God was worshipped by his Ammonite and Moabite wives, and another for Ashteroth or Astarte, the Moon-Goddess,[48] for the use of his Sidonian and Phœnician wives, and he, no doubt, himself took part in their worship, as indeed we are expressly told 'Solomon went after Ashtoreth the goddess of the Zidonians and after Molech the abomination of the Moabites';[49] and these high-places remained throughout the reigns of the most pious kings, until they were destroyed by Josiah[40] in the Great Reformation, after the finding of the Book of Deutero-

[42] J. iv. 20-24. [45] J. iv. 9. [48] 1 K. vii. 13, 14.
[43] 1 K. vi. 29, 32, 35, vii. 19, 20, 26, 36, 42. [46] 1 K. vii. 15-22. [49] 1 K. xi. 7.
[44] 2 K. xxiii. 13. [47] 1 K. xi. 5. [40] 2 K. xxiii. 13.

nomy, in the eighteenth year of his reign. And, that such high-places were frequented down to the latest days of the kingdom of Judah, is shown conclusively by the complaint which the Jewish women, who had escaped into Egypt after the destruction of Jerusalem, made to the prophet Jeremiah —' As for the word that thou hast spoken unto us in the name of JEHOVAH, we will not hearken unto thee. But we will certainly do whatsoever thing goeth forth out of our own mouth, to burn incense unto the Queen of Heaven and to pour out drink-offerings unto her, as we have done, we, and our fathers, our kings, and our princes, in the cities of Judah, and in the streets of Jerusalem: for then we had plenty of victuals and were well and saw no evil. But since we left off to burn-incense to the Queen of Heaven and to pour out drink-offerings unto her, we have wanted all things, and have been consumed by the sword and by the famine. And when we burned-incense to the Queen of Heaven, and poured out drink-offerings unto her, did we make her cakes to worship her and poured out drink-offerings unto her, without our men?'"[41]—that is, without the cognizance and consent of our husbands. These 'cakes' were buns,[42] marked with a cross or other symbol of Sun worship;[43] and from these have been derived our modern 'hot cross buns,' as the paschal eggs 'figured in the Chaldean rites just as they do now,'[44] and the worship of the Virgin has been substituted for the worship of the 'Queen of Heaven.' No doubt, it will surprise many in our own day—and perhaps offend some—to find that these and other practices of Christendom have been borrowed from heathen Sun worship. And so the great prophets of Israel, who were always striving to raise their people above the grovelling notions of the tribes around them to higher and truer ideas of the Deity, very naturally disavowed an idola-

[41] Jer. xliv. 16–19. [43] INMAN's *Ancient Faiths*, p. 378, &c.
[42] *Ib.* p. 407, &c.   [44] *Ib.* p. 378.

trous origin for the worship of JEHOVAH; and accordingly they speak everywhere of the heathen worship, or of Israelitish worship when practised with heathen rites, as worship of the Baal[46] or of Molech.[46] But, as we have seen,[47] the very same practices, which were used by the heathen in Baal-worship, are denounced in the Bible as habitually used in Israel, and countenanced and enforced by the examples of very many of their kings, and the great multitude of their priests and prophets. The grossest licentiousness was exhibited in close connection with the Temple-worship;[48] foul symbols, called *asheras*, and mistranslated in our English Version 'groves,' were set up by the altar of YAHVEH;[49] and sacrifices of first-born children were offered, down to the time of Josiah's Reformation.[50] So, when Jeremiah says in one place, 'As the number of thy cities, so are thy gods, O Judah,' he explains this elsewhere to mean that they had set up everywhere 'altars to that shame, altars to sacrifice unto the Baal.'[51] And Ezekiel must have witnessed with his own eyes such worship going on in the Temple itself, when he sees in his vision Jewish women 'weeping for Tammuz,' that is, for the dead Adonis or Lord, the Sun-God, for whom they wept as killed by a savage boar, but greeted with joy as restored to life on the third day, symbolising thus the passage of the Sun through the winter solstice,—as also when he sees men 'at the door of the Temple, between the porch and the altar, with their backs to the Temple and their faces towards the East, worshipping the Sun towards the East.'[52]

In short, it is plain that in the view of the people generally, whatever the prophets might say to the contrary, JEHOVAH or YAHVEH was identified with 'the Baal.' Accordingly, not

---

[46] Ju. ii. 11, 13, iii. 7, viii. 33, x. 6, 10, 1 S. vii. 4, xii. 10, &c.
[46] Jer. xxxii. 35, comp. L. xviii. 21, xx. 2-5.
[46] 1 K. xiv. 24, xv. 12, 2 K. xxiii. 7, comp. D. xxiii. 18.
[46] p. 265-6.   [46] Jer. ii. 28, xi. 13.
[47] p. 145-6.
[48] 2 K. xxi. 7, xxiii. 4, 6, 7.
[49] Ez. viii. 14, 16.

only in the rude time of the Judges a JOASH, though his own name begins with JEHO or JO, that is, with JEHOVAH, could have an 'altar of the Baal,' and call his son Jerub*baal*, that is, 'Baal shall contend'; [a] but, as we have seen,[b] in Samuel's age, when JEHOVAH was fully recognised as the National Deity of Israel, and the most strenuous efforts were made to establish His worship as such, Saul gave to his son the name Esh*baal*, 'man of Baal,' *Jo*nathan to his son the name of Meri*baal*, 'Baal is contending,' and David to his son the name *Baal*yadah, 'Baal knows,' instead of calling him *El*-yadah or *Jeho*iada. And so, on the other hand, Jezebel, the Tyrian princess, queen of Ahab, whose own name is compounded with Baal, as were those of her father, Eth*baal*,[c] and of her countrymen, Hanni*bal*, Asdru*bal*, Adher*bal*, who figure in Roman story, had her sons named Ahaz*iah*[d] and *Jo*ram,[e] and her daughter Athal*iah*,[f] all compounded with JEHOVAH or YAHVEH. This fact shows that there was no essential difference between the *Tyrian* Baal, Hercules, whose worship was introduced by Jezebel among the Israelites[g] and rooted out by Jehu,[h] and the *Syrian* Baal, YAHVEH or YAHUVEH, Iacchus or Bacchus, who was worshipped of old in Israel under the form of a calf.[i] The former worship was more stern and severe, the Sun-God being chiefly regarded on the more gloomy side of his character, being dreaded as having power to scorch and wither and destroy, and propitiated therefore with human sacrifices, not merely those of firstborn infants ; the latter was a more licentious and sensual worship, in which the Sun-God was hailed as the source of all life. But the Deity worship was the Sun-God still. And so, when Elijah slew the '450 prophets of the Baal,'[j]—that is, of the austere worship newly introduced by Jezebel—he did not slay

---

[a] Ju. vi. 25, 32.   [b] p. 79.   1 K. xvi. 31.   1 K. xxii. 51, 52.
2 K. iii. 1, 2.   2 K. viii. 18, 26.   1 K. xvi. 31, 32.   2 K. x. 18, 28.
Ex. xxxii. 4, 1 K. xii. 28, Hos. viii. 5, 6, x. 5, xiii. 2.   1 K. xviii. 19, 22, 40.

the '400 prophets of the *asheras*, who ate at Jezebel's table,⁴³ and belonged to the more genial worship of YAHVEH. And in like manner Jehu, when he 'destroyed the Baal out of Israel,'⁴⁴ destroyed only this foreign form of worship, but adhered himself to the national form of Baal-worship which had long been practised in Israel; for we read, 'Howbeit from the sins of Jeroboam, son of Nebat, who made Israel to sin, Jehu departed not from after them, to wit, the golden calves that were in Bethel and that were in Dan.'⁴⁵

Upon the whole, then, we conclude that the Israelites derived the name YAHVEH from contact with the tribes of Canaan, and that in the view of the people his worship was identified with that of the Baal, 'the God of the land.' They may have begun to use it soon after their entrance into Canaan, especially among the northern tribes; and hence we may account for the two or three names of persons belonging to those tribes, apparently formed with YAHVEH, which we find in the Book of Judges.⁴⁶ Under Saul, however, the *national life* of Israel began; and so under Saul YAHVEH appears to have been first distinctly recognised as the *national Deity* of Israel. And this took place, no doubt, under the direct influence of Samuel himself, who did so much to secure their temporal prosperity, and, as the tradition seems to imply, was equally zealous to promote their religious welfare, though the original account of Samuel's doings is very much coloured by later Deuteronomistic insertions.⁴⁷ It need not, of course, be supposed that Samuel's views of the Divine character, however elevated above that of his contemporaries,

---
⁴³ 1 K. xviii. 19, xxii. 6.   ⁴⁴ 2 K. x. 28.   ⁴⁵ v. 29.
⁴⁶ Joash, vi. 11, Jotham, ix. 5, Micah (?= Micaiah), xvii. 8: but the first two names may be otherwise derived, as *e.g.* Joseph is, and the derivation of the third is doubtful. N.B. Jonathan, xviii. 30, occurs in an interpolated verse.
⁴⁷ viz. 1 S. vii. 3-14, viii. 6-20, x. 8, 18, 19, 25, xii. 1-25, xiii. 8-15a.

had advanced to the height on which the Deuteronomist stood some centuries afterwards. But that such religious zeal was traditionally ascribed to Samuel is shown by these very insertions, as well as by the fact that he is classed with Moses by Jeremiah, the Deuteronomist himself, who says 'Though Moses and Samuel stood before Me, My mind could not be towards this people.'[68] For why should Moses and Samuel have been coupled thus together, unless in the view of Jeremiah there was some special relation between them? Does not this simple fact, in short, imply, that in Jeremiah's view Samuel was a lawgiver in the same sense as Moses—was *the* lawgiver, in fact, whose ordinances may very possibly be retained, as we saw in a former Lecture,[69] in that original code upon which in the Book of Exodus the covenant made between YAHVEH and Israel was based.

So, too, when Jeremiah says, 'YAHVEH thy Elohim is a Devouring Fire,'[70] or Isaiah asks, 'Who among us shall dwell with the Devouring Fire?'[71] this symbol of Fire—like that of Light, so often used by the greater prophets in speaking of YAHVEH[72]—is probably derived from the original connection of this name with the worship of the Sun-God. In like manner the Cross, which in pre-Christian times was used as the symbol of the Sun,[73] the 'light of this world,' has now been made the symbol of the spiritual Sun, that 'true Light which lighteth every man that cometh into the world.' As regards the outward decoration, the Christian female of the present day may be but following unconsciously the example of her sisters of old, in Alexandria and elsewhere. But for her the Cross has now a deeper meaning, not only as the symbol of light and life brought near to us in the Gospel of

---

[68] Jer. xv. 1.
[69] Is. xxxiii. 14.
[70] p. 135.
[71] Is. x. 17, Mic. vii. 8, Ps. iv. 6, xxvii. 1, &c.
[72] D. iv. 24, ix. 3.
[73] See App. III.

Christ, but as a reminder of the fact that the Great Light-bringer 'suffered even unto death, the death of the Cross,' and of the truth that they who would follow in his steps, the saviours and benefactors of mankind in all ages, must expect to share in their measure the lot of their Lord.

LECTURE XXII.

SUMMARY.

The O.S. of the Pentateuch composed in the age of Saul, David, and Solomon; its account of primeval times fictitious or mythical; indications of the fictitious character of the history of the patriarchal times in Genesis; the Elohistic Narrative contains very scanty details of the personal acts of the patriarchs, except the account of Abraham's purchasing a burying-place from the aboriginal inhabitants of the land of Canaan; the Elohist here lays special stress on Hebron, the original capital of David's Kingdom, as elsewhere he does on Bethel, the famous Sanctuary of the older times; his account of the origin of the names 'Bethel' and 'Israel' completely at variance with that of the Jehovist; it is doubtful if the forefathers of the Israelites of the Exodus ever really lived in Canaan; the story of Joseph also unhistorical, and perhaps fictitious; the real history of Israel begins with the Exodus; Hebrew Literature most probably originated in Samuel's prophetical schools where the O.S. was composed and was expanded into a complete narrative from the Creation to the first years of Solomon; this came into the hands of Jeremiah (the Deuteronomist) in Josiah's time, and was by him retouched and amplified, and extended to the time of the Captivity, and was subsequently enlarged during and after the Captivity, by the insertion of the priestly legislation; the strange legend about Ezra's having rewritten the Books of Moses by Divine inspiration, which was received generally by the Fathers of the Church, probably points to his activity in copying and commending the Law with its latest additions; what the Scriptures, when their origin is understood, may lose in miraculous character, they will gain in human interest.

THE HISTORICAL BOOKS FROM GENESIS TO THE SECOND BOOK OF KINGS.

I WILL now sum up briefly the results of my preceding Lectures with reference to the Composition of the Pentateuch and the other historical Books of the Bible before the Captivity. The oldest portion of the Pentateuch, the Elohistic Narrative, appears to have been written in the age of Samuel, and, if so, then most likely by Samuel's own hand.[1] The work was probably carried on by his disciples during the next age, the age of David and Solomon;[2] and so the Original Story of the Exodus was completed very much in the form in which it came into the hands of Jeremiah the Deuteronomist,[3] between three or four centuries afterwards. How much of that story, as it now lies before us, may have been derived from traditionary or legendary matter still floating in the folk-lore of Israel, and how much may be due to the writer's own imagination, it is, of course, impossible to say. We observe, however, that the different writers seem quite as much at home when narrating matters which occurred before the time of Abraham, or even before the Flood, as after it. For instance, they give long lines of patriarchs, with very definite but mani-

[1] p. 22-24, 38. [2] p. 39, 46-51, 57-67. [3] p. 148-52.

festly fictitious ages, ranging from 969 years downwards, and beginning with the first man Adam.[1] An attempt has been made to reduce these within ordinary limits by supposing that the 'year' in these instances means merely a 'month'; but this is set aside at once by observing that the writer mentions both 'year' and 'month' in speaking of Noah's age when the Flood began—'in the six hundredth year of Noah's life, in the second month, the seventeenth day of the month.'[2] As these ages, then, are undoubtedly unhistorical, such longevity being impossible on scientific grounds for human beings,[3] we may safely conclude that the conversations reported between the Deity and Adam, Eve, and Cain, and the words addressed to the serpent and Noah, are also unhistorical—that, in short, the whole history of the antediluvian world, with the accounts of the Creation, the Fall, and the Deluge, is purely mythical, and that the popular traditional dogmas founded upon them must be rejected, in the face of the certain results of Modern Science, from which we learn that the world was otherwise formed, that no such Flood ever covered the earth since the human race began to live upon it, and that animals of all kinds, and man himself, were in existence long ages before, according to the Scripture story, the Creation took place.

But, leaving these portions of Genesis, which, indeed, as we have seen,[4] contradict each other as well as the facts of Science, the question then arises as to the credibility of the later parts of that Book, those which describe the early sojournings in the land of Canaan of Abraham, Isaac, and Jacob, and the grandeur of Joseph in Egypt, which led to the settlement of the Hebrew people there. There would certainly be nothing strange in the supposition that real facts may lie at the foundation of these narratives—that, before the Israelites

---

[1] G. v. xl. 10-26.   [2] G. vii. 11, comp. viii. 5, 13, 14.
[3] Prof. Owen (*Fraser's Mag.*, Feb. 1873).   [4] p. 36.

entered Egypt, their forefathers might have lived for some time in the land of Canaan, not as masters of the country, but merely as strangers and sojourners, till at last they removed from Canaan into Egypt at the summons of Joseph, as the story is told in the Book of Genesis. But then we have to consider that, if these accounts are really based on facts, the Israelites must have been long enough in Egypt to have increased from the 'seventy souls' who went down with Jacob,[8] to a mighty nation;[9] and, further, that only those 'seventy souls,' many of them mere children, could have known anything personally about the land of Canaan, and that it is incredible that they should have handed down by word of mouth long accurate details of conversations and transactions, in which their ancestors took part some centuries previously. Such things may be *imagined*, as our great Scotch novelist has imagined them in stories referring to the times of Queen Elizabeth and James I. But no one supposes that such details could have been handed down correctly to his days, by mere traditionary reminiscences, from Elizabeth's time.

Moreover, the most ancient writer in Genesis has very little to say about either of the three patriarchs except Abraham, though he mentions carefully in each case the names of their wives and children. He tells us, for instance, that Abraham begat Ishmael and Isaac,[10] and that from Ishmael, the elder brother, were descended twelve Arabian tribes,[11] and so that Isaac begat Esau and Jacob,[12] and from Esau, again the elder brother, were derived the tribes of Edom,[13] and lastly that from Jacob sprang the twelve tribes of Israel.[14] But the real historical meaning of these statements may be this, that the Hebrews on their way to Canaan found already settled in

---

[8] G. xlvi. 27. [9] D. i. 10, x. 22, xxviii. 62. [10] G. xvi. 16, xxi. 3.
[11] G. xxv. 12-16. [12] D. 24-26. [13] G. xxxvi.
[14] G. xxxv. 22-26, xlvi. 8-27, E. i. 1-5.

those parts these Arabian and Edomite tribes, speaking substantially the same language with themselves and therefore manifestly of kindred origin, having migrated in fact from the same neighbourhood in the far East beyond the Euphrates,[15] like the Moabites and Ammonites, who for a like reason are referred—though by a shameful birth—to Lot, Abraham's nephew, as their father,[16] that is, to the same stock as the Hebrews. Besides these genealogies, however, he records how EL SHADDAI, 'ALMIGHTY GOD,' made a Covenant with Abraham 'to be a God to him and his seed after him,' and to give to 'him and to his seed after him' possession of the land of Canaan, and sealed it with the rite of circumcision,[17] and how He changed his name from 'Abram' to 'Abraham' on this occasion, and his wife's from 'Sarai' to 'Sarah,' and promised them a son in their old age,[18] and how He afterwards made a like promise of the land of Canaan to 'Jacob and his seed after him,' and changed his name to 'Israel,' and Jacob called the name of the place where ELOHIM spoke with him Beth El, that is, 'House of God.'[19] But the only transaction recorded by him, in which the patriarch himself takes a prominent part, is the purchase of a burying-place at Hebron from the old Hittite inhabitants of the land[20]—the object of which story may have been, as I have said,[21] merely to give the Israelites, as it were, a *seisin* in the land, by ancient purchase of the site of Hebron, David's royal city during the first years of his reign,[22] which was further made sacred for Israel by the fact, according to this writer, that Abraham and Sarah, Isaac and Rebekah, Jacob and Leah, all lay buried there.[23] And Bethel, no doubt, was a very famous ancient sanctuary, where there stood a sacred stone, set up for purposes of worship in primitive times beyond all memory

[15] p. 281, 291. [18] G. xii. 5, xix. 30–38. [17] G. xvii. 1–14.
[16] v. 5. 15–19. [19] G. xxxv. 9–15. [20] G. xxiii.
[21] p. 23. [22] 2 S. ii. 11. [23] G. xlix. 31, l. 13.

of man; and the writer here very naturally ascribes its preeminent sanctity to an act performed of old by Jacob. Here, however, Jacob sets up a pillar of stones, pours oil upon it, and calls the place 'Bethel,' and GOD at the same time changes his name to ' Israel,' on his return from Padan-Aram, whither his parents had sent him to procure a wife from thence, instead of marrying Hittite women as Esau had done.[14] But the later writer ascribes this journey of Jacob to dread of Esau's anger, and makes him perform the very same acts —*viz.* set up a pillar of stone, pour oil upon it, and call the place ' Bethel,'—on a totally different occasion, twenty years previously, on his way *to* Padan-Aram, when he had that vision of a ladder reaching from earth to heaven, 'and the angels of GOD ascending and descending upon it,' and consecrated the stone which he had used for his pillow.[15] And so the change of Jacob's name took place, according to this later writer, not at Bethel in the land of Canaan, *west* of the Jordan, but some time previously at Peniel, *east* of the Jordan, when GOD, or an Angel, had wrestled with him all night, and being worsted said, ' Thy name shall be called no more Jacob, but Israel; for as a prince hast thou power with GOD and men, and hast prevailed.'[16] The grotesqueness of this story is a clear proof that we have here only a fanciful attempt to derive the name ' Israel,' which really means ' EL is a prince,' instead of ' one who is a prince with EL.' But thus we see what has probably been done in a multitude of other cases, where names of persons and places, as the Israelites found them on taking possession of the land, are ingeniously made the scenes of events which are supposed to have given rise to the names in question. About the life of Isaac the Elohist tells us scarcely anything;[17] but the active invention and graphic pen of the later Jehovist has in some measure filled up the

[14] G. xxvi. 46, xxviii. 1-5, xxxv. 9-15.   [15] G. xxvii. 41-45, xxviii. 10-19.
[16] G. xxxii. 24-30.   [17] G. xxi. 2-5, xxv. 19, 20, 24, 26, xxxv. 27-29.

blank with the spirited story of Jacob obtaining by craft his brother's blessing,[50] and with some other incidents,[51] as he has also enlivened the older accounts of Abraham and Jacob with several episodes. But the very fact that he has introduced these incidents, unknown apparently to the more ancient writer,—still more, the fact that four centuries later still the Deuteronomist could insert in Genesis the account of a solemn vision in which JEHOVAH pledges himself once more to give the land of Canaan to Abraham [52]—is enough to show how much the imaginative faculty has been concerned in the composition of these narratives.

Upon the whole, it is very possible that these forefathers were never in the land of Canaan at all—that, in point of fact, they never really existed as individual men, but correspond to the mythical founders of other nations, whose histories are for the most part composed of fabulous narratives, which, so far as they are based at all on historical truth, shadow forth the doings of tribes and generations, instead of persons. Even the account of Joseph's being carried down as a slave to Egypt, and there rising to be Pharaoh's grand vizier, which led to his father and family settling in Egypt,[53] is in some of its statements so incredible that it is difficult to believe that we have here, any more than elsewhere in Genesis, veracious history. Thus the very basis of the whole story, the statement that, when there were seven successive years of dearth in Egypt, which in that land could only have arisen from deficient inundations of the Nile, there was also 'sore famine,' year after year, 'in all lands,'[54] which would have arisen from totally different causes, throws at once a grave doubt upon the historical character of the narrative. This detailed narrative, in fact, may be merely a work of imagination like the rest, which has been substituted for some brief notice which

[50] G. xxvii. 1-45. [52] G. xxv. 27-34, xxvi. [53] G. xv.
[51] G. xlv. 4-13. [54] G. xli. 54, 57.

the older writer had given of the way in which the Israelites came into Egypt, apparently on the summons of Joseph, since he speaks of him as already settled there,[n] and names him alone as of most importance when he writes—'And Joseph died and all his brethren and all that generation.'[14] Tradition said, and said truly, it would seem, as we have inferred from comparing the Egyptian records,[25] that the Hebrews had at one time been slaves in Egypt. But how they first arrived there was unknown; the tradition of that event had been lost in the course of time; as the Zulus have no recollection of the past beyond a few generations, and can tell us nothing of the cause—whether the pressure of other tribes behind them or the desire to find more ample grazing-grounds —which brought them down to these S.E. parts of Africa. Accordingly, the story of Joseph's doings may have been merely invented to account for the presence of the Hebrews in former time in Egypt, and to show that all the cruel treatment, which they had received at the hands of the Egyptians, was a most ungrateful return for the services rendered to the Pharaoh and people of other days by one of Hebrew blood. And very probably the writer of this section was one of the tribe of Joseph, an Ephraimite among the disciples of Samuel, who took thus an opportunity of lauding his own ancestor, or rather, of reflecting glory on the populous tribe of Ephraim, the powerful leader of the northern tribes.

However this may be, the real history of the Hebrews begins with the Exodus, and that of the Hebrew nation with the times of Saul and Samuel; and in that age also, as we have seen,[26] the idea of writing some popular account of the Exodus out of Egypt most probably originated and was carried into effect in the schools of the prophets, where also,

[n] Galvison, 27, E.i.5b.   [14] E.i.6.   [25] p. 279-282.   [26] p. 31.

no doubt, other literary works were composed, such as the
'Book of Jashar,'[37] that is, the 'Book of the Righteous
One,' viz. of the righteous people, Jeshurun[38] or Israel, and
the 'Book of the Wars of JEHOVAH,'[39] that is, of the wars of
Israel, whose cause was identified with that of its National
Deity, His people being supposed to fight His battles with
His strong co-operation as a 'Man of War'[40]—both which
books are now lost. To the same circle of writers may be
ascribed the most ancient portions of the Books of Judges and
Ruth, and of the two Books of Samuel—in fact, the whole
history in its original form, as it came into the hands of the
Deuteronomist, from G.i to 2S.xxiv, and even to 1K.ix.25,
after which we find no further trace of it. This work, which
now formed a continuous historical narrative from the
Creation downwards to the time of Solomon, perhaps lay
deposited in the Temple, or in the charge of the chief-priest,
till the days of Jeremiah, who retouched and enlarged it
throughout,[41] and especially wrote the main address of Moses
in Deuteronomy, the 'finding' of which in the Temple gave
rise to Josiah's Reformation.[42] To this he afterwards prefixed four introductory and appended two concluding chapters,[43] and he wrote also, as is generally agreed,[44] the rest of
the Books of Kings from the time of Solomon downwards,
for which he most probably had at his disposal some older,
perhaps official, records out of the different reigns. Accordingly the hand of one and the same writer can be distinctly traced, not only throughout almost the whole of
Deuteronomy, but in passages of Genesis, Exodus, Joshua,
Judges, the two Books of Samuel, and the first nine chapters
of Kings, as well as throughout the rest of the Books of
Kings and the prophecies of Jeremiah. In other words, it is

[37] J.x.13, 2S.L18.   [39] D.xxxii.15,xxxlii.5,26.   [40] N.xxi.14.
[38] E.xv.3,6, Pt.xxiv.8.   [41] p.150.   [42] p.152.
[43] p.158.   [44] Bishop Lord HERVEY (D.B.II.p.28).

plain that Jeremiah has either written or retouched and edited the whole of the history from G.i to 2K.xxv, which accordingly exhibits very clearly, wherever his hand has been at work, the stamp of his prophetical character.

Finally, during the first years of Jehoiachin's Captivity, Ezekiel followed Jeremiah's example, by writing L.xviii–xx and especially L.xxvi.[15] And his work was taken up during the Captivity and after it, by a series of priestly writers who have composed nearly half of the present Pentateuch, and made a few insertions, here and there, in the rest of the history as left by Jeremiah,[16] but who, in doing this, departed widely from the tone and spirit of the old prophetical writers, representing JEHOVAH as taking a special interest in a multitude of minute ritualistic observances, and ascribing to Divine authority a series of most stringent ordinances for maintaining the prerogatives of the priests and Levites, which whosoever should transgress 'shall surely die.'[17] Very probably, Ezra, about a century after the Captivity, had a large share in this work, which seems to have been brought very nearly to a close in his days, about B.C. 450, as far as the Hebrew Text is concerned, though it may have received some additions even after that time; for the numerous alterations in the Samaritan Text imply that the work of revision and correction was still going on more than a century afterwards, while the Septuagint Version shows plainly that the Greek Translators must have had before them copies of the Hebrew Scriptures differing in many respects materially from our own.

That something, however, was really done by Ezra, at least in editing and publishing the Law, seems to be implied by the Jewish tradition, which was adopted generally by the early Fathers, based probably upon the story told in the apocryphal

---

* p. 192.
* *e.g.* Ju. xviii. 30, xx. 27b, 28a, 1 K. iii. 16–28, iv. 24–34, v. 15–18, vi. 1, 11–14, viii. 4, 5, 10, 11, 6 b, 64, xii. 4–16.   * N. i. 51, iii. 10, 38, xvi. 40, xviii. 32.

Second Book of Esdras. Here Ezra says, 'Thy Law is burnt; therefore no man knoweth the things that are done of Thee or the works that shall begin. But, if I have found grace before Thee, send the Holy Ghost into me, that I may write all that has been done in the world since the beginning, which was written in Thy Law, so that they which live in the latter days may live.' And Ezra says that his prayer was heard, and he was told to retire into a private place with five men 'ready to write swiftly,' and with 'many box-wood tables to write upon.' 'So I took the five men as He bade me, and we went into the field and stayed there. And the next day lo! a voice called me saying, Ezra, open thy mouth, and drink that which I give thee to drink. Then I opened my mouth, and lo! he reached me a full cup, which was filled, as it were, with water, but the colour of it was like fire. And I took it and drank; and, when I had drunk of it, my heart uttered understanding, and wisdom grew in my breast; for my spirit strengthened my memory, and my mouth was opened and shut no more. The Highest gave understanding unto the five men, and they wrote the wonderful visions of the night that were told, which they knew not; and they sat forty days, and they wrote in the day and at night they ate bread.'[48]

Accordingly, JEROME[49] says, 'Whether you choose to say that Moses was the author of the Pentateuch or Ezra the restorer of that work, I have no objection'; while earlier Fathers speak more positively, as AUGUSTINE,[50] 'Ezra restored the Law, which had been burnt by the Chaldæans in the Temple archives, he being full of the same Spirit which had been in the Scriptures,' and CLEMENT[51] of Alexandria, 'When the Scriptures had been destroyed in the Captivity of Nebuchadnezzar, Ezra the Levite the priest, in the time of

---

[48] 2 Esdr. xiv. 21–42.
[49] *De mir. S.S.* ii. 33.
[50] *Ad. Heb.* III.
[51] *Strom.* I. xxii. 49.

Artaxerxes king of the Persians, having become inspired, reproduced prophetically all the ancient Scriptures,' and TERTULLIAN,[a] 'When Jerusalem was destroyed by the Babylonian storming, it is well known that every article of Jewish Literature was restored by Ezra,' and IRENÆUS,[b] 'Then, in the times of Artaxerxes king of the Persians, He inspired Ezra the priest of the tribe of Levi, to set in order again all the words of the former prophets, and restore for the people the Legislation of Moses.' So remarkable a story can hardly have originated without some strong tradition having pointed to Ezra having had a large share in writing the later portions of the priestly Law, or else to his having compiled that Law and exerted himself energetically in making it known to his contemporaries.

I have thus endeavoured to set before you as plainly as I can the main results of Modern Biblical Criticism as regards the composition of the Pentateuch. Doubtless, as the consequence of these conclusions, the popular ideas as to the nature of the Divine action among the Jews will have to be materially modified. The whole will become thoroughly humanised. The preternatural Divine influence will withdraw from the prominent place, which it occupies in the narrative as we read it, to that invisible action, which is familiarised to us by our own experience. But what the Scriptures may lose in revealing power, they will gain in human interest. The sacred history does indeed change its aspect under the influence of criticism. But it does not therefore cease to be a history, though a history whose importance is to be estimated rather by the ideas of which it records the rise and development, and the consequences that have flowed from them, than by any phenomena accompanying their introduction. Not the less does this history remain the preparatory stage for the

[a] *De hab. mul.* III. [b] *adv. hær.* III.xxi.2.

coming of that Divine Light which has 'lighted the Gentiles' ever since, at least over the whole Western World, and will yet be, as we trust, 'the glory of God's people Israel.' For, if their 'casting away,' as St. Paul says, became 'the reconciling of the world'[44]—if their blind attachment to the Law of Moses, which was in truth the work of their fathers when Moses had been in his grave for centuries, has hitherto kept them back as a body from the full enjoyment of that light, and of that liberty wherewith Christ has made us free as children of God,—may we not hope and believe that there is a development yet in store for them as well as for us, perhaps through the influence of that critical research, which seems to be crushing into powder the 'letter,' at once their trust and their chain,—that the time is coming when the more thorough union of Semitic faith with Aryan thought will be to the Church of the Living God as 'life from the dead'?[45]

[44] Rom. xi. 15.   [45] See *Spectator*, May 4, 1872, p. 571.

LECTURE XXIII.

SUMMARY.

The Church Fathers uncritical and credulous in adopting the fabulous story about Ezra; the apocryphal books of the O.T. regarded by the mass of Christendom as canonical, and in the Homilies of the Church of England as 'the Infallible Word of God'; the pretended commission of Artaxerxes, giving plenary powers to Ezra, altogether fictitious; this appears also from the disorders existing when Nehemiah came to Jerusalem; the Edict of Cyrus, allowing the Jews to return, quoted in part in Chronicles, is also fictitious; the whole of Ezra and half of Nehemiah due to the Chronicler; the letter to Artaxerxes and the royal rescript in Ezr.iv are authentic; these documents evidently refer to the building of the *walls* of Jerusalem, but are here erroneously transferred to the building of the *Temple* fifty years previously, which the writer represents as hindered by the enemies of Judah, in defiance of the facts of history, as shown by the prophet Haggai; this fiction he tries to support by a letter supposed to have been addressed to Darius, and the king's supposed reply, quoting a decree of Cyrus supposed to have been found in the royal archives—all which is a pure fiction; no dependence can be placed on the Chronicler's statements in these Books; nothing is certainly known about Ezra, whom Nehemiah does not even mention, though a priest of that name may have been zealously concerned in copying and introducing, and perhaps in part composing, the Levitical Law.

THE BOOKS OF EZRA AND NEHEMIAH.

IN my last Lecture I spoke of Ezra as having probably had a considerable share in composing the priestly portions of the Pentateuch; and I quoted a passage from the Second Book of Esdras asserting that Ezra had actually had the whole Law revealed to him afresh, when it had been destroyed and lost in the Babylonish Captivity, as also the statements of JEROME, AUGUSTINE, CLEMENT, TERTULLIAN, IRENÆUS, all to the same or similar purport. If, indeed, the authority of the Fathers of the Church is worth anything in such matters as these, it is difficult to see how a tradition so clear and so unanimously affirmed by so many of the most ancient, eminent, and learned of them, can be lightly rejected. Yet, I suppose, not the most zealous defender of traditionary views will now venture to maintain the historical veracity of these statements; though the Roman Church regards all the apocryphal books of the O.T., and the Greek Church regards most of them, as being equally Divine and infallible with the other Scriptures, a belief which prevailed also in the Church of England at the time when the Book of Homilies was written, in which we read, 'Almighty God by the Wise Man saith,'[1] referring to

[1] *Homilies* (Corrie's Ed.), p. 73.

the Book of Wisdom, and passages out of the Apocrypha are quoted as 'places of Scripture' in which 'the Holy Ghost doth teach,'[1] as 'the Word of God,'[2] 'the infallible and undeceivable Word of God.'[3] The Fathers in question have evidently copied from one another or from the story in the Book of Esdras (A.D. 100); and their statements serve only to show how unreasoning and credulous were these good men, and how little dependence therefore can be placed on their critical judgment in respect of any of the Canonical Books, either of the Old Testament or of the New.

But who was Ezra? The question might be easily answered, if we could trust to the data of the 'Book of Ezra,' which stands in our Bibles between the Books of Chronicles and the Book of Nehemiah. For this book tells us that Ezra was a 'priest the son of Aaron,'[4] and also 'a ready scribe in the Law of Moses,'[5] who went up from Babylon to Jerusalem at his own request in the seventh year of Artaxerxes, having 'prepared his heart to seek the Law of JEHOVAH and to do it, and to teach in Israel statutes and judgments.'[6] It states further that the king issued to him a formal commission, permitting any that pleased to go to Jerusalem with him, of the people, the priests, and the Levites, and authorising him to 'enquire concerning Judah and Jerusalem, according to the Law of his God which was in his hand,' and with 'the silver and gold which the king and his counsellors had freely offered unto the God of Israel whose dwelling was in Jerusalem,' in addition to the freewill offerings of his own people, to buy sacrifices for the Temple, together with their proper 'meal-offerings and drink-offerings,' and to spend the rest as he thought proper; and 'whatsoever more shall be needed for the House of thy God, which thou shalt have occasion to bestow, bestow it out of the king's treasury. And I, even I,

---

[1] *Homilies* (Corrie's Ed.), p.391.   [2] *Ib.* p.246,247.   [3] *Ib.* p.106.
[4] Ezr. vii. 1-5.   [5] *v.* 6.   [6] *v.* 6-10.

Artaxerxes the king, do make a decree to all the treasurers which are across the River, that whatsoever Ezra the priest, the scribe of the Law of the God of Heaven, shall require of you, it be done speedily. . . . Whatsoever is commanded by the God of Heaven, let it be diligently done for the House of the God of Heaven; for why should there be wrath against the realm of the king and his sons? Also we certify you that touching any of the priests and the Levites, choristers, gatekeepers, Nethinim, or servants of the House of God, it shall not be lawful to impose toll, tribute, or custom upon them. And thou, Ezra, after the wisdom of thy God that is in thine hand, set magistrates and judges, who may judge all the people that are across the River, all such as know the laws of thy God, and teach ye them that know them not. And whosoever will not do the law of thy God and the law of the king, let judgment be executed speedily upon him, whether it be unto death or to banishment or to confiscation of goods or to imprisonment.'[8]

Let us now consider a little the contents of this extraordinary commission, which, in the form of a letter to Ezra, invests this Jewish priest with plenary power over the lives and liberties and properties of all the king's subjects, not in Judah only, but in all the district 'across the River,' that is, in all the regions west of the Great River Euphrates, denouncing the most terrible penalties, not only against any who 'will not do the law of the king,' but also against all who 'will not do the law of Ezra's God.'[9] Very many of those to whom such a decree would have applied would most probably have been of the same religion as the king himself, and many also would have been Samaritans, who are represented in this book as living in bitter hostility to the Jews.[10] Can it be believed that Artaxerxes would have subjected all these to

[8] Ezr. vii. 11-26.   [9] v. 26.   [10] Ezr. iv. 1-16, 23, 24, v. 6, 17.

the penalty of death, if they disobeyed the 'Law of JEHOVAH' as taught by Ezra? Of the Law, probably, most of these people knew little or nothing. But they are here, it seems, to be converted to the Jewish religion—'teach ye them that know not the laws of thy God,'[11]—in true Mahommedan fashion, with the threat of imprisonment, confiscation, banishment, or death, if they did not receive it![12] Is this an edict of Artaxerxes or a mere dream of a later age? Moreover, Ezra is to appoint 'magistrates and judges, who shall judge all the people across the River, such as know already the laws of his God,'[13] and, of course, all the others when converted. Was, then, the priest Ezra to supersede the satraps and governors already ruling 'across the River,' by virtue of this letter addressed to himself? Yet the 'treasurers' across the River were, it seems, to remain in office, and to supply Ezra's demands for the Temple to any extent![14] Lastly, the king writes familiarly about 'the priests and the Levites,'[15] 'Judah and Jerusalem,'[16] 'the God of Israel, whose dwelling is in Jerusalem,'[17] 'meat-offerings and drink-offerings,'[18] and he exempts from payment of 'toll, tribute, or custom' the 'priests and Levites, choristers, gate-keepers, and Nethinim or menials of the Temple,'[19] writing just as if he had by heart the whole string of phrases of the Later Legislation; he enjoins that the 'bullocks, rams, and lambs,' required for the Levitical Sacrifices, shall be promptly purchased;[20] and he refers again and again to 'the Law,'[21] just as any well-trained Jew might have done. In short, it is clear that this 'letter' of Artaxerxes is a pure fiction, written with the view of magnifying the position and authority of 'Ezra the priest,' the renewer of the Law of Moses. But that Ezra had no such powers really committed to him is evident from the fact that Nehemiah, on

---

[11] Ezr. vii. 25.   [12] v. 26.   [13] v. 25.   [14] v. 21–23.
[15] v. 13, 14.   [16] v. 14.   [17] v. 15.   [18] v. 17.
[19] Ezr. vii. 24.   [20] v. 17.   [21] v. 12, 14, 21, 25, 26.

his arrival in Jerusalem twelve years afterwards, found the practice of usury existing among the Jews with gross oppression of their brethren,[72] in direct defiance of the Levitical Law,[73] which Ezra, with the 'Law of his God' in his heart, and with these summary powers in his hand, must be supposed during all this time to have overlooked or permitted.

This Book also professes to quote the very words of the Edict of Cyrus which allowed the Jews to return to their own land.[74] But, after the example which we have just had of the writer's practice of using his imagination freely in writing history, we shall have no difficulty in concluding that this Edict of Cyrus is just as fictitious as the Edict of Artaxerxes. It makes, for instance, the Persian king speak of JEHOVAH by name not only as 'the God of Israel,' but as the 'God of Heaven,' and say 'JEHOVAH He is the God,' 'JEHOVAH He hath given me all the kingdoms of the earth,'[75] as if he had actually himself adopted the faith of the Jews. It is plain that the writer has merely given in his own words the substance of some such a decree as he supposes Cyrus to have issued on this occasion. But a portion of this decree is also given at the end of the Second Book of Chronicles; and a close examination of the Books of Ezra and Nehemiah shows that almost all of the Book of Ezra and half of the Book of Nehemiah are the work of the Chronicler himself,[76] who wrote between one and two hundred years after the events which he here describes, or later still, and gives a thoroughly untrustworthy account of those events, inserting fictitious decrees,[77] letters,[78] prayers,[79] and speeches,[80] and colouring everything from a Levitical point of view.[81]

---

[72] Neh. v. 1-13. [73] L. xxv. 35-37. [74] Ezr. i. 2-4. [75] v. 2, 3.
[76] See Part VII of my work on the Pentateuch for proof of this.
[77] Ezr. i. 2-4, vi. 3-5, 6-12. [78] Ezr. v. 7-17, vii. 12-26.
[79] Ezr. ix. 6-15, Neh. ix. 5-38. [80] Ezr. ix. 1, 2, x. 2-4, 10-14.
[81] Ezr. i. 5, ii. 36-60, 61-63, 70, iii. 2-6, 8-13, vi. 16-20, vii. 1-7, viii. 2, 15-20, 24-30, 33-35. Neh. vii. 39, 62, 63, 65, 73, viii. x. 28-39, xi, xii, xiii. 5b, 9a, 10-13, 22a, 29-31a.

In one place, however, he really does quote what appears to be a genuine rescript of Artaxerxes, in reply to a representation made to him that the Jews were fortifying their city.[13] 'Be it known unto the king that the Jews which came up from thee to us are come unto Jerusalem, building [*i.e.* fortifying] that rebellious and bad city, and have set up its walls and joined the foundations. Be it known now unto the king that, if this city be builded, and the walls set up again, then will they not pay toll, tribute, and custom, and so thou shalt endanger the revenue of the kings.' And the king replies, 'Make a decree to cause these men to cease, and that this city be not builded, until commandment shall be given from me.'[14] No allusion is here made to the building of the *Temple* being stopped; nor was it likely that their conquerors should trouble themselves to interfere with *that* work. Moreover, Artaxerxes began to reign (B.C. 465) about seventy years after the return of the Jews from the Captivity (B.C. 536), and *fifty years after the Temple was actually finished* in the time of the prophets Haggai and Zechariah[15] (B.C. 515). Yet here the writer represents the 'adversaries of Judah and Benjamin' as conspiring to hinder the building of the Temple, and as succeeding in doing so by means of this very rescript of Artaxerxes,[16] written fifty years after the Temple was completed in the sixth year of Darius,[16] whom he actually supposes to have reigned *after* Artaxerxes,[17] instead of half a century before him! The prophet Haggai, however, says not a word about any such opposition on the part of the Jews' enemies to the building of the Temple, but ascribes the delay which had occurred wholly to the negligence, indifference, and luxury of the Jews themselves. 'This people says, The time is not come, the time when JEHOVAH'S House should be built. ... Is it a time for you, O ye, to dwell in your ceiled

---

[13] Ezr.iv.11-16.   [14] v.17-22.   [15] Hag.ii.6-9, Zech.vii.1-3.
[16] Ezr.iv.1-6,23,24.   [16] Ezr.vi.15.   [17] Ezr.iv.23,24.

houses, and this House lying waste? ... Ye looked for much, but lo! it came to little; and, when ye brought it home, I did blow upon it. Why? said JEHOVAH of Hosts. Because of Mine House that is waste, and ye run every man to his own house.'[a] The Chronicler must have had this prophecy before him when he wrote. But he was unwilling to allow that any delay—much more a delay of twenty years—had been caused by the lazy self-indulgence of the Jews themselves, and even while Zerubbabel and Joshua the chief-priest, who had led them from Babylon to Jerusalem, were still living.[b] So in the very teeth of Haggai's reproach he invents a series of vexatious hindrances from the enemies of Judah, suggested very probably by the opposition which was really made, more than half a century afterwards, in the days of Nehemiah, to the building of the *wall*.[c] For this purpose he uses these genuine letters to and from the king, which, however, speak only of 'the Jews who had come up from Artaxerxes' setting to work to 'build the rebellious and bad city, having completed the walls and joined the foundations,'[d] perhaps referring to Ezra and his party, who may have made some attempt, before Nehemiah's arrival, to fortify Jerusalem, so far as to 'complete' the walls, that is, lay the foundations all round—letters which he had obtained from some quarter or other, but of which he apparently wholly mistook the meaning.

Once more, in support of this fiction he has introduced another letter, purporting to have been sent to Darius the king by the Governor of the province to which Judæa belonged, acting in concert with certain Samaritans,[e] in which he reports the progress made in the building of the Temple, and states that the Jews appealed in support of their proceedings to a decree of Cyrus, which expressly ordered that

[a] Hag. i. 2. 4, 9.   [b] v. 1, comp. Ezr. iii. 2.   [c] Neh. i. 3, ii. 8, 13. 15. 17-20, iii, iv.
[d] Ezr. iv. 12.   [e] Ezr. v. 3. 17, comp. vi. 9, 10.

stones and timber should be supplied for the building and the expenses paid out of the revenues of the province, and suggests that this decree would probably be found in the king's treasury. Accordingly Darius, we are told, ordered a search to be made for the record in question, which was duly found,[14] and thereupon, in the second year of his reign, he issued a decree, which the writer here professes to quote at length, authorizing the completion of the Temple.[15]

But this letter and decree are evidently fictitious like the others; though, in imitation of the genuine letters to and from Artaxerxes, they are written in the Chaldee dialect, which differs from Hebrew much in the same sort of way that broad Scotch-English differs from common English. Would the Governor of the province have been ignorant that such a decree had been issued some sixteen years previously? O if he was, were there no royal counsellors alive who would have been aware of so notorious a fact which had so recently occurred, and would know that a large body of Jews had returned to Jerusalem in consequence, with free permission to rebuild their Temple? Was it necessary for the Governor to ask the king to have a search made for it among the archives of the Empire, as if it were some venerable charter issued in days of old beyond the memory of statesmen then living, when Zerubbabel had only to exhibit to all gainsayers the 30 golden chargers and 1,000 silver chargers or the '5,400 vessels of gold and silver' altogether,[16] which, we are told, Cyrus restored to him out of the spoils of the First Temple, as the best possible proof of his having sanctioned their undertaking? Or had Zerubbabel himself no copy of that decree, and during all this time had he never once appealed to it, to obtain from the Governor the help which he needed? How strange, too, that Haggai, who prophesied in this very same second year

[14] Ezr. vi. 1-5.   [15] v. 6-12.   [16] Ezr. i. 9-11.

of Darius,[16] makes no allusion whatever to the cheering circumstances under which the work would now go forward! Or, if we turn to the decree itself, as here quoted, can it be thought that Cyrus would have actually defined the very mode in which the Temple should be built, 'with three rows of great stones and a row of new timber,'[17] and have specified its exact dimensions, '60 cubits high and 60 cubits broad,'[18] that is, *twice as high and thrice as wide as the Temple of Solomon!*[19] Nothing is said about the length of it; but, supposing this to have been omitted by some careless copyist, and to have been in proportion to the height and breadth, would there then have been any ground for Haggai's saying, 'Who is left among you that saw this House in its former glory? and how do ye see it now? Is it not in your eyes as nothing in comparison of it?'[20] Or, again, is it credible that Darius would utter a prayer in this decree that 'the GOD who had caused His Name to dwell there'—where we recognise a well-known phrase of Deuteronomy[21]—'would destroy all kings and peoples who should put their hand to alter and to destroy this House of GOD which is at Jerusalem?'[22]

From all this it is plain that no dependence can be placed on any statements of the Chronicler contained in these Books, unless they are supported by other evidence—for instance, as to the details of the return from the Captivity,[23] the numbers and names of those who returned,[24] the building of the Temple and the ceremonies observed at its founding and dedication,[25] or the account of Ezra's journey from Babylon to Jerusalem,[26] eighty years after the return of Zerubbabel, with splendid presents for the Temple from 'the king and his counsellors and his lords and all Israel,'[27] and his proceedings on his

---

[16] Hag.i.1.
[17] 1K.vi.2.
[18] Ezr.vi.12.
[19] Ezr.iii.
[20] Ezr.vi.4.
[21] Hag.ii.3.
[22] Ezr.i.
[23] Ezr.vii.6—9,viii.
[24] v.3.
[25] D.xii.11,xiv.23,xvi.2,6,11,xxvi.2.
[26] Ezr.ii.
[27] Ezr.vii.15,16,viii.24-30,33,34.

arrival at Jerusalem, his mourning for the sin of those who had married heathen women,[58] his prayer and confession and exhortation,[59] and the effect which these had upon the people,[60] so that more than a hundred mentioned by name, who 'had taken strange wives, by some of whom they had children,' 'gave their hands that they would put away their wives, and being guilty offered a lamb of the flock for their trespass.' The whole of this rests on the Chronicler's testimony, and, from what we now know of his character as a historian, not a statement of his can be regarded as worthy of credence, unless it seems probable in itself or derives support from other independent sources. The very lists of names, which seem at first sight to guarantee the accuracy of his information and the truthfulness of his narrative, are found on examination to betray frequently the same unhistorical character which everywhere pervades the writings due to his hand.[61]

The first six chapters, however, of the Book of Nehemiah, the first few verses of the seventh, and most of the last chapter,[62] appear to be genuine extracts from some memoir of Nehemiah's doings written by his own hand, which, together with the genuine letter of Artaxerxes and the king's reply,[63] perhaps preserved also by Nehemiah, had come into the Chronicler's possession. But he has filled up the rest of this Book, as well as the whole Book of Ezra, with fictions composed in his own peculiar style, specially dignifying the priests and Levites. He tells us, for instance, how Ezra read the Book of the Law in the ears of the people 'on the first day of the month,'[64] and how they kept a solemn feast that day,[65] and the next day found 'written in the Law' the proper mode of keeping the Feast of Tabernacles,[66] which

---

[58] Ezr. ix. 1-4.   [59] Ezr. ix. 5-15,x.1-11.   [60] Ezr. x. 12-44.
    [61] See part VII for full proof of this.
[62] Neh. vii. 12,2 52,xiii.4 52,6-8,9b,14 21,22b 28,31b.   [63] Ezr. iv. 7 23.
[64] Neh. viii. 1-8   [65] v. 9-12.   [66] v. 13 18.

they accordingly observed duly for the first time in the history of Israel 'since the days of Joshua the son of Nun unto that day.'[67] After this he informs us how the Levites in a long supplication confessed God's Goodness and the people's sin,[68] and thereupon the people sealed a covenant that henceforth they would keep faithfully the Law of Moses,[69] and especially that they would maintain the sacrificial system as prescribed in the Later Legislation, and pay scrupulously the dues of the priests and Levites.[70] And then he gives long lists of names of priests and Levites,[71] which have probably no historical value whatever, except perhaps that of indicating the principal families existing in the writer's own time; and he goes on to describe, as if from the pen of Nehemiah,[72] the dedication of the walls,[73] along which two troops of choristers marched, setting out from one spot in opposite directions, Ezra heading his company of Levites, but Nehemiah following in the rear of his choir.[74] After all these accounts, however, of the activity and prominence of Ezra in the days of Nehemiah, it is somewhat remarkable that Nehemiah himself in his genuine memoirs does not even once mention his name. Still, as I have said,[75] the Jewish tradition seems to imply that there must have been some priest, named Ezra, after the Captivity, who took an active part in editing and publishing the Law of Moses, now increased with the Levitical Legislation, partly written by other priests in Babylonia, and partly perhaps by his own hand. More than this cannot be said with any confidence about Ezra's doings.

No doubt, it must at first sight seem somewhat extravagant to suppose that any nation would accept a vast system of minute legislative enactments as the regulations which had

---

[67] Neh. viii. 17.
[68] v. 32-39.
[69] Neh. xii. 27-43.
[70] Neh. ix. 4-38.
[71] Neh. xi. 10-23, xii. 1-26.
[72] v. 36, 38.
[73] Neh. x. 1-31.
[74] v. 31, 38, 40.
[75] p. 311.

been observed by their ancestors for ages, when in fact the details were mostly of modern introduction. Yet, as we have seen, it is the Jewish tradition that something very like this did actually take place after the return from the Babylonish Captivity, so that Ezra, in fact, appears in the Talmud as the very counterpart of Moses. What can have given rise to such a tradition but the knowledge of the fact that before this time the 'Law of Moses,' as we now possess it, was really unknown, that there were no copies which could be traced further back than that period, when, as all had to be organised anew among those who had grown up for two generations in a strange land, an opportunity occurred for introducing new rules under the garb of antiquity, such as has hardly occurred in the history of any other nation?[16] Among the returning exiles, if we can trust the statements in these Books, there was, as I have said,[17] one priest for ten laymen, and these last, most probably, more or less under priestly influence. As the result of this enormous preponderance of the priestly element, the reviving nation was easily taught to guard itself against unfaithfulness to its God in future by putting on the heavy clothing of a vast system of ecclesiastical observances, pervading the whole fabric of their lives. From this, thank God! the teaching of Christ has set us free. Nor will we now suffer ourselves and our children to be entangled again under the yoke of bondage, and make the due performance of rites and ceremonies, or the profession of an orthodox creed, of more consequence than that Divine Charity in which the life of the soul consists, and those fruits of the Spirit, 'love, joy, peace, longsuffering, gentleness, goodness, faith, meekness, temperance, against which there is no Law.'[18]

[16] *Spectator*, May 4, 1872, p. 570.   [17] p. 257.   [18] Gal. v. 22, 23.

LECTURE XXIV.

SUMMARY.

The Books of Chronicles fallacious and misleading; they have been the chief stay of the popular notion as to the Mosaic origin of the priestly legislation of the Pentateuch; in the older Lectionary no portion of these Books was ordered to be read, though much from the Apocrypha; Amos, Isaiah, Jeremiah, Ezekiel, show plainly that this Legislation did not in their time exist in the story of the Exodus; meaning of the phrase 'Law of JEHOVAH,' as used by these prophets; they refer to incidents of the O.S., but nowhere to the L.L.; even the later prophets speak of the priests as 'sons of Levi,' never as 'sons of Aaron'; the latter phrase is used habitually by the Chronicler, who also distinguishes the priests and the Levites, as in the L.L.; instances of his modifying the older history about the reign of David, to glorify the priests and Levites; special reason for his fiction about the Mosaic Tabernacle and Brazen Altar having been set up at Gibeon; he has left out whatever might be a reproach to David and Solomon, and has altered, in copying, the statements of Samuel and Kings, so as to represent the L.L. as in full force all along; his fictitious account of David's numbering the Levites, of his dividing the priests and choristers into courses and appointing the Levites to important offices, of his gifts to the Temple and his prayer of thanksgiving; the Chronicler's fictions in the history of the subsequent kings from Solomon downwards; he was probably a Levite chorister, writing long after the Captivity; some few of his notices, not found in Samuel and Kings, may have historical value, but as a whole his original statements are utterly untrustworthy; the grave nature of the Chronicler's conduct in deliberately falsifying the facts of history as known to himself; he has only followed the example of the priestly writers of the Pentateuch.

THE FICTIONS OF THE CHRONICLER.

HITHERTO I have made no use in these Lectures of the two Books of Chronicles, that is to say, I have never once appealed to them in support of my statements. The reason of this is obvious after what we have seen in the last Lecture of the Chronicler's mode of writing history in the Books of Ezra and Nehemiah. For in these Books he has not hesitated to insert letters and decrees which are thoroughly fictitious; and, generally, his accounts, when unsupported by other evidence, are worthless as history. The two Books of Chronicles exhibit the same fallacious and misleading character. They go over the same ground as that traversed by the Books of Samuel and Kings, though the writer confines himself chiefly to matters affecting the kingdom of Judah; and he not only had those older Books before him when he wrote, but he has very frequently copied their language word for word. And yet he has continually altered their statements or made his own additions to them, and usually in such a way as to magnify the office of the priests and Levites, and to represent the Levitical Law as in full force from the first, and the priestly ordinances as punctually obeyed.

This is a matter of grave importance, because it is really

the Chronicler who by these perversions of the fact has led
men all along to suppose that these prescriptions were
really ancient and even of Mosaic origin, instead of being
the product of a very late age. In the older Lectionary
of the Church of England not a single chapter was selected
for public reading, whether on Sundays and on holidays,
or in the common daily service, out of these two Books,
though so much was given from Esther and Ecclesiastes,
and even from the apocryphal books of Tobit, Judith,
Wisdom, Ecclesiasticus, and Baruch—nay, Bel and the
Dragon, and the story of Susannah. This cannot have
arisen from any lack of interesting matter in the Books of
Chronicles; on the contrary, the writer's style is of a very
decidedly religious and practical character, well suited,
as many would think, for the work of edifying. Accordingly
in the New Lectionary several chapters of the First Book are
appointed for Sunday Lessons, while others in the Second
Book appear in the columns for daily use. It is possible that
the framers of the older Lectionary were aware of the contradictions between the statements of the Chronicles and those
of the Books of Samuel and Kings, and thought it not good
to bring these differences into view before an ordinary congregation.[1] However this may be, the fact is that in the
Books of Chronicles the priests and the Levites, carefully distinguished from each other, fill the foreground of the picture
on various occasions, of which no example can be found in
the older histories, as also that the sacrificial system, as laid
down in the Levitical Law, is exhibited everywhere in full

---

[1] *e. g. comp.* 1Ch.i.1-12 with 1S.xxxi.1-13—xl.1-9 with 2S.v.1-3,6-10—
v.10-41a with 2S.xxiii.8-39—xiii.6-14 with 2S.vi.2,3,5-11—xlv.1-16 with 2S.
v.11-25—xvii,xviii,xix, with 2S.vii,viii,x—xx with 2S.xi.1,xii.30, 31,xxi.18-22—
xxi.1-27 with 2S.xxiv.1-4,9-25—2Ch.i.7-12 with 1K.iii.5-14—v.14-17 with
1K.x.26-29—iv.2-5 with 1K.vii.23-26—v.11-22 with 1K.vii.40-50—vii.11-22
with 1K.ix.1-9—viii with 1K.ix.10,17-28, &c., &c.; but see the full proof of the
statements made above in Part VII.

operation, of which no trace appears in the older prophets down to the Captivity.

Amos, for instance, is so far from blaming his people for disregard of the Levitical Law that he asks 'Was it sacrifices and offerings that ye brought near to me in the wilderness forty years, O House of Israel?'[1]—that is, 'Was that what I required of you then, that you think to pacify me now with such things?'—as if he knew nothing of any such Law, in which multitudinous sacrifices are said to have been enjoined in the wilderness. Isaiah says, 'I am full of the burnt-offerings of rams and the fat of fed beasts; and I delight not in the blood of bullocks or of lambs or of he-goats. When ye come to appear before Me, who hath required this at your hands that ye may tread My courts?'[2]— whereas in the Levitical Law these very things *were* expressly required of any who would 'tread the courts of JEHOVAH.' Jeremiah says, 'I spake not unto your fathers, nor commanded them, in the day that I brought them out of the land of Egypt, concerning burnt-offerings and sacrifices; but this thing I commanded them saying, Obey My voice, and I will be your God and ye shall be my people.'[3] But in the Levitical Law JEHOVAH does speak especially about 'burnt-offerings and sacrifices;' and such words could not have been written if the sacrificial laws of Exodus, Leviticus, and Numbers had either been actually prescribed in the wilderness, or had existed in Jeremiah's time in the story of the Exodus. Nor would Ezekiel have laid down his laws for the regulation of the priesthood, their office and income,[4] if these subjects had been fully treated of in the middle Books of the Pentateuch, or prescribed sacrifices at variance with those already prescribed in books regarded as Mosaic and Divine.[5] In short, the whole

---

[1] Am. v. 25.   [2] Is. i. 11, 12.
[3] Jer. vii. 22, 23.   [4] Ez. xliii. 18–27, xliv. 4–31.
[5] In Ez. xlv, *comp.* v. 23, 24 with N. xxviii. 19–22, v. 25 with N. xxix. 13–38; in Ez. xlvi, *comp.* v. 4 with N. xxviii. 9, v. 6 with N. xxviii. 11, v. 7 with N. xxviii. 12–14, v. 13 with E. xxix. 38–40, N. xxviii. 3 5

tone of the prophets differed utterly from that of the priestly mind, to which we owe the system of ritual enjoined in the Later Legislation ; and, accordingly, they repeatedly disparage, even contemptuously, the offering of sacrifices in comparison with moral rectitude and goodness.[7]

It is true, the expression 'Law of JEHOVAH' often occurs in ordinary translations of prophetical books.[8] But the Hebrew word for 'Law' means properly 'instruction, teaching,' and is used by the prophets to denote the teaching of themselves and their predecessors, which they called the 'teaching of JEHOVAH,' because JEHOVAH, as they believed, had put it into their hearts for the instruction of their brethren ; as where, for instance, Isaiah says, 'This is a rebellious people, lying children, children that will not hear the *instruction* of JEHOVAH, who say to the seers, See not, and to the prophets, Prophesy not unto us right things, speak unto us smooth things, prophesy deceits.'[9] And so, too, it is used for the 'instruction' which the priests, both before and after the Captivity, gave to pious enquirers, with reference to sacrifices of all kinds, vows, leprosy, &c.[10]

Again the prophets before the Captivity refer often to incidents which are mentioned in the Original Story of the Pentateuch.[11] But not one of them makes the least allusion to any part of the Levitical Law ; they never once mention the name of Aaron as priest, and know nothing of the distinction between priests and Levites ; though Ezekiel, as I have said,[12] shows a close connexion with the oldest portions of this Legislation, and after the Captivity Haggai

---

[7] Is.i.11–14,16,17, Hos.vi.6, Am.v.14,15,21–23.
[8] *e.g.* Is.i.10,ii.3,v.24,viii.16,20,xxx.9, Hos.iv.6,viii.1, Am.ii.4, Mic.iv.2.
[9] Is.xxx.9–11.
[10] Ex.xxii.26, Zeph.iii.4, Hag.ii.11–13, Mal.ii.7,9, *comp.* D.xxiv.8.
[11] Am.ii.9,10,iii.1,2,iv.11,v.25,26,vii.9, Hos.ii.14,15,ix.10,xi.1,8,xii.3,4,5,9, 12,13,xiii.4,5, Is.i.9,10,lii.9,x.24,26,xi.16,xii.2,5, Mic.vi.4,5,vii.15, Nah.i.3, Zeph.ii.9. [12] p.192

apparently makes a distinct reference to it.[13] Towards the end of the Captivity the Later Isaiah says that *all* Israelites shall be called 'priests of JEHOVAH,' 'ministers of our God,'[14] and that out of them—the Israelites generally—'JEHOVAH will take for priests, for Levites.'[15] Haggai and Zechariah, writing soon after the return from the Captivity, throw no light upon this question. But Malachi, probably a contemporary of Nehemiah, speaks of the 'sons of Levi' as priests, who shall be 'purged as gold and silver,' that they may 'bring-near to JEHOVAH an offering in righteousness';[16] and he refers to their having 'corrupted the Covenant of Levi,'[17] under which the whole tribe was appointed to act as priests for their brethren.[18] Nehemiah, however, in his genuine memoir,[19] speaks of the Levites, and also of the Nethinim,[20] as building their portion of the wall apart from the priests.[21] In his time, therefore, the distinction, it seems, was recognized; though Malachi, his contemporary, still speaks of the priests by the older designation 'the sons of Levi,'[22] instead of using the newly-coined phrase 'the sons of Aaron.'

We have already seen that in the Books of Samuel and Kings—except in one verse which is manifestly a later interpolation[23]—there is no trace of any distinction being made as yet between the priests and Levites, and that there is much, as in the account of Eli's time,[24] which is irreconcileable with the notion of the very existence of the Levitical Legislation. It is very different when we turn to the Books of Chronicles. Here constantly, as in the Books of Ezra and Nehemiah—about ninety times altogether—we find, exactly as in the Levitical Legislation, a strong

[13] Hag. ii. 11-13.
[14] Is. lxi. 6.
[15] Is. lxvi. 21.
[16] Mal. iii. 3.
[17] Mal. ii. 8.
[18] p. 238.
[19] p. 328.
[20] Neh. iii. 17, 22, 26, 28.
[21] v. 1, 22, 28.
[22] Mal. iii. 3.
[23] 1 K. viii. 4, see p. 252.
[24] p. 248.

line of demarcation drawn between the priests and the Levites, as forming two distinct orders of clergy, as also between both orders and the laity. Thus after Saul's death there come to David, among other supporters, 4,600 Levites and 3,700 'sons of Aaron,'[m] a designation which never once appears in the earlier historical books or in any of the prophetical writings. And yet, notwithstanding all this troop of priests and Levites, when a few years afterwards David undertakes to bring up the ark to Mount Zion, he employs only laymen for the work, and on that account solely, according to the Chronicler, the driver Uzza met with the accident which caused his death. It was only, he tells us, *after* the lesson taught by this sad event that David said, 'None ought to carry the ark of God but the Levites';[n] and so he summons them to bring up the ark on the second occasion saying, 'Ye are the heads of the fathers of the Levites; sanctify yourselves, ye and your brethren, that ye may bring up the ark of JEHOVAH the God of Israel to where I have prepared for it; for because ye did not at the first, JEHOVAH our God made a breach upon us, because we sought Him not after the due order. So the priests and the Levites sanctified themselves to bring up the ark of JEHOVAH the God of Israel. And the sons of the Levites bare the ark of God upon their shoulders with the staves thereon, as Moses commanded according to the word of JEHOVAH.'[o] Did, then, not one of the 3,700 priests and 4,600 Levites lift up his voice to warn the king against the profanity of his first attempt? And how was it that out of this large body, after such awful warning and the special summons of the king, only two priests and 862 Levites appear to have attended on the *second* occasion?[p]

[m] 1 Ch. xii. 26, 27.   [n] 1 Ch. xv. 2.   [o] v. 12-15.   [p] v. 4-11.

So, whereas the Book of Samuel tells us that 'David and all the House of Israel brought up the ark of JEHOVAH with shouting and with trumpet-sounds,'[29] the Chronicler informs us that 'David spake to the chief of the Levites to appoint their brethren to be the choristers with instruments of music, psalteries, and harps, and cymbals, sounding by lifting up the voice with joy,'[30] while seven priests 'did blow with the trumpets before the ark.'[31] And, instead of the statement in the older narrative, 'And David danced before JEHOVAH with all his might, and David was girded with a linen ephod,'[32] the Chronicler writes, 'And David was clothed with a robe of fine linen, and all the Levites that bare the ark and the choristers, and Chenaniah the song-master with the choristers, and David had upon him a linen ephod.'[33] In short, the story is turned into a glorification of these surpliced Levites; and the fact, that he gives the very names of the chief Levites and a number of others,[34] only shows more clearly the boldness of his genius; for names and numbers, as well as other details of the narrative as transformed by his hand, are all equally fictitious.[35]

Then he goes on to tell us how David set up a body of Levite choristers with Asaph at their head, playing with psalteries and harps and cymbals and trumpets, 'before the ark of the covenant of God' at Jerusalem,[36] and stationed at the same time Zadok and his brethren the priests, with Heman and Jeduthun and another troop of Levite choristers and gatekeepers, before the Mosaic Tabernacle in the high-place at Gibeon, to offer the Daily Sacrifice morning and evening 'according to all that is written in the Law of JEHOVAH which He commanded Israel.'[37] This fiction, however, of the Tabernacle with its Brazen Altar having been set up at

---

[29] 2 S. vi. 15.   [30] 1 Ch. xv. 16.   [31] v. 24.   [32] 2 S. vi. 14.
[33] 1 Ch. xv. 27.   [34] v. 5-11, 17-24.   [35] For the full proof of this see Part VII.
[36] 1 Ch. xvi. 4-6, 37.   [37] v. 38-42.

Gibeon,[38] has been introduced with the idea of accounting for the fact of Solomon's having sacrificed on that high-place,[39] contrary to the prescriptions of the Levitical Law, which required all sacrifices to be brought to the entrance of the Tabernacle, and the blood to be sprinkled upon the Brazen Altar in front of it,[40] and even contrary to the law in Deuteronomy, which confined all sacrifices to 'the place which JEHOVAH would choose.'[41] It is everywhere the same: while he carefully suppresses the account of David's adultery, treachery, and detestable act of murder,[42] and of Solomon's bloody king-craft, polygamy, and gross idolatry[43]—suppresses, in short, whatever could reflect reproach upon the founder and builder of the Temple—he has deliberately falsified the history of these kings and of the other kings throughout, so as to represent the ordinances of the Levitical Law as in full operation, and the Levites especially as in great request, from David's time downwards, in the very teeth of the more authentic narrative of the Books of Samuel and Kings, while yet in the main carefully following the statements, and often copying the identical words, of that narrative.

Thus in his old age David, he tells us, numbered the Levites 'from thirty years old and upwards,'[44] just exactly the age in the Book of Numbers,[45] though a later insertion in that Book reduces it to twenty-five years,[46] and the Chronicler makes David by 'his last words' reduce it to twenty years.[47] He finds 38,000 of them, and of these 24,000 were to oversee the Temple, 6,000 to be officers and judges, 4,000 to be choristers, and 4,000 to be gatekeepers,[48]—though in Zedekiah's unhappy time, it seems, there were only three gatekeepers.[49] He divides the priests into courses, sixteen of the house of

[38] 2 Ch. i. 3, 5, 6, 13.
[39] D. xii. 5, 6, 11, 13, 14.
[40] 1 Ch. xxiii. 3.
[41] 1 Ch. xxiii. 24-27.
[42] 1 K. iii. 4.
[43] 2 S. xi. 1-27.
[44] N. iv. 47.
[45] v. 3-5.
[46] L. xvii. 3-6.
[47] 1 K. li. 23-34, xi. 1-10.
[48] N. viii. 24.
[49] 2 K. xxiv. 18.

Eleazar and eight of that of Ithamar,[40] these two being named as 'sons of Aaron' in the Levitical Legislation.[41] He divides also into courses the choristers [42] and the gatekeepers.[43] But especially he sends out Levites everywhere in special positions of great authority—the sons of Izhar 'for the outward business over Israel as officers and judges,' the sons of Hebron, 1,700 of them, as officers west of the Jordan and 2,700 as rulers east of the Jordan 'for all matters pertaining to God and affairs of the king'[44]—of all which there is not a trace in the older history.

Again he tells us how David before his death gave to Solomon a prodigious amount of gold and silver for the Temple, *viz.* three thousand talents of gold (£15,000,000) and seven thousand talents of silver (£2,471,000), all 'of his own proper good,' besides what he had already 'prepared for the holy house,' *viz.* a hundred thousand talents of gold (£500,000,000) and a million talents of silver (£353,000,000) [45], and also 'patterns' for it and for its vessels, which JEHOVAH had 'made him understand in writing,'[46] and how his great men followed his example by making splendid offerings, five thousand talents of gold (£25,000,000) and ten thousand talents of silver (£3,530,000),[47] and David uttered a prayer of thanksgiving.[48] But the language of this prayer is wholly the Chronicler's own, as the psalm of praise, which he represents elsewhere as sung by David's order, is made up of pieces of later psalms.[49]

But time would fail to recount the endless perversions of the older more authentic history which we find in the Chronicler's narrative—how, when David sacrificed on the site of the future Temple, JEHOVAH 'answered him from heaven by fire

---

[40] 1 Ch. xxiv. 1-4.   [41] Lev. 6, 12, 16.   [45] 1 Ch. xxv. 53.
[42] 1 Ch. xxvi. 1-12.   [44] v. 29, 30.   [46] 1 Ch. ix. 3, 4, xxii. 14.
[43] 1 Ch. xxviii. 11-13, 19.   [47] 1 Ch. xxix. 6-9.   [48] v. 10-25.
[49] 1 Ch. xvi. 8-22, made up with some slight alterations from Ps. cv. 1-15, xcvi, cvii. 1, cvi. 47, 48.

upon the altar of burnt-offering,' and again at Solomon's Dedication of the Temple, 'fire came down from heaven and consumed the burnt-offering and the sacrifices, and the glory of JEHOVAH filled the House,'[60]—how Solomon appointed the priests and Levites to their charges, 'for so was the commandment of David the man of God,'[61]—how Abijah with 400,000 met Jeroboam with 800,000, and slew 500,000 of them,[62] after making a long speech to the enemy in which he says, 'Have ye not cast out the priests, the sons of Aaron? ... But as for us, JEHOVAH is our God and we have not forsaken Him, and the priests which minister unto JEHOVAH are the sons of Aaron, and the Levites wait upon their business,'[63] —how Jehoshaphat sent princes and Levites and priests, all named, to teach the Book of the Law in the cities of Judah,[64] and had a standing army of 1,160,000 soldiers, who 'waited on the king, *besides* those whom the king put in the fortresses throughout all Judea,'[65] and set Levites and priests as judges in Jerusalem,[66]—how Moab and Ammon and Edom came against Jehoshaphat,[67] and, as soon as the Levites began to sing and praise before his army, the Ammonites and Moabites fell upon the Edomites, and, 'when they had made an end of them, they helped to destroy one another. .... And Judah looked unto the multitude, and lo! they were dead bodies fallen to the earth, and none escaped'[68]—how Jehoshaphat made ships on the Red Sea to go *to* Tarshish in Spain,[69] where the Chronicler has made a curious mistake in copying the older writer, who only says that he made 'ships *of* Tarshish'[70] —that is, large merchant-ships, such as went the long voyage to Tarshish, as we should say 'Indiamen'—to go to Ophir,

---

[59] 1 Ch. xxi. 26, 2 Ch. vii. 1, *comp.* L. ix. 24.   [63] 2 Ch. viii. 14.
[60] 2 Ch. xiii. 3, 7.   [61] v. 9.   [64] 2 Ch. xvii. 7-9.
[62] v. 14-19.   [66] 2 Ch. xix. 8-11.
[67] 2 Ch. xx. 1, where read 'some of the Meunim (Edomites),' instead of 'beside the Ammonites,' E.V.
[68] v. 22-28.   [69] v. 36, 37.   [70] 1 K. xxii. 48.

very possibly the coast-line of the African gold-fields—how a letter, which is given at full length, came to Joram from Elijah the prophet,[71] who had been translated to heaven at least seven years previously [72]—how the zeal and courage of the priests and Levites, instead of the guards, as stated in the older history,[73] enabled Jehoiada to kill the wicked usurper Athaliah and restore the kingdom to the young prince Joash—how Joash levied the poll-tax which Moses laid upon Israel in the wilderness [74]—how Joash and Amaziah fell into idolatry and on *that* account [75] were killed by the hands of conspirators [76]—how king Uzziah wished to offer incense in the Temple, and the chief priest and eighty other priests withstood him and said, 'It is not for thee, Uzziah, to burn incense unto JEHOVAH, but for the priests the sons of Aaron: go out of the holy place, for thou hast trespassed,' and Uzziah was wroth, and *this* was the cause of his leprosy [77]—how Ahaz, because he was an idolatrous king, was attacked by Pekah king of Israel, who slew in one day 120,000 men of Judah, and led away captive 200,000 women and children, and abundance of spoil, but at the word of a prophet restored them all with the most fraternal tenderness [78]—how Hezekiah, with the help of the priests and Levites, reformed religion in Judah,[79] and kept a great passover, a century before Josiah's time,[80] and ordered the people to 'give the portion of the priests and Levites,' which they did faithfully, and the chief priest said, 'Since they began to bring the offerings into the House of JEHOVAH, we have had enough to eat, and have left plenty' [81] —how Manasseh for his sins was carried captive to Babylon, and there repented, and JEHOVAH brought him back to Jerusalem, and he cleared the Temple and the City of all

[71] 2 Ch. xxi. 12, 13.
[72] 2 Ch. xxiii. 2, 4-8, *comp.* 2 K. xi. 4-16.
[73] 2 Ch. xxiv. 2, 17-26, xxv. 2, 27, 28.
[74] 2 Ch. xxvi. 16-21, *comp.* 2 K. xv. 5.
[75] 2 Ch. xxix.
[76] 2 Ch. xxx.
[77] p. 161.
[78] 2 Ch. xxiv. 6, 9.
[79] 2 K. xii. 20, 21, xiv. 19.
[80] 2 Ch. xxviii. 5-15.
[81] 2 Ch. xxxi. 2-10.

idolatrous images and altars,[93] anticipating also Josiah's doings
—how Josiah himself in the *eighth* year of his reign 'began
to seek JEHOVAH,' and in the *twelfth* year 'began to purge
Judah and Jerusalem from the high-places and asheras and
images,'[94] while not a word is said by the Chronicler about
the Great Reformation in the *eighteenth* year of his reign,
which showed that all along, from the time of Solomon
downwards, the grossest idolatries were practised in Judah,[95]
—except that he mentions the passover kept at this time,
in which, of course, the priests and Levites are especially
prominent.[96]

Here is a mass of fictions, which we owe to the mistaken
zeal of this writer, probably himself a Levite chorister,[96] and
writing at the earliest 250[97]—perhaps 350—years after the
Captivity, and which have exercised a sort of glamour upon
the eyes of a multitude of pious readers ever since, of the
clergy as well as of the laity. Of course, the earlier historian, living before that dire catastrophe in which so many
records of preceding times must have perished, must have
had access to any documents from which, two or three centuries afterwards, the Chronicler might be thought to have
derived additional details. And, if *he* mentions none of these
things, nor even hints at the distinction between priests and
Levites or the conspicuous part they played throughout the
history, we may be sure that they were wholly unknown to
him, and are the offspring of the Chronicler's own imagination, reflecting the spirit of his later Levitical times. The
genealogies in 1Ch.i. are taken from the Book of Genesis, as

[93] 2Ch.xxxii.11-19.   [94] 2Ch.xxxiv.3-7.
[95] 2K.xxiii.1-25.   [96] 2Ch.xxxv.1-19.
[96] Observe the special interest which the writer shows in the Levite choristers,
1Ch.vi.31-48, xv.16-24, 27, 28, xvi.4-42, xxiii.5, xxv, 2Ch.v.12, 13, vii.6, xx.19, 21, 22,
xxiii.13, 18, xxix.22-28, xx, xxx.21, xxxi.2, xxxiv.12, xxxv.15.
[97] In Neh.xii.11 the descent is given of Jaddua, high-priest (according to
Josephus) in Alexander's time, B.C. 332; but some (as KUENEN) set the
Chronicler's age as low as B.C. 250.

are some of those in ch.ii, and most of those in ch.iii. from
the Books of Samuel and Kings. But, knowing what we
now do of his character, we can place no reliance on any of his
genealogical statements which are not supported by other
authorities, as, for instance, on his line of chief priests from
Aaron down to the Captivity.[18] He is capable of inventing
such genealogies, with a whole array of names and numbers,
to any extent, when the occasion seems to call for them.
Here and there experienced critics may detect a notice which
seems to have the ring of historical fact about it,[19] and which
he may have derived from some authentic source, like the
letters to and from Artaxerxes in Ezr. iv.[20] or the memoir of
Nehemiah.[21] But for ordinary readers, who wish to have a
true conception of the course of Hebrew history, the Books of
Chronicles must be set aside altogether, as not only untrustworthy, but utterly misleading.

The time is past for glossing over such conduct as the
Chronicler's with fair words, and ascribing to him only error
or exaggeration, but no intentional departure from the truth.
He has set himself down to reconstruct the history of his
people as known to himself in the older records, and he has
done this in the interest of the clerical body, to which in all
probability he himself belonged. If the Chronicler, indeed,
had been writing merely from tradition, it would not have
been surprising that he should have stereotyped in this manner what might have been the genuine convictions of himself
and of his age; as the writers of the earlier portions of the
Pentateuch, in trying to compose some accounts of the patriarchs, and the author of the Books of Kings, in embodying
with more veracious narratives the legendary tales about
Elijah[22] and Elisha[23] or the return of the sun's shadow ten

---
[18] 1 Ch. vi. 4-15. [19] *e.g.* 1 Ch. iv. 39-43. [20] p. 324, 5.
[21] p. 328. [22] 2 K. ii. 1-12.
[23] 2 K. ii. 14, 21, 24, iii. 16-24, iv. 1-7, 16, 17, 32-37, 38 41, 42 44, v. 8-14, 26, 27, vi.
5-7, 8-12, 13-18, 23, vii. 1, 6, 7, 17-20, viii. 1, 5, xiii. 14-19, 20, 21.

degrees upon the dial of Ahaz,[94] have not violated the laws of historical good faith, taking into account the times in which they lived. But, when we see the Chronicler with the older history before him, from which he is actually copying word for word, deliberately giving an entirely different representation of the whole course of events, with the purpose of leading his readers to believe that from the earliest times the Levitical Law was in full force in Judah, it is impossible, with a due regard to truth, to acquit him of the great crime of falsifying facts of history well known to him.

But the Chronicler had before him the example of the Later Legislation of the Pentateuch, where priestly writers of an age not very far distant from his own, had entirely modified the known facts of their national history, ascribing to JEHOVAH laws which they themselves had laid down, often for their own aggrandisement; and he resolved, it would seem, to take upon himself the task of supplying historical support for these pretensions. When, however, we consider that for 2,000 years the whole course of Jewish history has been thrown into confusion mainly by the acts of these writers, and that Christianity itself owes much of its past and present corruptions and superstitions,—such as the idea of the priestly office and the popular notion of the Atonement, based upon the supposed Divine origin of the sacrificial laws in the Pentateuch—to the existence of these priestly and Levitical fictions, it is not easy to speak lightly of a fraud which has had such enormous and far-reaching evil consequences; while we find here another warning—unhappily by no means unneeded in the present age—that 'lies spoken in the name of the Lord,'[95] however well meant, can never work out the good of man or the righteousness of God.

[94] 2 K. xx. 8-11.   [95] Zech. xiii. 3.

LECTURE XXV.

SUMMARY.

The Psalms, Proverbs, Canticles, Lamentations, Job, Esther, Ecclesiastes, contain no allusion to the L.L.; the very late Book of Daniel refers to it; the story of the discovery and destruction of the Moabite Stone; the characters engraved upon it; its contents; signs of progress in writing in an early age, so that the O.S. may have been composed in the days of David and Solomon; the language shows the close affinity of the Moabites to the Hebrews; Moab seems to have thrown off the yoke of Solomon at the same time with Edom and Syria; 'forty years' used in the Stone for an indefinite long period; Chemosh, the Sun-God of Moab, fills the same place in this inscription as YAHVEH, the Sun-God of Canaan, does in the Bible; the worship of Chemosh is substance identical with that of YAHVEH, who is here recognised as the National Deity of the *Ten Tribes*; the name YAHVEH known to the Moabites, and therefore spoken by the Israelites of that age; striking discrepancy between the Hebrew and Moabite records about Mesha and his conflicts with Israel; extravagance of the Hebrew story; the two accounts have been reconciled by assuming that the one takes up the narrative where the other leaves it; improbability of this supposition; the Bible, with all its defects and faults, the mightiest instrument in the hands of the Divine Teacher for revealing to us His True Name.

THE MOABITE STONE.

THE Book of Psalms contains compositions of all ages, from the time of David — possibly even Samuel — downwards, till that of the Maccabees,[1] about B.C. 175, three centuries and a half after the return from Babylon. In some of these allusions are made to Aaron as Priest,[2] to the distinction between the priests and the Levites,[3] to the 'precious ointment that ran down upon the beard of Aaron and went down to the skirts of his garments,'[4] or to some other feature of the Levitical Legislation.[5] But such allusions occur only in very late psalms written after the Captivity, as the most eminent scholars allow.[6] The Book of Proverbs consists of seven Parts, of which the first five were written before the Captivity and the last two after it;[7] but throughout we find no trace whatever of the Levitical Legislation. The Song of Solomon, a beautiful idyll, intended apparently to exhibit the superiority of pure wedded love, though in humble circumstances, to all considerations of mere earthly wealth and grandeur,

---

[1] See Part VII for the proof of this.
[2] Ps. xcix. 6(?), cvi. 16, cxv. 10, 12, cxviii. 3, cxxxv. 19.
[3] Ps. cxxxv. 19, 20.   [4] Ps. cxxxiii. 2, comp. E. xxx. 25, 30.
[5] Ps. lxxxi. 3, comp. L. xxiii. 24, 39, 41. N. xxix. 1; Ps. xcv. 10, 11, comp. N. xiv. 33, 34; Ps. cvi. 32, 33, comp. N. xx. 2-12; Ps. cvi. 29, 30, comp. N. xxv. 6-13.

was probably written in the northern kingdom under the reign
of Jeroboam II. (B.C. 800),[1] but contains not the least allusion
to the Levitical Law. Then come in order of age the Lamentations, probably composed by Jeremiah, partly during the
siege of Jerusalem, partly after it (B.C. 588–6)[1]—the Book of
Job, written about a century afterwards or even later[1]—the
Book of Esther, an extravagant romance, written about two
centuries later still[1]—Ecclesiastes, about B.C. 200[1]—in none
of which is there any reference to the Levitical Law. Lastly,
we have the Book of Daniel, written under the form of prophecies ascribed to Daniel, to support the faith and courage
of the Jews under the oppressive measures of Antiochus
Epiphanes (B.C. 165);[1] and in this we find some allusions
to the priestly Law,[6] which was at that time in full force. If
we add that in none of the older prophets before Jeremiah
do we find any trace of acquaintance with the Book of
Deuteronomy, it will be seen that we have here indirectly very
strong additional support for the conclusions, that Deuteronomy was written in the age and apparently by the hand
of Jeremiah himself, and that the Levitical Legislation was
begun by Ezekiel and completed by priests of that age and
after it.

Let us now consider what further light is thrown upon the
subjects discussed in these Lectures by that most interesting
relic of antiquity which has been lately found, the Moabite
Stone. I will first give a brief account of its discovery,[7] and
then of its contents, and afterwards draw some inferences from
them in connexion with these enquiries.

In August, 1868, a German Missionary[8] was in the land
of Moab, which lies along the eastern side of the Dead Sea,

---

[6] Dan. ix. 11, 13, 'Law of Moses'—Dan. viii. 12–13, xi. 31, xii. 11, 'continual sacrifice,' ix. 21, 'evening oblation,' comp. E. xxix. 38–42, N. xxviii. 3–8.

[7] The facts in this Lecture are mainly derived from Dr. GINSBURG's admirable work on the Moabite Stone, 2nd Ed., to which G. refers in the notes below.

[8] The Rev. F. KLEIN of the Church Missionary Society.

a country little visited by Europeans, and, when near Dibon, he was informed by an Arab Sheikh, his friend and protector, that hardly ten minutes off there was a black basalt stone inscribed with ancient characters. He found it lying among the ruins of Dibon, perfectly exposed and with its face uppermost, about 3*ft*. 10*in*. high, 2*ft*. broad, and 14½*in*. thick, rounded at top and bottom, and containing thirty-four lines of inscription running across the Stone. The Missionary did not appreciate the immense importance of this discovery, and merely copied a few words from the Stone and compiled an alphabet; though he took measures at once to secure it for the Berlin Museum, which, in consequence of the conflicting powers and repeated absences of the different Pachas concerned, proved a very tedious and intricate business. For nearly three thousand years that stone had lain exposed to all the elements uncared for: but now the Moabites found that it was very valuable, and worth, as they supposed, its weight in gold. A few weeks afterwards a man came purposely to inform the agent of the Palestine Exploration Society[9] of its existence: but he, knowing that the Prussian Consul was moving in the matter, would take no action about it. In the spring of 1869, however, he learnt with astonishment, as did also a member of the French Consulate at Jerusalem,[10] that no copy or 'squeeze' of the inscription had been taken. In July, 1869, the former had to leave for the Lebanon; but the latter, with indiscreet zeal, not only sent men to obtain squeezes, who quarrelled in the presence of the Arabs, but offered for the Stone the sum of £375, whereas £80 had been already promised by the Prussian authorities and had been at last agreed to by those who held it, after long and wearisome negotiations, the sum of £1000 having been

---

[9] Capt. WARREN.   [10] M. CLERMONT-GANNEAU.

asked for it at one time. But now the Governor of Nablûs interposed and demanded this splendid prize for himself; and the Moabites, exasperated with this claim, in November, 1869, 'sooner than give it up, put a fire under it, and threw cold water on it, and so broke it, and then distributed the bits among the different families, to be placed in the granaries and act as blessings upon the corn; for they said that without the Stone a blight would fall upon their crops.'[11] Of these fragments twenty are now in the French savant's possession, containing in all 613 letters; while eighteen small pieces are held by the Palestine Exploration Society, containing 56 letters, making a total of 669 out of 1,100, which the entire Stone must have contained—that is to say, about two-thirds of the whole inscription. Most of the missing letters, however, have been recovered from the squeezes taken before and after the Stone was broken, so that only 35 words, 15 half-words, and 18 letters—less than one-seventh of the whole—remain to be supplied from conjecture, but are often clearly suggested by the context; and it is just to say that the person, who has most successfully laboured at this restoration of the entire inscription, is the French archæologist himself.

This Stone records three series of events in the reign of Mesha king of Moab, who is mentioned in the Bible[12] as having rebelled against Israel after the death of Ahab, B.C. 898, and who lived therefore about B.C. 900, only 75 years after Solomon's time, and may have erected this Stone about B.C. 890. The First Part of this Inscription runs as follows:—

'I Mesha am son of Chemosh-Gad king of Moab the Dibonite. My father reigned over Moab thirty years, and I reigned after my father. And I erected this Stone to

[11] G. p. 10.   [12] 2 K. iii. 4, 5.

Chemosh at Korcha, a *Stone of Salvation*, for he saved me from all despoilers and made me see my desire upon all my enemies, even Omri king of Israel. Now they afflicted Moab many days, for Chemosh was angry with his *land*. His son succeeded him, and he also said, I will afflict Moab. In my days he said *Let us go* and I will see my desire on him and his house, and Israel—I shall destroy it with an everlasting destruction. Now Omri took the land of Medeba, and *the enemy* occupied it in *his days and in* the days of his son, forty years. And Chemosh *had mercy* on it in my days; and I fortified Baal-Meon and made therein the tank, and I fortified Kiriathaim. For the men of Gad dwelt in the land of *Ataroth* from of old, and the *king of I*srael fortified for himself Ataroth, and I assaulted the wall and captured it, and killed all the wa*rriors of* the wall for the well-pleasing of Chemosh and Moab; and I removed from it all the spoil, and *offered* it before Chemosh in Kirjath; and I placed therein the men of Siran (? Sebam) and the *men of* Mochrath. And Chemosh said to me, Go, take Nebo against Israel. *And I* went in the night, and I fought against it from the break of dawn till noon, and I took it and slew in all seven thousand *men, but I did not kill* the women, *and* maidens, for *I* devoted them to Ashtar-Chemosh; and I took from it *the vessels of* YAHVEH and offered them before Chemosh. And the King of Israel fortified Jahaz and occupied it, when he made war against me; and Chemosh drove him out before *me, and* I took from Moab two hundred men, all its poor, and placed them in Jahaz, and took it to annex it to Dibon.'

The Second Part describes the public works undertaken by Mesha after his deliverance from his Jewish oppressors,[12] and the Third records his successful wars

---

[12] ' I built Korcha, the wall of the forest, and the wall of the city, and I built the gates thereof, and I built the towers thereof, and I built the palace, and I

against the Edomites."[14] But these two Parts have no special interest for us in connexion with our present subject; we will confine our attention to the First Part of the Inscription.

(i) Here, first, we notice that the art of writing must have already far advanced in that early age, B.C. 900, since this stone is clearly and distinctly engraved, with no sign of rudeness and imperfection in the work, the words being carefully separated by points and the clauses by vertical strokes, and the story is recorded in a plain and perspicuous style and in a perfectly grammatical form. There is therefore no reason to doubt that the art of writing may have been freely practised among the Hebrews in the time of Solomon and David, *comp.* 2 S. xi. 14, 15; and that in that age the Original Story of the Pentateuch may have been written.

(ii) Next, the letters engraved on this Stone, as I have said, are not the later square Chaldee characters as in our printed Hebrew Bibles, but the Phœnician, called also the Samaritan, which were used by the Hebrews before the Captivity. These characters, says GINSBURG, were common before B.C. 700 to all the races of W. Asia, and were used in Nineveh, Phœnicia, Jerusalem, Samaria, Moab, Cilicia, Cyprus; so that we have here the alphabet 'from which the Greek, the Roman, and all other European alphabets

---

made the prisons for the *criminals* within *the* walls. And there was no cistern in the wall at Korcha, and I said to all the people, make for yourselves everyman a cistern in his house. And I dug the ditch for Korcha with the *chosen* men of *Israel.* I built Aroer, and I made the road across the Arnon. I built Beth-Bamoth, for it was destroyed; I built Bezer, for it was cut *down* by the armed men of Dibon, for all Dibon was now loyal; and I reigned from Bikran which I added to my land, and I built *Beth-Gamul* and Beth-Diblathaim and Beth-Baal-Meon, and I placed there the *poor people of* the land.'

[14] ' And as to Horonaim *the men of Edom* dwelt therein *on the descent from of old.* And Chemosh said to me, Go down, make war against Horonaim and take it. And I assaulted it, and I took it, and Chemosh *restored it* in my days. Wherefore I made . . . your . . and I . . .'

have been derived, the veritable prototype of modern writing.' As we find among them representatives of all the *twenty-two* letters of the ancient Semitic alphabet, the story, that only *sixteen* were brought into Greece from Phœnicia, falls at once to the ground, and, doubtless, the whole Phœnician alphabet was taken over by the Greeks from Kadmus, that is, 'the man of the east,' for *kedem* in Hebrew means 'the east.' The language, however, though closely akin to that found in Phœnician inscriptions, is still more nearly allied to Biblical Hebrew, and almost, indeed, identical with it. In fact, 'the whole vocabulary of the Moabite Stone is to be found in the Hebrew Scriptures';[15] while certain shades of meaning are for the first time supplied for certain Hebrew words. This shows how closely related were the Hebrews to the Phœnicians and Moabites, and, no doubt, to the Ammonites and Edomites, and other tribes in the midst of which they settled down when they came out of Egypt. And so David allied himself closely with the Phœnicians,[16] whom according to the Pentateuch he was bound to have utterly destroyed;[17] and he was himself of Moabite descent through his ancestress Ruth,[18] and, when threatened by Saul, he sent his parents to the care of the king of Moab.[19]

(iii) We are not told why David afterwards 'smote Moab' and slew in cold blood two-thirds of the population, and reduced the whole land to subjection.[20] But at some time or other after this the Moabites must have shaken off the yoke of Judah, since, according to this Stone, Omri, Ahab's father, conquered them again about fifty or sixty years after Solomon's time. Most probably they revolted from Solomon at the time when Edom and Syria appear to have regained their independence, after the death of David and Joab, in the

[15] G. p. 29.   [16] 2 S. v. 11, 1 K. v. 1.   [17] D. xx. 16, *comp.* J. xiii. 6.
[18] R. iv. 13–17.   [19] 1 S. xxii. 3, 4.   [20] 2 S. viii. 1, 2.

very beginning of Solomon's reign.[11] But, according to the Stone, they were liberated once more by Mesha, and they seem to have maintained their independence of Israel ever afterwards.

(iv) Omri is here said to have taken from Moab the land of Medeba and with his son Ahab to have held it 'forty years.' But Omri reigned only *twelve* years and Ahab *twenty-two* years;[12] so that they reigned altogether only at most *thirty-four* years, and the conquest will hardly have been made in the very first year of Omri. In other words, the term of 'forty years' seems to be used here, as it is with reference to the wanderings in the wilderness and often elsewhere in Scripture,[13] for an indefinite long time, perhaps in this case twenty or thirty years.

(v) Again, the name of the Sun-God, Chemosh, the National Deity of Moab,[14] is used in this inscription just exactly as JEHOVAH or YAHVEH, the name of the National Deity of the Hebrews, the Sun-God of Canaan,[15] was used by the Hebrews. Thus the name of Mesha's father, Chemosh-Gad, is compounded with Chemosh, as so many Hebrew names are compounded with JEHOVAH.[16] Moreover, Gad was the God of good-fortune, acknowledged by all the Canaanite nations; so that Chemosh-Gad means 'Chemosh is the God of good-fortune,' just as in the Bible Gaddiel means[17] 'Gad is ELOHIM,' or Baal-Gad[18] means 'Baal is Gad,' or Baal-Yah[19] means Baal is YAHVEH.' So Mesha erects this 'Stone of Salvation' to Chemosh, 'for he saved me from all despoilers'; just as Samuel sets up a 'Stone of Help,' Eben-ezer, saying, 'Hitherto hath JEHOVAH helped us,'[20] or as David set up a memorial 'when he returned from smiting the Syrians in the

---

[11] 1 K. xi. 14-25, see p. 58.   [12] 1 K. xvi. 23, 29.   [13] p. 284.
[14] N. xxi. 29, Ju. xi. 24, 1 K. xi. 7, 33, 2 K. xxiii. 13, Jer. xlviii. 7, 13, 46.
[15] p. 77.   [16] p. 79.   [17] N. xiii. 10.
[18] J. xi. 17, xii. 7, xiii. 5.   [19] 1 Ch. xii. 5.   [20] 1 S. vii. 12.

Valley of Salt.'[31] Chemosh here lets Mesha 'see his desire upon his enemies'; and so the Psalmist says, 'God shall let me see my desire upon mine oppressors,'[32] and again, 'I shall see my desire upon my enemies.'[33] Chemosh 'was angry' with his land, and allowed Israel to oppress it: and so 'the anger of JEHOVAH was kindled against Israel, and He delivered them into the hands of spoilers that spoiled them.'[34] But Chemosh again has mercy upon his land, and gives Mesha the victory over his foes; and the Israelites upon the wall are killed 'for the well-pleasing of Chemosh and Moab,' where Chemosh is identified with Moab, as JEHOVAH is with Israel;[35] the spoil is offered before Chemosh, as David offers his spoil to JEHOVAH;[36] Chemosh 'said to Mesha, Go, take Nebo against Israel,' as JEHOVAH 'said to David, Go, and smite the Philistines,'[37] and sends Saul to smite Amalek.[38] And Mesha does this and kills all the men, but devotes the women and children to Ashtar-Chemosh, that is, reserves them for the foul orgies of Sun-worship, of which we see plain traces in the Bible as practised down to a late age in Israel.[39] So Mesha takes the 'vessels of JEHOVAH and offers them before Chemosh,'[40] and Chemosh drives out Israel from before him at Jahaz.[41] In short, 'if we did not know the nature of the Moabite religion from other sources, and if the name of JEHOVAH were substituted for that of Chemosh, this Inscription would read like a chapter in the Book of Kings.'[42]

(vi) Once more, 'these vessels of JEHOVAH,' which Mesha captures at Nebo and dedicates to Chemosh, show that the Deity worshipped by the Israelites at such high-places as that at Nebo was really JEHOVAH, though a Hebrew prophet would probably have called them 'vessels of the Baal'; and 'the

---

[31] 2S. viii. 13, where the E.V. has 'gat him a name.'
[32] Ps. cxviii. 7.
[33] 2S. viii. 11.
[34] Jn. ii. 13, comp. iii. 8, 2K. xiii. 3.
[35] 1S. xxlii. 2.
[36] 2K. xxiii. 7, comp. D. xxiii. 18.
[37] E. xxlii. 29, 30, xxxiv. 11, Ju. ii. 3, vi. 9.
[38] Ps. lii. 11.
[39] J. lv. 12, 13.
[40] 1S. xv. 2, 3.
[41] comp. 1K. vii. 51, 2S. viii. 11.
[42] G. p. 38.

fact, that these vessels, used in the service of JEHOVAH, could so easily be converted into the worship of Chemosh, shows beyond doubt that the special part of the ritual for which they were designed was common to the religion both of the Hebrews and of the Moabites.'[45] Rather, there was probably no essential difference between the worship of Chemosh and that of JEHOVAH carried on at the high-places of Judah and Jerusalem. Hence the *Jewess* Naomi, though a worshipper of JEHOVAH, without any scruple bids Ruth the *Moabitess*, her widowed daughter-in-law, after she had been married ten years to her son, and had probably conformed to his religion, to return unto her own people and unto her Elohim Chemosh, as her sister had done; but Ruth refuses and says, 'Thy people shall be my people and thy Elohim my Elohim.'[44] Hence, too, Solomon built a high-place for Chemosh, to oblige his Moabite wives, on the Mount of Olives, in full view of the Temple of JEHOVAH.[45] And we observe that in this Inscription JEHOVAH is spoken of as the National Deity of the *Northern* Kingdom, where, therefore, under the form of a calf JEHOVAH or YAHVEH must have been worshipped at Bethel or Dan;[46] so that, when it is said 'Jeroboam drave Israel from following JEHOVAH,'[47] it is meant that by setting up his calves he hindered them from serving the God of Israel with a higher spiritual worship, undefiled by the gross symbols and the lascivious and bloody rites of heathenism.

(vii) Further, the name 'JEHOVAH' was in later days only allowed to be used in the priestly benediction in the Temple; and when, on the Great Day of the Atonement, the High-Priest uttered it, while confessing the sins of the nation, 'all the priests and people in the outer court who heard it had to kneel down, bow, and fall upon their faces, exclaiming, 'Blessed be the glorious Name of His Majesty for ever!,'

---

[43] G. p. 22.
[44] R. i. 15, 16.
[45] 2 K. xxiii. 13.
[46] 1 K. xii. 28, 29.
[47] 2 K. xvii. 21.

while any layman who pronounced it forfeited his life both in this world and in the world to come."⁴⁸ Accordingly this Name is never employed in the Septuagint Version or in the Apocryphal Books, where *Kurios* or Lord is always used for it, from which has been derived 'the LORD' of the English Bible. Now tradition maintains that this superstitious dread of pronouncing the Name dates after the time of Moses and that the Law itself distinctly forbids it. And tradition was, no doubt, right in supposing that the practice was forbidden, or at least discouraged, in that passage of Leviticus, where JEHOVAH orders a man to be stoned to death for blaspheming '*the Name*,'⁴⁹ the very expression used by the Samaritans and later Jews instead of uttering the Divine Name. But then this passage of Leviticus was not written 'in the time of Moses': it is one of the latest portions of the Levitical Law. Perhaps the Jews, who were settled in Egypt after the Captivity, adopted this superstition from the Egyptians, who never uttered the names of certain deities, and passed it on to the Jews in Palestine. At all events, this Stone shows that the Name was well known to the Moabites B.C. 900, as that of the National Deity of Israel, and therefore, no doubt, in that age it was freely pronounced by the Israelites.

(viii) Lastly, we must compare the Moabite record with the Hebrew account of this same Mesha and his relations with Israel.⁵⁰ In this we read that Mesha was rich in flocks, and paid an annual tribute to the king of Israel of 100,000 wethers and 100,000 rams with their wool,—that he rebelled after Ahab's death, and that Joram son of Ahab, with his allies, Jehoshaphat king of Judah and his tributary, the king of Edom, marched against him by a circuitous route, seven days through the wilderness of Edom. The three allies, however, with their troops and cattle, were nearly perishing for want of water

⁴⁸ G. p. 22. ⁴⁹ L. xxiv. 11-16. ⁵⁰ 2 K. iii. 4-27.

when Jehoshaphat found that Elisha was living near at hand and went down to consult him. Elisha at first bids Joram go to the prophets of his father Ahab and his mother Jezebel; but at last for Jehoshaphat's sake he enquires of JEHOVAH, and for reply bids them 'make the valley full of ditches,' for without wind or rain it should be filled with water, and Moab also should be delivered into their hands, and they 'should smite every fenced city and every choice city, and fell every good tree, and stop every well of water, and mar every good piece of land with stones.' And lo! in the morning there came streams by the way of Edom, and the country was filled with water; and, when the Moabites saw it ruddy with the rays of the rising sun, they thought it was blood. So, taking it for granted that the three allied armies had smitten one another, they rushed in full force to the spoil; but, when they reached the camp of Israel, the Israelites rose up and smote them, and chased them into their own land, slaughtering without mercy, beating down the cities, marring the land with stones, stopping the wells, and felling the fruit-trees, till they drove the king of Moab into a strong-hold where he maintained himself, while the slingers went about and smote it. At last, being hard pressed, he sallied out with seven hundred men and tried to break through the besieging force, but failed; whereupon he 'took his eldest son that should have reigned in his stead, and offered him for a burnt-offering upon the wall. And there was great indignation against [or upon] Israel, and they departed from him, and returned to their own land.

We have here a very different story from that recorded on the Moabite Stone, and the question is, Can these two accounts in any way be reconciled? The contrast between them is certainly as great as possible. In the one we have a simple, unvarnished tale of struggles and conquests beginning with the admission of Moab's long subjection and ending with its liberation from the yoke of Israel, but all told in the most natural manner, without the least sign of a desire to adorn the narrative with fictitious or miraculous incidents: in the other we have a series of incredible statements, beginning with an annual tribute from Moab of 100,000 wethers and 100,000 rams, enormously out of proportion to the extent of the country (about forty miles long by ten broad), and ending with the Moabites mistaking the water in the morning sunlight for blood, and hastily concluding that 'the kings are surely slain, and they have smitten one another,'—as if, supposing some of them for a moment to have been possessed by such a delusion, it would not have been dispelled long before they reached the Camp of Israel and fell helplessly into their enemies' hands! In short, the whole Hebrew story, as it now stands, is a manifest fiction, apparently part of some legendary account of Elisha's doings, which, like that about Elijah, Jeremiah[81] has adopted into his history of the kings, retouching it here and there with his own hand.

But may this extravagant story after all have been based on some real historical fact? It has been suggested[82] that the Scripture narrative has taken up the account of Mesha's doings just where the Moabite Stone has left it, each record having suppressed altogether the facts which would have redounded to the glory of the enemy, so that here we have only two parts of the same campaign described from two opposite points of view, like English and French accounts of the Battle of Waterloo. Mesha, it is said, may have really freed his country *north* of the Arnon, as stated on the Stone, during the short reign of Ahaziah, Ahab's eldest son and successor;[83] and then, after his death, his successor Joram may have fortified Jahaz *south* of the Arnon, as here mentioned, and tried to stem his progress in that direction, but, finding him too strong, was obliged to withdraw his force without a battle, or, as the

---

[81] See Part VII for the proof that Jeremiah wrote the Books of Kings.
[82] G. p. 17-19.
[83] 1 K. xxii. 51, 2 K. i. 1.

Stone says, 'Chemosh drave him out.' But after this he may have summoned his allies, as the Bible tells us, and, going round by the south, may have utterly overthrown Mesha, ravaging his land and shutting him up in his last fortified place, from which he tried to break out, but failed, and then, by the sacrifice of his son raised such a fury in his people that they attacked and routed the Israelites, or, in the euphemistic language of the Bible, 'there was great indignation against Israel, and they departed from him and returned to their own land.'

This ingenious explanation may possibly be true. Yet, considering the fictitious character of most of the details of the Hebrew story, this seems very doubtful in face of the fact that not the slightest hint of Mesha's disasters, of his having lost his towns and had his land ravaged, and been driven to sacrifice his firstborn son, appears on the Stone. Perhaps the notorious fact of Moab having thrown off under Mesha the yoke of Israel alone gave rise to the Scripture story. In order to account for the Israelites having permitted such a revolt, they are here represented as having first by miraculous aid, vouchsafed for the good Jehoshaphat's sake, chastised the rebellious Moabites and reduced them to uttermost distress and despair, and having then abandoned their conquest in consternation and commiseration, as Josephus[14] and many commentators explain it, at the horrible deed committed before their eyes.

However this may be, it is plain that the Moabite Stone, if even its contents can be reconciled at all with the Hebrew story, lends no support whatever to the traditional view as to the Divine infallibility of the Bible, much less as to the Mosaic origin and Divine authority of the Pentateuch, while in various ways it indirectly confirms the views I have set before you in these Lectures. For all this, however, the Bible,

[14] *Ant.* IX. iii.

relieved from a merely superstitious view of its character, does not cease to be 'profitable for doctrine, reproof, correction, instruction in righteousness.' It still remains for us that Book, which, whatever intermixture it may show of human elements—of error, infirmity, passion, or ignorance—has yet through God's gracious Providence and the working of the Divine spirit on the minds of its writers, been the means of revealing to us His True Name, the Name of the Living God, and has all along been, and, as far as we know, will never cease to be, the mightiest instrument in the hand of the Divine Teacher for awakening in our minds just conceptions of His character and of His Goodness towards the children of men.

LECTURE XXVI.

SUMMARY.

There will be no need in future to hold or teach that slavery is enjoined in the Bible by Divine authority; we are not surprised to find in it numerous discrepancies, and very different readings in the Sam. and Sept. Versions, the last of which is habitually quoted in the N.T., and comprised the Apocrypha of the O.T., as having like authority with the Canonical Books of the English Bible; in all State-aided schools the truths of Science must be taught, though often at variance with Scripture; fictions must not be imposed on ignorant heathen 'in the name of the LORD,' nor miraculous stories be matched with those of more civilised heathens; a miracle would in our days be appalling, as it would shake our whole faith in the orderly government of the Universe; since the popular notion of the Divine infallibility of the Bible is contradicted by the plainest scientific conclusions, Biblical Criticism is a blessed gift, which shows that such a notion is a mere delusion; some great social questions will now be treated on their own merits, without appealing to supposed Divine dicta in respect of them, e.g., capital punishments, marriages of affinity, the treatment of polygamist converts from heathenism, Sunday observance; when the L.L. is shown to be of post-Captivity origin, the whole priestly system falls to the ground, and its complement, the ritualistic system, with its doctrine of sacrifices; Bishop BROWNE on dogmatic teaching; the power of the Cross lies not in dogma; the life and death of Jesus revealed the Father to men, as men must reveal the Father to each other.

CONCLUDING REMARKS.

 SHALL now close this series of Lectures by considering some of the more important consequences which follow from the results which have been set before you. That we shall be relieved in future from the necessity of holding and teaching the revolting doctrine that the practice of slavery may be supported by express Divine utterances, like that which permits a master to flog his slave to death, provided he or she 'continue a day or two, for he is his money,'[1] or that which bids a Hebrew slave go out free at the end of six years' service, but leave behind as slaves his wife and children,[2] or that which speaks of 'JEHOVAH'S tribute' of thirty-two female slaves, to be the perquisite of the priests,[3] is obvious at once; and the clergy of all denominations will surely rejoice to have overwhelming evidence laid before them that passages such as these form no portion of that Divine Law, which they are bound to present to their flocks as the Word of the Living God.

Moreover, we are now able to regard the numerous discrepancies and contradictions, which a thoughtful student of the Bible cannot fail to have noticed, perhaps with pain, in different parts of it, as only the natural consequence of the

[1] E.xxi.20,21.   [2] v.4.   [3] N.xxxi.40.

conditions under which it has been composed, by fallible men like ourselves, however inspired with Divine Life, writing in different ages and from very different points of view—not to speak of the fact that the Greek Version and the Samaritan Text give evidence of the existence of very ancient copies of the Hebrew Scriptures, containing very considerable variations from the Hebrew Text, which in those days were regarded as authoritative records of the Jewish Religion, and as such are habitually quoted in the New Testament. Nay, the Apocryphal Books of the Old Testament were all received by those ancient Alexandrian Jews as equally 'canonical' with the other Scriptures, as they are still by the Roman Church and most of them by the Greek Church, and were not very long ago by the Reformed Church of England.[1]

Again, there are few intelligent Christians who have not of themselves been brought to the conviction that the statements of the Bible are frequently opposed to the plain conclusions of Modern Science in almost every department, Geology, Astronomy, Geography, History, Ethnology, Physiology, Chemistry, &c. Must our children learn in the day-school elementary truths, which will flatly contradict the teaching of the Pulpit and the Sunday-School? And must we not expect that, as the result of such confusing lessons, they will be in very great danger of parting with religion itself, and making shipwreck of faith altogether? Or shall we be justified in supporting schools where, in the vain hope of avoiding or at least staving off this danger, under the anxious care of religious bodies, Church of England or otherwise, 'lies' shall be habitually 'taught in the name of the Lord,'[2] on matters which concern their moral growth and intellectual development and their best interests as social beings?

And the heathen, to whom we send our Missionaries—who are not yet drugged with the results of past centuries of

[1] p. 319. [2] Zech. xiii. 3.

dogmatic teaching, but are ready to open their hearts to us, and receive as messages from a higher sphere the word which we bring to them,—*what right* have we to begin our work among them by laying down a basis of falsehood, and, while professing to be servants of the God of Truth, with our own eyes already in some measure opened to the light, to insist on loading their minds with superstitions, preparing thus a future harvest—here also, as elsewhere—of miserable doubt or irremediable unbelief? Can we expect any blessing from above on such proceedings?

Or, in the case of more highly civilised heathens, must we attempt to rival them in quoting one miracle after another, a belief in which is to be regarded as an essential part of Christian Faith?—when to us, grown up and nurtured amongst the secrets of Nature, now revealed, with our extended knowledge of the laws, the order, of this wondrous universe, so manifold, so diverse, yet all tending to unity, to one great central Cause, a miracle, if really witnessed, would be like a jarring discord in the midst of a mighty music—not a sign of the master-musician's presence, but a token that for once he had failed to subdue the rebellious elements—would, in short, be simply frightful. Must we really give up all faith in our Father in Heaven, 'all our dearest hopes and consolations,'— must we turn a deaf ear to the Divine Teachings of the Son of Man, the way to the Father, the truth and the life—are all those words of power to become unmeaning, to lose their sense for us, now that the light of science or critical research compels us to give up the setting of the jewel, the antique moulding, peculiar and suitable to the times in which it was cast, which has surrounded the pearl of great price for so many centuries?

Shall we not rather bless God devoutly that in this our wondrous mother-age He has awakened among us the gift of *critical* Science, as well as the rest—so that, whereas in former days, when comparatively little was known about the universe, it was possible by a few adroit words to silence enquiry about the meaning of the first chapters of Genesis, and so little harm was done comparatively by those appearances of conflict between Scripture and Science which were even then observed by a few, *now*, however, when the light shines roundabout us and penetrates every corner, the results of Modern Biblical Criticism come to relieve us from the miserable necessity of choosing between the Book of Nature and the Book of God, and we are able to receive joyfully illumination from whatever source it reaches us, from the Bible and from the Church, as also from the rich outflowings of Literature and Science, with which the 'Father of Lights' has blessed us in this our day? Shall we not be thankful that the idol, which tradition had set up by its notion of Infallible Inspiration, is for ever upset and annihilated, like the brazen serpent, which the Israelites worshipped in blind superstition as the work of Moses in the wilderness, but which Hezekiah broke in pieces and called it 'Nehushtan—a piece of brass'?* That notion of Scripture Infallibility is clearly seen to be a mere human invention and absolutely false. There is no infallible Book for our guidance, as there is no infallible Church or infallible Man. The Father of spirits has not willed it thus, who knows best what is needed for the training of each individual soul, as well as for the education of the race. But He gives us light enough upon our path that we may rejoice before Him and do our work faithfully day by day, and fear no evil here or hereafter. And the pure and loving in heart and true in life will see God face to face in many a passage of the Sacred Book—will recognize the Divine revealing Itself in the Human in all that is good throughout it from beginning to end—will hear God's voice

---

* 2K. xviii. 4.

CONCLUDING REMARKS.

in it speaking to the soul, through the ministry of frail and faulty fellow-men, of like passions as we are and subject to like infirmities—will feel His Living Word come home to the heart, and that it must be obeyed.

Again, some questions of great public importance will now be relieved from the incubus which has hitherto weighed down the discussion of them through the notion that there were religious difficulties in the way, that the Divine Voice had uttered an authoritative dictum, which must either preclude any free discussion, or else must be explained away, before such subjects could be discussed at all. It will probably be no longer urged, as it has been in former days, that all wilful heretics and obstinate unbelievers should be destroyed, as JEHOVAH commanded the Canaanites to be,[7] that all wizards and witches should be put to death,[8] or that a stubborn son should be brought out by his father and mother, 'and all the men of his city shall stone him with stones that he die.'[9] Yet capital punishments are still maintained in the case of murderers upon the notion that the words in Genesis, ' Whoso sheddeth man's blood, by man shall his blood be shed,'[10] were really uttered by Almighty Wisdom, instead of their merely expressing the views of a pious Hebrew of old, or perhaps recording the actual practice of an age, when Samuel 'hewed Agag to pieces before JEHOVAH,'[11] and David sawed asunder, harrowed, chopped in pieces, and burnt, his Ammonite captives[12]—acts which can hardly be regarded as models for Christian times.

Further, the question of marriages of affinity is complicated in the minds of many with the consideration of a certain law in Leviticus[13]—which appears, however, only to forbid a man marrying his wife's sister while the wife herself is living,—as if it had Divine authority, and was anything more than a rule

---

[7] D. vii. 2, xx. 16, 17.   [8] E. xxii. 18, L. xx. 27.   [9] D. xxi. 18-21.
[10] G. ix. 6.   [11] 1 S. xv. 33.   [12] 2 S. xii. 31.   [13] L. xviii. 18.

existing among the polygamist Jews at the time of the Captivity; though it did not prevent a writer in David's age from representing their forefather Jacob as having married two sisters at once. And so, too, the question of the proper mode of dealing with polygamist converts from heathenism has been considered not only under the influence of that strong feeling of monogamy which has characterised the Teutonic race from the earliest times,[14] and of that still higher feeling which springs from appreciating the true place of woman under the teaching of Christianity, but under the notion that to suffer a native convert to remain in the state in which the Word of God had found him, though with more than one wife, is opposed to the Great Marriage Law of Paradise,[15] as if this were an infallible Divine command, which must be enforced at all sacrifices, and at the cost of that sense of justice and tenderness towards wives and children, which is of the very essence of Christianity —though such a command must appear to them in puzzling contradiction to the conduct of Abraham the 'father of the faithful' and David the 'man after God's own heart,' if the facts of their histories are honestly brought before them as recorded in the Bible.

It may be that these and other like questions will in future be treated purely on their own merits as civil and social questions, without appealing to supposed religious sanctions of the most stringent kind, which are now shown to be of no authority whatever. Of the same nature, but frequently far more serious, is the evil caused by the solemn recitation of the Ten Commandments, with their Sabbath-law, as words uttered by the Divine Voice; whereas, as we have seen,[16] they are only a summary by a later Jewish prophet of what *he* deemed the most essential things to be observed in Israel, departing, however, in respect of the Sabbath from the older custom,

---

[14] *Tac. Germ.* xviii.   [15] G. ii. 24.   [16] p. 138.

which made the New Moon of more importance than ordinary Sabbaths, as the *first* Sabbath of the month, which regulated the rest, and was therefore honoured with far larger sacrifices.[17]

But, perhaps, the most important effect of the criticism of the Pentateuch is this, to strike a death-blow at the whole sacerdotal system, which mainly rests on the supposition that the Levitical Laws in the Books of Exodus, Leviticus, and Numbers are really of Mosaic or, rather, of Divine origin. We have seen that these are all without exception the product of a very late age, during or after the Captivity,[18] and for the most part express merely the hopes and ambitious pretensions of the very numerous body of priests, lording it over the consciences of the comparatively small number of devoted laity, who returned from the Captivity to Jerusalem,[19] and make the position of the priest, his rank and power, his action and influence, of supreme importance to the whole community. We have seen what a plentiful provision is made for their support[20]—how strong a line of separation is drawn not only between the clergy and the laity, but even between the priests and the Levites,[21] of which no sign appears before the Captivity, when the very name 'sons of Aaron' was utterly unknown, which replaces Ezekiel's 'sons of Zadok'[22] throughout the Levitical Legislation and the Chronicler's writings,[23] but occurs nowhere else in the whole of the Old Testament, except in a few of the later Psalms[24]—and how in the Books of Chronicles, the fitting pendant to these priestly laws, the priests and the Levites are perpetually brought upon the stage, with almost ludicrous eagerness.[25] We have seen also that this sacerdotal yoke was fastened upon the necks of the people at a time when the prophet's voice was rarely heard to

[17] p. 175.
[18] p. 221.
[19] p. 205-8.
[20] p. 193-4.
[21] p. 190, 337.
[22] p. 349.
[23] p. 267, 33.
[24] p. 104, 255.
[25] p. 337-40.

disturb their self-complacent slumbers,[96] until true spiritual life became at last deadened in them, and so, when the Great Prophet came, they blinded their eyes and stopped their ears, that the Truth might not reach them, and the multitude urged on by the priests cried 'Crucify him! Crucify him!,' and 'the voices of them and of the chief priests prevailed.'[97]

But with the priesthood comes also to the ground the whole ritualistic system, with its multitude of sacrifices expressly contrived, not merely for the relief of the burdened conscience of the sinner, but for the benefit of the priest. How, indeed, could these narrow priestly notions set forth in any way the sacrifice of Christ, that living sacrifice of loving obedience, faithful unto death, the death of the cross, amidst seemingly blighted hopes and disappointed efforts and the bitterest contempt and hatred in return for lifelong labours of self-sacrificing love—the sacrifice which Jesus offered in his life and death, and which in their measure all his true followers must be ready to offer also, as parts of that 'daily sacrifice' to be presented by the 'Israel of God,' the good and true of all ages and climes and under all religions, the savour of which mounts up to Heaven as holy incense, and helps to keep the whole world sweet!

Lastly, the time is surely come when in all State-assisted schools children shall be supplied with instruction in full agreement with the advanced knowledge of the times, without having their intellects and their hearts and consciences stunted and deformed by the cramping effects of dogmatic teaching. A Bishop of the Church of England has lately said, speaking on behalf of the National-School system, 'We have not troubled their little brains, as some people seem to think, with all kinds of dogmatic theology; though by the bye I don't think people know what dogmatic theology means. The fact

[96] p. 210.   [97] Luke xxiii. 23.

that there is a God is dogmatic theology. The fact that there
is a heaven, a hell, that our Saviour came down to save us,
that is dogmatic theology. Of course, in that way we have
taught them dogmatic theology.'[20] These little ones, then,
are taught about 'hell'—that is to say, not about death and
the grave, which are facts before their eyes continually, or
about a righteous judgment for faults committed against the
better knowledge which they possess, to which even the conscience of a child will bear witness—but about the everlasting
torments of hell-fire, that revolting and blasphemous dogma,
which dooms to never-ending woe the vast majority of human
beings, of men, women, and children with whom they meet
upon their daily pathway—which makes the God and Father
of our Lord Jesus Christ, 'the Father of mercies and the God
of all consolation,' into a very Moloch, reigning upon a throne
of glory, while shrieks and groans are ever resounding from
the bottomless abyss, and, as some teach,[21] the cries of little
innocent unbaptized babes among the rest—'and the smoke
of their torments goes up for ever and ever'!

No! the fact that there is a God is not dogmatic theology,
except for those who are subjected to such teaching as this.
It may be made so, of course, if men will seek to commend
belief in this fact, by denouncing the terrors of 'hell' against
all who refuse to believe it, or by holding out the joys of
'heaven' as a reward for those who are willing to receive it.
But it need not be so, and it should not be so, when a Christian Teacher is seeking to carry home that truth to the heart,
for instance, of a little child or of an ignorant heathen.
Rather, he will feel within himself, what is ready to be
awakened in every intelligent human being, the sense of a
Mighty Presence about us which cannot be put by, the sense
of dependence upon an Unseen Father and Friend, a longing

---

[20] Bishop (BROWNE) of Ely, (*Guardian*, Nov. 14, 1870).
[21] See *Natal Sermons*, First Series, p.130-4.

desire to find Him who 'is not far from any one of us,' in whom we 'live and move and have our being.' It is no 'dogmatic teaching' to say that in the light of that Presence, in the conscious enjoyment of it, must be Heaven, the life and blessedness of the creature, or that in the loss of that light, the conscious sense of the Divine displeasure, must be the very sum of wretchedness, more awful than any physical pain or contact with devils, or all the machinery of the popular 'hell.' To teach that Jesus is the Saviour of men is not to lay down a number of tenets respecting his person and nature, as taught by 'dogmatic theologians' and enforced in the so-called Athanasian Creed. We need not require on pain of perdition a belief in miracles, whether those of the Pentateuch or those which the Gospels represent as specially endorsing the mission of Jesus to mankind, whose doings, however, we now see but indistinctly through the mist of those many years which had elapsed between the time when Jesus lived on earth and the time when those narratives were written. It does not seem that those 'mighty works' produced any permanent effect on the men of that age. Where were the multitudes that saw those wonders, that were healed themselves or had their dear ones healed,—the five thousand that were fed with five loaves or the four thousand with seven,—when 'all his disciples forsook him and fled,' or when a few dejected followers and a few trembling broken-hearted women stood or sat down beneath his bloody Cross?

Ah! but from that Cross has gone forth a power to subdue and to regenerate the world. God's strength was made perfect in that weakness. The sight of love so pure, so patient, so tried with suffering, so triumphant in death, has given us such a glimpse of the *Divine* Love, with which the whole soul of Jesus was filled, as had never been revealed to man before. It was the Love of God which poured itself out in the life and death of Jesus upon all the sorrowful and sinstricken, the waifs and strays of humanity, the prodigal and the outcast, the publican and the sinner, as well as upon the best and noblest of our race. It is the Love of God also which is manifested even now in their lives and deaths, in those of all his true followers, the faithful and good of all ages. This teaching is simple enough, and brings its own evidence to the soul. There is no need to enforce it by damnatory clauses and the threat of hell-fire. When once this idea has fully possessed us—when once we hear the Divine Voice saying to us by the lips of Jesus, not ' Blessed are those who keep undefiled all the articles of this creed,' but ' Blessed are the meek, the merciful, the pure in heart, the peacemakers, those who hunger and thirst after righteousness,'—when once we realize that God Himself is speaking to us by every word or act of truth and goodness which His Spirit helps us, as His own dear children, to put forth in daily intercourse one with another, revealing thereby, each in his measure, even as Jesus did, the Father to men—it is all clear as day to us, it is as if our eyes were opened, as if, having been born blind, we are able now to see of ourselves that the whole world—in spite of all seeming contradictions—is full of the Glory and Goodness of God.

APPENDIX.

APPENDIX I.

THE ELOHISTIC NARRATIVE.

N.B.—The sign | denotes that here an interpolation occurs in the present Book of Genesis.

GENESIS.

These are the generations of the Heaven and the Earth in the day of their being created.*

2. ¹ In the beginning of ELOHIM'S creating the Heaven and the Earth, ² when the Earth was waste and void, and darkness upon the face of the deep, and the spirit of ELOHIM hovering upon the face of the waters, ³ then ELOHIM said, 'Let there be light,' and there was light. ⁴ And ELOHIM saw the light that it was good, and ELOHIM divided between the light and the darkness. ⁵ And ELOHIM called the light 'Day,' and the darkness He called 'Night.' And it was evening and it was morning—one day.

⁶ And ELOHIM said, 'Let there be an expanse in the midst of the waters, and let it be dividing between waters and waters.' ⁷ And ELOHIM made the expanse, and divided between the waters which were under the expanse and the waters which were above the expanse; and it was so. ⁸ And ELOHIM called the expanse 'Heaven.' And it was evening and it was morning—a second day.

⁹ And ELOHIM said, 'Let the waters under the Heaven be gathered unto one place, and let the dry land appear'; and it was so. ¹⁰ And ELOHIM

---

* These words, which now appear in G.ii.4a, seem to have formed a part originally of the Elohistic Narrative, having been prefixed as a heading to the account of the Creation in G.i, as in other similar instances in that narrative, G. v. 1, vi. 9, xi. 10, 27, xxv. 12, 19, xxxvi. 1, 9, xxxvii. 2a.

called the dry *land* 'Earth,' and the gathering of waters called He 'Seas'; and ELOHIM saw that it was good. 11 And ELOHIM said, 'Let the Earth vegetate vegetation, the herb seeding seed, the fruit-tree making fruit after its kind, whose seed is in it, upon the Earth'; and it was so. 12 And the Earth brought-forth vegetation, the herb seeding seed after its kind, and the tree making fruit, whose seed is in it, after its kind; and ELOHIM saw that *it was good*. 13 And it was evening and it was morning—a third day.

14 And ELOHIM said, 'Let there be luminaries in the expanse of the Heaven, to divide between the day and the night, and let them be for signs, and for seasons, and for days and years; 15 and let them be for luminaries in the expanse of Heaven, to give light upon the Earth'; and it was so. 16 And ELOHIM made the two great luminaries,—the greater luminary for the rule of the day, and the lesser luminary for the rule of the night,—and the stars. 17 And ELOHIM put them in the expanse of the Heaven, to give light upon the Earth, 18 and to rule over the day and over the night, and to divide between the light and the darkness; and ELOHIM saw that *it was good*. 19 And it was evening and it was morning—a fourth day.

20 And ELOHIM said, 'Let the waters swarm with swarming-things of living soul, and let fowl fly over the Earth upon the face of the expanse of the Heaven.' 21 And ELOHIM created the great monsters, and every living soul that moveth, which the waters swarmed after their kind, and every fowl of wing after its kind; and ELOHIM saw that *it was good*. 22 And ELOHIM blessed them, saying, 'Be fruitful and multiply, and fill the waters in the Seas, and let fowl abound in the Earth.' 23 And it was evening and it was morning—a fifth day.

24 And ELOHIM said, 'Let the Earth bring-forth living soul after its kind, cattle, and moving thing, and living-thing of the Earth after its kind'; and it was so. 25 And ELOHIM made the living-thing of the Earth after its kind, and the cattle after its kind, and every moving-thing of the ground after its kind; and ELOHIM saw that *it was good*. 26 And ELOHIM said, 'Let us make man in our image, after our likeness; and let them have-dominion over the fish of the Sea, and over the fowl of the Heaven, and over the cattle, and over every living-thing of the Earth, and over every moving-thing that moveth upon the Earth.' 27 And ELOHIM created man in His image; in the image of ELOHIM created He him; male and female created He them. 28 And ELOHIM blessed them, and ELOHIM said to them, 'Be fruitful and multiply, and fill the Earth, and subdue it; and have-dominion over the fish of the Sea, and over the fowl of the Heaven, and over every living-thing that moveth upon the Earth.' 29 And ELOHIM said, 'Lo! I give you every herb seeding seed, which is on the face of all the Earth, and every tree in which is the fruit of a tree seeding seed; to you it shall be for food: 30 and to every living-thing of the Earth, in which is a living soul, *I give* every green herb for food'; and it was so. 31 And ELOHIM saw all that He had made, and lo! *it was* very good. And it was evening and it was morning—a sixth day.

II. 1 And the Heaven and the Earth were finished, and all their host. 2 And ELOHIM finished on the seventh day His work which He had made, and rested on the seventh day from all His work which He had made. ³And ELOHIM blessed the seventh day, and sanctified it; for on it He rested from all His work which ELOHIM created and made.|

V. ¹This is the book of the generations of Adam in the day of ELOHIM'S creating Adam; in the likeness of ELOHIM made He him. ²Male and female created He them and blessed them, and He called their name Adam in the day of their being created.

³And Adam lived a hundred and thirty years, and begat in his likeness, according to his image; and he called his name Seth. ⁴And the days of Adam, after his begetting Seth, were eight hundred years, and he begat sons and daughters. ⁵And all the days of Adam which he lived were nine hundred and thirty years, and he died.

⁶And Seth lived a hundred and five years, and begat Enos. ⁷And Seth lived, after his begetting Enos, eight hundred and seven years, and begat sons and daughters. ⁸And all the days of Seth were nine hundred and twelve years, and he died.

⁹And Enos lived ninety years, and begat Kenan. ¹⁰And Enos lived, after his begetting Kenan, eight hundred and fifteen years, and begat sons and daughters. ¹¹And all the days of Enos were nine hundred and five years, and he died.

¹²And Kenan lived seventy years, and begat Mahalaleel. ¹³And Kenan lived, after his begetting Mahalaleel, eight hundred and forty years, and begat sons and daughters. ¹⁴And all the days of Kenan were nine hundred and ten years, and he died.

¹⁵And Mahalaleel lived sixty-and-five years, and begat Jared. ¹⁶And Mahalaleel lived, after his begetting Jared, eight hundred and thirty years, and begat sons and daughters. ¹⁷And all the days of Mahalaleel were eight hundred and ninety-five years, and he died.

¹⁸And Jared lived a hundred and sixty-two years, and begat Enoch. ¹⁹And Jared lived, after his begetting Enoch, eight hundred years, and begat sons and daughters. ²⁰And all the days of Jared were nine hundred and sixty-two years, and he died.

²¹And Enoch lived sixty-and-five years, and begat Methuselah. ²²And Enoch walked with ELOHIM, after his begetting Methuselah, three hundred years, and begat sons and daughters. ²³And all the days of Enoch were three hundred and sixty-five years. ²⁴And Enoch walked with ELOHIM, and he was not, for ELOHIM took him.

²⁵And Methuselah lived a hundred and eighty-seven years, and begat Lamech. ²⁶And Methuselah lived, after his begetting Lamech, seven hundred and eighty-two years, and begat sons and daughters. ²⁷And all the days of Methuselah were nine hundred and sixty-nine years, and he died.

²⁸And Lamech lived a hundred and eighty-two years, and begat [Noah, p. 35].] ²⁹And Lamech lived, after his begetting Noah, five hundred and ninety-five years, and begat sons and daughters. ³¹And all the days of Lamech were seven hundred and seventy-seven years, and he died.

⁵²And Noah was five hundred years old, and Noah begat Shem, Ham, and Japheth.]

VI. ⁹These are the generations of Noah. Noah was a man just and perfect in his generations: Noah walked with ELOHIM. ¹⁰And Noah begat three sons, Shem, Ham, and Japheth. ¹¹And the Earth had become-corrupt before ELOHIM, and the Earth was filled with violence. ¹²And ELOHIM saw the Earth, and lo! it had become-corrupt; for all flesh had corrupted its way upon the Earth.
¹³And ELOHIM said to Noah, 'The end of all flesh has come before Me, for the Earth is full of violence because of them; and lo! I will destroy them with the Earth. ¹⁴Make thee an Ark of cypress-wood; with cells shalt thou make the Ark, and shalt pitch it within and without with pitch.[¹⁷And I, lo! am bringing the Flood of waters upon the Earth, to destroy all flesh in which is a living spirit from under the Heaven; all which is in the Earth shall die. ¹⁸But I establish My covenant with thee; and then shalt go into the Ark, thou, and thy sons, and thy wife, and thy sons' wives with thee. ¹⁹And out of every living-thing out of all flesh, two out of all shalt thou bring into the Ark, to keep-alive with thee; male and female shall they be. ²⁰Out of the fowl after its kind, and out of the cattle after its kind, out of every moving-thing of the ground after its kind, two out of all shall come unto thee, to keep-alive. ²¹And then—take thee out of all food which is eaten, and thou shalt gather it unto thee, and it shall be to them and to them for food.' ²²And Noah did according to all which ELOHIM commanded him, so did he.]

VII. ⁶And Noah was six hundred years old when the Flood of waters was upon the Earth. ⁷And Noah went, and his sons, and his wife, and his sons' wives with him, into the Ark, because of the waters of the Flood. ⁸Out of the clean cattle and out of the cattle which are not clean, and out of the fowl and all that moveth upon the ground, ⁹two and two, they came unto Noah into the Ark, male and female, as ELOHIM commanded Noah.]

¹¹In the six-hundredth year of Noah's life, in the second month, in the seventeenth day of the month, on this day were broken up all the fountains of the great deep, and the windows of the Heaven were opened.] ¹³On this very day went Noah, and Shem and Ham and Japheth, Noah's sons, and Noah's wife, and his sons' three wives with them, into the Ark; ¹⁴they, and every living-thing after its kind, and all the cattle after its kind, and every moving-thing that moveth upon the Earth after its kind, and all the fowl after its kind, every fowl of every wing. ¹⁵And they came unto Noah into the Ark, two and two, out of all flesh in which is a living spirit. ¹⁶ᵃAnd those coming, male and female out of all flesh they came, as ELOHIM commanded him.]

¹⁸ᵃAnd the waters were mighty, and multiplied greatly upon the Earth,] ¹⁹, and all the high mountains that were under all the Heaven were covered.] ²¹And all flesh died that moved upon the Earth, fowl and cattle and living-thing and all the swarming-things that swarm upon the Earth, and all man. ²²All in whose nostrils was the breath of a living spirit, out of all which was in the dry land, died.; ²³ᵇAnd only Noah was left and what was with him

in the Ark. ⁸⁴And the waters were mighty upon the Earth a hundred and fifty days.|

VIII. ¹ And ELOHIM remembered Noah and every living-thing and all the cattle that was with him in the Ark; and ELOHIM caused-to-pass-over a wind upon the Earth, and the waters subsided. ² And the fountains of the deep were stopped and the windows of the Heaven; | ³ᵃand the waters decreased at the end of a hundred and fifty days,| ⁴ᵇIn the seventh month, in the seventeenth day of the month.| ⁵And the waters were decreasing continually until the tenth month: in the tenth *month*, in the first of the month, the tops of the mountains were seen.| ¹³ᵃAnd it came to pass in the six hundred and first year, in the first *month*, in the first of the month, that the waters were dried-up from off the Earth: | ¹⁴ and in the second month, in the seventeenth day of the month, the Earth was dry.

¹⁵ And ELOHIM spake unto Noah, saying, ¹⁶ 'Go-forth out of the Ark, thou, and thy wife, and thy sons and thy sons' wives with thee. ¹⁷ Every living-thing that *is* with thee out of all flesh, fowl, and cattle, and every moving-thing that moveth upon the Earth, bring-forth with thee; and let them swarm in the Earth, and be fruitful and multiply upon the Earth.' ¹⁸ And Noah went-forth, and his sons, and his wife, and his sons' wives with him. ¹⁹ Every living-thing, every moving-thing, and every fowl, everything moving upon the Earth—after their families they went-forth out of the Ark.|

IX. ¹ And ELOHIM blessed Noah and his sons and said to them, 'Be fruitful and multiply and fill the Earth. ² And the fear of you and the dread of you shall be upon every living thing of the Earth, and upon every fowl of the Heaven, upon all that moveth upon the ground, and upon all the fishes of the Sea; into your hand they are given. ³ Every moving-thing that liveth, to you it shall be for food: as the green herb I give to you all. ⁴ Only flesh with its soul, its blood, ye shall not eat. ⁵ And surely your blood of your souls will I require; from the hand of every living-thing will I require it, and from the hand of man; from the hand of a man's brother will I require the soul of man. ⁶ Whoso sheddeth man's blood, by man shall his blood be shed: for in the image of ELOHIM made He man. ⁷ And you, be fruitful and multiply, swarm in the Earth and multiply in it.'

⁸ And ELOHIM said unto Noah and unto his sons with him, saying, ⁹ 'And I, lo! I will establish My covenant with you and with your seed after you, ¹⁰ and with every living soul which is with you, fowl and cattle and every living-thing of the Earth with you, from all going-forth out of the Ark to every living-thing of the Earth. ¹¹ And I establish My covenant with you, and all flesh shall not be again cut off through the waters of the Flood, and there shall not be again a Flood to destroy the Earth.'

¹² And ELOHIM said, 'This is the sign of the Covenant which I will put between Me and you and every living soul that is with you, for perpetual generations. ¹³ My bow do I put in the cloud, and it shall be for a sign of a Covenant between Me and the Earth. ¹⁴ And it shall be, at My bringing-a cloud upon the Earth, when the bow shall appear in the cloud, ¹⁵ then I will remember My Covenant which is between Me and you and every living soul

among all flesh; and the waters shall not become again a Flood to destroy all flesh. ¹⁶ And, when the bow shall be in the cloud, then I will see it, to remember the perpetual Covenant between ELOHIM and every living soul among all flesh that is upon the earth. ¹⁷ And ELOHIM said unto Noah, 'This is the sign of the Covenant which I establish between Me and all flesh that is upon the Earth.'|

²⁸ And Noah lived after the Flood three hundred and fifty years. ²⁹ And all the days of Noah were nine hundred and fifty years, and he died.|

XI. ¹⁰ These are the generations of Shem.

Shem was a hundred years old, and begat Arphaxad two years after the Flood. ¹¹ And Shem lived, after his begetting Arphaxad, five hundred years, and begat sons and daughters.

¹² And Arphaxad lived five-and-thirty years, and begat Salah. ¹³ And Arphaxad lived, after his begetting Salah, four hundred and three years, and begat sons and daughters.

¹⁴ And Salah lived thirty years, and begat Heber. ¹⁵ And Salah lived, after his begetting Heber, four hundred and three years, and begat sons and daughters.

¹⁶ And Heber lived four-and-thirty years, and begat Peleg. ¹⁷ And Heber lived, after his begetting Peleg, four hundred and thirty years, and begat sons and daughters.

¹⁸ And Peleg lived thirty years, and begat Reu. ¹⁹ And Peleg lived, after his begetting Reu, two hundred and nine years, and begat sons and daughters.

²⁰ And Reu lived two-and-thirty years, and begat Serug. ²¹ And Reu lived, after his begetting Serug, two hundred and seven years, and begat sons and daughters.

²² And Serug lived thirty years, and begat Nahor. ²³ And Serug lived, after his begetting Nahor, two hundred years, and begat sons and daughters.

²⁴ And Nahor lived nine-and-twenty years, and begat Terah. ²⁵ And Nahor lived, after his begetting Terah, a hundred and nineteen years, and begat sons and daughters.

²⁶ And Terah lived seventy years, and begat Abram, Nahor, and Haran.

²⁷ And these are the generations of Terah.

Terah begat Abram, Nahor, and Haran; and Haran begat Lot.| ³¹ And Terah took Abram his son, and Lot, the son of Haran, his son's son, and Sarai his daughter-in-law, the wife of Abram his son, and they went-forth with them together out of Ur of the Chaldees to go to the land of Canaan, and they went as far as Charran and dwelt there. ³² And the days of Terah were two hundred and five years, and Terah died in Charran.|

XII. ⁴ᵇ And Abram was seventy-five years old at his going-forth out of Charran. ⁵ And Abram took Sarai his wife, and Lot his brother's son, and all their gain which they had gotten, and the souls which they had made in Charran, and they went-forth to go to the land of Canaan, and they came to the land of Canaan.| **XIII.** ⁶ And the land did not bear them to dwell to-

THE ELOHISTIC NARRATIVE.

gether; for their gain was much, and they were not able to dwell together.| ¹² Abram dwelt in the land of Canaan, and Lot dwelt in the cities of the circuit.|

XVI. ¹ Now Sarai, Abram's wife, bare not to him, and she had a maid, an Egyptian, and her name was Hagar.| ² And Sarai, Abram's wife, took Hagar the Egyptian, her maid, at the end of ten years of Abram's dwelling in the land of Canaan, and gave her to Abram her husband to him for wife.| ¹⁵ And Hagar bare to Abram a son, and Abram called the name of his son, which Hagar bare, Ishmael. ¹⁶ And Abram was eighty-and-six years old at Hagar's bearing Ishmael to Abram.|

XVII. ¹ And Abram was ninety-and-nine years old, and JEHOVAH* appeared unto Abram and said unto him, 'I am EL-SHADDAI: walk before Me, and be thou perfect. ² And I will put my Covenant between Me and thee, and I will very greatly multiply thee.'

³ And Abram fell upon his face, and ELOHIM spake with him saying, ⁴ 'I—lo! My Covenant is with thee, and thou shalt be a father of a multitude of nations. ⁵ And thy name shall not be called any longer Abram, but thy name shall be Abraham; for I put thee as a father of a multitude of nations. ⁶ And I will make thee very fruitful and will put thee for nations, and kings shall go-forth out of thee. ⁷ And I will establish My Covenant between Me and thee and thy seed after thee in their generations for a perpetual Covenant, to be to thee ELOHIM and to thy seed after thee. ⁸ And I will give to thee and to thy seed after thee the land of thy sojournings, the whole land of Canaan, for a perpetual possession, and I will be to them ELOHIM.'

⁹ And ELOHIM said unto Abram, 'And thou—My Covenant shalt thou keep, thou and thy seed after thee in their generations. ¹⁰ This is My Covenant which they shall keep between Me and you and thy seed after thee—to be circumcised among you every male. ¹¹ And ye shall circumcise the flesh of your foreskin, and it shall be for a sign of a Covenant between Me and you. ¹² And every male in your generations, eight days old, shall be circumcised among you—child of the house, and purchase of silver from any son of

---

* This is the only instance where, in the present Hebrew copies of the Bible, 'JEHOVAH' occurs in the whole Elohistic Narrative before the revelation in E.v..2–5. The proper formula of the Elohist is seen in G.xxxv.9. 'And ELOHIM appeared unto Jacob,' identical with that before us, except in respect of the Divine Name. Since, therefore, 'ELOHIM' is used everywhere else (87 times) in the Elohistic Narrative and *ten* times in this very chapter, it seems very probable that it stood originally in v. 1, and has been accidentally changed to 'JEHOVAH'—perhaps by an oversight of some copyist. In fact, the 'ELOHIM' of v. 3 apparently presupposes 'ELOHIM' also in v. 1.

It is not *necessary*, however, to suppose such an error in copying; since the Elohist himself knew and used the name JEHOVAH, as appears from E.vi.2–5, and therefore may have inadvertently employed it here in his history, 'JEHOVAH appeared unto Abram,' though he does not place it in the mouth of the Deity, 'I am JEHOVAH,' or of any other speaker before the revelation to Moses.

the stranger, which is not of thy seed. ¹³Circumcised shall he surely be, child of thy house and purchase of thy silver; and My Covenant shall be in your flesh for a perpetual Covenant. ¹⁴And an uncircumcised male, whose flesh of his foreskin is not circumcised, that soul shall be cut off from his people; he hath broken My Covenant.'

¹⁵And ELOHIM said unto Abraham, 'Sarai thy wife—thou shalt not call her name Sarai; for Sarah is her name. ¹⁶And I will bless her, and also I will give to thee out of her a son, and I will bless her, and she shall become nations, kings of peoples shall be out of her.']*

¹⁸And Abraham said unto ELOHIM, 'Would that Ishmael may live before Thee!' ¹⁹And ELOHIM said, 'Truly Sarah thy wife shall bear to thee a son, and thou shalt call his name Isaac; and I will establish My Covenant with him for a perpetual Covenant to his seed after him. ²⁰And as for Ishmael, I have heard thee. Lo! I bless him and make him fruitful and multiply him exceedingly; twelve princes shall he beget, and I give him for a great nation. ²¹But My Covenant will I establish with Isaac, whom Sarah shall bear to thee at this season in the following year.' ²²And ELOHIM finished to speak with him, and ELOHIM went up from Abraham.

²³And Abraham took Ishmael his son, and all the children of his house, and all the purchase of his silver, every male among the men of Abraham's house; and he circumcised the flesh of his foreskin on that very day, as ELOHIM had spoken to him. ²⁴And Abraham was ninety-and-nine years old at his being circumcised in the flesh of his foreskin. ²⁵And Ishmael his son was thirteen years old at his being circumcised in the flesh of his foreskin. ²⁶On that very day was Abraham circumcised, and Ishmael his son. ²⁷And all the men of his house, child of the house and purchase of silver from the son of a stranger, were circumcised with him.|

XIX. ²⁹And it came to pass, at ELOHIM'S destroying the cities of the circuit, then ELOHIM remembered Abraham, and He sent forth Lot out of the midst of the overthrow at His overthrowing the cities in which Lot dwelt.|

XXI. ²And Sarah conceived and bare a son to his old-age, according to the season which ELOHIM had spoken of with him. ³And Abraham called the name of his son that was born to him, whom Sarah bare to him, Isaac. ⁴And Abraham circumcised his son Isaac, eight days old, as ELOHIM had commanded him. ⁵And Abraham was a hundred years old at Isaac his son's being born to him.|

XXIII. ¹And the life of Sarah was a hundred and twenty and seven years, the years of the life of Sarah. ²And Sarah died in Kirjath-Arba| in the land of Canaan; and Abraham came to mourn over Sarah and to weep for her. ³And Abraham arose from before his dead, and spake unto the sons of Heth, saying, ⁴'A sojourner and dweller am I with you: give me a possession of a burial-place with you, and I will bury my dead from before me.'

---

* v. 17 seems to be interpolated, since Abraham has already 'fallen upon his face' in v. 3, and the phrase 'say in his heart' is used in xxvii.41(J)), and nowhere else in the Pentateuch.

⁵ And the sons of Heth answered Abraham, saying, 'Pray hear us, my lord: a prince of ELOHIM art thou in the midst of us: in the choice of our burial-places bury thy dead; no man of us will hold-back his burial-place from thee, that thou shouldst not bury thy dead.' ⁷ And Abraham arose and bowed-himself before the people of the land, to the sons of Heth. ⁸ And he spake with them, saying, 'If it is your (soul) pleasure for me to bury my dead from before me, hear me and entreat for me to Ephron son of Zohar, ⁹ that he may give me the cave of Machpelah which is his, which is in the extremity of his field: for full silver shall he give it me in the midst of you for a possession of a burial-place.' ¹⁰ Now Ephron was dwelling in the midst of the sons of Heth. And Ephron the Hittite answered Abraham in the ears of the sons of Heth, before all entering at the gate of his city, saying, ¹¹ 'Nay, my lord! hear me: the field I give thee, and the cave which is in it, to thee I give it; in the presence of the sons of my people I give it thee; bury thy dead.' ¹² And Abraham bowed-himself before the people of the land. ¹³ And he spake to Ephron in the ears of the people of the land, saying, 'If thou art indeed *for giving it*, pray hear me: I give the silver of the field: take it from me, that I may bury my dead there.' ¹⁴ And Ephron answered Abraham, saying, ¹⁵ 'Pray, my lord! hear me: the land is four hundred shekels of silver: between me and thee what is that? so bury thy dead.' ¹⁶ And Abraham hearkened unto Ephron; and Abraham weighed for Ephron the silver which he spake in the ears of the sons of Heth, four hundred shekels of silver, current with the trader. ¹⁷ And the field of Ephron which was in Machpelah, which was (before) east of Mamre, the field, and the cave that was in it, and all the trees that were in the field, that were in all its border roundabout, stood ¹⁸ to Abraham for a purchase in the presence of the sons of Heth, among all entering at the gate of his city. ¹⁹ And afterwards Abraham buried Sarah his wife in the cave of the field of Machpelah eastward of Mamre] in the land of Canaan. ²⁰ And the field, and the cave that was in it, stood to Abraham for a possession of a burial-place from the sons of Heth.]

XXV. ⁷ And these *are* the days of the years of the life of Abraham which he lived, a hundred and seventy-and-five years. ⁸ And Abraham gave-up-the-ghost, and died in good grey hairs, old and full *of years*, and was gathered unto his people. ⁹ And Isaac and Ishmael, his sons, buried him in the cave of Machpelah, in the field of Ephron son of Zohar the Hittite, which *was* east-ward of Mamre, ¹⁰ the field which Abraham bought from the sons of Heth: there was buried Abraham and Sarah his wife.]

¹² And these *are* the generations of Ishmael, the son of Abraham, whom Hagar the Egyptian, Sarah's maid, bare to Abraham.

¹³ And these *are* the names of the sons of Ishmael, by their names, according to their generations: the firstborn of Ishmael, Nebaioth, and Kedar, and Adbeel, and Mibsam, ¹⁴ and Mishma, and Dumah, and Massa, ¹⁵ and Hadar, and Tema, Jetur, Naphish, and Kedemah. ¹⁶ These *are* the sons of Ishmael, and these *are* their names, by their villages and by their kraals, twelve princes after their folks.

¹⁷ And these *are* the years of the life of Ishmael, a hundred and thirty-and-

THE ELOHISTIC NARRATIVE.

seven years; and he gave-up-the-ghost and died, and was gathered to his people.|

¹² And these are the generations of Isaac the son of Abraham. Abraham begat Isaac. ²⁰ And Isaac was forty years old at his taking him for wife Rebekah, the daughter of Bethuel the Syrian, out of Padan-Aram, the sister of Laban the Syrian.| ²¹ᵇ And Rebekah his wife conceived; | ²⁴ and her days were fulfilled to bear, and lo! twins in her womb! ²⁵ And the first came-forth red, all of him, as a mantle of hair, and they called his name Esau. ²⁶ And afterwards came-forth his brother, and his hand grasping upon the heel of Esau; and (one called his name —) his name was called Jacob; and Isaac was sixty years old at her bearing them.|

XXVI. ³⁴ And Esau was forty years old and he took to wife Judith, the daughter of Beeri the Hittite, and Basmath, the daughter of Elon the Hittite. ³⁵ And they were a bitterness of spirit to Isaac and to Rebekah.

XXVII. ¹ And Isaac called unto Jacob, and blessed him, and charged him, and said to him, 'Thou shalt not take a wife out of the daughters of Canaan. ² Arise, go to Padan-Aram, to the house of Bethuel thy mother's father; and take to thee from thence a wife out of the daughters of Laban thy mother's brother. ³ And EL-SHADDAI bless thee, and make thee fruitful, and multiply thee, that thou mayst become a company of peoples, ⁴ and give thee the blessing of Abraham, to thee and to thy seed with thee, to thy inheriting the land of thy sojournings which ELOHIM gave to Abraham!' ⁵ So Isaac sent-away Jacob, and he went to Padan-Aram, unto Laban, the son of Bethuel the Aramæan, the brother of Rebekah, the mother of Jacob and Esau.

⁶ And Esau saw that Isaac had blessed Jacob, and had sent-him-away to Padan-Aram, to take him from thence a wife—in blessing him too he charged him, saying, 'Thou shalt not take a wife out of the daughters of Canaan'— ⁷ and Jacob hearkened unto his father and unto his mother, and went to Padan-Aram. ⁸ And Esau saw that the daughters of Canaan were evil in the eyes of Isaac his father. ⁹ And Esau went unto Ishmael, and took him to wife Mahalath, the daughter of Ishmael, the son of Abraham, the sister of Nebaioth, besides his *other* wives.|

[Here occurs the first hiatus in the Elohistic Narrative, the original account of Jacob's marriage—probably as brief as that of Isaac's marriage in xxv. 16—having apparently been removed, to make way for the circumstantial narrative of the Jehovist in xxix. Some fragments, however, of the older story seem to have been retained, as below; and probably the births of all Jacob's sons, including *Benjamin*, xxxv. 24, were here given, though now much overlaid by Jehovistic insertions. Thus xxx. 22 is *certainly* Elohistic, *comp.* G. viii. 1, xix. 29, E. ii. 24; and, as the story now stands, the names of Zebulun and Joseph are *twice* derived.]

XXIX. ²⁴ And Laban gave to her Zilpah his maid, to Leah his daughter for maid.| . . . ²⁹ And Laban gave to Rachel his daughter Bilhah his maid for maid.| . . . ³²ᵃ And Leah conceived and bare a son, and she called his

THE ELOHISTIC NARRATIVE.   391

name Reuben.| ³³ᵇAnd she conceived again and bare a son,| and she called his name Simeon. ³⁴ᵃAnd she conceived again and bare a son,| . . . ³⁵ᵃAnd she conceived again and bare a son,| . . . and she stood from bearing.

XXX. ¹ᵃ And Rachel saw that she bare not to Jacob,| ⁴ and she gave to him Bilhah her maid for wife.| ⁵ And Bilhah conceived and bare to Jacob a son. ⁶ᵃ And Rachel said, 'Elohim hath judged me.'| . . . ⁷ And Bilhah, Rachel's maid, conceived again, and bare a second son to Jacob. ⁸ᵃ And Rachel said, 'With wrestlings of ELOHIM have I wrestled with my sister,'| and she called his name Naphtali.

⁹ And Leah saw that she had stood from bearing; and she took Zilpah her maid, and gave her to Jacob for wife. ¹⁰ And Zilpah, Leah's maid, bare to Jacob a son. ¹¹ And Leah said, 'A troop!' and she called his name Gad. ¹² And Zilpah, Leah's maid, bare a second son to Jacob. ¹³ And Leah said, 'My blessing! for daughters will bless me'; and she called his name Asher.|

¹⁷ And ELOHIM hearkened unto Leah, and she conceived, and bare to Jacob a fifth son. ¹⁸ And Leah said, 'ELOHIM hath given me my hire, because I have given my maid to my husband'; and she called his name Issachar. ¹⁹ And Leah conceived again, and bare a sixth son to Jacob. ²⁰ And Leah said, 'ELOHIM hath presented me with a good present,'| and she called his name Zebulun. ²¹ And afterwards she bare a daughter, and she called her name Dinah.

²² And ELOHIM remembered Rachel, and ELOHIM hearkened unto her, and opened her womb. ²³ And she conceived and bare a son, and she said, 'ELOHIM hath gathered my reproach!" ²⁴ And she called his name Joseph.|

XXXI. ¹⁷ᵃ And Jacob arose,| . . . ¹⁸ and he led away all his cattle, and all his gain which he had gotten, the cattle of his property, which he had gotten in Padan-Aram, to go unto Isaac his father, to the land of Canaan.|

XXXV. ⁹ And ELOHIM appeared unto Jacob again,* at his coming from Padan-Aram, and spake with him. ¹⁰ And ELOHIM said to him, 'Thy name is Jacob; thy name shall not be called any longer Jacob, but Israel shall be thy name'; and He called his name Israel. ¹¹ And ELOHIM said to him, 'I am EL-SHADDAI: be fruitful and multiply: a nation and a company of nations shall be out of thee, and kings shall go forth out of thy loins. ¹² And the land which I gave to Abraham and to Isaac, to thee will I give it, and to thy seed after thee will I give the land.' ¹³ And ELOHIM went up from him in the place where He spake with him. ¹⁴ And Jacob set up a pillar in the place where He spake with him, a pillar of stone; and he dropped upon it a drink-offering, and poured oil upon it. ¹⁵ And Jacob called the name of the place where ELOHIM spake with him Beth-El.

¹⁶ᵃ And they set off from Beth-El, and it was still a space of land to come

---

* This seems to mean that this was a *second* appearance of ELOHIM, and this time He appeared to Jacob, and made a fresh promise of the land to him and to his seed, as formerly to Abraham and Isaac and their descendants, xvii. 1, 8, 19. There is no record of any 'appearance' to Isaac, *comp.* xxviii. 4.

to Ephrath.| ¹⁹ And Rachel died, and was buried in the way of Ephrath.| ²⁰ And Jacob set-up a pillar upon her grave.|

²²ᵃ And the sons of Jacob were twelve; ²³ the sons of Leah, Jacob's firstborn, Reuben, and Simeon, and Levi, and Judah, and Issachar, and Zebulun; ²⁴ the sons of Rachel, Joseph and Benjamin; ²⁵ and the sons of Bilhah, Rachel's handmaid, Dan and Naphtali; ²⁶ and the sons of Zilpah, Leah's handmaid, Gad and Asher. These are the sons of Jacob, which were born to him in Padan-Aram.

²⁷ And Jacob came unto Isaac his father, to Mamre, the city of Arba,| where Abraham sojourned, and Isaac. ²⁸ And the days of Isaac were a hundred and eighty years. ²⁹ And Isaac gave-up-the-ghost, and died, and was gathered unto his people, old and full of days; and Esau and Jacob, his sons, buried him.

XXXVI. ¹ And these are the generations of Esau, that is, Edom.

² Esau took his wives of the daughters of Canaan, Adah, daughter of Elon the Hittite, and Aholibamah, daughter of Anah, son of Zibeon the Hivite, ³ and Basmath, daughter of Ishmael, sister of Nebaioth. ⁴ And Adah bare to Esau Eliphaz, and Basmath bare Reuel, ⁵ and Aholibamah bare Jeush, and Jaalam, and Korah. These are the sons of Esau, which were born to him in the land of Canaan.

⁶ And Esau took his wives and his sons and his daughters, and all the souls of his house, and his cattle and all his beasts, and all his gain which he had gotten in the land of Canaan, and went unto the land [of Seir] because of Jacob his brother. ⁷ For their gain was plentiful above living together, and the land of their sojourning was not able to bear them because of their cattle. ⁸ And Esau dwelt in Mount Seir: Esau, he is Edom.

⁹ And these are the generations of Esau, the father of Edom, in Mount Seir.

¹⁰ These are the names of the sons of Esau—Eliphaz, the son of Adah, Esau's wife, Reuel, the son of Basmath, Esau's wife.

¹¹ And the sons of Eliphaz, Teman, Omar, Zepho, and Gatam, and Kenaz. ¹² And Timnah was concubine to Eliphaz, Esau's son, and she bare to Eliphaz Amalek. These are the sons of Adah, Esau's wife.

¹³ And these the sons of Reuel, Nahath and Zerah, Shammah and Mizzah. These were the sons of Basmath, Esau's wife.

¹⁴ And these were the sons of Aholibamah, the daughter of Anah, granddaughter of Zibeon, Esau's wife. And she bare to Esau Jeush and Jaalam and Korah.

¹⁵ These are the dukes (? clans) of the sons of Esau. The sons of Eliphaz, Esau's firstborn, duke Teman, duke Omar, duke Zepho, duke Kenaz, ¹⁶ duke Korah, duke Gatam, duke Amalek. These are the dukes of Eliphaz in the land of Edom; these are the sons of Adah.

¹⁷ And these the sons of Reuel, Esau's son, duke Nahath, duke Zerah, duke Shammah, duke Mizzah. These are the dukes of Reuel in the land of Edom; these are the sons of Basmath, Esau's wife.

THE ELOHISTIC NARRATIVE.

¹⁸ And these are the sons of Aholibamah, Esau's wife, duke Jeush, duke Jaalam, duke Korah. These are the dukes of Aholibamah, daughter of Anah, Esau's wife.

These are the sons of Esau, and these their dukes: he is Edom. [

³¹ And these are the kings who reigned in the land of Edom, before the reigning of a king over the children of Israel. ³² And there reigned in Edom Bela the son of Beor, and the name of his city was Dinhabah.

³³ And Bela died, and there reigned in his stead Jobab the son of Zerah, out of Bozrah.

³⁴ And Jobab died, and there reigned in his stead Husham, out of the land of the Temanite.

³⁵ And Husham died, and there reigned in his stead Hadad the son of Bedad, [and the name of his city was Avith.

³⁶ And Hadad died, and there reigned in his stead Samlah, out of Masrekah.

³⁷ And Samlah died, and there reigned in his stead Saul, out of Rehoboth of the River.

³⁸ And Saul died, and there reigned in his stead Baal-Hanan son of Achbor.

³⁹ And Baal-Hanan son of Achbor died, and there reigned in his stead Hadad, and the name of his city was Pau, and the name of his wife was Mehetabel, daughter of Matred, granddaughter of Mezahab.

⁴⁰ And these are the names of the dukes of Esau, according to their families, according to their places, by their names:—duke Timnah, duke Alvah, duke Jetheth, ⁴¹ duke Aholibamah, duke Elah, duke Pinon, ⁴² duke Kenaz, duke Teman, duke Mibzar, ⁴³ duke Magdiel, duke Iram. These are the dukes of Edom, according to their dwellings in the land of their possession: he is Esau, the father of Edom.

XXXVII. ¹ And Jacob dwelt in the land of his father's sojournings, in the land of Canaan.

² These are the generations of Jacob.

Joseph, seventeen years old, was tending with his brethren among the flocks, and he was a lad with the sons of Bilhah and with the sons of Zilpah, his father's wives. [* . . . ²⁸ᵃ And there passed-over Midianites, merchantmen. [

---

* No part of the present history of Joseph before Jacob's descent into Egypt, xlvi. 6, 7, belongs to the Elohist, except v. 2a and perhaps v. 28a, 36, as above, where 'Midianites' are named instead of 'Ishmaelites,' as in v. 25, 27. The 'sons of Bilhah and sons of Zilpah,' v. 2a, appear no more in the story. As the Elohist knows nothing of any ill-blood between Sarah and Hagar, Ishmael and Isaac, Esau and Jacob, Leah and Rachel, so he probably knew of none between Joseph and his brethren, and may have represented Joseph as having been merely kidnapped and carried off into Egypt by the Midianites, while out one day, with only four of his brethren, tending his father's sheep. A very few words may have sufficed for this, e.g., 'and there passed-over Midianites, merchantmen, [and they saw Joseph and laid hold on him and took him,] and the Midianites sold him into

THE ELOHISTIC NARRATIVE.

⁶⁰ And the Midianites sold him into Egypt, to Potiphar, an officer of Pharaoh, captain of the guard.] . . .

XLVI. ⁶ And they took their cattle and their gain which they had gotten in the land of Canaan, and they came to Egypt, Jacob and all his seed with him. ⁷ His sons and his sons' sons with him, his daughters and his sons' daughters, and all his seed, brought he with him to Egypt.

⁸ And these are the names of the sons of Israel that came to Egypt, Jacob and his sons; Jacob's firstborn, Reuben; ⁹ and the sons of Reuben, Enoch and Pallu, Hezron and Carmi. ¹⁰ And the sons of Simeon, Jemuel, and Jamin, and Ohad, and Jachin, and Zohar, and Saul son of the Canaanitess. ¹¹ And the sons of Levi, Gershon, and Kohath, and Merari. ¹² And the sons of Judah, Er, and Onan, and Shelah, and Pharez, and Zarah.] ¹³ And the sons of Issachar, Tola, and Phuvah, and Job, and Shimron. ¹⁴ And the sons of Zebulun, Sered, and Elon, and Jahleel. ¹⁵ These are the sons of Leah, which she bare to Jacob in Padan-Aram, and Dinah his daughter, all the souls of his sons and daughters, thirty-three.

¹⁶ And the sons of Gad, Ziphion, and Haggi, Shuni, and Ezbon, Eri, and Arodi, and Areli. ¹⁷ And the sons of Asher, Jimnah, and Ishuah, and Isui, and Beriah, and Serah their sister; and the sons of Beriah, Heber and Malchiel. ¹⁸ These are the sons of Zilpah, whom Laban gave to Leah his daughter, and she bare these to Jacob, sixteen souls.

¹⁹ The sons of Rachel, Jacob's wife, Joseph and Benjamin. ²⁰ And there were born to Joseph in the land of Egypt, whom Asenath daughter of Potipherah priest of On bare to him, Manasseh and Ephraim. ²¹ And the sons of Benjamin, Bela, and Becher, and Ashbel, Gera, and Naaman, Ehi and Rosh, Muppim, and Huppim, and Ard. ²² These are the sons of Rachel, which were born to Jacob, all the souls fourteen.

²³ And the sons of Dan, Hushim. ²⁴ And the sons of Naphtali, Jahzeel, and Guni, and Jezer, and Shillem. ²⁵ These are the sons of Bilhah, whom Laban gave to Rachel his daughter, and she bare these to Jacob, all the souls seven.

²⁶ All the souls of Jacob that came to Egypt, coming-forth out of his loins,] all the souls were sixty-and-six. ²⁷ And the sons of Joseph, which were born to him in Egypt, were two souls. All the souls of the house of Jacob that came to Egypt were seventy.]

XLVII. 7 And Joseph brought Jacob his father, and stationed him before Pharaoh, and Jacob blessed Pharaoh. ⁸ And Pharaoh said unto Jacob, 'About what are the days of the years of thy life?' ⁹ And Jacob said unto Pharaoh, 'The days of the years of my sojournings are a hundred and thirty years; few and evil have been the days of the years of the life of my fathers in the days of their sojournings.' ¹⁰ And Jacob blessed Pharaoh, and went-forth from before Pharaoh.

Egypt, &c.' The Elohist must then have stated how Joseph came to be high in office under Pharaoh, and how his father and brethren heard of his being alive, and went down to settle in Egypt—these points being referred to in the following portion of the Elohistic Narrative.

ⁱⁱᵃᵈ And Joseph settled his father and his brethren | in the land of Rameses; |
²⁷ᵇ and they were fruitful and multiplied exceedingly. ²⁸ And Jacob lived in
the land of Egypt seventeen years, and Jacob's days of the years of his life
were a hundred and forty-seven years. |

XLVIII. ³ And Jacob said unto Joseph, 'EL-SHADDAI appeared unto me
at Luz in the land of Canaan and blessed me, ⁴ and said unto me, "Lo! I will
make thee fruitful and multiply thee, and (give) make thee for a company of
peoples; and I will give this land to thy seed after thee, a perpetual possession." ⁵ And now, thy two sons, which were born to thee in the land of
Egypt before my coming unto thee to Egypt, they are mine, Ephraim and
Manasseh; even as Reuben and Simeon they shall be mine. ⁶ And thy offspring, which thou hast begotten after them, shall be thine; by the names of
their brothers shall they be called in their inheritance. ⁷ And I, at my
coming from Padan,—Rachel died beside me in the land of Canaan, when
there was yet a space of land to come to Ephrath, and I buried her in the
way to Ephrath.' |

XLIX. ¹ᵃ And Jacob called unto his sons, | ²⁹ and he charged them, and
said unto them, 'I shall be gathered to my people; bury me unto my fathers
in the cave that is in the field of Ephron the Hittite, ³⁰ in the cave that is in
the field of Machpelah, which is east of Mamre, in the land of Canaan, which
Abraham bought with the field from Ephron the Hittite for a possession of a
burial-place. ³¹ There they buried Abraham and Sarah his wife; there they
buried Isaac and Rebekah his wife; and there I buried Leah. ³² The purchase
of the field and of the cave that is in it was from the sons of Heth.' ³³ And
Jacob ended to charge his sons, and he was gathered unto his people. |
L. ¹³ And his sons carried him to the land of Canaan, and buried him in the
cave of the field of Machpelah, which Abraham bought with the field for a
possession of a burial-place from Ephron the Hittite, east of Mamre. |

EXODUS.

I. ¹ And these are the names of the children of Israel, who came to
Egypt with Jacob, each and his house they came—² Reuben, Simeon, Levi, and
Judah, ³ Issachar, Zebulun, and Benjamin, ⁴ Dan and Naphtali, Gad and
Asher. ⁵ And all the souls that went-forth out of Jacob's thigh were seventy
souls; and Joseph was in Egypt.

⁶ And Joseph died, and all his brethren, and all that generation. ⁷ And
the children of Israel were fruitful and teemed and multiplied, and were ex-
ceedingly mighty; and the land was filled with them. | ¹³ And the Egyptians
made the children of Israel to serve with rigour. | II. ²³ᵇ And the children
of Israel sighed because of the service, and they cried; and their wail went-
up unto ELOHIM because of the service. ²⁴ And ELOHIM heard their sighing,
and ELOHIM remembered His covenant with Abraham, with Isaac, and with
Jacob. ²⁵ And ELOHIM saw the children of Israel, and ELOHIM knew. |

THE ELOHISTIC NARRATIVE.

vi. ² And ELOHIM spake unto Moses* and said unto him, 'I am JEHOVAH. ³ And I appeared unto Abraham and unto Isaac and unto Jacob by the name EL-SHADDAI; but by My name JEHOVAH I did not make-myself known to them. ⁴ And I have also established My Covenant with them, to give to them the land of Canaan, the land of their sojournings in which they sojourned. ⁵ And I have also heard the sighing of the children of Israel, whom the Egyptians make to serve, and I have remembered My Covenant. . . .

[Here the Elohistic Narrative ends abruptly, having been broken off perhaps through the sickness or death of the writer, or perhaps because he had completed the special work which he had set himself to do, viz. to record the history of the primeval times, down to the revelation of the name Jehovah at the time of the Exodus.]

---

* The Elohist here mentions Moses for the first time in what now remains of his work, and may have given a short notice about his birth between this passage and ii. 23b-25, which the Jehovist has replaced by his more circumstantial narrative. But this assumption is not absolutely necessary. We see that Joshua is introduced quite as abruptly by the Jehovist in E. xvii. 9 and Hur in v. 10.

APPENDIX II.

THE ORIGINAL STORY OF THE EXODUS.

N.B. The sign | denotes that here an interpolation occurs in the Original Story. The passages within [ ] belong to the Elohistic Narrative.

I. [¹And these are the names of the children of Israel, who came to Egypt with Jacob,—each and his house they came: ²Reuben, Simeon, Levi, and Judah, ³Issachar, Zebulun, and Benjamin, ⁴Dan and Naphtali, Gad and Asher. ⁵And all the souls that went-forth out of Jacob's thigh were seventy souls; and Joseph was in Egypt.

⁶And Joseph died, and all his brethren, and all that generation. ⁷And the children of Israel fructified and teemed and multiplied, and were exceedingly mighty; and the land was filled with them.] ⁸And there arose a new king over Egypt, who knew not Joseph. ⁹And he said unto his people, 'Lo ! the people of the children of Israel *are* more numerous and mighty than we. ¹⁰Come on ! let us deal-wisely with it, lest it multiply, and it come-to-pass, when war happeneth, that it join-itself, it also, to our foes, and fight against us, and go-up out of the land.' ¹¹And they placed over it princes of tribute so as to afflict it with their burdens ; and it built store-cities for Pharaoh, Pithom and Rameses. ¹²And, as they afflicted it, so it multiplied, and so it broke-forth ; and they were vexed because of the children of Israel. [¹³And the Egyptians made the children of Israel to serve with rigour.*] ¹⁴And they embittered their lives with hard service, in clay, and in brick, and in all *kind of* service in the field : all their service, which they (served) laid upon them, *they laid* with rigour. †

---

* This would be tame, if written by the *same* hand which had already written v. 11.

† J. explains here the statement of E. in v. 13, showing in what the 'service' consisted, in agreement with his own previous words in v. 11.

"And the king of Egypt said to the Hebrew midwives, (of whom the name of the one was Shiphrah, and the name of the second was Puah), and he said, 'When ye help the Hebrew-women to bear, and see at the troughs, if it is a son, then put-him to-death, and, if it is a daughter, then let her live.' And the midwives feared Elohim, and did not do as the king of Egypt spake unto them, but let the boys live. And the king of Egypt called for the midwives and said to them, 'Why have ye done this thing, and let the boys live?' And the midwives said unto Pharaoh, 'Because the Hebrew-women are not as the Egyptian-women, for they are lively : before the midwife cometh-in unto them they have borne.'

And ELOHIM did-good to the midwives, and the people multiplied, and they were very mighty. And it came-to-pass, because the midwives feared ELOHIM, that He made for them households. And Pharaoh commanded all his people saying, 'Every son that is born—ye shall cast him into the River, and every daughter ye shall let live.'

11. 'And there went a man of the house of Levi, and took to wife a daughter of Levi.* 'And the woman conceived and bare a son, and she saw that he was fair, and she hid him three months. 'And she was not able to hide him any longer, and she took for him an ark of rushes, and daubed it with bitumen and with pitch, and placed the boy in it, and placed it in the weeds by the brink of the River. 'And his sister stood some-way-off, to know what would be done to him.

'And the daughter of Pharaoh came down to bathe by the River, and her damsels were walking by the side of the River ; and she saw the ark in the midst of the weeds, and sent her handmaid, and took it. 'And she opened and saw him, the boy, and lo ! a child weeping ! and she had pity on him and said, 'This is one of the boys of the Hebrews.' 'And his sister said unto Pharaoh's daughter, 'Shall I go and call thee a suckling-woman of the Hebrews, that she may suckle the boy for thee ?' 'And Pharaoh's daughter said to her, 'Go !' and the maiden went, and called the boy's mother. 'And Pharaoh's daughter said to her, 'Take this boy away, and suckle him for me, and I—I will give thy hire' ; and the woman took the boy and suckled him. 'And the boy grew, and she brought-him-in to Pharaoh's daughter, and he was to her for a son ; and she called his name Moses (*Mosheh*), and said, 'Because I have drawn (*mashah*) him out of the water.'

"And it came to pass in those days that Moses grew, and he went-forth unto his brethren, and looked at their burdens, and he saw an Egyptian man smiting a Hebrew man, one of his brethren. And he turned-his-face here and there, and saw that there was no man, and smote the Egyptian, and hid him in the sand. And he went-forth on the second day, and lo ! two men, Hebrews, were con-tending ; and he said to the wrong-doer, 'Wherefore smitest thou thy neighbour?' And he said, 'Who placed thee as a prince and a judge over us ? Art thou thinking to slay me as thou didst slay the Egyptian?' And Moses feared and

---

* The writer, who speaks merely of a 'man of the house of Levi,' and who calls the woman 'a daughter of Levi,' 'the woman,' v. 2, 9, 'the child's mother,' v. 8, evidently knew nothing of the *names* of their parents 'Amram' and 'Joche-bed,' which are due to the L.L, vi. 20, N. xxvi, 59.

said, 'Surely the matter is known.' ¹⁵ And Pharaoh heard of this matter and thought to slay Moses; and Moses fled from the face of Pharaoh, and dwelt in the land of Midian.

And he sat down by the well. ¹⁶ Now a prince of Midian had seven daughters; and they came and drew and filled the troughs, to water their father's flock. ¹⁷ And the shepherds came and drove-them-away; and Moses arose and saved them, and watered their flock. ¹⁸ And they came-in to Reuel, their father, and he said, 'Why have ye hastened to come-in to-day?' ¹⁹ And they said, 'An Egyptian man delivered us out of the hands of the shepherds, and also drew plentifully for us, and watered the flock.' ²⁰ And he said unto his daughters, 'And where is he? Wherefore *is* this *that* ye left the man? call him that he may eat bread.' ²¹ And Moses was willing to dwell with the man, and he gave Zipporah his daughter to Moses. ²² And she bare a son, and she called him Gershom; for he said, 'A sojourner (*ger*) have I been in a strange land.'

²³ And it came to pass in those many days that the king of Egypt died. [And the children of Israel sighed because of the service,* and they cried; and their wail went-up unto ELOHIM because of the service. ²⁴ And ELOHIM heard their sighing, and ELOHIM remembered His covenant with Abraham, with Isaac, and with Jacob. ²⁵ And ELOHIM saw the children of Israel, and ELOHIM knew.]

III. ¹ And Moses was feeding the flock of Jethro his father-in-law, prince of Midian; and he led the flock behind the wilderness, and came unto the Mount of ELOHIM. | ² And there appeared unto him an angel of YAHVEH in a flame of fire out of the midst of the thorn-bush; and he saw and lo! the thorn-bush was burning with fire, and the thorn-bush was not devoured. ³ And Moses said, 'Let me turn-aside, I pray, and see this great appearance, why the thorn-bush is not burnt.' ⁴ And YAHVEH saw that he turned-aside to see, and ELOHIM called unto him out of the midst of the bush and said, 'Moses! Moses!' And he said, 'Behold me!' ⁵ And He said, 'Come not near hither; cast thy shoes from off thy feet, for the place on which thou art standing is holy ground.' ⁶ And He said, 'I *am* the Elohim of thy father, the Elohim of Abraham, the Elohim of Isaac, and the Elohim of Jacob.' And Moses hid his face, for he was afraid to behold ELOHIM. ⁷ And YAHVEH said, 'I have verily seen the affliction of My people who *are* in Egypt, and their cry have I heard because of its exactors; for I know its woes. ⁸ And I have come-down to deliver it out of the hand of the Egyptians, and to bring-it-up out of that land unto a land good and large, unto a land flowing with milk and honey.| ⁹ And now, lo! the cry of the children of Israel has come-in unto me, and I have also seen the oppression wherewith the Egyptians *are* oppressing them. ¹⁰ And now, come, and I will send thee unto Pharaoh, and bring-thou-forth My people, the children of Israel, out of Egypt.' ¹¹ And Moses said unto ELOHIM, 'Who *am* I that I should go unto Pharaoh, and that I should bring-forth the children of Israel out of Egypt?' ¹² And He said, 'For I will be with thee; and this *shall be* the sign for thee that I have sent thee: at thy bringing-forth the people out of Egypt, ye shall serve ELOHIM by this Mount.' ¹³ And Moses said unto ELOHIM, 'Lo! *when* I come unto the children

---

* This so obviously refers to the words in L 13, and not ii. 1-23a, that the interpolation of the Jehovist is distinctly betrayed.

of Israel, and shalt say to them, the Elohim of your fathers hath sent me unto you, and they shall say to me, What is His Name? what shall I say unto them?' [13] And ELOHIM said unto Moses, 'I AM WHO I AM': and He said, 'Thus shalt thou say to the children of Israel, I AM hath sent me unto you.'

[15] And ELOHIM said again unto Moses, 'Thus shalt thou say unto the children of Israel, YAHVEH, the Elohim of your fathers, the Elohim of Abraham, the Elohim of Isaac, and the Elohim of Jacob, hath sent me unto you: this is My Name for ever, and this My memorial for generation *and* generation. [16] Go, and thou shalt gather the elders of Israel, and thou shalt say unto them, YAHVEH, the Elohim of your fathers, hath appeared unto me, the Elohim of Abraham, Isaac, and Jacob, saying, I have surely visited you, and that which is done to you in Egypt. [17] And I have said, I will bring-you-up out of the affliction of Egypt | unto a land flowing with milk and honey. [18] And they shall hearken to thy voice, and thou shalt go-in, thou and the elders of Israel, unto the king of Egypt, and ye shall say unto him, YAHVEH, the Elohim of the Hebrews, hath met with us ; and now, let us go, we pray, a journey of three days into the wilderness, and sacrifice to YAHVEH our Elohim. [19] And I—I know that the king of Egypt will not (give) allow you to go, not even by a strong hand. [20] And I will put-forth My hand, and will smite Egypt with all My marvels, which I will do in the midst of it, and afterwards he will let-you-go. [21] And I will put the favour of this people in the eyes of the Egyptians, and it shall come to pass, when ye go, that ye shall not go empty ; [22] and every woman shall ask from her neighbour, and from her who sojourneth in her house, articles of silver and articles of gold and garments, and ye shall place them on your sons and on your daughters, and ye shall spoil the Egyptians.'

IV. [1] 'And Moses answered and said, 'But lo ! they will not believe me, and they will not hearken unto my voice, for they will say YAHVEH hath not appeared unto thee.' [2] 'And YAHVEH said unto him, 'What is this in thy hand?' And he said, 'A staff.' [3] And He said, 'Cast it to the earth'; and he cast it to the earth, and it became a serpent, and Moses fled from its presence. [4] 'And YAHVEH said unto Moses, 'Put-forth thy hand, and lay-hold on its tail,'—and he put-forth his hand, and laid-hold on it ; and it became a staff in his palm—[5] 'so that they may believe that YAHVEH the Elohim of their fathers, the Elohim of Abraham, the Elohim of Isaac, and the Elohim of Jacob, hath appeared unto thee.'

[6] And YAHVEH said unto him again, 'Put-in, I pray, thy hand into thy bosom'; and he put-in his hand into his bosom, and he brought-it-forth, and lo ! his hand *was* leprous like snow. [7] 'And He said, 'Put-back thy hand into thy bosom,'— and he put-back his hand into his bosom, and he brought-it-forth from his bosom, and lo ! it had returned like his *other* flesh—[8] 'and it shall come to pass, if they will not believe thee, and will not hearken to the voice of the first sign, that they will believe the voice of the second sign.' [9] And it shall come to pass, if they will not believe also these two signs, and will not hearken to thy voice, that thou shalt take of the waters of the River and pour on the dry-land ; and it shall be, the water which thou shalt take out of the River,—yea, it shall become blood upon the dry-land.'

[10] And Moses said unto YAHVEH, 'Oh my Lord ! I *am* not a man of words either yesterday or before, or since Thy speaking unto Thy servant ; for I *am* slow of mouth and slow of tongue.' [11] And YAHVEH said unto him, 'Who has

THE ORIGINAL STORY OF THE EXODUS. 401

(placed) made a mouth for man? or who shall make dumb or deaf or open-eyed or blind? is it not YAHVEH? ¹² And now, go, and I will be with thy mouth, and will direct thee what thou shalt speak.' ¹³ And he said, 'O my Lord I send, I pray, by the hand *of him whom* Thou wilt send.' ¹⁴ And YAHVEH's anger was kindled against Moses, and He said, 'Is not Aaron the Levite thy brother? I know that he will certainly speak, and also, lo ! he cometh-forth to meet thee, and he will see thee and rejoice in his heart. ¹⁵ And thou shalt speak unto him, and thou shalt place words in his mouth, and I will be with thy mouth and with his mouth, and will direct you what ye shall do. ¹⁶ And he shall speak for thee unto the people, and it shall come to pass that he shall become to thee a mouth and thou shalt become to him ELOHIM. ¹⁷ And this staff thou shalt take in thy hand, wherewith thou shalt do the signs.'

¹⁸ And Moses went and returned unto Jethro his father-in-law, and said to him, ' Let me go, I pray, and return to my brethren who *are* in Egypt, and see whether they are yet alive.' And Jethro said to Moses, 'Go in peace.' *¹⁹ And YAHVEH said to Moses in Midian,* 'Go, return to Egypt, for all the men are dead who sought thy life.' ²⁰ And Moses took his wife and his sons (? son), and made them ride on the ass, and returned to the land of Egypt, and Moses took the staff of ELOHIM in his hand. ²¹ And YAHVEH said unto Moses, ' At thy going to return to Egypt, see, all these wonders that I put in thy hand, that thou do them before Pharaoh ; but I will harden his heart, and he will not let the people go. ²² And thou shalt say unto Pharaoh, ' Thus saith YAHVEH, My son, My firstborn, *is* Israel. ²³ And I say unto thee, Let My son go that he may serve Me ; but, refuse to let him go, lo ! I slay thy son, thy firstborn.' ²⁴ And it came to pass in the way, at the resting-place, that YAHVEH lighted on him, and sought to kill him. ²⁵ And Zipporah took a flint, and cut-off the foreskin of her son, and threw it at his feet, and said, ' Surely a bridegroom of blood art thou to me.' ²⁶ And He desisted from him ; then she said, ' a bridegroom of blood,' because of the circumcision.

²⁷ And YAHVEH said unto Aaron, 'Go to the wilderness to meet Moses' ; and he went, and lighted on Moses at the Mount of ELOHIM and kissed him. ²⁸ And Moses told to Aaron all the words of YAHVEH with which He had sent him, and all the signs which He had commanded him. ²⁹ And Moses went and Aaron, and they gathered all the Elders of the children of Israel. ³⁰ And Aaron spake all the words which YAHVEH had spoken with Moses, and he [Moses] did the signs before the eyes of the people. ³¹ And the people believed, and they heard that YAHVEH had visited the children of Israel, and that he had seen their affliction, and they bowed-the-head and worshipped.

V. ¹ And afterwards Moses and Aaron went-in and they said unto Pharaoh, ' Thus saith YAHVEH, the Elohim of Israel, Let My people go, that they may keep a Feast to Me in the wilderness.' ² And Pharaoh said, ' Who is YAHVEH, that I should hearken to His voice to let Israel go? I know not YAHVEH, and also Israel I will not let go.' ³ And they said, ' The Elohim of the Hebrews hath

---

* The previous call of Moses, and the directions given to him, were, therefore, only preparatory ; when the proper moment was come, Moses received a divine notice ' in Midian,' where he was with Jethro, having already obtained his consent to his going.

D D

met with us: let us go, we pray, a journey of three days in the wilderness and sacrifice to YAHVEH our Elohim, lest He fall upon us with pestilence or with sword.' ⁵ And the king of Egypt said unto them, 'Wherefore do ye, Moses and Aaron, set the people free from its works? go ye to your burdens.' ⁵ And Pharaoh said, 'Lo! numerous now is the people of the land, and ye make them rest from their burdens.'

⁶ And Pharaoh commanded on that day the exactors among the people and its officers, saying, ⁷ 'Ye shall not add to give straw to the people for the making of bricks as heretofore; let them go and collect straw for themselves. ⁸ And the tale of brick which they were making heretofore shall ye lay upon them, ye shall not diminish from it; for idle are they: therefore are they crying, saying, Let us go, let us sacrifice to our Elohim. ⁹ Let the service be heavy upon the men, and let them work at it, and let them not regard lying words.'

¹⁰ And the exactors of the people and its officers went-forth and said unto the people, saying, 'Thus saith Pharaoh, I give you no straw: ¹¹ do ye go, take for yourselves straw from what ye find; for there is nothing diminished from your service.' ¹² And the people was scattered through all the land of Egypt, to collect stubble for straw. ¹³ And the exactors were urgent, saying, 'Finish your works, the matter of a day in its day, as when there was straw.' ¹⁴ And the officers of the children of Israel, whom Pharaoh's exactors had placed over them, were beaten, saying, 'Why have ye not finished your portion, in making-bricks as heretofore, both yesterday and to-day?' ¹⁵ And the officers of the children of Israel came-in and cried unto Pharaoh, saying, 'Wherefore doest thou thus to thy servants? ¹⁶ Straw has not been given to thy servants, and they are saying to us, Make-bricks; and lo! thy servants are beaten, but thy people have done the wrong.' ¹⁷ And he said, 'Idle are ye, idle! therefore are ye saying, Let us go, let us sacrifice to YAHVEH. ¹⁸ And now, go ye, serve! for straw shall not be given to you, yet the tale of bricks shall ye give.'

¹⁹ And the officers of the children of Israel saw that they were in evil case, (saying) it being said, 'Ye shall not diminish from your bricks, the matter of a day in its day.' ²⁰ And they lighted upon Moses and Aaron standing to meet them at their coming-forth from Pharaoh. ²¹ And they said unto them, 'Let YAHVEH look upon you and judge; for ye have made our savour to stink in the eyes of Pharaoh and in the eyes of his servants, to give a sword into their hand to slay us.'

²² And Moses returned unto YAHVEH and said, 'O Lord, wherefore hast Thou done evil to this people? Wherefore is this that Thou sentest me? ²³ For since I went-in unto Pharaoh to speak in Thy name, he has done-evil to this people, and Thou hast not at all delivered thy people.' VI. ¹ And YAHVEH said unto Moses, 'Now shalt thou see what I will do to Pharaoh; for through a strong hand shall he let them go, and through a strong hand shall he drive them out of his land.' [² And Elohim spake unto Moses and said unto him, 'I am YAHVEH. ³ And I appeared unto Abraham, and unto Isaac, and unto Jacob, by EL-SHADDAI; but by my Name YAHVEH I did not make-Myself-known to them. ⁴ And I have also established My covenant with them, to give to them the land of Canaan, the land of their sojournings in which they sojourned. ⁵ And I have also heard the sighing of the children of Israel, whom the Egyptians make to serve, and I have remembered My covenant.'] | ⁶ And Moses spake

so unto the children of Israel: and they hearkened not unto Moses for straitness of spirit and for hard service.|

VII. ¹⁴ And YAHVEH said unto Moses, 'Pharaoh's heart is heavy; he refuseth to let the people go. ¹⁵ Go unto Pharaoh in the morning: lo! he goeth forth to the water: and thou shalt stand to meet him by the brink of the River, and the staff, which was turned to a serpent, thou shalt take in thy hand. ¹⁶ And thou shalt say unto him, 'YAHVEH, the Elohim of the Hebrews, hath sent me unto thee, saying, Let My people go that they may serve Me in the wilderness; and lo! thou hast not hearkened hitherto. ¹⁷ Thus saith YAHVEH, By this shalt thou know that I am YAHVEH: lo! I smite with the staff that is in my hand upon the waters that are in the River, and they shall be turned to blood. ¹⁸ And the fish that are in the River shall die, and the River shall stink, and the Egyptians shall loath to drink water out of the River.'| ²⁰ᵇ And he lifted-up with the staff and smote the waters that were in the River before the eyes of Pharaoh and before the eyes of his servants, and all the waters that were in the River were turned to blood. ²¹ And the fish that were in the River died, and all the River stank; and the Egyptians were not able to drink water out of the River, and the blood was in all the land of Egypt.| ²³ And Pharaoh turned and went-into his house, and did not set his heart even to this. ²⁴ And all the Egyptians dug round-about the River water to drink, for they were not able to drink of the waters of the River.

²⁵ And there were fulfilled seven days after YAHVEH's smiting the River. VIII. ¹ 'And YAHVEH said unto Moses, 'Go unto Pharaoh and say unto him, Thus saith YAHVEH, Let My people go that they may serve Me. ² And if thou refuse to let them go, lo! I smite all thy borders with frogs. ³ And the River shall teem with frogs, and they shall come-up and go-in into thy house, and into thy bed-room, and upon thy bed, and into the house of thy servants and upon thy people, and into thy ovens, and into thy trays. ⁴ And upon thee and upon thy people and upon thy servants shall the frogs come up.'* . . . | ⁸ And Pharaoh called to Moses and to Aaron and said, 'Make-entreaty unto YAHVEH that He take-away the frogs from me and from my people, and I will let the people go, that they may sacrifice to YAHVEH.' ⁹ And Moses said to Pharaoh, '(Honour thyself over me—) Honour me by saying for when I shall make entreaty for' thee and for thy servants and for thy people, to cut-off the frogs from thee and from thy house; only in the River shall they be left.' ¹⁰ And he said, 'For to-morrow'; and he said, 'According to thy word ! in order that thou mayest know that there is none like YAHVEH our Elohim. ¹¹ And the frogs shall go away from thee and from thy houses, and from thy servants, and from thy people; only in the River shall they be left.' ¹² And Moses and Aaron went-forth from Pharaoh, and Moses cried unto YAHVEH about the matter of the frogs which He had laid on Pharaoh. ¹³ And YAHVEH did according to the word of Moses; and the frogs died out of the houses, out of the villages, and out of the field. ¹⁴ And they collected them in heaps, heaps, and the land stank. ¹⁵ᵃ And Pharaoh saw that there was breathing-time and he made-heavy his heart.|

²⁰ And YAHVEH said unto Moses, 'Rise-early in the morning, and station thyself

* Here the original account of the frogs being brought-up either by Moses acting with his rod or by a direct act of YAHVEH, as in viii. 24, ix. 6, xii. 29, has been struck out by L.L., to make room for the magnification of Aaron in v. 5-7.

before Pharaoh: lo! he goeth-forth to the water; and thou shalt say unto him, 'Thus saith YAHVEH, Let My people go that they may serve Me. ¹² For if thou let not My people go, lo! I send on thee and on thy servants and on thy people and on thy houses the cockroach; and the houses of the Egyptians shall be full of the cockroach, and also the ground on which they are. ¹³ And I will distinguish in that day the land of Goshen, on which My people stand, that there be no cockroach there; so that thou mayest know that I am YAHVEH in the midst of the land; ¹⁴ and I will place a division between My people and thy people: to-morrow shall this sign be.' ¹⁵ And YAHVEH did so; and there came-in the cockroach in multitudes into the house of Pharaoh and into the house of his servants, and into all the land of Egypt; the land was corrupted because of the cockroach. ¹⁶ And Pharaoh called unto Moses and to Aaron and said, 'Go ye, sacrifice to your Elohim in the land.' ¹⁷ And Moses said, 'It is not right to do thus; for we shall sacrifice the abomination of the Egyptians to YAHVEH our Elohim. Lo! shall we sacrifice the abomination of the Egyptians before their eyes, and will they not stone us? ¹⁸ A journey of three days will we go in the wilderness, and sacrifice to YAHVEH our Elohim, as He shall say to us.' ¹⁹ And Pharaoh said, 'I will let-you-go, that ye may sacrifice to YAHVEH your Elohim in the wilderness; only do not go very far away. Make-entreaty on my behalf.' ²⁰ And Moses said, 'Lo! I go-forth from thee, and will make-entreaty unto YAHVEH that the cockroach may go-away from Pharaoh, and from his servants, and from his people, to-morrow. Only let not Pharaoh add to act-deceitfully, so as not to let the people go to sacrifice to YAHVEH.' ²¹ And Moses went-forth from Pharaoh, and made-entreaty unto YAHVEH. ²² And YAHVEH did according to the word of Moses, and he took-away the cockroach from Pharaoh, from his servants, and from his people; not one was left. ²³ And Pharaoh made-heavy his heart at this time also, and he did not let the people go.

IX. ¹ And YAHVEH said unto Moses, 'Go-in unto Pharaoh, and thou shalt speak unto him, Thus saith YAHVEH the Elohim of the Hebrews, Let My people go that they may serve Me. ² For, if thou refuse to let them go, and wilt still keep thy hold on them, ³ lo! the hand of YAHVEH is upon thy cattle which is in the field, upon horses, upon asses, upon camels, upon oxen, and upon sheep—a very grievous pestilence. ⁴ And YAHVEH will distinguish between the cattle of Israel and the cattle of the Egyptians; and there shall not a thing die of all which belongs to the children of Israel.' ⁵ And YAHVEH set an appointed-time, saying, 'To-morrow YAHVEH will do this thing in the land.' ⁶ And YAHVEH did that thing on the morrow, and all cattle of the Egyptians died, and of cattle of Israel died not even one. ⁷ And Pharaoh sent, and lo! there was not dead out of the cattle of the children of Israel even one: but the heart of Pharaoh was heavy, and he did not let the people go.

¹³ And YAHVEH said unto Moses, 'Rise-early in the morning, and present-thy-self before Pharaoh, and thou shalt say unto him, Thus saith YAHVEH, the Elohim of the Hebrews, Let My people go that they may serve Me. ¹⁴ For at this time I will send all My plagues upon thy heart, and on thy servants, and on thy people, so that thou mayest know that there is none like Me in all the earth. ¹⁵ For now I had put-forth My hand, and smitten thee and thy people with pestilence, and thou hadst been cut-off from the earth. ¹⁶ Nevertheless, on account of this I have let thee stand, in order that I may make thee see My power, and in

order to declare My name in all the earth. ¹⁸ As yet thou exaltest thyself against My people not to let them go. ¹⁹ Lo! I will make-it-rain about this time to-morrow very heavy hail, such as has not been in Egypt since the day of its foundation even until now. ²⁰ And now, send, secure thy cattle and all which thou hast in the field: all the men and beasts which are found in the field and are not gathered into the house—the hail shall come-down upon them and they shall die.' ²¹ He who feared the word of YAHVEH of the servants of Pharaoh, made his servants and his cattle flee into the houses. ²² And he who set not his heart unto the word of YAHVEH, left his servants and his cattle in the field. ²³ And YAHVEH said unto Moses, 'Stretch out thy hand towards heaven, that there may be hail in all the land of Egypt, on man and on beast and on every herb in the field in the land of Egypt.' ²⁴ And Moses stretched out his staff towards heaven, and YAHVEH sent thunderings and hail, and the fire went towards the earth; and YAHVEH rained hail upon the land of Egypt. ²⁵ And there was hail and fire continual in the midst of the hail, very grievous, such as there was none like it in all the land of Egypt since it became a nation. ²⁶ And the hail smote in all the land of Egypt all that was in the field, from man even unto beast; and every herb of the field the hail smote, and every tree of the field it broke. ²⁷ Only in the land of Goshen, where the children of Israel were, was there no hail. ²⁸ And Pharaoh sent and called to Moses and to Aaron, and said unto them, 'I have sinned this time: YAHVEH is the righteous, and I and my people are the guilty. ²⁹ Make-entreaty unto YAHVEH, and let there be enough of there being thunders of ELOHIM and hail; and I will let you go, and ye shall not any longer stay.' ³⁰ And Moses said unto him, 'At my going-forth from the city, I will spread-out my hands unto YAHVEH; the thunders shall cease and the hail shall be no more, in order that thou mayest know that the earth is YAHVEH's. ³¹ But thou and thy servants—I know that ye will fear not yet because of YAHVEH-ELOHIM.' ³² Now the flax and the barley were smitten; for the barley was in the ear, and the flax was in the flower. ³³ But the wheat and the spelt were not smitten, for they were dark. ³⁴ And Moses went-forth from Pharaoh out of the city, and he spread-out his hands unto YAHVEH; and the thunders and the hail ceased; and the rain was not poured-out to the earth. ³⁵ But, when Pharaoh saw that the rain ceased and the hail and the thunders, he sinned yet more and made-heavy his heart, he and his servants.

X. 'And YAHVEH said unto Moses, 'Go-in unto Pharaoh, for I have made-heavy his heart and the hearts of his servants, that so I may set these my signs in the midst of him, ² and that so thou mayest relate to the ears of thy son and thy son's son what I have wrought-reproachfully in Egypt, and my signs which I have placed among them, that ye may know that I am YAHVEH.' ³ And Moses went-in and Aaron unto Pharaoh, and they said unto him, 'Thus saith YAHVEH the Elohim of the Hebrews, How long dost thou refuse to humble-thyself before Me? Let My people go that they may serve Me. ⁴ For, if thou refusest to let My people go, lo! I bring to-morrow the locust on thy border. ⁵ And it shall cover the eye of the land, and thou shalt not be able to see the land, and it shall eat the remnant of that which is escaped, which is left to you by the hail, and it shall eat every tree which groweth or you out of the field. ⁶ And it shall fill thy houses, and the houses of all thy servants, and the houses of all the Egyptians, which neither thy fathers nor thy fathers' fathers have seen since the day of their being on the ground unto this day.' And he turned-his-face and went-forth from Pharaoh. ' And the servants of Pharaoh said unto him, 'How long shall this (man) become a snare for us? Let the men go that they may serve Yahveh their Elohim. Knowest thou not yet that Egypt has perished?' ⁸ And Moses and Aaron were brought back to Pharaoh, and he said unto them, 'Go ye, serve YAHVEH your Elohim; who and who are those going?' ⁹ And Moses said, 'With our young and with our old will we go; with our sons and with our daughters, with our flocks and with our herds, will we go; for we have a Feast to YAHVEH.' ¹⁰ And he said unto them, 'YAHVEH be so with you, as I will let you go and your little ones! Look ye! for evil is over-against you. ¹¹ Not so! go ye, I pray, the men, and serve YAHVEH; for that were ye seeking.' And one drove them from the presence of Pharaoh. ¹² And YAHVEH said unto Moses, 'Stretch-out thy hand over the land of Egypt for the locust, that it may come-up over the land of Egypt, and eat every herb of the land, all which the hail has left.' ¹³ And Moses stretched-forth his staff over the land of Egypt, and YAHVEH guided an east-wind over the land all that day and all the night; the morning was, and the east-wind brought the locust. ¹⁴ And the locust came-up over all the land of Egypt, and rested in all the border of Egypt, very grievous; before it was no such locust as it, and after it there shall not be such. ¹⁵ And it covered the eye of all the land, and the land was darkened; and it ate every herb of the land and every fruit of the trees which the hail had left, and there was not left any green-thing in the trees and in the herb of the field in all the land of Egypt. ¹⁶ And Pharaoh hastened to call Moses and Aaron and said, 'I have sinned against YAHVEH your Elohim and against you. ¹⁷ And now, forgive, I pray, my sin only this time, and make-entreaty to Yahveh your Elohim that he may take-away from me only this death.' ¹⁸ And he went-forth from Pharaoh and made-entreaty unto YAHVEH. ¹⁹ And YAHVEH turned a strong west-wind, and it took-up the locust and threw it into the Red Sea; there was not left one locust in all the boundary of Egypt. ²⁰ But YAHVEH hardened Pharaoh's heart, and he did not let the people of Israel go.

²¹ And YAHVEH said unto Moses, 'Stretch-out thy hand over the heaven, that there may be darkness over the land of Egypt, that one may feel darkness.' ²² And Moses stretched-forth his hand over the heaven, and there was darkness, thick darkness, in all the land of Egypt three days. ²³ They saw not one his brother, and they arose not each from his place three days; but for all the children of Israel there was light in their dwellings. ²⁴ And Pharaoh called unto Moses and said, 'Go ye, serve YAHVEH! only your flocks and your herds shall be stayed; also your little-ones shall go with you.' ²⁵ And Moses said, 'Thou also shalt give into our hand sacrifices and burnt-offerings, that we may offer to YAHVEH our Elohim. ²⁶ And also our cattle shall go with us, not a hoof shall be left; for we shall take of it to serve YAHVEH our Elohim; and we know not with what we shall serve YAHVEH until our coming thither.' ²⁷ But YAHVEH hardened Pharaoh's heart, and he would not let them go. ²⁸ And Pharaoh said to him, 'Begone from me! beware-thee that thou see not my face again; for in the day of thy seeing my face thou shalt die.' ²⁹ And Moses said, 'So hast thou spoken! I will not see thy face any more.'

XI. ¹ Now YAHVEH had said unto Moses, 'Yet one stroke more will I bring upon Pharaoh and upon the Egyptians; afterwards he will let you go hence: at his letting you go, he will surely drive you away hence altogether. ² Speak now in the ears of the people, and let them ask, each from his neighbour and each woman from her neighbour, articles of silver and articles of gold.'" ² 'And YAHVEH had put favour for the people in the eyes of the Egyptians: also the man Moses was very great in the land of Egypt, in the eyes of Pharaoh's servants, and in the eyes of the people. ⁴ And Moses said,† 'Thus saith YAHVEH, About midnight I go-forth in the midst of Egypt.‡ ⁵ And every firstborn shall die in the land of Egypt, from the firstborn of Pharaoh who sits upon his throne unto the firstborn of the maidservant who is behind the millstones, and every firstborn of cattle. ⁶ And there shall be a great cry in all the land of Egypt, such as there has been none like it, nor shall be like it anymore. ⁷ But against any of the children of Israel not a dog shall sharpen his tongue, even from man unto beast, that so ye may know that YAHVEH distinguisheth between the Egyptians and Israel. ⁸And all these thy servants shall come-down unto me and bow-down to me, saying, Go-forth, thou, and all the people which is at thy feet! and afterwards I will go-forth.' And he went-forth from Pharaoh in heat of anger.‖ XII. ²⁹ And it came to pass that at midnight YAHVEH smote every firstborn in the land of Egypt, from the firstborn of Pharaoh that sat on his throne unto the firstborn of the captive who was in the dungeon, and every firstborn of cattle. ³⁰ And Pharaoh rose-up in the night, he and all his servants and all the Egyptians; and there was a great cry in Egypt; for there was not a house where there was not one dead. ³¹ And he called for Moses and for Aaron in the midnight, and said, 'Arise! go-forth from the midst of my people, both you and the children of Israel, and go, serve YAHVEH as ye have spoken. ³² Also your flocks and your herds take, as ye have spoken, and go, and bless me also.' ³³ And the Egyptians pressed-hard upon the people, to hasten to let them go out of the land, for they said, 'We are all of us dead men!' ³⁴ So the people took their dough before it was leavened, their kneading-troughs being bound-up in their garments on their shoulders. ³⁵ And the children of Israel did according to the word of Moses; and they asked of the Egyptians articles of silver and articles of gold, and garments. ³⁶ And YAHVEH put favour for the people in the eyes of the Egyptians, and they gave them gladly, and they spoiled the Egyptians.

³⁷ And the children of Israel journeyed from Rameses to Succoth, about six hundred thousand men on foot, besides children. ³⁸ And also a great rabble went-up with them, and flocks and herds, very much cattle. ³⁹ And they baked the dough which they brought-forth out of Egypt with mazzoth (unleavened) cakes, for it was not leavened; for they were driven-away out of Egypt, and were not able to tarry, and also they had not made for themselves food-for-the-way.‖

XIII. ¹ And YAHVEH spake unto Moses saying, ²'Sanctify for me all the first-

---

* The writer here recalls to the reader's recollection the words in iii. 20–22, iv. 22, 23, supposed to have been spoken long ago, at the very commencement of the movement which led to the Exodus.

† Moses says this before going out from Pharaoh, in continuation of his words in x. 29.

‡ These words in xi. 4, compared with xii. 29, imply beyond any doubt that the final stroke would be given on the midnight *next following*: and they would be so understood by every reader but for the difficulties, introduced by the *interpolation* of the L.L., about the Passover, &c., xii. 1–28, see p. 3, 6.

born, that openeth any womb among the children of Israel among men and cattle: it is mine.'* . . .|

¹¹ And it came-to-pass, at Pharaoh's letting the people go, that ELOHIM did not lead them by the way of the land of the Philistines, for that was near, for ELOHIM said, 'Lest the people repent at their seeing war and they return to Egypt.' ¹⁸But ELOHIM took the people roundabout by the way of the wilderness of the Red Sea: and the children of Israel went-up arrayed out of the land of Egypt. ¹⁹ And Moses took the bones of Joseph with him; for he had strictly sworn the children of Israel, saying, 'ELOHIM will certainly visit you, and ye shall bring-up hence my bones with you.' ²⁰ So they broke-up from Succoth, and camped at Etham at the extremity of the wilderness. ²¹ And YAHVEH was going before them by day in a pillar of cloud to lead them the way, and by night in a pillar of fire to give them light, to go by day and by night. ²² He removed not the pillar of cloud by day and the pillar of cloud by night before the people.

XIV. ¹ And YAHVEH spake unto Moses, saying, ² 'Speak unto the children of Israel that they return and camp before Pi-hahiroth between Migdol and the Sea, before Baal-Zephon: over-against it camp ye by the Sea. ³ For Pharaoh hath said of the children of Israel, They are entangled in the land: the wilderness hath shut upon them. ⁴ But I have hardened Pharaoh's heart that he may pursue after them; and I will get-myself honoured upon Pharaoh and on all his force, and the Egyptians shall know that I am YAHVEH.' And they did so.

⁵ And it was told to the king of Egypt that the people had fled; and the heart of Pharaoh and his servants was turned against the people, and they said, 'What is this we have done? for we have let Israel go from serving us?' ⁶ And he harnessed his chariot, and he took his people with him; ⁷ and he took six hundred chosen chariots, even all the chariots of Egypt, and captains over them all.| ⁹ And the Egyptians pursued after them, and they overtook them camping by the Sea,—all the chariot-horses of Pharaoh, and his horsemen, and his force, —by Pi-hahiroth before Baal-Zephon.

¹⁰ And Pharaoh drew-near, and the children of Israel lifted up their eyes, and lo! the Egyptians journeyed after them; and they feared greatly, and the children of Israel cried unto YAHVEH. ¹¹ And they said unto Moses, 'Because there were no graves in Egypt, hast thou taken us to die in the wilderness? ¹² Is not this the thing that we spake unto thee in Egypt, saying, Cease from us, and let us serve the Egyptians? for it is better for us to serve the Egyptians than our dying in the wilderness.' ¹³ And Moses said unto the people, 'Fear ye not; stand, and see

---

* The O.S., which in v. 1, 2, has grounded the dedication of the first-borns in Israel, both of man and beast, upon the fact of the first-borns of man and beast being killed in Egypt, as a memorial of that event, intended, no doubt, to ground also the observance of the Feast of Mazzoth upon the fact of the Israelites being compelled, for want of time, to take their bread out of Egypt unleavened, upon which such very particular stress is laid in xii. 34, 39. It probably did once contain a short passage to that effect after v. 1, 2, which D. has replaced by his own language in v. 3-16, instituting the Feast of Mazzoth in v. 3-10, and in v. 11-16 explaining and softening the abrupt words of the O.S. in v. 2, which, as they stand, seem to imply that the firstlings of man and beast were to be dealt with alike, and 'sanctified to YAHVEH' by being sacrificed.

THE ORIGINAL STORY OF THE EXODUS.

the salvation of YAHVEH, which He will (do) work for you to-day; for the Egyptians, whom ye have seen to-day, ye shall see them no more for ever. ¹⁴ YAHVEH fighteth for you, and ye, be still!' ¹⁵ And YAHVEH said unto Moses, 'Why cryest thou unto Me? Speak unto the children of Israel that they break-up (=march). ¹⁶ And thou, lift-up thy staff, and stretch-out thy hand over the Sea, and cleave-it; and the children of Israel shall go-in in the midst of the Sea on dry-land. ¹⁷ And I—lo! I harden the heart of the Egyptians, and they shall go-in after them; and I will get-myself honoured on Pharaoh, and on all his force, on his chariots and on his horsemen. ¹⁸ And the Egyptians shall know that I am YAHVEH, when I get-myself-honoured on Pharaoh, on his chariots, and on his horsemen.' ¹⁹ And the angel of ELOHIM, that was going before the Camp of Israel, journeyed and went behind them; and the pillar of cloud journeyed from before them and stood behind them; ²⁰ and it came between the Camp of the Egyptians and the Camp of Israel; and there was the cloud and the darkness, and it gave light by night; and one drew not near unto the other all the night.

²¹ And Moses stretched-out his hand upon the Sea, and YAHVEH made the Sea go by a strong east wind all the night, and (placed) made the Sea become dry-land, and the waters were cleft. ²² And the children of Israel went-in in the midst of the Sea on dry-land; and the waters were for them a wall on their right and on their left. ²³ And the Egyptians pursued and went-in after them, every horse of Pharaoh, his chariots and his horsemen, unto the midst of the Sea. ²⁴ And it came-to-pass in the morning watch that YAHVEH looked unto the Camp of the Egyptians through the pillar of fire and cloud, and troubled the Camp of the Egyptians. ²⁵ And He turned-aside the wheels of their chariots, and they guided them with difficulty, and the Egyptians said, 'Let us flee before Israel! for YAHVEH fighteth for them against us.' ²⁶ And YAHVEH said unto Moses, 'Stretch-out thy hand over the Sea, that the waters may return upon the Egyptians, upon their chariots, and upon their horsemen.' ²⁷ And Moses stretched-out his hand over the Sea, and the Sea returned at the turning of the morning to its usual-power, and the Egyptians were fleeing to meet it, and YAHVEH overthrew the Egyptians in the midst of the Sea. ²⁸ And the waters returned, and covered the chariots and the horsemen of the whole host of Pharaoh that came-in after them in the Sea: there was not left among them even one. ²⁹ And the children of Israel went on dry-land in the midst of the Sea: and the waters were for them a wall on their right and on their left. ³⁰ And YAHVEH saved Israel on that day out of the hand of the Egyptians; and Israel saw the Egyptians dead upon the brink of the Sea. ³¹ And Israel saw the great (hand) work which Yahveh did upon the Egyptians, and the people feared YAHVEH, and believed in Yahveh and Moses His servant.

XV. ¹ Then sang Moses and the children of Israel this Song * to YAHVEH, and they said, saying:—

---

* This 'Song of Moses' seems to have been inserted by an afterthought, as an expansion of the Song of Miriam in v. 21, and probably by the same hand which had completed the original account of the Exodus. This will explain the fact that in v. 16 there appears certainly to be a reference to the passage of the Jordan, which the writer (as we suppose) had already described—

'Till Thy people, YAHVEH, *pass-over*,
Till this people *pass-over* whom Thou hast purchased.'

' I will sing to YAHVEH,
   For He hath triumphed excellently;
   The horse and his rider hath He thrown into the Sea.
' My Strength and my Song is JAH,
   And He became for me Salvation;
   This is my El, and I will glorify Him,
   The Elohim of my father, and I will exalt Him.
' YAHVEH is a man of war;
   Yahveh is His name.
' The chariots of Pharaoh and his force hath He thrown into the Sea,
   And the choice of his captains have sunk in the Red Sea.
' The depths do cover them;
   They went-down in the depths like a stone.
' Thy right-hand, YAHVEH!
   Is become glorious in power;
   Thy right-hand, YAHVEH!
   Doth dash-in-pieces the enemy.
' And in the abundance of Thy excellency
   Thou overthrowest those that rise against Thee;
   Thou sendest-forth Thy wrath;
   It consumes them as stubble.
' For by the wind of Thy nostrils
   The waters were piled;
   The floods stood as a heap;
   The depths were congealed in the heart of the Sea.
' The enemy said, ' I will pursue, I will overtake;
   I will divide spoil, my soul shall be filled with them;
   I will draw-out my sword;
   My hand shall destroy them.'
¹⁰ Thou didst blow with Thy wind;
   The Sea covered them;
   They sank like lead in the mighty waters.
¹¹ Who is like Thee among the gods, YAHVEH?
   Who is like Thee, glorious in holiness,
   Fearful in praises, doing wonders?
¹² Thou stretchedst-out Thy right-hand;
   The earth swallowed them.
¹³ Thou hast led in Thy mercy
   The people whom Thou hast redeemed;
   Thou hast guided them in Thy strength
   Unto the habitation of Thy holiness.
¹⁴ The peoples heard, and were afraid;
   Anguish seized on the inhabitants of Philistia.
¹⁵ Then were the dukes of Edom amazed;
   The mighty-ones of Moab—trembling seizes them,
   All the inhabitants of Canaan are melted.
¹⁶ There shall fall upon them terror and dread;
   Through the greatness of Thine arm they shall be dumb as a stone,—
   Till Thy people pass-over, YAHVEH!
   Till this people pass-over whom Thou hast purchased.

THE ORIGINAL STORY OF THE EXODUS.   411

" Thou shalt bring-them-in and plant-them
  In the mountain of Thine inheritance,—
  The fixed-place, YAHVEH ! *which* Thou hast made for Thine abode,—
  The Sanctuary, O Lord ! *which* Thy hands have prepared.*
¹⁸ YAHVEH shall reign for ever and ever !'

¹⁹ For Pharaoh's horse went-in with his chariots, and with his horsemen in the Sea, and YAHVEH brought-back upon them the waters of the Sea, and the children of Israel went on dry-land in the midst of the Sea.

²⁰ And Miriam, the prophetess, Aaron's sister, took the timbrel in her hand, and all the women went-forth after her with timbrels and with dances. ²¹ And Miriam answered them—

  'Sing ye to YAHVEH, for He hath triumphed gloriously !
  The horse and his rider hath He thrown into the Sea.'

²² And Moses made Israel break-up from the Red Sea, and they went-forth unto the wilderness of Shur ; and they went three days in the wilderness and found no water.   ²³ And they came to Marah, and they were not able to drink waters out of Marah, for they were bitter ; therefore one called its name Marah. ²⁴ And the people murmured against Moses, saying, 'What shall we drink ?' ²⁵ And he cried unto YAHVEH, and YAHVEH showed him a tree, and he cast it into the waters, and the waters were made sweet.‡ ²⁷ And they came to Elim, and there were there twelve springs of water, and seventy palm-trees, and they camped there by the water. XVI. ¹ And all the Assembly of the children of Israel journeyed from Elim, and came into the wilderness of Sin, which *is* between Elim and Sinai.‖

XVII. ¹ And all the Assembly of the children of Israel journeyed from the wilderness of Sin according to their journeyings by the mouth of YAHVEH, and they camped at Rephidim, and there was no water for the people's drinking. ² And the people strove with Moses and said, 'Give us water that we may drink.' And Moses said to them, 'Why do ye strive with me? Why do ye tempt YAHVEH?' ³ And the people thirsted there for water, and the people murmured against Moses, and said, 'Why is this that thou hast brought-us up out of Egypt to put (me) as to death and (my) our children and (my) our cattle with thirst ?'

⁴ 'And Moses cried unto YAHVEH, saying, 'What shall I do to this people ? yet a little and they will stone me.' ⁵ And YAHVEH said unto Moses, 'Pass-over before the people, and take with thee of the Elders of Israel, and thy staff, with which thou smotest the River, take in thy hand and go. ⁶ Lo ! I stand before thee there by the rock,‖ and thou shalt smite on the rock, and water shall come forth out of it, and the people shall drink.' And Moses did so before the eyes of the Elders of Israel. ⁷ And one called the name of the place Massah (temptation) and Meribah (strife), on account of the strife of the children of Israel and on account of their tempting YAHVEH, saying, ' Is YAHVEH in the midst of us or not ?'

⁸ 'And Amalek came and fought with Israel at Rephidim. ⁹ And Moses said unto Joshua,† 'Choose for us men and go-forth, fight with Amalek ; to-morrow I

---

* These words point to an author who lived after the establishment by David of the Sanctuary on Mount Zion, which was meant from the first to be, as it became ultimately, a central place of worship for all Israel.

† Joshua is here mentioned abruptly for the first time, as Hur is in v. 10, (and Moses by the Elohist in vi. 2) without any previous words of introduction.

stand on the top of the hill, and the staff of ELOHIM in my hand.' ¹⁰ And Joshua did as Moses said to him, to fight with Amalek: and Moses, Aaron, and Hur went-up to the top of the hill. ¹¹ And it came-to-pass, when Moses lifted-up his hand, that Israel prevailed, and when he rested his hand that Amalek prevailed. ¹² And the hands of Moses were heavy, and they took a stone, and placed it under him, and he sat upon it; and Aaron and Hur took-hold on his hands, on this *side* one and on this *side* one, and his hands were steady till the going-in of the sun. ¹³ And Joshua weakened Amalek and his people with the edge of the sword.¶ ¹⁴ And Moses built an altar and called its name YAHVEH-Nissi (YAHVEH is my banner), ¹⁶ and said, 'The hand on the banner of JAH! War for YAHVEH with Amalek from generation to generation!'

XVIII. ¹ And Jethro, prince of Midian, father-in-law of Moses, heard all that ELOHIM had done for Moses and for Israel his people, that YAHVEH had brought-forth Israel out of Egypt. ² And Jethro, the father-in-law of Moses, took Zipporah the wife of Moses, after his sending-her-away, ³ and her two sons, of whom the name of the one was Gershom,—for he said, 'A sojourner was I in a strange land,'—⁴ and the name of the other Eliezer,—'for the ELOHIM of my father *was* for my help, and delivered me from the sword of Pharaoh.' ⁵ And Jethro, the father-in-law of Moses, came, and his sons, and his wife, unto Moses, unto the wilderness where he was camping, to the Mount of ELOHIM. ⁶ And he said unto Moses, 'I thy father-in-law Jethro come unto thee, and thy wife and her two sons with her.' ⁷ And Moses went-forth to meet his father-in-law, and he bowed-himself and kissed him, and they asked one another of welfare, and they came unto the tent. ⁸ And Moses recounted to his father-in-law all that YAHVEH had done to Pharaoh and to the Egyptians on account of Israel, all the travail which had found them in the way, and YAHVEH had delivered them. ⁹ And Jethro rejoiced over all the good which YAHVEH had done for Israel, whom He had delivered out of the hand of the Egyptians. ¹⁰ And Jethro said, 'Blessed be YAHVEH, who hath delivered you out of the hand of the Egyptians and out of the hand of Pharaoh, who hath delivered the people from under the hand of the Egyptians! ¹¹ Now I know that great *is* YAHVEH above all the ELOHIM—yea, in the thing in which they dealt proudly against them.' ¹² And Jethro, the father-in-law of Moses, took a burnt-offering and sacrifices for ELOHIM; and Aaron came, and all the elders of Israel, to eat bread with the father-in-law of Moses before ELOHIM.

¹³ And it came-to-pass on the morrow that Moses sat to judge the people, and the people stood by Moses from the morning until the evening. ¹⁴ And the father-in-law of Moses saw all that he *was* doing for the people and said, 'What is this thing which thou *art* doing for the people? Why art thou sitting by thyself, and all the people standing by thee from morning until evening?' ¹⁵ And Moses said to his father-in-law, 'Because the people cometh unto me to seek ELOHIM. ¹⁶ If they shall have a matter, they come unto me that I may judge between a man and his neighbour, and that I may make them know the statutes of ELOHIM and His laws.' ¹⁷ And the father-in-law of Moses said unto him, 'The thing is not good which thou *art* doing. ¹⁸ Thou wilt surely wear-away, both thou and this people that *is* with thee; for the thing is too heavy for thee; thou wilt not be able to do it by thyself. ¹⁹ Now hearken unto my voice: let me counsel thee, and ELOHIM be with thee! Be thou for the people towards ELOHIM, and bring-in thou the matters unto ELOHIM, ²⁰ and that thou mayest enjoin them the statutes and the laws, and mayest make them know the way in which they shall go and the work

which they shall do. ²¹ And thou shalt look-out from all the people men of force, fearing ELOHIM, men of truth, hating lucre; and thou shalt set *them* over them as captains of thousands, captains of hundreds, captains of fifties, and captains of tens. ²² And they shall judge the people at all times; and it shall come-to-pass *that* every great matter they shall bring unto thee, and every small matter they shall judge; so lighten it from off thee, and they shall bear with thee. ²³ If thou wilt do this thing, and ELOHIM command thee, then thou wilt be able to stand, and all this people shall go to their place in peace.'

²⁴ And Moses hearkened to the voice of his father-in-law, and did all he said. ²⁵ And Moses chose men of force out of all Israel, and appointed them as heads over the people, captains of thousands, captains of hundreds, captains of fifties, and captains of tens. ²⁶ And they judged the people at all times: the hard matter they brought unto Moses, and every small matter they judged. ²⁷ And Moses sent-away his father-in-law, and he gat him unto his land.

XIX. | ¹ And they journeyed from Rephidim, and came to the wilderness of Sinai, and camped in the wilderness, and Israel camped there before the Mount. ³ᵃ And Moses went-up unto ELOHIM. | ⁹ᵃ And YAHVEH said unto Moses, 'Lo! I am coming unto thee in a thick cloud, in order that the people may hear at My speaking with thee and also may believe in thee for ever.'| ¹⁰ And YAHVEH said unto Moses, 'Go unto the people, and sanctify them to-day and to-morrow, and let them wash their clothes. ¹¹ And let them be ready for the third day; for on the third day YAHVEH will come-down in the sight of all the people on Mount Sinai. ¹² And thou shalt set-bounds to the people roundabout, saying, Take-heed to yourselves as to going-up on the Mountain or touching its extremities; every-one that toucheth the Mountain shall surely die. ¹³ Let no hand touch it; for he shall be certainly stoned or shot-through; whether beast or man he shall not live; at the drawing-out of the ram's-horn, they shall go-up on the Mount.' ¹⁴ And Moses went-down from the Mount unto the people, and sanctified the people, and they washed their clothes. ¹⁵ And he said unto the people, 'Be ye ready for the third day: come-not near to a woman.'

¹⁶ And it came-to-pass on the third day, when the morning was, that there were (voices) thunderings and lightnings, and a heavy cloud upon the Mount, and the sound of a trumpet very loud; and all the people trembled that were in the Camp. ¹⁷ And Moses brought-forth the people to meet ELOHIM out of the Camp; and they stationed-themselves underneath the Mount. ¹⁸ And Mount Sinai was all of it smoke, because YAHVEH had come-down upon it in fire; and its smoke went-up as the smoke of the furnace, and the whole Mount trembled greatly. ¹⁹ And the sound of the trumpet was going very much louder and louder; Moses spake, and ELOHIM answered him by a (voice) thundering.] XX.* ¹⁸ And all the people were seeing the (voices) thunderings and the flashes and the sound of the trumpet and the Mountain smoking; and, when the people saw, they shrunk-back and

---

* If YAHVEH in the O.S. had uttered in the hearing of the people the Ten Words, 'with a great voice out of the midst of the fire,' how is it that in v. 18 there is nothing said about this—no reference to their having heard the loud-spoken '*words*,' as well as the 'thunderings' and the 'sound of the trumpet'—and that not the slightest allusion is made to them in all the 'words' and 'judgments' which follow, xx. 22–xxiii. 21?

stood at a distance. ²⁰And they said unto Moses, 'Speak thou with us, and we will hear; but let not ELOHIM speak with us, lest we die.' ²¹And Moses said unto the people, 'Fear ye not; for in order to prove you hath ELOHIM come, and in order that His fear may be before your face, that ye sin not.' ²¹And the people stood at a distance, and Moses approached unto the thick darkness where ELOHIM was.*

²²And YAHVEH said unto Moses, 'Thus shalt thou say unto the children of Israel—Ye have seen that out of heaven I have spoken with you.† ²³Thou shalt not make with Me gods of silver, and ye shall not make you gods of gold. ²⁴An altar of earth shall ye make for Me, and thou shalt sacrifice upon it thy burnt-offerings and thy peace-offerings, thy sheep and thine oxen: in every place where ye make-mention of My Name, I will come unto thee and I will bless thee. ²⁵And, if thou shalt make for Me an altar of stones, thou shalt not build them of hewn-stones; if thou hast waved thy tool upon it, then thou shalt defile it. ²⁶And thou shalt not go-up by steps upon My altar, that thy nakedness be not revealed upon it.

XXI. ¹'And these are the judgments which thou shalt place before them.

²'When thou buyest a Hebrew servant, six years shall he serve, and in the seventh he shall go-forth free for nothing. ³If by himself he came-in, by himself shall he go-forth; if he was a married man, then his wife shall go-forth with him. ⁴If his lord shall give him a wife, and she bear to him sons or daughters, the woman and her children shall be her lord's, and he shall go-forth by himself. ⁵And if the servant shall positively say, I love my lord, my wife, and my children, I will not go-forth free, ⁶then his lord shall bring-him-nigh unto ELOHIM, and shall bring-him-nigh unto the door or unto the side-post, and his lord shall bore his ear with an awl, and he shall serve him for ever.

⁷'And when a man selleth his daughter for a handmaid, she shall not go-forth according to the going-forth of the men-servants. ⁸If she be evil in the eyes of her lord, who hath betrothed her to himself, he shall let her be redeemed; to a strange people he shall have no power to sell her, at his dealing-faithlessly with her. ⁹And if he shall betroth her to his son, according to the right of daughters shall he do to her. ¹⁰If he shall take another for him, her food, her clothing, and her cohabitation, he shall not diminish. ¹¹And, if he will not do these three to her, then she shall go-forth for nothing, without money.

¹²'He that smiteth a man that he die shall surely be put to death. ¹³And he who hath not lain-in-wait, but ELOHIM lets fall into his hand, I will appoint for thee a place whither he shall flee. ¹⁴But, when a man shall act wickedly against his neighbour to slay him with guile, from My altar shalt thou take him for death. ¹⁵And he that smiteth his father or his mother shall be surely put to death. ¹⁶And he that stealeth a man and selleth him, or if he be found in his hand, shall surely be put to death. ¹⁷And he that curseth his father or his mother shall surely be put-to-death. ¹⁸And, when men shall strive, and a man shall smite his neighbour with a stone or with his fist, and he dieth not, but falls a-bed, ¹⁹If he arise, and walk-about abroad upon his staff, then the smiter shall be acquitted: only he shall

---

* It will be seen that the command (of the L. L.) in xix. 24, that Moses should go down and come up with *Aaron*, is never carried out.

† YAHVEH had 'spoken with them' by the 'voice' or thundering in xix. 19.

pay his resting, and shall have him thoroughly healed. ²⁰ And, when a man shall smite his servant or his handmaid with a rod, and he die under his hand, he shall certainly be punished. ²¹ Only if he shall stand a day or two days, he shall not be punished, for he is his money. ²² And, when men shall strive and shall smite a pregnant woman, and her children go-forth, and there be no mischief, he shall certainly be mulcted as the woman's husband shall lay upon him, and he shall give it by the judges. ²³ But, if there shall be mischief, then thou shalt give life for life, ²⁴ eye for eye, tooth for tooth, hand for hand, foot for foot, ²⁵ burning for burning, wound for wound, stripe for stripe. ²⁶ And, when a man shall smite the eye of his servant or the eye of his handmaid, and shall destroy it, he shall let him go free for his eye. ²⁷ And, if he shall smite-out the tooth of his servant or the tooth of his handmaid, he shall let him go free for his tooth. ²⁸ And when an ox shall gore a man or a woman and die, the ox shall be surely stoned, and its flesh shall not be eaten, and the owner of the ox *shall be* acquitted. ²⁹ And, if the ox was goring aforetime, and it has been testified against its owner, and he have not watched it, and he kill a man or a woman, the ox shall be stoned, and also its owner shall be put to death. ³⁰ If an atonement is laid upon him, then he shall give the ransom of his life according to all that shall be laid upon him. ³¹ Whether it shall gore a son or shall gore a daughter, according to this judgment it shall be done to him. ³² If the ox shall gore a manservant or a handmaid, thirty shekels of silver shall he give to his master, and the ox shall be stoned. ³³ And, when a man shall open a pit, or when a man shall dig a pit, and shall not cover it, and an ox or an ass fall therein, ³⁴ the owner of the pit shall repay; money shall he return to its owner, and the dead shall be his. ³⁵ And, when a man's ox shall hurt his neighbour's ox and it die, then they shall sell the living ox and halve its silver, and also the dead shall they halve. ³⁶ Or should it be known that the ox was goring aforetime, and its owner hath not watched him, he shall certainly repay ox for ox, and the dead shall be his.

XXII. ¹ ' When a man shall steal an ox or a sheep, and slaughter it or sell it, five oxen shall he repay for the ox and four sheep for the sheep. ² When the thief shall be found breaking-in and he be smitten that he die, there is no blood for him. ³ If the sun had risen upon him, there is blood for him: he shall certainly repay; if he have nothing, then he shall be sold for his theft. ⁴ If theft be certainly found in his hand, whether it be ox or ass or sheep, alive, he shall repay double.

⁵ ' When a man shall eat-off a field or a vineyard, and shall let loose his beast that it eat-off in the field of another, the best of his field and the best of his vineyard shall he repay. ⁶ If fire goeth-forth and catch thorns, so that stack or standing-corn or field be devoured, he that kindled the conflagration shall certainly repay. ⁷ When a man shall give unto his neighbour silver or vessels to keep, and it shall be stolen out of the man's house, if the thief be found, let him repay double. ⁸ If the thief be not found, then the master of the house shall be brought-near unto ELOHIM, *to swear* that he hath not put his hand to his neighbour's property. ⁹ For all matter of transgression, for ox, for ass, for sheep, for raiment, for anything lost of which one shall say this is it, unto ELOHIM shall come the matter of both of them: whom ELOHIM shall pronounce-to-fault, he shall repay double to his neighbour. ¹⁰ When a man shall give unto his neighbour ass or ox or sheep, or any beast, to keep, and it die, or be hurt, or be plundered, none seeing, ¹¹ an oath of YAHVEH shall be between them both, that he has not put his

hand to his neighbour's property, and its owner shall take it, and he shall not repay. ¹² But, if it be certainly stolen from him, he shall repay its owner. ¹³ If it be torn in pieces, then let him bring it as a witness: the torn he shall not repay. ¹⁴ When a man shall ask of his neighbour, and it be hurt or have died, its owner not being with it, he shall surely repay. ¹⁵ If its master was with it, he shall not repay: if it was hired, it came for its hire.

¹⁶ ' And when a man shall entice a virgin who is not betrothed, and lie with her, he shall certainly endow her for himself for wife. ¹⁷ If her father utterly refuse to give her to him, he shall weigh-out money according to the dowry of virgins.

¹⁸ ' A witch thou shalt not let live.

¹⁹ ' Everyone lying with a beast shall surely be put-to-death.

²⁰ ' He that sacrificeth to ELOHIM shall be (devoted) utterly-destroyed, except to YAHVEH only.

²¹ ' And the sojourner thou shalt not afflict or oppress him; for sojourners were ye in the land of Egypt. ²² Any widow and orphan thou shalt not afflict. ²³ If thou at all afflict them, surely if at all he cry unto Me, I will hear his cry; ²⁴ then My wrath shall be kindled, and I will slay you with the sword, and your wives shall be widows and your children orphans.

²⁵ ' If silver thou shalt lend to My people that is poor with thee, thou shalt not be to him as an usurer; thou shalt not lay upon him interest. ²⁶ If thou takest in pledge at all thy neighbour's raiment, by the going-in of the sun thou shalt return it to him. ²⁷ For that is his covering only: it is his raiment for his skin; wherewith shall he lie down? and it shall come-to-pass, when he crieth unto Me, that I will hear, for gracious am I.

²⁸ ' ELOHIM shalt thou not revile, and the prince among thy people shalt thou not curse. ²⁹ Thy fulness and thy (tears) juice thou shalt not delay: the first-born of thy sons thou shalt give to Me. ³⁰ So shalt thou do with thy ox, with thy sheep: seven days shall it be with its dam; on the eighth day thou shalt give it to Me. ³¹ And men of holiness shall ye be for Me; and flesh in the field, *that is* torn, shall ye not eat; to the dog shall ye cast it.

XXIII. ¹ ' Thou shalt not raise a false report: put not thy hand with the wicked to be a witness of violence. ² Thou shalt not be after many to do evil: and thou shalt not answer about a suit to turn aside after many to turn-aside *justice*. ³ And a poor man shalt thou not respect in his suit.

⁴ ' When thou shalt meet thine enemy's ox or his ass straying, thou shalt certainly take-it-back to him. ⁵ When thou seest the ass of him that hateth thee lying under its burden, and wilt refrain from unloosing for it, thou shalt certainly unloose with him.

⁶ ' Thou shalt not turn-aside the judgment of thy poor in his suit. ⁷ From a false matter thou shalt keep-at-a-distance; and the innocent and righteous shalt thou not slay: for I will not justify the wicked. ⁸ And a bribe shalt thou not take; for the bribe blindeth the seeing, and perverteth the words of the righteous.

⁹ ' And a sojourner thou shalt not oppress; for ye know the soul of the sojourner, for sojourners were ye in the land of Egypt.

¹⁰ ' And six years shalt thou sow thy land, and shalt gather its produce. ¹¹ And the seventh year thou shalt let it [*i.e.* 'its produce'] rest and lie still; that the poor of thy people may eat, and their leaving the beast of the field shall eat: so shalt thou do to thy vineyard, to thy oliveyard.

⁹ ' Six days thou shalt do thy work, and on the seventh day thou shalt rest, that

so thine ox and thine ass may repose, and the son of thy handmaid and the sojourner may be refreshed.

¹⁴ 'Three times shalt thou keep-feast to me in the year. ¹⁵ The Feast of Maẓẓoth shalt thou keep, at the season of the month of (green-ears) Abib, for in it thou camest-forth out of Egypt, ¹⁶ and the Feast of Harvest, the firstfruits of thy work which thou shalt sow in the field, and the Feast of Ingathering, at the end of the year, at thy gathering thy work out of the field. ¹⁷ Three times in the year shall every male of thine appear before the Lord YAHVEH, and they shall not appear before Me empty.'*

¹⁸ 'Thou shalt not sacrifice with leaven the blood of My sacrifice, and the fat of My Feast shall not remain until the morning.

²⁰ 'Lo! I send an Angel before thee to keep thee in the way, and to bring thee unto the place which I prepared. ²¹ Be watchful before him, and hearken to his voice: embitter him not, for he will not pardon your transgression, for My Name is in him.'

XXIV. ¹ And unto Moses He said, 'Come-up unto YAHVEH, thou and Aaron, Nadab and Abihu, and seventy of the Elders of Israel, and ye shall worship at a distance. ² And Moses shall draw near by himself unto YAHVEH, but they shall not draw-near; and the people shall not come-up with him.'

³ And Moses came and related to the people all the words of YAHVEH and all the judgments; and all the people answered with one voice, and they said, 'All the things, which YAHVEH hath spoken, will we do.' ⁴ And Moses wrote all the words of YAHVEH; and he rose-early in the morning, and built an altar under the Mountain, and twelve pillars according to the twelve tribes of Israel. ⁵ And he sent young-men of the children of Israel,† and they offered-up burnt-offerings and sacrificed peace-offerings to YAHVEH, steers. ⁶ And Moses took half of the blood, and placed it in basons, and half of the blood he sprinkled upon the altar. ⁷ And he took the book of the Covenant, and read in the ears of the people, and they said, 'All which YAHVEH hath spoken will we do and we will hearken.' ⁸ And Moses took the blood, and sprinkled upon the people, and he said, 'Lo! the blood of the Covenant which YAHVEH hath made with you concerning all these words.'

⁹ And Moses went-up, and Aaron, Nadab, and Abihu, and seventy of the Elders of Israel. ¹⁰ And they saw the ELOHIM of Israel, and under His feet like a work of transparent sapphire, and as the body of heaven for clearness. ¹¹ And upon the nobles of the children of Israel He put not forth His hand; and they beheld ELOHIM, and they ate and drank.

¹² And Moses arose and Joshua his minister, and Moses went-up unto the Mount of ELOHIM. ¹³ And unto the Elders he said, 'Stay for us here, until we return unto you: and lo! Aaron and Hur are with you; whoever has matters, let him draw-near unto them.' ¹⁵ And Moses went-up into the Mount, and the cloud covered the Mount. ¹⁸ And Moses went into the midst of the cloud, and he went-up into the Mount, and Moses was in the Mount forty days and forty nights.

---

* These words, 'and they shall not appear before Me empty,' clearly belong to the end of v. 17: in the place where they now stand, at the end of v. 15 (E.V.), they break the connection between v. 15a and v. 16, since the same verb, 'thou shalt observe,' is meant to govern the three accusatives, 'the Feast of Maẓẓoth,' 'the Feast of Harvest,' 'the Feast of Ingathering.'

† Where were 'the priests, who draw-near to YAHVEH,' expressly mentioned in xix. 24 (L. L.), that they did not assist on this occasion?

XXX. " And He gave unto Moses, when He had finished to speak with him on Mount Sinai, two tables of the Testimony, tables of stone, written with the finger of ELOHIM."

XXXII. ' And the people saw that Moses delayed to come-down from the Mount, and the people gathered-together against Aaron, and they said unto him, ' Arise ! make us an ELOHIM who shall go before us : for this Moses, the man who brought-us-up out of the land of Egypt, we know not what has become of him.' ² And Aaron said unto them, ' Strip-off the rings of gold which are in the ears of your wives, of your sons, and of your daughters, and bring-them unto me.' ³ And all the people stripped themselves of the rings of gold which were in their ears, and brought it unto Aaron. ⁴ And he took it out of their hands, and formed it with a graver, and made it a molten calf ; and they said, ' This is thy ELOHIM, O Israel, who brought-thee-up out of the land of Egypt ! ' ⁵ And Aaron saw it, and he built an altar before it ; and Aaron proclaimed and said, ' A Feast of YAHVEH to-morrow ! ' ⁶ And they rose-early on the morrow ; and they offered-up burnt-offerings and brought-near peace-offerings ; and the people sat-down to eat and drink, and they arose to play.⁷

¹⁵ And Moses turned and went-down from the Mount, and the two tables of the Testimony were in his hand, tables written on both their sides, on this side and on that were they written. ¹⁶ And the tables—they were the work of ELOHIM, and the writing—it was the writing of ELOHIM, graven upon the tables. ¹⁷ And Joshua heard the sound of the people at their shouting, and he said unto Moses, ' A sound of war is the camp ! ' ¹⁸ And he said, ' No sound of crying victory and no sound of crying defeat—the sound of singing do I hear.' ¹⁹ And It came-to-pass, as he came-near unto the Camp, that he saw the calf and dances ; and the anger of Moses was kindled, and he cast-out of his hand the tables, and broke them under the Mount. ²⁰ And he took the calf which they had made, and burnt it with fire, and ground it¦o powder, and sprinkled on the surface of the water, and made the children of Israel drink. ²¹ And Moses said unto Aaron, ' What hath this people done to thee, that thou hast brought upon it a great sin ? ' ²² And Aaron said, ' Let not my lord's anger be kindled ! thou knowest the people that it is set on evil. ²³ And they said to me, Make us an ELOHIM who shall go before us ; for this Moses, the man who brought-us-up out of the land of Egypt, we know not what has become of him. ²⁴ And I said to them, Whoever has gold, let them strip-themselves and give it to me ; and I cast it into the fire, and there came forth this calf.'

²⁵ And Moses saw the people that it was unbridled, for Aaron had made it unbridled for a shame among their adversaries. ²⁶ And Moses stood at the gate of the Camp, and he said, ' Who is for YAHVEH—to me ! ' and all the sons of Levi gathered unto him. ²⁷ And he said to them, ' Thus saith YAHVEH, the ELOHIM of Israel ! Place-ye each his sword upon his thigh ; pass-over and return from gate to gate in the Camp, and slay each his brother and each his friend and each his neighbour.' ²⁸ And the sons of Levi did according to the word of Moses ; and there fell of the people on that day about three thousand men. ²⁹ For Moses said, ' [Fill your hands—] Consecrate-yourselves this day to YAHVEH, yes, each on his son and on his brother, and to bring upon yourselves this day a blessing.' *

---

* There were probably some words in the O.S., in connexion with this speech of Moses to the Levites and their zealous execution of his command, appointing them

THE ORIGINAL STORY OF THE EXODUS 419

⁩⁰ And it came-to-pass on the morrow that Moses said unto the people, 'Ye—ye have sinned a great sin; and now I will go-up unto YAHVEH; perhaps I shall atone for your sin.' ³¹ And Moses returned unto YAHVEH and said, 'Lo! this people hath sinned a great sin, and they have made themselves an ELOHIM of gold. ³² And now, if Thou wilt forgive their sin—and if not, wipe-me-out, I pray, from Thy book which Thou hast written.' ³³ And YAHVEH said unto Moses, 'Whosoever hath sinned against Me, him will I blot out of My book.' ⁋ ³⁵ And YAHVEH plagued the people because they had made the calf which Aaron made.

XXXIII. ¹ 'And YAHVEH spake unto Moses, 'Go, go-up from hence, thou and the people which thou hast brought-up out of the land of Egypt, into the land which I sware to Abraham, to Isaac, and to Jacob, saying, To thy seed will I give it.' ⁋ ⁷ 'And Moses took the Tent and pitched it without the Camp, a little way off from the Camp, and one called it Tent of Meeting; and it came-to-pass *that* every one seeking YAHVEH went-forth unto the Tent of Meeting which *was* without the Camp. ⁸ And it came-to-pass, when Moses went-forth unto the Tent, that all the people arose, and they stood each at the opening of his tent, and they looked after Moses until his going into the Tent. ⁹ And it came-to-pass, when Moses went into the Tent, that the pillar-of-cloud came down, and stood at the opening of the Tent, and He spake with Moses. ¹⁰ And all the people saw the pillar of cloud standing at the entrance of the Tent. And all the people arose and worshipped, each at the entrance of his tent. ¹¹ And YAHVEH spake unto Moses face unto face, as a man speaketh unto his friend; and he returned unto the Camp; and his minister, Joshua, son of Nun, a young-man, did not depart out of the Tent.

¹² And Moses said unto YAHVEH, 'See! Thou sayest unto me, Bring-up this people; and Thou hast not made-me-know whom Thou wilt send with me; and Thou hast said, I know thee by name, and also thou hast found grace in Mine eyes. ¹³ And now, if, I pray, I have found grace in Thine eyes, make-me-to-know, I pray, Thy way, that I may know Thee; that so I may find grace in Thine eyes; for see that this nation is Thy people!' ¹⁴ And He said, 'My Presence shall go, and I will make thee rest.' ¹⁵ And he said unto Him, 'If Thy Presence go not, carry-us-not-up hence. ¹⁶ And by what shall it indeed be known that I have found grace in Thine eyes, I and Thy people? Is it not in Thy going with us? And so shall we be distinguished, I and Thy people, from all the people which *is* on the face of the ground.' ¹⁷ And YAHVEH said unto Moses, 'Also this thing, which thou hast said, will I do; for thou hast found grace in Mine eyes, and I know thee by name.' ¹⁸ And he said, 'Make-me-see, I pray, Thy glory.' ¹⁹ And He said, 'I will make all My goodness to pass before thee, and I will call upon the name of YAHVEH before thee, and I will be gracious to whom I will be gracious, and will compassionate whom I will compassionate.' ²⁰ But He said, 'Thou art not able to see My face; for man shall not see Me and live.' ²¹ And YAHVEH said, 'Lo! there is a place with Me, and thou shalt take thy station by the rock. ²² And it shall come-to-pass, at the passing-over of My glory, then I will place thee in a cleft of the rock, and will cover My palm upon thee until I have passed over. ²³ And I will take-away My hand, and thou shalt see My back, but My face shall not be seen.'

---

henceforth to be the priestly tribe in Israel, to which reference seems to be made in D. x. 8, 9, J. xlii. 14, 33, but which were necessarily struck-out by the writer of the I.-I., to make way for the elaborate priestly system in E. xxviii, &c.

XXXIV. ¹ 'And YAHVEH said unto Moses, 'Hew thee two tables of stone like the first, [and make thee an ark of wood].ª and I will write upon the tables the words which were upon the first tables which thou brakedst, [and thou shalt place them in the ark].ª ² 'And be ready for the morning, and thou shalt come-up in the morning unto Mount Sinai, and thou shalt stand before Me there upon the top of the Mount. ³ 'And no man shall go-up with thee, and also no man shall be seen in all the Mount; also the flocks and the herds—let them not feed opposite to that Mount.' ⁴ [And he made an ark of shittim-wood,]ª and he hewed him two tables of stone like the first; and Moses rose-early in the morning, and went-up unto Mount Sinai, as YAHVEH commanded him, and he took in his hand the two tables of stone.

⁵ 'And YAHVEH came-down in the cloud, and stood with him there, and he called on the name of YAHVEH. ⁶ For YAHVEH passed-over before him and called, 'YAHVEH, YAHVEH, EL merciful and gracious, slow of anger and abundant in kindness and truth, ⁷ keeping kindness for thousands, forgiving iniquity and transgression and sin, but who will not wholly acquit, visiting the iniquity of the fathers upon children and upon children's children, upon the third *generation* and upon the fourth.' ⁸ And Moses hastened and bowed his head to the earth, and worshipped.| ²⁸ And he was there with YAHVEH forty days and forty nights; bread he ate not, and water he drank not; and He wrote upon the tables the words of the Covenant.| [And YAHVEH gave them unto Moses; and he turned, and went-down from the Mount, and put them into the ark which he had made, as YAHVEH commanded him.ª]

²⁹ And it came-to-pass, when Moses came-down from Mount Sinai, and the two tables of the Testimony *were* in the hand of Moses at his coming-down from the Mount, that Moses did not know that the skin of his face shone at His speaking with him. ³⁰ And Aaron and all the children of Israel saw Moses, and lo! the skin of his face shone, and they feared to draw-near unto him. ³¹ And Moses called unto them, and Aaron and all the Assembly came-back unto him, and Moses spake unto them. ³² And afterwards all the children of Israel drew-near, and he commanded them all which YAHVEH spake with him in Mount Sinai.|

NUMBERS.

X. ²⁹ And Moses said to Hobab son of Reuel the Midianite, father-in-law of Moses, 'We are journeying unto the place of which YAHVEH said, I will give it to you; come with us and we will do thee good, for YAHVEH hath spoken good concerning Israel. ³⁰ And he said unto him, 'I will not go, but to my land and to my kindred will I go.' ³¹ And he said, 'Forsake us not, I pray; for therefore hast thou known our camping in the wilderness, that thou mayest be to us for

---

ª See Lect. XVII for the reasons which lead to the conjecture that this passage originally contained the four clauses within [ ] in v. 1, 4, 28,—which were necessarily struck-out by the writer of the L.L., when he inserted E. xxv, &c.

eyes. ⁹⁰ And it shall come-to-pass, if thou wilt go with us, yea, it shall come-to-pass that the good, which YAHVEH will do with us, we will do to thee.'

³³ And they journeyed from the Mount of YAHVEH a way of three days, and the ark of the Covenant of YAHVEH * was journeying before them a way of three days to search-out for them a resting-place.† ³⁴ And the cloud of YAHVEH was over them by day at their journeying from the Camp. ³⁵ And it came-to-pass at the journeying of the ark that Moses said—

> 'Arise, YAHVEH, and let Thine enemies be scattered,
> And let those that hate Thee flee before thee!' ‡

³⁶ And at its resting he said—

> 'Return, YAHVEH,
> Thou ten thousands of the thousands of Israel!'

XI. ¹ 'And the people was as men complaining of evil in the ears of YAHVEH; and YAHVEH heard, and His anger was kindled, and the fire of YAHVEH burnt among them, and devoured at the extremity of the Camp. ² And the people cried unto Moses, and Moses prayed unto YAHVEH, and the fire was quenched. ³ And one called the name of that place Taberah (i.e. ' burning '), for the fire of YAHVEH burnt among them.

⁴ And the rabble which was among them lusted a lust, and also the children of Israel wept again § and said, ' Who will make-us-eat flesh? ⁵ We remember the fish which we ate in Egypt for nothing, the cucumbers, and the melons, and the leeks, and the onions, and the garlick. ⁶ And now our soul is dry; there is nothing except this manna before our eyes.' ⁷ Now the manna was as coriander seed, and its (eye) colour as the (eye) colour of bdellium. ⁸ The people turned-aside, and gathered it, and ground it with millstones or pounded it in a mortar, and boiled it in the pan, and made it into cakes; and its taste was as the taste of the moisture of oil. ⁹ And, at the coming-down of the dew upon the camp at night, the manna came-down upon it. ¶

¹⁰ And Moses heard the people weeping according to their families, each at the entrance of his tent; and the anger of YAHVEH was kindled greatly, and in the

---

* The O.S. uses here, v. 33, for the *first* time, ' Ark of the Covenant of YAHVEH,' which it employs again in xiv. 44, an expression which the L.L. never uses. The L.L. says invariably 'ark of the Testimony,' E. xxv. 22, xxvi. 33, 34, &c.

† The ark is here carried *before* the host; but in ii. 17 (L.L.) the 'Tent of Meeting' is to march ' *in the midst of the camps*,' that is, between Reuben, v. 16, and Ephraim, v. 18, the *second* and *third* of the four camps of Israel. In x. 17, however, the 'Tabernacle' is to march between Judah and Reuben, the *first* and *second* of the four camps, whereas the 'holy things,' including the Ark, are to march between Reuben and Ephraim, v. 21, as before, the former going-on in front in order that the Tabernacle might be set up against the others ' came ' with the 'holy things,' v. 21.

‡ See Lect. VII, pp. 86–90, on the identity between this passage and Ps. lxviii. 1.

§ 'Again'—that is, after the 'complaining' just mentioned in v. 1, for which they had been so severely punished.

¶ The L.L. repeats this story of the manna in E. xvi.

eyes of Moses it was evil. ¹¹ And Moses said unto YAHVEH, 'Wherefore hast Thou done-evil to Thy servant, and wherefore have I not found grace in Thine eyes, to place the burden of all this people upon me? ¹² Have I conceived all this people, or have I begotten it, that Thou shouldst say unto me, Bear it in thy bosom, as the nursing-father beareth the suckling, to the ground which Thou swarest to its fathers? ¹³ Whence have I flesh to give to all this people? for they weep against me, saying, Give us flesh, that we may eat. ¹⁴ I am not able alone to bear all this people, for *it is* too heavy for me. ¹⁵ And, if Thou doest thus to me, slay me, I pray, outright, if I have found grace in Thine eyes, and let me not look at my wretchedness.'

¹⁶ And YAHVEH said unto Moses, 'Gather me seventy men of the Elders of Israel, as to whom thou knowest that they are elders of the people and its officers; and take thou them unto the Tent of Meeting, and let them present-themselves there with thee. ¹⁷ And I will come-down * and I will speak with thee there; and I will take-back of the spirit which is upon thee, and place *it* upon them, and they shall bear with thee of the burden of the people, and thou shalt not bear it alone. ¹⁸ And unto the people thou shalt say, Sanctify-yourself for to-morrow and ye shall eat flesh, for ye have wept in the ears of YAHVEH saying, Who will make-us-eat flesh? for it was good for us in Egypt; (and) so YAHVEH shall give you flesh that ye may eat. ¹⁹ Not one day shall ye eat, and not two days, and not five days, and not ten days, and not twenty days, ²⁰ *but* unto a whole month, until it come-forth out of your nostrils, and it become to you loathsome; because ye have rejected YAHVEH who is among you, and ye wept before Him saying, Wherefore *is* this *that* we have come-forth out of Egypt?' ²¹ And Moses said, 'Six hundred thousand on foot *are* the people among whom I *am*: and Thou—Thou hast said, Flesh will I give them, that they may eat a whole month. ²² Shall the flocks and herds be slaughtered for them, that one may find for them? or shall all the fish of the sea be gathered for them, that one may find for them?' ²³ And YAHVEH said unto Moses, 'Is the hand of YAHVEH short? Now shalt thou see if my words shall meet thee or not.'

²⁴ And Moses went-forth † and spake unto the people the words of YAHVEH, and gathered seventy men of the Elders of the people, and made them stand around the Tent. ²⁵ And YAHVEH came-down in the cloud, and spake unto him; and He took-back of the spirit which was upon him, and put *it* upon the seventy men, the Elders; and it came-to-pass, when the spirit rested upon them, that they prophesied, and (added not) not again. ²⁶ And there were left two men in the Camp, the name of the one Eldad, and the name of the second Medad, and the spirit rested upon them—for they *were* among those written, but they went not forth to the Tent,—and they prophesied in the Camp. ²⁷ And a young-man ran and told it to Moses and said, ' Eldad and Medad *are* prophesying in the Camp !' ²⁸ And Joshua son of Nun, the minister of Moses, *one* of his young men, answered and said, 'My lord Moses, restrain them !' ²⁹ And Moses said to him, 'Art thou jealous for me? Would that all the people of YAHVEH were prophets, that

---

* In the L.L. the cloud 'abides' upon the Tabernacle, ix. 18, Exl 37; the idea of YAHVEH 'coming-down' as here, and 'coming-down in the cloud,' v. 25, is peculiar to the O.S., E. xxxiii. 9, xxxiv. 5, N. xii 5, D. xxxi. 15, *comp.* E. xix. 9.

† This expression, here and in v. 26, *comp.* also v. 30, shows that the 'Tent of Meeting' was supposed to be *outside* the Camp, as in E. xxxiii. 7-11, not in the very centre of it, as in the L. L. (N. ii. 3, 10, 18, 25).

THE ORIGINAL STORY OF THE EXODUS.

YAHVEH would put His spirit upon them!' ²⁸ And Moses (gathered) betook himself into the Camp, he and the Elders of Israel.

³¹ And a wind journeyed from YAHVEH, and brought-over quails from the Sea, and left them by the Camp, about a day's journey here and about a day's journey there roundabout the Camp, and about two cubits high upon the face of the earth. ³² And the people arose all that day and all that night and all the day of the morrow, and gathered the quails; he who had little gathered ten homers; and they spread them out everywhere for themselves roundabout the Camp.

³³ While the flesh was yet between their teeth, before it was cut-off, then the anger of YAHVEH was kindled against the people, and YAHVEH smote among the people with a very great smiting. ³⁴ And one called the name of that place Kibroth-hattaavah (graves of lust), for there they buried the people who had lusted.

³⁵ And from Kibroth-hattaavah the people journeyed to Hazeroth, and they were at Hazeroth. XII. ¹ And Miriam spake and Aaron against Moses on account of the Cushite woman whom he had taken, for he had taken a Cushite woman. ² And they said, 'Only by Moses hath YAHVEH spoken? Hath he not spoken also by us?'—and YAHVEH heard. ³ Now the man Moses was very humble, more than any of the men who were on the face of the ground. ⁴ And YAHVEH said suddenly unto Moses, and unto Aaron, and unto Miriam, 'Come-forth, ye three, unto the Tent of Meeting!'—and they three went-forth. * ⁵ And YAHVEH came-down in the pillar of cloud, and stood at the opening of the Tent, and called Aaron and Miriam, and they two went-forth.* ⁶ And He said, 'Hear now, I pray, My words. If there shall be a prophet of YAHVEH of yours, in a vision will I make-myself-known unto him, in a dream will I speak by him. Not so My servant Moses: in all My house is he faithful. ⁷ Mouth unto mouth will I speak with him, and with an appearance, and not in riddles, and the form of YAHVEH shall be beheld: and why have ye not feared to speak against My servant, against Moses?' ⁹ And the anger of YAHVEH was kindled against them, and He went. ¹⁰ And the cloud departed from over the Tent,† and behold! Miriam was leprous as snow; and Aaron turned towards Miriam, and behold! she was leprous. ¹¹ And Aaron said unto Moses, 'O my lord! lay not, I pray, upon us sin, in what we have done-foolishly and in what we have sinned. ¹² Let her not, I pray, be as one dead, half of whose flesh is devoured at his coming-forth from his mother's womb.' ¹³ And Moses cried unto YAHVEH saying, 'O EL, I pray, give-healing, I pray, to her!' ¹⁴ And YAHVEH said unto Moses, 'And, had her father but spit in her face, would she not be ashamed seven days? Let her be shut seven days without the Camp, and afterwards let her be gathered.' ¹⁵ And Miriam was shut without the Camp seven days, and the people journeyed from Hazeroth, and camped in the wilderness of Paran.

---

* In v. 4 YAHVEH calls all three to 'come-forth'—i.e. out of the Camp—'unto the Tent of Meeting,' which was set-up outside the Camp, E. xxxiii. 7. In v. 5 YAHVEH descends at the entrance of the Tent, and calls Miriam and Aaron who 'came-forth' from where they were standing, i.e. came-forward at the summons, leaving Moses standing as before.

† But, according to the L.L., the cloud was always 'upon the Tabernacle, to dwell upon it,' in. 22.

XIII. ¹ 'And YAHVEH spake unto Moses, saying, ² "Send-thee-forth men and search-out the land of Canaan which I give to the children of Israel; one man for each tribe of their fathers shall ye send, everyone a prince among them." ³ 'And Moses sent-them-forth from the wilderness of Paran by the mouth of YAHVEH, all those men heads of the children of Israel. ǁ ¹⁷ And Moses sent-them-forth to search-out the land of Canaan, and said unto them, 'Go-up this way by the Negeb, and go-up into the mountain; ¹⁸ and see the land what it is, and the people that dwelleth upon it, whether it is strong or weak, whether few or many; ¹⁹ and what the land *is* upon which they dwell, whether it is good or evil, and what the cities in which they dwell, whether in encampment or in fortresses; ²⁰ and what the land *is*, whether it is fat or lean, whether there is wood in it or not; and be ye (strong) courageous, and take of the fruit of the land.' Now the days were the days of the firstfruits of the grapes. ǁ ²² So they went-up by the Negeb, and came to Hebron, and there were Ahiman, Sheshai, and Talmi, offspring of the Anak; and Hebron was built seven years before Zoan of Egypt. ²³ And they came to the brook Eschol and cut-down from thence a branch and one cluster of grapes, and they bare it on a pole by two *men*, and of the pomegranates, and of the figs. ²⁴ That place one called the brook Eschol (*i.e.* 'cluster'), on account of the cluster which the children of Israel cut down from thence. ǁ

²⁶ And they went and came unto Moses and unto Aaron and unto all the Assembly of the children of Israel, unto the wilderness of Paran ǁ; and they brought-back word to them and to all the Assembly, and they showed them the fruit of the land. ²⁷ And they related to him and said, 'We came unto the land to which thou sentest-us-forth, and truly it is flowing with milk and honey, and this *is* its fruit. ²⁸ Nevertheless, the people is strong that dwells in the land, and the cities are fortified, very great, and also the sons of Anak we saw there. ²⁹ Amalek dwells in the land of the Negeb, and the Hittite, and the Jebusite, and the Amorite dwell in the Mountain, and the Canaanite dwells by the Sea, and by (hand) side of Jordan.

³⁰ And Caleb stilled the people before Moses, and he said, 'Let us surely go-up and possess it; for we shall certainly be able for it.' ³¹ And the men who went-up with him said, 'We are not able to go-up unto the people, for it is stronger than we. ǁ ³³ And there we saw the giants, sons of Anak of the giants; and we were in our eyes as grasshoppers, and so were we in their eyes.'

XIV. ¹ 'And all the Assembly lifted-up and gave-forth their voice, and the people wept that night. ǁ ¹¹ And YAHVEH said unto Moses, 'How long will this people despise Me? and how long will they not believe in Me for all the signs which I have done among them? ¹² I will smite it with pestilence and dispossess it, and I will make thee become a nation greater and mightier than it.' ¹³ And Moses said unto YAHVEH, 'The Egyptians have both heard that Thou broughtest-up this people from the midst of it by Thy power, ¹⁴ and they have told *it* unto the inhabitants of this land: they have heard that Thou, YAHVEH, art among this people, that Thou art seen, YAHVEH, eye to eye, and Thy cloud stands over them, and in a pillar of cloud Thou goest before them by day and in a pillar of fire by night. ¹⁵ And, if Thou shalt put-to-death this people as one man, then the nations who have heard Thy fame will (say) speak saying, ¹⁶ Because of YAHVEH'S not being able to bring-in this people unto the land which He sware to them, therefore He slaughtered them in the wilderness. ¹⁷ And now, I pray, let the power of my Lord be great as Thou hast spoken, saying ¹⁸ YAHVEH, slow of anger and abundant in kindness, forgiving iniquity and transgression, but *who will not wholly acquit*, visiting the iniquity of fathers upon children, upon the third generation and upon the fourth. ¹⁹ Pardon, I pray, the iniquity of this people, for Thy kindness is great, and as Thou hast forgiven this people from Egypt even until now.' ²⁰ And YAHVEH said, 'I will pardon according to thy word. ²¹ Notwithstanding, as I live, the whole earth shall be filled with the glory of YAHVEH. ²² For all these men, who saw My glory and My signs which I did in Egypt and in the wilderness, and have tempted Me these ten times, and have not hearkened unto My voice,—²³ they shall not see the land which I sware to their fathers, and all that despise Me shall not see it.' ²⁴ But my servant Caleb, because another spirit was with him, and he fulfilled after Me, therefore will I bring him unto the land whither he went, and his seed shall possess it. ²⁵ Now the Amalekite and the Canaanite dwell in the (valley) hollow. To-morrow turn and take-your-journey into the wilderness by the way of the Red Sea.'‡

³⁹ And Moses told these words unto all the children of Israel, and the people be-wailed greatly. ⁴⁰ And they rose early in the morning, and went-up unto the top of the mountain saying, ' Here we *are*, 'and let us go-up unto the place which YAHVEH said, for we have sinned.' ⁴¹ And Moses said, ' Wherefore *is* this *that* ye are transgressing the (mouth) word of YAHVEH? Yet it shall not prosper. ⁴² Go-not-up, for YAHVEH is not among you, that ye may not be smitten before your enemies. ⁴³ For the Amalekite and Canaanite *are* there before you, and ye shall fall by the sword ; for therefore have ye turned-back from after YAHVEH that YAHVEH may not be among you.' ⁴⁴ And they presumed to go-up unto the top of the mountain ; but the ark of the Covenant of YAHVEH and Moses departed not out of the midst of the Camp.† ⁴⁵ And the Amalekite came-down and the Canaanite that dwelt in that mountain, and smote them, and beat-them-down, unto Hormah.¦

XVI. ¹ And there rose-up ¦ Dathan and Abiram, sons of Eliab, son of Pallu, son of Reuben;¦ ² and they (rose-up before –) resisted Moses.¦ ³ For Moses sent to call Dathan and Abiram, sons of Eliab ; and they said, ' We will not come-up. ¹³ Is it little that thou hast brought-as-up out of a land flowing with

* The O.S. in v.30-24 says nothing about the *forty years'* wandering in the wilderness.

† Not a word is here said about *Aaron* or about the Levites being in attendance to carry the ark, as the L.L. would have required. The statement, that the ark and Moses ' departed not *out of the midst of* the Camp,' does not imply that they were in the *centre* of it, in accordance with N. iii. 38, any more than the similar expression in E. xxxiii. 11 implies that Joshua took post in the *centre* of the Tent of Meeting. In fact, the ' Tent,' according to the O.S., was, strictly speaking, *outside* the Camp, E. xxxiii. 7, ' afar off,' says the E. V., but rather ' a short distance off,' ' some little way off, as it were a bow-shot,' G. xxi. 16 ; and Moses, accordingly, went ' out of the Camp ' each time that he went to consult YAHVEH. But in a looser sense, and with reference to the expedition of the Israelites to the top of the Mountain, the ' Tent ' would be reckoned as within the whole encampment. The meaning of the passage is plain ; neither Moses nor the ark marched out with the warriors.

‡ GRAF reads, as here, ' son of Pallu, son of Reuben,' for ' and On, son of Peleth, sons of Reuben.'

milk and honey to put-us-to-death in the wilderness, that thou wilt altogether
make-thyself-prince over us? ¹⁴ Also thou hast not brought us into a land flowing
with milk and honey, and given us an inheritance of field and vineyard. Wilt thou
pierce-out the eyes of these men? We will not come-up.' ¹⁵ And it (anger) was
kindled to Moses greatly, and he said unto YAHVEH, 'Turn-not Thou unto their
offering; not one ass have I taken from them; I have not done evil to one of them.'|
¹⁶ And YAHVEH spake unto Moses saying, ²⁴ 'Speak unto the Assembly saying,
Get-ye-up from around the tabernacle of | Dathan and Abiram.' ²⁵ And Moses
rose-up and went unto Dathan and Abiram, and the Elders of Israel went after
him. ²⁶ And he spake unto the Assembly saying, 'Go-aside, I pray, from beside
the tents of these wicked men, and touch not anything that is theirs, lest ye be
taken-off in all their sin.' ²⁷ And they went-up from beside the tabernacle of |
Dathan and Abiram roundabout; and Dathan and Abiram came-forth, standing
at the entrance of their tents, and their wives, and their children, and their little-
ones. ²⁸ And Moses said, 'By this shall ye know that YAHVEH hath sent me to
do all these works, that not of my heart *have I done them*. ²⁹ If like the death of
all men these shall die, and a visitation of all men shall be visited upon them,
YAHVEH hath not sent me. ³⁰ But, if YAHVEH shall create a (creature) new-thing,
and the ground open its mouth and swallow them, and all that they have, and
they go-down alive to the grave, then ye shall know that these men have despised
YAHVEH.' ³¹ And it came-to-pass, at his finishing to speak all these words, that
the ground, which was under them, was cleft asunder. ³² And the earth opened
her mouth, and swallowed them and their households, both all the men | and all
the substance. ³³ And they went-down, and all which they had, alive to the
grave; and the earth covered over them, and they perished from the midst of the
Congregation. ³⁴ And all Israel, who were roundabout them, fled at the (voice)
cry of them, for they said, 'Lest the earth swallow us!' |

XX. ¹ And the children of Israel, all the Assembly, came into the wilderness of
Zin in the first month;* and the people dwelt in Kadesh,† and Miriam died there
and was buried there.| ¹⁴ And Moses sent messengers out of Kadesh unto the
king of Edom, saying, 'Thus saith thy brother Israel, Thou—thou knowest all
the travail which hath found us. ¹⁵ For our fathers went-down to Egypt, and we
dwelt in Egypt many days, and the Egyptians did evil to us and to our fathers.
¹⁶ And we cried unto YAHVEH, and He heard our voice, and sent an Angel, and
brought-us-forth out of Egypt; and lo! we are at Kadesh, a city on the extremity
of thy territory. ¹⁷ Let us pass-over, I pray, through thy land; we will not pass-
over through field or vineyard, and we will not drink water of the well; by the
king's way will we go; we will not turn-aside right or left, until we shall pass-
over thy territory.' ¹⁸ And Edom said unto him, 'Thou shalt not pass-over
through me, lest with sword I go-forth to meet thee.' ¹⁹ And the children of

---

* The 'first month' is evidently the first month of the *second* year; whereas on
the traditionary view it is apparently the second month of the *fortieth* year, that is,
there must be supposed either here, or at v. 14, a sudden leap without notice of
thirty-eight years.

† This 'Kadesh' in the 'wilderness of Zin' is undoubtedly Petra, near Mount
Hor, v. 22, and so in xxxiii. 36, D.i. 40; whereas 'Kadesh' in the 'wilderness of
Paran,' xiii. 26, xxxii. 8, D.i. 19, ix. 23, is distinguished as 'Kadesh-Barnea.'

Israel said unto him, 'By the high-road will we go-up, and, if we drink of thy water, I and my cattle, then I will give its pay: only it is nothing—let me pass-over on foot.' ²⁰ And he said, 'Thou shalt not pass-over;' and Edom went-forth to meet him with (heavy) much people and with a strong hand. ²¹ And Edom refused to give Israel passage-over through his territory; and Israel turned-aside from beside him. ²² And they journeyed from Kadesh, and they came, the children of Israel, all the Assembly, to Mount Hor.]

XXI. ¹ Now the Canaanite, king of Arad, dwelling in the Negeb, had heard that Israel came by the way of the spies,* and had fought with Israel, and had taken captive some of them. ² And Israel vowed a vow to YAHVEH and said, 'If Thou wilt indeed give this people into my hand, then I will utterly destroy their cities.' ³ And YAHVEH hearkened unto the voice of Israel, and gave the Canaanite, and he utterly-destroyed them and their cities, and one called the name of the place Hormah (utter-destruction).

'And they journeyed from Mount Hor by the way of the Red Sea to go-round the land of Edom; and the soul of the people was (shortened) distressed by the way. ⁵ And the people spake against ELOHIM and against Moses, 'Wherefore have ye brought-us-up out of Egypt to die in the wilderness? for there is no bread and no water, and our soul loathes at the light bread.' ⁶ And YAHVEH sent among the people fiery serpents, and they bit the people, and much people died out of Israel. ⁷ And the people came unto Moses and said, 'We have sinned, for we have spoken against YAHVEH and against thee; pray unto YAHVEH that He may take-away from us the serpents;' and Moses prayed on behalf of the people. ⁸ And YAHVEH said unto Moses, 'Make-thee a fiery-serpent, and place it on a pole: and it shall come-to-pass that every-one, who is bitten, shall look at it and live.' ⁹ And Moses made a serpent of brass, and placed it on the pole; and it came-to-pass, if the serpent stung a man, then he looked at the serpent of brass and lived.

¹⁰ And the children of Israel journeyed and camped at Oboth. ¹¹ And they journeyed from Oboth, and camped at Ije-Abirim, in the wilderness which is before Moab, towards the rising of the sun. ¹² From thence they journeyed, and camped at the brook Zared. ¹³ From thence they journeyed and camped on the other side of Arnon, which is in the wilderness that goeth-forth out of the border of the Amorite; for Arnon is the border of Moab, between Moab and the Amorite. ¶ ¹⁶ And from thence to Beer; that is the well (beer), of which YAHVEH said to Moses, 'Gather the people, and I will give them water.' ¹⁷ Then Israel sang this song:—

> 'Spring up, O well!
> Sing thus to it!
> The well, the princes digged it,
> Nobles of the people bored it,
> With the ruler's-staff, with their staves.'

[And the children of Israel journeyed from the wells of Bene-Jaakan to Moserah: there died Aaron, and he was buried there. From thence they

---

* That is, the way by which the spies had entered Canaan just before, xiii. 22, and by which the Israelites went up, xiv. 44, and were defeated by the Amalekites and Canaanites=the king of Arad, v. 45.

journeyed to Gudgodah, and from Gudgodah to Jotbathah, a land of springs of water,]* and from the wilderness to Mattanah, ¹⁹ and from Mattanah to Nahaliel, and from Nahaliel to Bamoth, ²⁰ and from Bamoth to the valley which is in the field of Moab, the top of Pisgah, and looketh towards the front of (Jeshimon) the wilderness.

²¹ And Israel sent messengers unto Sihon king of the Amorites saying, ²² 'Let me pass-over through thy land; we will not turn-aside through field or vineyard; we will not drink water of the well; by the king's way will we go, until we pass-over thy territory.' ²³ And Sihon did not give Israel passage-over through his territory; and Sihon gathered all his people, and went-forth to meet Israel to the wilderness, and came to Jahzah, and fought with Israel. ²⁴ And Israel smote him with the edge of the sword, and possessed his land from Arnon unto Jabbok, unto the children of Ammon; for the border of the children of Ammon was strong. ²⁵ And Israel took all these cities, and Israel dwelt in all the cities of the Amorites, in Heshbon and in all its (daughters) villages. ²⁶ For Heshbon was the city of Sihon king of the Amorites, and he had fought with the former king of Moab, and had taken all his land out of his hand unto Arnon.¶ ³¹ So Israel dwelt in the land of the Amorites. ³² And Moses sent to spy-out Jaazer, and they captured its (daughters) villages, and dispossessed the Amorites who were there.

³³ And they turned and went-up the way of Bashan: and Og, king of Bashan, went-forth to meet them, he and his people, to war at Edrei. ³⁴ And YAHVEH said unto Moses, 'Fear him not; for into thy hand have I given him and all his people and all his land; and thou shalt do as thou hast done to Sihon, king of the Amorites, who dwelt in Heshbon.' ³⁵ And they smote him and his sons, and all his people, until one left him no remnant, and they possessed his land.

XXII. ¹ ² And Balak, son of Zippor, saw all that Israel had done to the Amorites. ³ And Moab was exceedingly afraid because of the people, for it was numerous, and Moab was distressed because of the children of Israel. ⁴ And Moab said unto the Elders of Midian, 'Now shall this congregation lick-up all that is round-about us, as the ox licketh-up the verdure of the field;' and Balak, son of Zippor, was king of Moab at that time. ⁵ And he sent messengers unto Balaam, son of Beor, to Pethor, which is by the River of the children of his people, to call for him saying, 'Lo! a people hath come-forth out of Egypt; lo! it hath covered the eye of the land, and it is dwelling over-against me. ⁶ And now, I pray you, curse for me this people, for it is mightier than I; perhaps I may be able that we smite it, and I may drive it out of the land; for I know that whom thou blessest is blessed, and whom thou cursest is cursed.'

⁷ And the Elders of Moab and the Elders of Midian went, and rewards-of-divination in their hands; and they came unto Balaam, and spake unto him the words of Balak. ⁸ And he said unto them, 'Lodge here to-night, and I will bring you back word, as YAHVEH shall speak unto me;' and the princes of Moab dwelt with Balaam. ⁹ And ELOHIM came unto Balaam and said, 'Who are these men with thee?' ¹⁰ And Balaam said unto ELOHIM, 'Balak, son of Zippor, king of Moab, hath sent unto me, saying, ¹¹ Lo! the people that is coming-forth out of Egypt, and it covers the eye of the land—now come, pierce it for me; perhaps I

---

* This passage, which now stands in a most unsuitable place, D. x. 6, 7, probably stood originally somewhere in this chapter; see Lect. XVII. p. 238. But some other fragments of this itinerary may be missing.

may be able to fight with it, that I may drive it out.' ¹² And ELOHIM said unto Balaam, 'Thou shalt not go with them; thou shalt not curse the people; for it is blessed.' ¹³ And Balaam rose-up in the morning, and said unto the princes of Balak, 'Go into your land, for YAHVEH refuses to let me go with you.' ¹⁴ And the princes of Moab rose-up, and came unto Balak and said, 'Balaam refuseth to come with us.'

¹⁵ And Balak sent princes again, more numerous and more honourable than they. ¹⁶ And they came unto Balaam and said to him, 'Thus saith Balak, son of Zippor, Be not, I pray, withheld from coming unto me. ¹⁷ For I will greatly honour thee, and all which thou shalt say unto me I will do: and come, I pray, pierce for me this people.' ¹⁸ And Balaam answered and said unto the servants of Balak, 'If Balak would give-me the fulness of his house of silver and gold, I may not transgress the (mouth) word of YAHVEH my ELOHIM, to do a small thing or a great. ¹⁹ And now abide, I pray, here, you also, to-night, and I shall know what YAHVEH speaks again with me.' ²⁰ And ELOHIM came unto Balaam by night, and said to him, 'If the men have come to call for thee, arise, go with them; but only the thing which I shall speak with thee, it shalt thou do.'

²¹ And Balaam arose in the morning, and saddled his ass, and went with the princes of Moab. ²² And the anger of ELOHIM was kindled because he was going, and the angel of YAHVEH stood in the way for an adversary to him; and he was riding upon his ass, and two young men with him. ²³ And the ass saw the Angel of YAHVEH standing in the way and his sword drawn in his hand; and the ass turned-aside out of the way, and went in the field, and Balaam smote the ass to make her turn-aside into the way. ²⁴ And the Angel of YAHVEH stood in a narrow-path of the vineyards, a fence on this side and a wall on that. ²⁵ And the ass saw the Angel of YAHVEH, and pressed herself against the wall, and he smote her again. ²⁶ And the Angel of YAHVEH passed-over again, and stood in a strait place, where there was no turning-aside to the right-hand or to the left. ²⁷ And the ass saw the Angel of YAHVEH, and she lay down under Balaam, and Balaam's anger was kindled, and he smote the ass with a stick. ²⁸ And YAHVEH opened the mouth of the ass, and she said to Balaam, 'What have I done to thee, that thou hast smitten me these three times?' ²⁹ And Balaam said to the ass, 'Because thou hast played-tricks with me: would that there were a sword in my hand, for now had I killed thee!' ³⁰ And the ass said unto Balaam, 'Am I not thine ass upon which thou hast ridden ever since thou wast unto this day? Have I been at all accustomed to do this to thee?' And he said, 'No.' ³¹ And YAHVEH opened the eyes of Balaam, and he saw the Angel of YAHVEH standing in the way, and His sword drawn in His hand; and he bowed his head and worshipped on his face. ³² And the Angel of YAHVEH said unto him, 'For what hast thou smitten thine ass these three times? Lo! I have come-forth for an adversary: for thy way hath been perverse before Me. ³³ And the ass saw Me, and turned-aside before me these three times; perhaps, she hath turned aside because of My presence; for now both thee had I slain and her had I let live.' ³⁴ And Balaam said unto the Angel of YAHVEH, 'I have sinned, for I knew not that Thou wast standing to meet me in the way; and now, if it is evil in thine eyes, I will get-me back.' ³⁵ And the Angel of YAHVEH said unto Balaam, 'Go with the men; only the word that I shall speak unto thee, that shalt thou speak.' And Balaam went with the princes of Balak.

³⁶ And Balak heard that Balaam had come, and he went-forth to meet him unto

the city of Moab which is on the border of Arnon, which *is* on the extremity of the border. ³⁷ And Balak said unto Balaam, 'Have I not earnestly sent unto thee to call for thee? Wherefore hast thou not come unto me? Shall I not truly be able to honour thee?' ³⁸ And Balaam said unto Balak, 'Lo! I have come unto thee: now shall I be able at all to speak anything? the word which ELOHIM shall place in my mouth, that shall I speak.' ³⁹ And Balaam went with Balak, and they came to Kirjath-Huzoth. ⁴⁰ And Balak sacrificed oxen and sheep, and sent for Balaam, and for the princes who *were* with him. ⁴¹ And it came-to-pass in the morning that Balak took Balaam and brought-him-up to Bamoth-Baal, and he saw from thence the extremity * of the people.

XXIII. ¹ And Balaam said unto Balak, 'Build-me here seven altars, and prepare for me here seven steers and seven rams.' ² And Balak did as Balaam spake; and Balak and Balaam offered-up a steer and a ram upon each altar. ³ And Balaam said to Balak, 'Stand by the burnt-offering, and I will go; perhaps YAHVEH will (meet) come to meet me, and the word—what he shall show me—then I will tell to thee;' and he went to an eminence. ⁴ And ELOHIM met Balaam, and he said unto Him, 'The seven altars I have arranged, and I have offered a steer and a ram upon each altar.' ⁵ And YAHVEH placed a word in Balaam's mouth, and said, 'Return unto Balak, and thus shalt thou speak.' ⁶ And he returned unto him, and lo! he was standing by his burnt-offering, he and all the princes of Moab. ⁷ And he lifted-up his parable and said—

'From Aram doth Balak lead me,
The king of Moab from the mountains of the East, *saying*,
Come curse for me Jacob,
And come, execrate Israel.
⁸ How shall I pierce whom EL hath not pierced?
And how shall I execrate whom YAHVEH hath not execrated?
⁹ For from the tops of the rocks I see him,
And from the heights I behold him;
Lo! the people dwelleth alone,
And among the nations it doth not reckon-itself.
¹⁰ Who hath counted the dust of Jacob,
Or the number of the fourth of Israel?
May my soul die the death of the upright,
And may my last end be like him!'

¹¹ And Balak said unto Balaam, 'What hast thou done to me! To pierce mine enemies I took thee, and lo! thou hast altogether blessed!' ¹² And he answered and said, 'What YAHVEH shall place in my mouth, shall I not observe to speak?' ¹³ And Balak said unto him, 'Come, I pray, with me unto another place, from whence thou shalt see him; only his extremity shalt thou see, and of all of him thou shalt not see; and pierce him for me from thence.' ¹⁴ And he took him to the field of Zophim, unto the top of Pisgah; and he built seven altars, and offered a steer and a ram upon each altar. ¹⁵ And he said unto Balak, 'Stand thus by thy burnt-offering, and I will meet thus.' ¹⁶ And YAHVEH met Balaam, and placed a word in his mouth, and said, 'Return unto Balak, and thus shalt

---

* Balaam saw 'the extremity,' *i.e.*, the farthest portion—and therefore the whole—of the people.

thou speak.' ¹⁶ And he came unto him, and lo! he was standing by his burnt-
offering, and the princes of Moab with him; and Balak said to him, 'What hath
YAHVEH spoken?' ¹⁸ And he took-up his parable and said:—

    'Arise, Balak, and hear!
      Give-ear to me, thou son of Zippor!
  ¹⁹ EL is not a man, that He should lie,
      Nor a son of man, that He should repent;
      Hath He not said, and shall He not do—
      And spoken, and shall He not confirm?
  ²⁰ Lo! to bless have I received;
      He hath blessed, and I will not reverse.
  ²¹ He hath not beheld iniquity in Jacob,
      And He hath not seen perverseness in Israel;
      YAHVEH his ELOHIM is with him,
      And the shout of a King is in him.
  ²² EL brought-them-forth out of Egypt;
      He has like a buffalo's speed.
  ²³ For there is no enchantment against Jacob,
      And there is no divination against Israel.
      At the *proper* time it shall be said of Jacob and of Israel,
      What hath EL wrought!
  ²⁴ Lo! the people as a lioness shall arise,
      And as a lion shall lift-itself-up;
      He shall not lie-down till he devour the prey,
      And the blood of the slain shall he drink.'

²⁵ And Balak said unto Balaam, 'Neither pierce it all, nor bless it all.' ²⁶ And
Balaam answered and said unto Balak, 'Spake I not unto thee, saying, All
that YAHVEH shall speak with me, that will I do?' ²⁷ And Balak said unto
Balaam, 'Come, I pray, I will take thee unto another place; perhaps, it will be
right in the eyes of ELOHIM to curse it for me from thence.' ²⁸ And Balak took
Balaam to the top of Peor, that looketh (in front) east of the wilderness (Jeshimon). ²⁹ And Balaam said unto Balak, 'Build me here seven altars, and prepare
me here seven steers and seven rams.' ³⁰ And Balak did as Balaam said, and
offered a steer and a ram upon each altar.

XXIV. ¹ And Balaam saw that it was good in the eyes of YAHVEH to bless
Israel; and he went not, as time by time, to meet enchantments, but he set his
face towards the wilderness. ² And Balaam lifted-up his eyes, and saw Israel
tabernacling by its tribes, and the spirit of ELOHIM was upon him, ³ and he took-
up his parable and said:—

    'Balaam, the son of Beor, affirms,
      And the man, whose eyes are shut, affirms,
    ⁴ He who hears the words of EL, affirms,
      Falling *into a trance*, but with eyes uncovered—
    ⁵ How goodly are thy tents, O Jacob,
      Thy tabernacles, O Israel!
    ⁶ As valleys are they stretched out,
      As gardens by the River,

As aloes *that* YAHVEH has planted,
As cedars by the waters.
'He maketh waters flow from his buckets,
And his seed is in many waters;
And higher than Agag* shall be his king,
And his kingdom shall be exalted.
'EL brings-him-forth out of Egypt,
He has like a buffalo's speed;
He shall eat-up nations his adversaries,
And their bones shall be break,
And *with* his arrows shall be smite.
'He stooped, he lay-down as a lion,
Even as a lioness—who shall rouse him?
Those blessing thee shall be blessed,
And those cursing thee shall be cursed.'

¹⁰ And Balak's anger was kindled against Balaam, and he smote his hands; and Balak said unto Balaam, 'To pierce mine enemies have I called thee, and lo! thou hast altogether blessed them these three times.' ¹¹ And now, flee-thee unto thy place; I said, I would altogether honour thee, but lo! YAHVEH hath kept-thee-back from honour.' ¹² And Balaam said unto Balak, 'Did I not speak unto thy messengers, whom thou sentest unto me, saying, ¹³ If Balak would give me the fulness of his house of silver and gold, I shall not be able to go-beyond the (mouth) word of YAHVEH, to do a good-thing or an evil out of my heart; what YAHVEH shall speak, that will I speak? ¹⁴ And now, lo! I go to my people; come, let me counsel thee what this people shall do to thy people in the latter-end of the days.' ¹⁵ And he took-up his parable and said:—

'Balaam, the son of Beor, affirms,
And the man, whose eyes are shut, affirms,
¹⁶ He, who hears the words of EL, affirms,
And who knows the knowledge of the Highest,
Who sees the visions of Shaddai,
Falling *into a trance*, but with eyes uncovered—
¹⁷ I see him, but not now!
I behold him, but not near!
A Star has (stepped-forth) appeared out of Jacob,
And a Sceptre has arisen out of Israel,
And hath smitten the (corners) temples of Moab,
And the crown of the head of all the sons of pride.
¹⁸ And Edom shall be a possession,
Yea, Seir shall be a possession—his enemies;
But Israel shall be (making) gaining force.†

---

* We have here a sign of the age when this passage was written, in connexion with 1 S. xv, viz., about the time when the glory of Agag had just passed away and was remembered as a thing of the last generation.

† The manifest allusions in v. 17-19 to David and his conquests over Moab, Edom, &c., seem plainly to show that this prophecy of Balaam was composed in

THE ORIGINAL STORY OF THE EXODUS.

¹⁹ And one shall rule out of Jacob,
    And shall destroy the remnant out of the city.'

²⁰ And he saw Amalek, and he took-up his parable and said :—

    'The beginning of the nations is Amalek,
    And his end—he perisheth for ever.'

²¹ And he saw the Kenite, and he took-up his parable and said : —

    'Strong is thy dwelling,
    And *thou* puttest in the rock thy nest (*ken*) ;
    ²² Yet (*K'ain*) the Kenite shall be for sweeping-away ;
    How long ere Asshur carries-thee captive !'

²³ And he took-up his parable and said :—

    'Alas ! who shall live after EL's (placing) ordaining this !
    ²⁴ And ships from the (hand) coast of Chittim,
    And they shall humble Asshur, and they shall humble Eber,
    And also it perisheth for ever !'

²⁵ And Balaam arose, and he went and returned to his place,* and also Balak went-his-way.

XXV. ¹ And Israel dwelt in Shittim, and the people began to commit-whoredom with the daughters of Moab. ² And they called for the people to the sacrifices of their Elohim. ³ And Israel joined-itself to Baal-Peor, and the anger of YAHVEH was kindled against Israel. ⁴ And YAHVEH said unto Moses, 'Take all the heads of the people, and hang them † before YAHVEH over-against the sun, that the fierceness of YAHVEH'S anger may turn-back from Israel.' ⁵ And Moses said unto the Judges of Israel, 'Slay ye each his men, those joined to Baal-Peor.' ‖

XXXII. ¹ And the children of Reuben and the children of Gad had much cattle, very mighty, and they saw the land of Jazzer and the land of Gilead, and behold ! the place was a place for cattle. ³³ And Moses gave to them—to the children of Gad and to the children of Reuben and to the half-tribe of Manasseh son of Joseph —the kingdom of Sihon king of the Amorites and the kingdom of Og king of Bashan, the land with its cities in the coasts, the cities of the land roundabout. ‡ ‖

¹⁶ And they came near unto him and said, 'Folds for sheep let us build for our cattle here and cities for our little-ones. ¹⁷ And we will arm ourselves in full panoply before the children of Israel, until we have brought them unto their place ; and our little-ones shall dwell in the fortified cities because of the inhabitants of the land. ¹⁸ We will not return to our houses, until the children of Israel have inherited each his inheritance. ¹⁹ For we will not inherit with them across the Jordan

---

David's age, at a time when his might was still advancing, and Edom had not yet been subdued, 2 S. viii. 14. nor Ammon conquered. See Lect. VII. pp. 94–6.

* That is, he returned to his home beyond the Euphrates, xxii. 5. The O.S. therefore knew nothing about Balaam's evil counsel, or of his fate and the war against Midian, which belong to the L.L. (xxxi. 8, 16).

† 'Take all the heads of the people,' *i.e.* with thee as witnesses or counsellors, comp. E. xvii. 5, N. xi. 25, 'and hang them,' *i.e.* the offenders.

‡ See (VI. 120) for the reasons which support the conjecture that v. 33 followed originally v. 1.

F F

and further on: for our inheritance has come to us across the Jordan eastward. ²⁰ And Moses said unto them, 'If ye will do this thing—if ye will arm-yourselves before YAHVEH for war, ²¹ and every armed-man of you pass-over the Jordan before YAHVEH, until He have expelled His enemies before Him, ²² and the land be subdued before YAHVEH—then afterwards ye shall return and be guiltless with YAHVEH and with Israel ; and this land shall be to you a possession before YAHVEH. ²³ But, if ye will not do so, lo ! your sin is against YAHVEH, and know that your sin it will find you. ²⁴ Build yourselves cities for your little-ones and folds for your sheep : and what goeth out of your mouth do.'|

³⁴ So the children of Gad built Dibon, and Ataroth, and Aroer, ³⁵ and Atroth, Shophan, and Jaazer, and Jobehah, ³⁶ and Beth-Nimrah, and Beth-Haran—fenced cities and folds of sheep.

³⁷ And the children of Reuben built Heshbon, and Elealeh, and Kiriathiam, ³⁸ and Nebo, and Baal-Meon (changed as to name), and Sibmah ; and they called by names the names of the cities which they built.

³⁹ And the children of Machir, son of Manasseh, went to Gilead, and captured it ; and he dispossessed the Amorite who was in it. ⁴⁰ And Moses gave Gilead to Machir, son of Manasseh, and he dwelt in it.

⁴¹ And Jair, son of Manasseh, went and captured their small towns (havvoth), and he called them Havvoth-Jair.

⁴² And Nobah went and captured Kenath and her (daughters) villages, and called Nobah by his name. |

DEUTERONOMY.

XXXI. ¹⁴ And YAHVEH said unto Moses, ' Lo ! thy days have come to die : call Joshua, and take-your-stand in the Tent of Meeting, and I will command him.' And Moses went, and Joshua, and took-their-stand in the Tent of Meeting. ¹⁵ And YAHVEH appeared in the Tent in a pillar of cloud, and the pillar of cloud stood at the entrance of the Tent.| ²³ And He commanded Joshua, the son of Nun, and said, ' Be strong and be firm ; for thou shalt bring the children of Israel into the land which I sware to them, and I will be with thee.' |

XXXIV. ⁵ And Moses, the servant of YAHVEH, died there in the land of Moab by the mouth of YAHVEH. ⁶ And one buried him in a valley in the land of Moab, opposite to Beth-Peor ; but no man knoweth of his grave unto this day. | ¹⁰ And there arose not a prophet any more in Israel like Moses, whom YAHVEH knew face unto face.

The passages in the Book of Joshua belonging to the O.S. are as follows :—i. 1-2, ii. 1-24, iii. 1, 5-9, 11-17, iv. 1-12, 14-18, 20-23, v. 1, 9, 13-15, vi. 1-18, 20-24ᵃ, 25-27, vii. 2-6, 10-26 (except v. 25ᵇ), viii. 1-29, ix. 3-15ᵃ, 16, 22-27ᵃ, x. 1-11, 15-43, xi. 1, 2, 4-20, xiii. 1-21ᵃ, 23-31, 33, xv, xvi, xvii. 1, 2, 7-18, xviii, xix. 1-50, xxii. 7, xxiv. 28-30, 32.

APPENDIX III.

THE PRE-CHRISTIAN CROSS, ITS UNIVERSALITY AND MEANING.

From the Edinburgh Review for January, 1870.

'From the dawn of organised Paganism in the Eastern world to the final establishment of Christianity in the Western, the CROSS was undoubtedly one of the commonest and most sacred of symbolical monuments. . . . Apart from any distinctions of social and intellectual superiority, of caste, colour, nationality, or location in either hemisphere, it appears to have been the aboriginal possession of every people in antiquity. . . . Diversified forms of the symbol are delineated more or less artistically, according to the progress achieved in civilisation at the period, on the ruined walls of temples and palaces, on natural rocks and sepulchral galleries, on the hoariest monoliths and the rudest statuary, on coins, medals, and vases of every description, and, in not a few instances, are preserved in the architectural proportions of subterranean as well as superterranean structures, of tumuli as well as fanes. . . . Populations of essentially different culture, tastes, and pursuits—the highly-civilised and the demi-civilised, the settled and nomadic—vied with each other in their superstitious adoration of it, and in their efforts to extend the knowledge of its exceptional import and virtue amongst their latest posterities.

'Of the several varieties of the Cross still in vogue, as national and ecclesiastical emblems, and distinguished by the familiar appellations of St. George, St. Andrew, the Maltese, the Greek, the Latin, &c., &c., there is not one the existence of which may not be traced to the remotest antiquity. They were the common property of the Eastern nations. . . . That each known variety has been derived from a common source, and is emblematical therefore of one and the same truth, may be inferred from the fact of forms identically the same, whether simple or complex, cropping up in contrary directions, in the Western as well as in the Eastern hemisphere.

'Amongst the earliest known type is the *crux ansata*, vulgarly called 'the key of the Nile,' because of its being found sculptured or otherwise represented so frequently upon Egyptian and Coptic monuments. It has, however, a very much older and more sacred signification than this. It was the symbol of symbols, the mystical Tau, 'the hidden wisdom,' not only of the ancient Egyptians, but also of the Chaldæans, Phœnicians, Mexicans, Peruvians, and of every other ancient people commemorated in history, in either hemisphere; and is formed very similarly to our letter T, with a *roundlet* or *oval* placed immediately above it. . . . The most curious exhibition of it may be seen on a stele from Khorsabad, whereon is depicted an eagle-headed man holding the *circle* in his right hand and the *tau* in his left hand. . . . It seems to us almost indisputable that the *oval* or *roundlet* constitutes an integral part of the symbol, and is not an accidental or convenient addition to it.

'When the Spanish Missionaries first set foot upon the soil of America, in the fifteenth century, they were amazed to find that the Cross was as devoutly worshipped by the Red Indians as by themselves. . . . The hallowed symbol challenged their attention on every hand and in almost every variety of form. . . . And, what is still more remarkable, the Cross was not only associated with other subjects corresponding in every particular with those delineated on Babylonian monuments, but it was also distinguished by the Catholic appellations, "the tree of subsistence," "the wood of health," "the emblem of life."

'Another form of the Cross common to both hemispheres was the Maltese, the four delta-like arms of which, in the oldest known occurrences, are conjoined to or issue from the nave of a wheel or diminutive *circle*. . . . It figures on the breasts of the most powerful monarchs pourtrayed on the Nineveh remains, now in the British Museum, of which the colossal tablet from Nimroud, bearing the superscription of Ashur-Idanni-pal, is a notable example.* It depends, with other sacred emblems, from the neck of the king. . . . And, when inserted in a *roundlet*, as may be seen in the left-hand corner of the stele just mentioned, is emblematical of Saml. or the *Sun* dominating the earth as well as the heavens.'

N.B.—For further information on this subject reference may be made to Part VI. App. 122.

---

* This Tablet is represented in the Frontispiece, and is described in the Guide, printed by order of the Trustees of the British Museum, as 'a high arched slab, having in front a bas-relief of the King, with various Sacred symbols, and on the sides and back an invocation to the Assyrian gods, and a chronicle of the King's conquests.' The name of this King is now read as ' Assur-lair-pal, or Assur-nazirpal, the earliest Assyrian monarch of whom any large monuments have been procured, and who is believed to have reigned about B.C. 880.'

www.ingramcontent.com/pod-product-compliance
Lightning Source LLC
Chambersburg PA
CBHW020537300426
44111CB00008B/697